October 10–12, 2013
Orlando, Florida, USA

I0054879

**Association for
Computing Machinery**

Advancing Computing as a Science & Profession

CARIBE ROYALE
SUITES · CONVENTION CENTER · VILLAS
ORLANDO

SIGITE'13

Proceedings of the 2013 ACM SIGITE Annual Conference on
Information Technology Education

Sponsored by:
ACM SIGITE

Supported by:
EMC Academic Alliance, NetApp, Oracle Academy, ABET, & University of South Florida

**Association for
Computing Machinery**

Advancing Computing as a Science & Profession

The Association for Computing Machinery
2 Penn Plaza, Suite 701
New York, New York 10121-0701

Notice to Past Authors of ACM-Published Articles
ACM intends to create a complete electronic archive of all articles and/or other material previously published by ACM. If you have written a work that has been previously published by ACM in any journal or conference proceedings prior to 1978, or any SIG Newsletter at any time, and you do NOT want this work to appear in the ACM Digital Library, please inform permissions@acm.org, stating the title of the work, the author(s), and where and when published.

ISBN: 978-1-4503-2239-3 (Digital)

ISBN: 978-1-4503-2676-6 (Print)

Additional copies may be ordered prepaid from:

ACM Order Department
PO Box 30777
New York, NY 10087-0777, USA

Phone: 1-800-342-6626 (USA and Canada)
+1-212-626-0500 (Global)
Fax: +1-212-944-1318
E-mail: acmhelp@acm.org
Hours of Operation: 8:30 am – 4:30 pm ET

Printed in the USA

SIGITE/RIIT 2013 Chair's Message

Welcome to Orlando!

We are happy to welcome you to the 13th Annual Conference on Information Technology Education and the 2nd Annual Research in IT Conference, hosted by the University of South Florida. This year continues our IT Research conference, which was introduced last year to significant interest and participation.

Those of you who attended last year's conference in Calgary may remember a questionnaire you were asked to complete about the 2013 conference. Well, we listened. The most noticeable change from last year is the addition of a third parallel session track, providing more flexibility and, in future years, an increased number of papers at the conferences. For this year, its chief effect has been an increase in the time allotted to each paper presentation. Many of you said you might bring the family, which certainly affected our choice of conference city as well as our selection of an all-suite conference hotel that provides free shuttle service to Disney theme parks.

This year's SIGITE theme is making lemonade from the lemon grove that is our collective, resource-constrained education enterprise – in short, doing more with less. As higher education is increasingly challenged financially – a trend that shows no signs of abating – we need to open the door to economies of scale and collaborative ventures. Entrepreneurism is no longer simply something to be taught, but must be an approach to maximizing our resources and squeezing every drop of lemonade out of each lemon. And (I can't resist asking) where better to talk about lemons and lemonade than central Florida, the heart of the citrus industry?

SIGITE/RIIT 2013 kicks off with a provocative keynote by Sam Esfahani, CIO of PSCU, the leading service organization in the credit union industry. Sam is a turnaround specialist who blends innovative thinking with an uncommon ability to build high performing teams, and has been instrumental in leading PSCU's transformation as a technology leader in the credit union industry. Titled "Digit Shift: Leverage or Get Leveled," Sam's talk focuses on industry/academia collaboration, why it is so essential for the future health for both, and ways it can be cost-effectively implemented.

SIGITE/RIIT 2013 is a true team effort, and we would like to acknowledge and thank the people who have made this year's conferences possible. Rob Friedman and Ken Baker served as Program Co-Chairs, and successfully dealt with the many challenges that program chairs must. Rob, of course, also serves as SIG Chair, so had to handle twice as many questions!

Conferences are expensive events, and registration fees do not cover everything. The critically important job of garnering external support for our conferences was accomplished in great form by Sponsorship Co-Chairs Amber Settle and Terry Steinbach. To the sponsors that Amber and Terry signed up go our thanks for their generous support. Essential support has also been provided by the host for the conference, the University of South Florida, including financial support for program printing provided by the College of Engineering and audio-visual and computing support provided by Information Technology.

Behind the scenes are many others whose efforts are essential for a successful event. These people deserve special thanks, and include Abdel Ejnioui as Treasurer, Phil DuMas as Registration Chair, Colin Arnold as Local Sponsorship Chair, April Mosqus at ACM for assistance with overall planning, Lisa Tolles at Sheridan Communications for organizing the proceedings, Steven Houston for putting up all authors and presentations on our conference website, and Janet Gillis and Michelle King for designing and producing our printed conference program. Randy Connolly, last year's conference chair and the SIG's Information Director, also assisted with website matters at critical points.

Over the years, we have found our conference to be both a wellspring of ideas to address current issues and a much-needed opportunity to network and bond with fellow IT educators. We hope you find this year's conference as beneficial and rewarding as the many we have attended in the past.

Dave Armitage
Conference Chair, SIGITE/RIIT 2013

SIGITE/RIIT 2013 Program Chairs' Message

There's been a lot of change for SIGITE over the years – growth in membership, increased cooperation with other SIGs, sponsorship of affiliated conferences, and new IT programs from around the world contributing to a steadily enhanced stature for IT as a computing subarea, just to name a few. Last year's inauguration of the Research in Information Technology (RIIT) conference as a co-located event with the annual SIGITE conference is one change that has proved warranted, given the number and quality of the submissions we received this year and last. The RIIT thread complements the more widely known and more heavily subscribed SIGITE conference, given the increased interest industry continues to show in partnering with academia to address collaboratively applied research advances in areas related to our five curricular pillars. As Dave Armitage and Jeff Brewer wrote in last year's Program Chairs' message, "With a hands-on flavor and stronger connections with industry, [research in IT] is clearly differentiating itself from research in more traditional computing disciplines, and is deserving of its own conference venue."

As authors and reviewers no doubt noticed, we changed conference management systems this year. Several years ago, Grinnell University's Henry Walker was kind enough to mirror his databases and web forms used to organize SIGCSE to accommodate SIGITE, and we appreciate his consistent support. This year, however, we opted for change in this area, too. Colleagues in SIGKDD developed and manage the Microsoft CMT application we selected to use. Although there were a few bumps in the transition, most of our contributors and volunteers found it to be an easy-to-use system. 12 RIIT reviewers made recommendations on 24 submissions to RIIT, and 64 peer reviewers scored and commented on 70 submissions to SIGITE.

The number and substance of these submissions, in relation to the venue of this year's conferences, provided yet other opportunities for change in the conferences. These include providing more panel discussions, more workshops and more time allotted for individual paper presentations. As interest grows in SIGITE/RIIT, we're able to be more selective and more inclusive at the same time. 28 technical papers will be presented at SIGITE, which will significantly reduce our acceptance rate from a 6-year average of 54% to 40% this year, while RIIT's acceptance rate came in at 50%. We are able to provide inclusivity by offering 24 authors – a four-fold increase over last year – the opportunity to present their work as poster papers that are included in the ACM Digital Library. We would like to thank a highly responsive group of 76 peer reviewers, several of whom got tagged late in the process to review more papers than they bargained for.

Perhaps the most significant change to the proceedings is that they are available for download to conference registrants for two weeks preceding and two weeks following the conference dates, thus providing more opportunity for conversation among authors and attendees. From a community building perspective, this is a tremendous opportunity for advancement provided by the ACM Publications Board.

As you look through the schedule of events, you'll notice that we have doubled the panel session time from 30 to 60 minutes, and these panels will run concurrently and not opposite any technical papers, so you can participate and contribute to the topic that is most important to you. We have also moved the workshops to Saturday morning in an attempt to make the best use of a time block that in the past has not been well attended. We know that Orlando attractions beckon, but please consider taking advantage of the workshops.

All of us on the organizing committees would like to hear from you about these changes so that we can continue to innovate and provide SIGITE/RIIT attendees with the best experience possible.

We welcome you to SIGITE 2013 and RIIT 2013. Engage the panels and the paper and poster authors, meet new colleagues and reengage with old friends. Thanks for attending!

Ken Baker and Rob Friedman
SIGITE/RIIT Program Co-Chairs

Table of Contents

Paper Session G1: Student Perceptions

Session Chair: Joel Larson *(University of Washington Tacoma)*

Paper Session G2: Interdisciplinarity

Session Chair: J. Ekstrom *(Brigham Young University)*

Poster Session

Workshop 1

Workshop 2

Paper Session H1: Pedagogy

Session Chair: Chi Zhang *(Southern Polytechnic State University)*

Paper Session H2: Games and MOOCs

Session Chair: Randy Connolly *(Mount Royal University)*

Paper Session J1: Innovation & VoIP

Session Chair: Ken A Baker *(Ch Mack/Capella University)*

Paper Session J2: Program Change

Session Chair: Craig Miller *(DePaul University)*

Author Index

SIGITE/RIIT 2013 Conference Organization

General Chair: William D. Armitage, *University of South Florida, USA*

Program Co-Chairs: Rob Friedman, *University of Washington Tacoma, USA*
Ken Baker, *CH Mack, USA*

Sponsorship Co-Chairs: Amber Settle, *DePaul University, USA*
Terry Steinbach, *DePaul University, USA*

Treasurer: Abdel Ejnioui, *University of South Florida, USA*

Registration Chair: Phil DuMas, *University of South Florida, USA*

Local Arrangements Committee: Colin Arnold, *University of South Florida, USA*
Phil DuMas, *University of South Florida, USA*
Abdel Ejnioui, *University of South Florida, USA*
Steven Houston, *University of South Florida, USA*

Program Design and Printing: Janet Gillis & Ryan Wakefield, *University of South Florida, USA*

Steering Committee Chair: Rob Friedman, *University of Washington Tacoma, USA*

Steering Committee: Ken Baker, *CH Mack, USA*
Randy Connolly, *Mount Royal University, Canada*
Richard Helps, *Brigham Young University, USA*
Rick Lee Homkes, *Purdue University, USA*
Jim Leone, *Rochester Institute of Technology, USA*
Barry Lunt, *Brigham Young University, USA*
Mihaela Sabin, *University of New Hampshire, USA*
Mark Stockman, *University of Cincinnati, USA*

Reviewers:

Sohaib Ahmed, *Massey University*
Hend Al-Khalifa, *KSU*
Peter Alston, *Edge Hill University*
Larry Booth, *CSU*
Thomas Borrelli, *Rochester Institute of Technology*
Lynn Braender, *The College of New Jersey*
Jeff Brewer, *Purdue University*
Rob Byrd, *Abilene Christian University*
Sam Chung, *University of Washington Tacoma*
Randy Connolly, *Mount Royal University*
Jean Coppola, *Pace University*
Mónica Costa, Unknown
Michele Dijkstra, *Pacific Lutheran University*
Nalaka Edirisinghe, *Temasek Polytechnic*
Abdel Ejnioui, *University of South Florida*
Joseph Ekstrom, *Brigham Young University Provo*
Alan Fedoruk, *Mount Royal University*
Alessio Gaspar, *University of South Florida*
Rick Gee, *Okanagan College*
Thomas Gibbons, *The College of St. Scholastica*
Bryan Goda, *Kyushu Institute of Information Science*
Mingwei Gong, *Mt. Royal University*
Richard Helps, *Brigham Young University, IT*
Lawrence Hill, *Rochester Institute of Technology*
Ricardo Hoar, *Mount Royal University*
Edward Holden, *Rochester Institute of Technology*
Arno Hollosi, *FH CAMPUS 02*
Rick Homkes, *Purdue University*
Janet Hughes, *University of Dundee*
Michael Jonas, *University of New Hampshire*
Jane Kochanov, *Penn State Harrisburg*

Deborah Labelle, *Nazareth College*
Séamus Lawless, *Trinity College Dublin*
Jim Leone, *Rochester Institute of Technology*
Sergio Lopes, *University of Minho*
Jitendra Lulla, *Chelsio Communications*
Barry Lunt, *Brigham Young University*
Cynthia Marcello, *SUNY Sullivan*
Kevin McReynolds, *LDS Business College*
Craig Miller, *DePaul University*
Selvarajah Mohanarajah, *Edward Waters College*
Yousif Mustafa, *SimplexSystems, Inc.*
Besim Mustafa, *Edge Hill University*
Yin Pan, *Rochester Institute of Technology*
Junfeng Qu, *Clayton State University*
Hugo Rehesaar, *Griffith University*
Janet Renwick, *Univ of Arkansas - Fort Smith*
Rebecca Rutherfoord, *Southern Polytechnic State University*
Etienne Schneider, *Independent*
Amber Settle, *DePaul University*
Zaffar Shaikh, *IBA Karachi*
Edward Sobiesk, *USMA*
Mark Stockman, *University of Cincinnati*
Andrew Suhy, *Ferris State University*
Kevin Tew, *Brigham Young University*
Xinli Wang, *Michigan Tech University*
Elissa Weeden, *Rochester Institute of Technology*
James Woolen, *Ferris State University*
Nima Zahadat, *George Washington University*
Chi Zhang, *Southern Polytechnic State University*

SIGITE/RIIT 2013 Sponsor & Supporters

Sponsor:

Supporters:

Digit Shift: Leverage or Get Leveled

How the Business and Academia Can Collaborate

Sam Esfahani
Chief Information Officer, PSCU
560 Carillon Pkwy, St Petersburg, FL 33716
(800) 443-7728
Sesfahani@pscu.com

ABSTRACT

We are facing extraordinary change in technology and its impacts on business. The fierce competitive environment and ability to rapidly deliver products and service to market have posed tremendous challenges for many companies. These issues coupled with rising expectations in consumer demands and progression of a global economy have accentuated the need for top talents.

Finding these top talents with fundamental skills such as critical thinking, an innovative mind set, communication, collaboration, and entrepreneurship have been on the minds of many CIOs in the past few years.

My talk today is about how the partnership between business and academia can prepare students for the job market, and how the business can profit from a well- prepared workforce supplied by Universities – a workforce that can provide both technical contributions and thought leadership to the business.

Categories and Subject Descriptors

K.3.1 [Computers and Education]: General

Keywords

Commercialization, Investment, Education

Bio

Sam Esfahani is Chief Information Officer (CIO) for PSCU, the leading service organization in the credit union industry, and has been instrumental in leading PSCU's transformation as a technology leader in the credit union industry. He believes in and practices an inclusive style of management that is structured yet enables talent to move freely forward and unencumbered, by endorsing risk-taking as the path to high performance rewards. Mr. Esfahani has a broad academic background, having earned bachelors' degrees in Mechanical Engineering and Industrial Engineering Technology and an M.S. in Business Administration.

SIGITE'13, October 10–12, 2013, Orlando, Florida, USA.
ACM 978-1-4503-2239-3/13/10.
http://dx.doi.org/10.1145/2512276.2512277

Training Cyber-Defense and Securing Information Assets Using Student Blue Teams

Scott Pack
Brigham Young University
spack3@byu.edu

Dale C. Rowe, Ph.D
Brigham Young University
dale_rowe@byu.edu

ABSTRACT
In this paper, we discuss the creation of a student Blue Team to assist campus organizations with security incident response. We also explore approaches for establishing a relationship with university information technology staff, informing blue team members of professional and ethical responsibilities, and aiding system administrators with incident response and system hardening. Finally, we discuss the benefits to students taking part in these activities, as well as their contributions to improving an organizations security posture.

Categories and Subject Descriptors
K.6.5 [**Security and Protection**]: Authentication, Insurance, Invasive Software, Physical Security, and Unauthorized Access.
K.6.1 [**Project and People Management**]: Staffing, Systems Analysis and Design, Training

Keywords
Security, Education, Training, Blue-Team, Forensics, Incident Response

1. INTRODUCTION
Students attempting to enter the information security industry are often faced with position requirements such as "three years of work experience in the security industry required." As a result, students search for part-time security work or other experience to increase their security work experience. This is not always easy to come-by on a part-time basis as relationships allowing students to work with confidentiality, trust and expertise often require significant time to foster.

At the same time, university organizations are inundated with attacks on information assets on a daily basis. As is the case in most organizations, university information technology personnel are spread thin. Even in organizations with dedicated information

security teams, the requirements of maintaining existing security infrastructure, performing analysis of previous incidents, and monitoring the network for new intrusions can be burdensome. In a recent interview with a security analyst it was revealed that it is typical for a university to experience attacks requiring a configuration change to occur on average over two hundred and fifty times per day. Although automated tools in many cases can be used to detect and prevent network attacks, human intervention is still required when an attack results in a breach of information, disruption of services, or site defacement.

In addition to providing a short-term fix to address the problem at hand, an analysis is frequently undertaken to determine the attack vector used and what measures should be taken to prevent future exploitation of similar vulnerabilities. As many systems may be outside the administrative domain of the university information technology group, the actual work of securing information assets often falls to departmental system administrators and developers; in many situations these individuals are full-time students who may not have the requisite knowledge or skills to prevent attack recurrence.

While many consider this barrage of attacks as a hindrance to smooth university operation, we propose it can be leveraged as a learning tool. Information Technology students build a foundation of knowledge through classes in web application development, databases, networking, and system administration, the pillars upon which information systems are based. By organizing a team of security-minded Information Technology students to act as an incident response arm of a campus IT Security Team, or student "Blue Team," some of the duties of campus security can be offloaded. This helps alleviate the first issue discussed, that of increasing relevant security experience for students.

A typical process for this team would involve gathering sufficient information on the environment (including logs, packet captures drive images etc.), the Blue Team analyzes the data and prepares a list of recommendations, customizes an implementation guide, and assists with the deployment of recommended security measures. The Blue Team can also provide training to inform system administrators and developers of common security risks, and how to address them. Suggestions and implementation assistance for creating backups, monitoring, and an incident response plan are also made, ensuring that departmental IT staff is prepared to defend against, detect, and react to future problems.

By providing security assistance in a variety of deployment scenarios, Blue Team members not only provide a valuable service to the university, but also gain the following benefits:

- Authentic exposure to the same attack methods encountered in industry
- Proficiency with incident assessment and response
- Exposure to prevention controls
- Experience with monitoring tools and methodologies
- Situations by which theoretical knowledge can be put in context.

These benefits as well as others increase their proficiency and marketability in a world that has a growing need of defensive cyber security professionals [5].

2. BACKGROUND

Academically, most Information Assurance oriented programs expose students to security first to a theoretical approach; by studying the history and vocabulary. Many IT Security programs have adapted lab approaches in which students build upon this theoretical knowledge. In such an approach students are provided with a task or problem, and are expected to apply a methodology to find or build a solution. Many institutions found that security labs have special requirements such as "root" system privileges [6]. In a security scenario the subject matter may include live malware and tools that could be hazardous to information infrastructure, and may trigger mechanisms that prevent other legitimate users from accessing network resources [3]. Since security research can be volatile, and malware and infected hosts may react in unexpected ways, much security research takes place in isolated labs [2] or virtual environments [7]. This protects the surrounding network infrastructure, but also cuts out many of the variables that affect security in a large organization, such as network broadcasts, removal of remote command and control (C2), and normal user traffic. Some events are organized to place students in a situation which simulates these variables [1], but are time-limited to the duration of the event.

3. BLUE TEAM CREATION

After the creation of a student Red Team in 2011 [4], several penetration tests were carried out and the results presented to the parties that had requested the security assessment. As client organizations reviewed the penetration test result and the list of vulnerabilities, of which many had been successfully exploited, they found that while now aware of the problems they were unsure as to how to go about fixing these holes. To assist organizations with response to both incidents caused by malicious attackers and vulnerabilities discovered by the Red Team, the Blue Team was created.

4. BLUE TEAM ORGANIZATION

Prior to establishment of the Blue Team, a relationship was fostered between faculty, several students and members of the campus IT security team. The campus security team nominated a senior analyst to act as a communication point between campus-wide IT services and the Blue Team. This individual is a regular attendee of Blue Team meetings where possible and also provides briefs on recent campus security events, incident response protocols, and forensics procedures.

The team is operated and organized under the direction of a member of the IT faculty who invites students to the team, provides mentorship and advisement, and communication with the campus organizations (in particular, the IT security analyst) as needed.

A senior or experienced student is assigned to act as Blue Team Lead. Their responsibilities include soliciting work from various departments and IT security services, working closely with the security-team analyst, overseeing projects and activity logistics planning.

To recruit students to the Blue Team, announcements were made in IT course lectures as well as meetings of the IT Student Association and Cyber Security Student Association meetings. In this announcement students were made aware of the goals of the Blue Team including:

- Stay abreast of current threats in information security.
- Provide clients with detailed and actionable security direction.
- Perform forensic analysis of security incidents.
- Represent the technical expertise and professionalism of the Information Technology program.

Application forms were provided to those interested on which they supplied names, academic year, and relevant security experience. From these applicants were selected several individuals from a range of classes, and differing experience. The intent of selecting both upper and lower classmen was to create senior and junior members which would roll over in future years, creating a persistent Blue Team and allowing more seasoned Blue Team members to pass on contacts and experience. We have found a team of 6 students to be an appropriate number in balancing management and capabilities and use a 2-2-2 breakdown of skill levels, meaning two more experienced students, two junior members and two apprentices.

The Blue Team Lead is responsible for planning and conducting regular training meetings, ensuring that client engagements are making regular progress, and maintaining communication with clients in addition to regular member responsibilities. Training meetings include reviews of pen-test results and application logs, discussing hardening techniques, exploring forensics, and sharing useful security tools.

Blue Team members are responsible for researching security topics relevant to ongoing Blue Team engagements, training other members on the use of tools with which they are familiar, and writing portions of the recommendations report and implementation guide given to clients.

Consideration was given to split the Blue Team into smaller specialty groups that can be assigned to focus on a particular technology or client as has been done elsewhere [3], but given that the Blue Team is an ongoing commitment, it proved difficult to recruit and manage the large number of individuals required for such an organizational hierarchy.

In order to sufficiently assist client organizations in the hardening process, Blue Team members are often exposed to sensitive information such as passwords, infrastructure details, student information, etc. To ensure that each Blue Team member is aware of the ethical and professional responsibilities of their position, new Blue Team members are given a document detailing what constitutes appropriate and inappropriate use and disclosure of information and required to sign a non-disclosure agreement (NDA). Upon reading and signing this document, as well as obtaining a signed faculty endorsement, individuals are admitted to the Blue Team.

5. FINDING BLUE TEAM ENGAGEMENTS

For the Blue Team to be of use, departments need to be made aware of and offered its services. Blue Team-Client engagements currently can start one of four ways:

5.1 Office of Information Technology Relay

The BYU Office of Information Technology (OIT) Security Team logs traffic that comes in and out of the network, which is monitored and analyzed by an Intrusion Detection System (IDS) as well as by manual inspection. Many exploits are recognizable to the IDS via attack signatures and statistical analysis. When the IDS detects that an exploit has been performed, a security analyst confirms whether or not the host has been compromised. A confirmed intrusion is communicated to the departmental system administrators, and where deemed appropriate, Blue Team services are offered. If accepted, the Blue Team is put into communication with the affected department.

5.2 Campus Network Community

BYU has several resources available to web developers and system administrators, such as web community meetings, a campus-wide ticketing system, and email distribution lists. By connecting with the rest of the university as a whole via these methods, the Blue Team is able to be kept aware of what issues are being confronted by different organizations. A brief notice and Blue Team contact information is also given to newly hired employees via the Campus Web Developer meeting held each month.

5.3 Response to a Security Assessment

When the BYU Red Team is commissioned by an organization to perform a penetration test, Blue Team services are offered at the scope-defining stage. If accepted, the Blue Team is put within the scope of "Trusted Parties" of the engagement agreement. This allows Blue Team members to be present for the duration of the penetration test, as well as allows Blue Team members to review the assessment results. Access to Pen-Test results allows the Blue Team to ensure that the most glaring problems are addressed quickly, fitting with the end-goal of locating and removing potentially exploitable vulnerabilities. Our experience has shown the coupling both teams in this manner to be an excellent and very effective method for increasing security across campus departments.

5.4 Public Cyber Intel Gathering

While the Blue Team does not have direct access to network and IDS logs, it does have access to search publically available information, such as pages crawled by searched engines, a practice colloquially referred to as "Google hacking." In a January report by the National Post, a student was ejected from enrollment for using a vulnerability scanner. As vulnerability scanners make the step from public information gathering to fingerprinting, which can cause service disruption, they are prohibited for use by the Blue Team (unless requested in writing in an engagement proposal). By filtering search results to search for defaced sites within the University domain the Blue Team can locate defaced webservers and contact the appropriate departmental system administrator. Thus the blue team can also be effective in detecting previously undetected breaches.

6. BLUE TEAM APPROACH

Once the Blue Team enters into an engagement a topology and all information related to the vulnerable systems within scope is collected. This includes:

- Service logs
- Running services
- List of web applications
- Open ports
- Database Schema
- Firewall configuration
- Packet captures where available
- File system trees and timestamps
- Other situation-specific material

An intrusion report and service requirements are collected by interview. This data is analyzed to determine the attack vector that was used, where security principles of Least Privilege and Segregation of Duties are being implemented or neglected, and recommendations to remediate these issues are organized and proposed.

If the department elects to implement these recommendations, the Blue Team acts as an advisory group, not implementing the changes themselves, but training system administrators and developers to do it themselves. This takes place in the form of providing implementation guides, being present or available during the deployment period, and providing guidance as issues arise. This results in system administrators and developers that are more aware of how their work has an impact on the security of their information systems.

In addition to addressing the problem-at-hand, the Blue Team will also discuss with system administrators on whether or not it may be appropriate to set up additional hardening, redundancy, or monitoring solutions such as Tripwire, Fail2Ban, backup procedures, and RAID configurations to further increase the confidentiality, integrity, and availability of their computer systems and data.

7. BLUE TEAM RESOURCES

As the Blue Team is often asked to assist with system hardening on platforms with which they have little previous experience, a private cloud solution has been within which Blue Team members may deploy operating systems, test software configurations, and gain familiarity with security tools. For example, if a server suffers an intrusion and logs reveal that the exploit targeted an un-sanitized input in a web application, a Blue Team member can start an instance, write a small application in the same language, and learn how to sanitize inputs in that language.

The Blue Team operates as an organizational arm of the BYU Cyber Security Research Lab. This provides facilities such as an isolated private-cloud, lab workspace and a conference room for research and team meetings. If an investigation requires the copying of running configurations to this environment, written permission must be sought due to the multi-purpose nature of this lab equipment and lab space. This allows an approximation of a client's environment where issues can more easily be identified, and solutions demonstrated.

8. LEARNING EFFECTIVENESS

The aforementioned studies have explored the use of using short-term simulated environments to teach information assurance, and have shown that providing students with an environment to get hands-on experience are effective. Increasing the authenticity of the situation by causing Blue Team members to react to actual security events in an existing information infrastructure causes them to get experience in an atmosphere that more accurately represents a situation in industry. In such an environment Blue Team members encounter the following issues that are unlikely to be present in a lab environment.

- Dealing with personnel issues that can arise from security-sensitive issues. (For example, a developer who upon becoming aware of programming errors becomes defensive).
- Lack of documentation increasing difficulty of administration (this is a frequent occurrence in a campus environment where many tasks are performed by part-time student employees).
- The justification of security policy, planning and equipment as part of a risk management exercise to help organizations get the funding required to provide adequate security.
- Pressure to maintain application availability
- Working under strict confidentiality and non-disclosure style environments where trust is paramount.

Blue Team members gain experience in network defense and are in a position to observe both positive and negative examples of security practices. By working with production systems, Blue Teams are pushed to understand the feel of an organization under the pressure of an information attack. By establishing the Blue Team in continuous operation and interfacing with several departments, the Blue Team creates a reputation of technical ability and professional behavior which Blue Team members will be expected to uphold. These factors result in more authentic learning that will be valuable to Blue Team members in industry.

9. CONCLUSION

Information Technology students have the foundation of knowledge that makes them a potentially valuable resource for university security teams. By organizing security-minded IT students into a Blue Team, students not only provide a valuable service to the university offloading work of the university security team, but they also train campus developers and system administrators in concepts and practices that result in more secure computer systems.

Through this process Blue Team members are exposed to a number of security incidents, for which they research forensics, countermeasures, and general hardening techniques. Working with non-simulated systems suffering from authentic attacks places knowledge gained in classroom and lab environments in context, and further prepares students for security work in real-world environments.

10. REFERENCES

[1] Conklin, A. 2006. Cyber defense competitions and information security education: An active learning solution for a capstone course. *System Sciences, 2006. HICSS'06. Proceedings of ....* 00, C (2006), 1–6.

[2] Hill, J.M.D., Carver, C. a., Humphries, J.W. and Pooch, U.W. 2001. Using an isolated network laboratory to teach advanced networks and security. *ACM SIGCSE Bulletin*. 33, 1 (Mar. 2001), 36–40.

[3] Jr, R.D. 2003. Organization and training of a cyber security team. *Systems, Man and ....* (2003).

[4] Kercher, K. and Rowe, D. 2012. Risks, Rewards and Raising Awareness: Training a Cyber Workforce Using Student Red Teams. *SIGITE*. (2012).

[5] Rowe, D. 2012. Cyber-Security, IAS and the Cyber Warrior. *The Colloquium for Information Systems Security ....* (2012).

[6] Vigna, G. 2003. Teaching Hands-On Network Security: Testbeds and Live Exercises. *Journal of Information Warfare*. 2, 3 (2003), 8–24.

[7] Wang, X., Hembroff, G.C., Yedica, R., Ave, N.M. and Bay, G. 2008. Using VMware VCenter Lab Manager in Undergraduate Education for System Administration and Network Security Categories and Subject Descriptors. *CISSE* (2008), 43–51.

Cyber-Physical System Concepts for IT Students

Richard Helps, Ph.D.
BYU
265 CTB, Provo UT, 84602
+1 801-422-6305
richard_helps@byu.edu

Scott Pack
BYU
265 CTB, Provo UT, 84602
+1 801-822-2529
scottjpack@gmail.com

ABSTRACT

Cyber-Physical Systems (CPS), a.k.a. embedded systems, are becoming increasingly important within Information Technology. As the "Internet of Things" and ubiquitous mobile devices impact an ever-increasing segment of IT, it becomes imperative for IT students and professionals to appreciate the key concepts of CPS so that they can design IT systems. Special consideration should include aspects of networking, security and HCI within CPS and mixed systems.

This report presents an introductory experience, targeted at first-year students in IT, to help them understand the key concepts of CPS that are relevant to IT professionals. The experience is offered within the context of a first-year class where a single lecture and a single short lab experience are assigned to introduce CPS concepts. The lecture and lab are designed to engage the students, help them understand the relevance of this discipline to IT professionals and give to them a taste of designing and working with CPS.

The lab and lecture was designed as a combination demonstration and development experience. In the experience, students developed a working system within the one-hour lab available and explored several CPS and related IT concepts. Details of the lab design are presented. Student learning was assessed and learning results and student responses are presented.

Categories and Subject Descriptors

C.3 [Computer Systems **Organization**]: Real-time systems and embedded systems, Process Control Systems

K.3.2 [**Computers and Information Science Education**]: Curriculum

K.3.m [**Miscellaneous**]: Computer Literacy

General Terms

Design, Experimentation, Human Factors.

Keywords

Cyber-Physical Systems, CPS, Embedded computer Systems, laboratory design, Instructional Design, Internet of Things

1. INTRODUCTION

Cyber-Physical computer systems (CPS), a.k.a. embedded computer systems, are gaining increasing prominence in computing in general[1] and research in this area is growing. Small, embedded systems, based on microcontrollers, have outsold general-purpose desktops and laptops for many years. These smaller systems are often equipped with communication capabilities connecting them with a much wider world. Their connection to the Internet raises questions of security, software design, human-computer interaction and systems integration, all of which are of considerable interest to professionals within the IT domain.

The term Cyber-Physical Systems is replacing "embedded systems" in general use, which more strongly emphasizes their interaction with the physical world, with the associated requirements for reliability, real-time response and responsibility for human lives and equipment. The term "cyber" also indicates the connection to the world of computing. Finally emphasizing "systems" in the title is an indicator of the complex heterogeneous nature of design in this domain.

"Systemization" is apparent in two different (overlapping) aspects of this domain.

Internet and Intranet Communication: Many CPS have networking capabilities. This capability is seen in microcontrollers, single-board computers and Compact Mobile Platforms (CMP) (I.E. smartphones, tablets etc.). These systems are found in many products and larger systems, such as industrial control, consumer electronics, transportation networks, appliances, security systems, point-of-sale systems, health systems, and more. All of these systems are frequently connected to the Internet or to intranets. These types of systems continue to play a larger role in computing. A recent report by IDC[*] indicated that tablet computers suppliers will ship more systems than portable PCs (notebook computers) in 2013, and more than the entire PC market by 2015.

Distributed Function Among Distinct Devices: Many CPS are becoming complex heterogeneous systems. For example, within industrial control systems independent microcontrollers link back to a centralized proprietary controller, which in turn is networked back to other controllers and linked upstream to MMI supervisory systems, and they in turn are linked through the Internet to corporate systems. Thus many different types of systems, each with their own operating system and their own communication and security capabilities all communicate and interact, leading to a complex and heterogeneous system.

---

[*] http://www.idc.com/getdoc.jsp?containerId=prUS24129713

The net result of these trends is that system design is more complex and challenging. When embedded systems provide isolated intelligence to appliances they can successfully be designed by vertical market specialists, such as a sole electronic hardware designer. In the changing design space broader system needs must be addressed. Multiple researchers have explored the problems and importance of cyber-physical design[2-6]. These attempts at formal analysis of CPS design point to the need for a more systems-oriented approach to design in this domain.

Some aspects of cyber-physical systems design require professionals in the areas of integrative systems design, Human-Computer Interaction (HCI), Information Assurance and Security (IAS), reliability, networking, web interactions and much more. Since these skills are all part of the IT university curriculum, IT professionals have a significant role to play in the design of these complex systems. Most of these skills are part of the pillars and central themes of IT education[7]. It is revealing that the respected annual survey sponsored by EE Times and others[8] indicate that over 50% of the projects include networking and more than 30% include wireless, but in this report the designers are classified as hardware, software or firmware engineers and their lists of design tasks do not include issues related to IAS, HCI, or other IT-related issues.

Future IT professionals are facing a far more diverse IT future than one dominated by a very few system configurations and two or three operating systems. Despite this trend CPS concepts are not traditionally emphasized or even addressed in IT programs. To address this need a combined class and lab experience was designed for first-year students in an IT program. The class and lab, taught in a single two-hour block exposes them to fundamental concepts in CPS and introduces the relationship between CPS and IT. Other classes later in the curriculum enable students to explore these ideas in greater depth.

2. DESIGN OF THE LAB AND CLASS

2.1 Objectives of the Class and Lab

The overarching objective is to design a student experience so that early students in an IT program understand some basic principles of CPS and realize the importance of the relationship between CPS and IT. Several aspects of CPS are addressed. This includes technical and development issues, such as the real-world interface (sensors and actuators) and development issues. Then contextual issues, such as application domain, cost and computing power are considered. Finally some specific IT-oriented issues such as web systems, networking and security are included. In this simple two-hour experience other important aspects such as real-time systems, information management, and HCI are only addressed lightly.

Thus the specific goals of the instructional design were as follows:

Incorporate CPS principles:

- Use a small, non-desktop system interacting with the real world through sensors and actuators. Include both digital and analog sensed variables.

- Develop an application for the CPS using a Software Development Kit (SDK) environment I.E. a separate development computer and a target computer. Students should realize that the target computer does not have the capability to act as a development machine and that the development computer does not have the capability to act as a cyber-physical interaction system.

Incorporate system, networking, world-wide-web and security principles:

- The small system is networked to a desktop computer running a browser. Security issues are demonstrated.

There are also pedagogical and practical goals:

- Engaging: The lab should be engaging and memorable to raise the students' awareness and enthusiasm and thus to encourage learning.

- Experiential and Creative: The students should have the opportunity to design and implement part of the system, in keeping with the experiential nature of the learning model favored by technology disciplines. The creative aspect will move the learning experience further up the scale in Bloom's taxonomy[9].

An earlier version of this course[13] formed the foundation for the current design. This extended version incorporates more IT issues.

2.2 Course Structure and Constraints

The class presentation and lab was administered as part of a first-year course that attempts to address a variety of subjects for IT students. The course was designed to offer students entering the IT program early experiences in a variety of IT-related topics and to ensure that all students had a minimum level of understanding in basic IT concepts. Although quite similar to a survey class in IT, this course goes beyond that by requiring the students to complete meaningful, although introductory, laboratory and other assignments in the basic areas of the discipline.

Although the class is offered as a first-year course, in fact the class participants are distributed between first and fourth year levels. This arises because most students selecting IT as a major have transferred from other disciplines at some stage of their college career, thus have sufficient credit hours to qualify as sophomores, juniors and seniors. Although the distribution is not even, there are substantial representatives of each year in the class. All students entering the IT major are required to take the introductory class.

There are significant time and facility constraints in this course. Typically fifty to seventy students take the course in a semester and lab facilities for each topic area are provided by using the labs used by the advanced classes, which are normally much smaller classes with 10 to 20 lab stations. To manage the numbers of students the labs are scheduled in smaller groups and are limited to one-hour experiences. For this CPS lab, 15 workstations are available, students are teamed and two one-hour sections are scheduled. The complete CPS experience is taught in a single two-hour block. Time constraints are managed by splitting the class into two at the beginning of the first hour and having half the class do the lab followed by the classroom presentation and the other half do the class, followed by the lab.

Splitting the class to accommodate lab constraints also means that the some of the students are introduced to the concepts in the class presentation and then strengthen their understanding with a practical experience in the lab, while other students get the lab experience first and then have the class discussion to help them put their lab experience into context with the concepts of CPS.

3. MEASUREMENTS

3.1 Data collection

Data was collected from the students using surveys. Pre- and post surveys were used to measure the students' technical background, their knowledge of CPS and how much they changed through the two-hour experience. The surveys were anonymous and pre and post surveys were not matched with the same students. A group of questions relating to CPS concepts and questions, related to the relationship between CPS and IT, were duplicated in both the pre- and post-surveys so changes in the students' understanding could be detected, and a question added to the post survey to gauge the students' degree of learning.

The responses from the two groups of students were recorded separately so differences relative to the lab-first or class-first experience might be detected. Unfortunately, as discussed in "Distortion of Data" below circumstances rendered some aspects of this separate data of limited value.

3.2 Survey Format

Data collection was also constrained by the need to administer both of them within the limited time of the two-hour class and lab. Accordingly the survey was constructed mostly as a set of Likert-style question,[14] that could be answered in just a few minutes at the beginning and end of the two-hour block. The questions addressed the students' technical background, based on the IT pillars[7], their familiarity with developing CPS, and their understanding of CPS system characteristics, as well as their opinion of the significance of CPS to IT. The questions are, of course, not isolated, merely asking the questions heightens the students' awareness of the topics and helps them to be more aware of the topics in the discussion and lab that immediately follows. The post-survey repeated several of the pre-survey questions and also asked the students to assess how much they had learned.

3.3 Distortion of the Data

All the students were asked to complete both pre and post surveys, however not all students completed both surveys. Since the class was spilt into two ad-hoc sections half the class completed the pre-survey at the start of the lab portion and half completed it at the start of the class portion. At the end of the experience the students completed the post-survey at the end of the class and lab sections respectively.

The experience was intended for half the class to start in the lab and complete their assignment within an hour. Due to technical difficulties many of the students could only start the lab after about 20 minutes and so the lab ran late. Several of the second lab group then arrived and we told to come back to complete the lab on another day and not all the students who in the lab-first group attended the class in the second hour. This led to some confusion and uneven numbers of post surveys were completed and submitted. Students who did the lab the following week were also asked to complete the post surveys, however the large gap between the class and lab probably impacted the data.

Examining the data from the lab-first and class-first groups no clear differences could be determined. We were unable to conclude if there were no real differences or if the difficulties in administering the labs obscured any differences. Consequently most of the results treated the data as a single large group and conclusions were based on the students' overall experiences, rather than their experiences as two separate groups. Data for the separate halves was gathered and, mostly, combined into a single data set for analysis.

4. THE LAB AND CLASS DESIGN

4.1 Class Segment

The class addresses a variety of CPS concepts and illustrates them with examples of applications. Students are invited to share their own experiences with systems that go beyond conventional desktop and notebook computers and the structure of typical heterogeneous cyber-physical systems is presented and discussed. IT aspects such as networking, security, programming, HCI design and systems integration are included. CPS issues such as typical system size, cost and power are combined with discussions of development environments. The one-hour class discussion serves as an introduction for the first half of the class prior to their doing the lab portion, and as a concluding and integrating discussion for the second half of the class who have just completed the lab portion of the experience.

4.2 Lab Segment

The lab portion of the class needs to reveal to students one practical example of a CPS design and engage them in creating some aspects of that design. The strong time constraint (one hour) requires the lab to be carefully designed and pre-configured so that the students can have a successful experience, while still doing some meaningful creative work.

The device used for this lab is a PIC32-based microcontroller equipped with Ethernet and USB interfaces, connected to several buttons, LEDs, a piezoelectric speaker, and a pair of flex-potentiometers. A demo unit is also equipped with a WiFi (802.11a/b) card. The microcontroller is pre-programmed with a routine that starts a webserver, rendering a speedometer to any connected browser. The development environment is MPIDE, an Arduino-compatible system for PIC microcontrollers.

The context of the lab is found in the movie "Back to the Future." The idea is introduced with a brief movie clip that shows scenes from the movie, and emphasizing the time machine with its time-traveling "flux capacitor." The students then watch a demonstration of a "working" flux capacitor. The potentiometers connected to the PIC32 act as pedal sensors, controlling the speed of Doc Brown's famous DeLorean sports car. As the accelerator potentiometer is pressed the speedometer rendered in a browser reflects an increased speed, and the inverse is seen with the brake. A two-way communication channel exists between the CPS unit and the browser running on a remote computer. This demonstrates significant networking aspects between the analog inputs and the CPS unit, as well providing a background of the integration between CPS devices and the Internet at large. As students discover the connection between the accelerator/brake and speedometer, they are instructed to bring the DeLorean to "88 miles per hour" as illustrated in the previously shown movie clips and push a button to "engage the flux capacitor". When this is done a LED display flashes and a tune plays indicating that the flux capacitor is activated and time travel is about to happen.

An important aspect of this is that the relationship between the physical world and the CPS unit is demonstrated, as is the relationship between the CPS unit and the broader networked world. Students can see that action taken on the browser directly affects physical actions on the CPS and similarly real-world sensors can be monitored in real-time on an ordinary browser.

Once the basic functionality of the system has been demonstrated the lab instructor briefly indicates the structure of the WiFi link and invites students to "hack" the link. This can easily be done with any WiFi device, including students' smartphones. When the system's resources are saturated by a very simple denial-of-service attack it quickly fails to respond promptly to requests, and the browser times out. This leads to a brief discussion about the need for security, which will be discussed in depth in later classes.

This fictional setup appeals to the students. It also incorporates all the elements of a heterogeneous system of a CPS system linked to both the physical world and to the Internet.

One concern that the developers had was that most of the students in the class were not born when the "Back to The Future" movies were made, however an informal poll of showed that the vast majority of the students had watched and enjoyed the movies. In addition the short movie clips shown illustrated the essential concepts needed for the lab, for any students not familiar with the movies.

Once the system had been demonstrated the development SDK is introduced. An important pedagogical goal here was to emphasize the separation between the development system and the target system. The students' development task in the lab was to create software to program their own LED flux capacitors and also to create a suitable sound accompaniment, preferably synchronized to the LED display. Previous experiences over several years with similar types of labs have shown that if the students are given a software framework with some basic functions that almost every student can complete the assignment within the one-hour time frame, regardless of their previous programming experience. Teaching assistants help the students with initial problems and also look for the more experienced students. The more experienced students are challenged to complete more complex tasks involving more complex sound effects and sophisticated lighting effects, and even to attempt more complex network interactions. The best creations are shared with the class as a whole to increase student feedback and awareness of the possibilities inherent in the system; this also serves as a reward mechanism for the more advanced students.

Students worked in teams of two. Previous experience with similar labs has shown that the dynamic interchange between two students is more productive than students working alone.

4.3 Hardware Configuration
As always, cost is a significant constraint, particularly as 15 workstations were required. The CPS system was the PIC32 based Microchip 32 bit development board, from Digilent, which was running an Arduino-compatible software suite. The analog accelerator and brake input sensors were created using resistive flex sensors. The sensors, flux capacitor LEDs and sound actuator were deliberately mounted on a custom-built separate board, connected by a ribbon cable to the CPS CPU board to visually emphasize the separation of physical world elements from computing elements. Similarly the programming connection (cable) between the desktop development station and CPU board emphasizes the separation between development and target units. Using available parts and hand-building the sensor-actuator boards enabled us to create each student workstation for less than $200, not including the desktop system. The desktop systems were standard lab computers running free Arduino-compatible development packages from Diligent, the suppliers of the CPU board.

5. RESULTS
The results showed that initial understanding of IT concepts from the pillars of IT[7] was low, which agrees with our general understanding of what is expected from students in an introductory class. The questions in this area covered topics such as web systems, programming, databases and system administration. On a 0-5 scale, with 5 being very good, the average scores ranged from 0.95 to 2.67, with an average of 1.55. The students scored comparatively well on "Helping People with their computers" (3.2/5). Apparently, and unsurprisingly, being involved in a computing major makes a student the computing expert within her community. Scores on CPS items were even lower, ranging from 0.2 to 1.0. However, despite their lack of knowledge, their opinion of the importance of this field was relatively high, at 3.2 (on a 0-4 Likert scale). In the post survey test the students rated this importance of the field at 3.4, a slight rise from the already high level. It is interesting to contrast these figures with those from the previous version of this experiment[13] where the initial scores (normalized to the same scale) were 2.9, rising to 3.2 in the post-assessment. It seems reasonable to assume that these scores between the two versions of the class are generally comparable, since the assessments were administered under similar conditions to similar groups of students. On that assumption it appears that student expectation of the relevance of CPS is high and increasing.

Student learning was measured by the responses to 17 questions that appeared on both the pre- and post-tests, relating to aspects of CPS systems and the relationship between CPS and other IT systems. In all cases the average responses improved, with values ranging from 4 to 36% improvement in their scores. The biggest improvements were in the areas related to CPS characteristics (where their initial understanding of CPS was very low). The improvements in their understanding of the relationship between IT and CPS were largest in the areas demonstrated in the lab. While this result is not surprising it does indicate the value to addressing CPS topics for IT students with an experiential learning design.

Open feedback from the students was strongly positive. Student comments indicated that they found the lab both challenging and interesting. Students commented that they felt a significant feeling of accomplishment by being able to program the system and then seeing the LEDs and sound system respond. They strongly appreciated the experiential nature of the instructional approach and looked forward to further explorations of CPS in later classes. The few negative comments from the open feedback related to the problems with the administration of the lab and not the content. Some students expressed the wish that more time be allocated to the lab—a wish that the faculty would agree with, if the practical constraints could reasonably be overcome.

6. CONCLUSIONS
The development of this lab and class experience showed that it is possible to introduce key concepts of cyber-physical systems to a first-year class of IT students in a single two-hour block. Careful design and administration of the experience allowed IT and CPS concept relationships to be demonstrated and experienced by the students. The confluence of design between IT and CPS has been discussed elsewhere[15].

Measurements from the experience showed that students learned successfully and also that students strongly valued the introduction of CPS into IT.

Students showed a strong awareness of the value of CPS within the IT discipline, and a strong desire to see more of this topic introduced into IT coursework. The design and thinking skills that IT students develop makes them excellent candidates to participate in CPS design, and the IT aspects of cyber-physical systems requires those skills for the growing development of the Internet of Things[16] and future heterogeneous cyber-systems.

7. REFERENCES

[1] Jianhua, S., Wan, J., Yan, H. and Suo, H. *A Survey of Cyber-Physical Systems*. City, 2011. □

[2] Dumitrache, I. The next generation of Cyber-Physical Systems *Journal of Control Engineering and Applied Informatics*, 2 2010), 3-4. □

[3] Lee, E. A. *Cyber Physical Systems: Design Challenges*. City, 2008. □

[4] Henzinger, T. and Sifakis, J. *The Embedded Systems Design Challenge* □ *FM 2006: Formal Methods*. Springer Berlin / Heidelberg, City, 2006. □

[5] Davies, N. and Gellersen, H.-W. Beyond Prototypes: Challenges in Deploying Ubiquitous Systems. *IEEE Pervasive Computing* (January-March 2002 2002). □

[6] Edwards, S., Lavagno, L., Lee, E. A. and Sangiovanni-Vincentelli, A. Design of embedded systems: formal models, validation, and synthesis. *Proceedings of the IEEE*, 85, 3 1997), 366-390.

[7] Lunt , B. M., Ekstrom, J. J., Gorka, S., Hislop, G., Kamali, R., Lawson, E. A., LeBlanc, R., Miller, J. and Reichgelt, H. *Information Technology 2008: Curriculum Guidelines for Undergraduate Degree Programs in Information Technology*. ACM, IEEE-CS, 2008.

[8] Electronic Engineering Times, E. *Embedded Market Study 2011*. City, 2011.

[9] Anderson, L. W., Krathwohl, D. R. and Bloom, B. S. *A taxonomy for learning, teaching, and assessing: a revision of Bloom's taxonomy of educational objectives*. Longman, New York, 2001. □

[10] Marwedel, P. *Embedded System Design: Embedded Systems Foundations of Cyber-Physical Systems*. Springer, 2010

[11] Bhave, A., Krogh, B., Garlan, D. and Schmerl, B. Multi-domain Modeling of Cyber-Physical Systems Using Architectural Views. In *Proceedings of the Analytic Virtual Integration of Cyber-Physical Systems Workshop (AVICPS)* (San Diego, November 30, 2010, 2010). □

[12] Israr, A. and Huss, S. A. Specification and design considerations for reliable embedded systems. In *Proceedings of the conference on Design, Automation and Test in Europe* (Munich, Germany, 2008). ACM □

[13] Blanked to preserve anonymous review

[14] Likert, Rencis, 1932, A Technique for the Measurement of Attitudes. *Archives of Psychology*, 22, 140 (1932), 55.

[15] Blanked to preserve anonymous review

[16] Gershenfeld, N., Kikorian, R. and Cohen, D. *The Internet of Things*. Scientific American, 2004. □

Leveraging HCI in Teaching Mobile, "Anytime and Everywhere" IT

Rich Halstead-Nussloch
Southern Polytechnic State University
1100 South Marietta Parkway
Marietta, GA 30060
+01.678.915.5509
rhalstea@spsu.edu

Han Reichgelt
Southern Polytechnic State University
1100 South Marietta Parkway
Marietta, GA 30060
+01.678.915.7399
hreichge@spsu.edu

ABSTRACT

Within our IT program, we have been working on constructive ways to teach HCI for the past five years; so, when the mobile revolution caught fire, we already had been working on better ways to incorporate HCI-related learning outcomes in our curricula. In the course of this activity, we have identified leverage points to meaningfully teach the important HCI concepts and skills listed below. These points provide a means for those interested in effective IT administration, accreditation and teaching to manage the increasing importance, complexity, and methodological diffusion of HCI in the mobile environment. This paper compiles and assesses the top seven of these leverage points.

HCI topics required in the curriculum include:

- Human Factors
- HCI Aspects of Application Domains
- Human-Centered Evaluation
- Developing Effective Interfaces
- Accessibility
- Emerging Technologies
- Human-Centered Computing

Categories and Subject Descriptors

H.1.2 [**Information Systems**]: User/Machine Systems – *human factors, human information processing, software psychology.*

Keywords

Accreditation, Curriculum, HCI, Mobile, Smart Phone.

1. INTRODUCTION

In their overview of the past, present and future of HCI, Churchill, Bowser and Preece [1] describe HCI as a domain of computing that is of ever-increasing importance and also ever-increasingly dynamic. For purposes of this paper, we will take a broad view of HCI, seeing it as a domain of computing complete

SIGITE'13, October 10–12, 2013, Orlando, Florida, USA.
Copyright © 2013 ACM 978-1-4503-2239-3/13/10...$15.00.
http://dx.doi.org/10.1145/2512276.2512295

with methods, a body of knowledge, issues, experts, etc. In short, HCI has become a true pillar of computing, and is recognized as such in the ACM/IEEE-CS Model Curriculum for Information Technology [7]. Moreover, one can only expect the importance of HCI to increase in the near future, we would argue because of two developments that are already taking place, or are likely to take place in the near future.

First, computing is seeing a crossover from personal computers to personal devices, predominately smart phones that occurred near the end of 2011 [2, 3]; to have a networked computing device available at all times has become the normal mode of computing.

Second, we are also seeing a transition of sales leadership of smart phones from the developed to the developing world; this transition appears to have taken place in 2012 [2, 4, 5]. Moreover, perhaps because the mobile device is the only computing device available to many in the developing world, we are also seeing the development of many innovative applications of the technology. For example, we have seen the development of completely new payment systems in East Africa where clients now routinely pay for services in particular through the transfer of pre-paid minutes on their mobile devices.

From our perspective, these transitions constitute a (historical) phase change in the nature and identity of computing. In the prior phase, computing was more of an elite human activity, and came with more exclusive norms and a cadre of professional users, servants and creators. In the new phase, computing is becoming more ordinary, a commodity of sorts necessary to maintain everyday life throughout the planet, leaving computing professionals to face challenges that are new to them, such as commoditization.

Continuing the description of our perspective, the growth of mobile computing also has thrown a major disruption into human-computer interaction (HCI). Indeed, the SIGITE 2013 call for papers states it well in only 10 words: "in these days of mobile computing, what does HCI mean?" This phrase captures that HCI has exploded in many directions with many implications for teaching and learning HCI within information technology (IT). Among these implications are three that we have found from our perspective to be critical to successfully manage IT curricula and education: 1) HCI is much more important in mobile computing; 2) Simultaneously, HCI is much more complex now; 3) Prior methods of incorporating good HCI into IT systems are less likely to work in the mobile environment, that is, mobile computing has caused the diffusion of HCI methods.

Clearly, these changes are likely to require significant changes in the way in which computer professionals think about and design interfaces, and these changes in turn are likely to have significant implications for computing education.

Historically speaking, computing educators have had some difficulties implementing effective HCI education. Indeed, Manaris' [X] 2003 editorial on HCI education explains that despite multiple efforts, computing educators were slow in recognizing the importance of HCI and incorporating it effectively in the computing curriculum. In our perspective, these difficulties stem from many sources, e.g., the unique and "soft" features of HCI being foreign to the "hard" nature of computing; nonetheless they do continue to call out for change in HCI education.

This paper describes our perspective and efforts to reflect both the historical difficulties and this new reality that surround effectively incorporating HCI in our undergraduate programs in Information Technology.

2. THE ISSUE

The curriculum development work described in this paper was undertaken in the normal course of course assessment and curriculum improvement to

- Improve student outcomes
- Align our curriculum with the 2008 IT Curriculum
- Better manage scheduling, staffing and operation of the IT courses
- Improve alumni competitiveness in the rapidly changing IT environment

Moreover, all of this was accomplished in a resource-limited environment. Like most other public universities, our institution received less and less financial support from the state. Moreover, we thought it neither desirable nor feasible by shifting the cost to students. Again, like most other universities, our students simply did not have the resources to cover significantly increases in tuition, especially in light of the simultaneous inflation in the cost of text books. The work described in this paper aimed to accomplish the above four goals with respect to the field of HCI.

When our undergraduate degree in information technology was formed ten years ago, we utilized existing courses in a computing curriculum, primarily to minimize the cost of adding a new degree program. This, our IT program included a 4-credit hour course originally designed for our Software Engineering program to cover HCI.

However, it had become clear that the continued use of the software engineering HCI course to cover HCI was both undesirable and unnecessary.

For example, analysis of student feedback revealed that those IT students nearing graduation often felt that too much time (4 semester credit hours) had been spent on HCI, which also meant they were unable to take full advantage of advanced or current topics such as Linux deployment or virtualization. Furthermore, students wanted HCI covered from an IT system implementation perspective as opposed to the system development perspective taken by the original course.

The obvious solution of replacing the software engineering focused HCI course by an IT focused HCI course was not optimal either.

For example, our enrollment had grown to the point where a full set of core and a rich set of elective IT classes could be offered each term and receive full enrollment, and it was not clear that using some of our faculty members to deliver an IT focused HCI course was in the best way to meet the demands for a richer set of electives by our students, or by potential employers of our students.

Finally, and crucially, the HCI knowledge area in the 2008 IT Model Curriculum [7,pp 71-75], a document that many institutions have used to guide them in the design of their IT program , includes the following topic areas Human Factors

- HCI Aspects of Application Domains
- Human-Centered Evaluation
- Developing Effective Interfaces
- Accessibility
- Emerging Technologies
- Human-Centered Computing

The document recommends a minimum of 20 lecture hours, or their equivalent, to cover the knowledge area, or less than half a semester course. While the document obviously does not prevent schools from offering a full course in HCI, many programs may wish to put a greater emphasis on other knowledge areas covered in the IT model curriculum, such as information assurance and security, and might therefore look for other ways of covering the required minimum knowledge of HCI rather than introduce a full three semester hour course.

3. THE SOLUTION

Having decided that a full-blown HCI course was neither desirable nor necessary, we attempted to match the HCI related learning outcomes in the IT Model Curriculum to our existing IT baccalaureate courses. This exercise showed that there was a fairly direct correspondence with outcomes for our required IT management course and a somewhat more indirect correspondence for a few other courses, e.g., electronic commerce. This alignment resulted in the decision that the HCI outcomes could be embedded within our required IT management course.

Moreover, an informal survey of forecasts for HCI capabilities for IT professionals showed that a robust and dynamic set of skills will be necessary to maintain professional standards. These include being able to research for the latest best practices; maintaining flexibility to align with rapidly advancing interaction technology, the informed use of HCI principles in the management of experts/non-experts who implement and use IT systems, and the ability to maintain high levels of HCI service through secondary actions, e.g., not actually doing usability testing, but recognize when it needs to be and has been done. In short, a key HCI capability for an IT manager is to learn how to learn to keep up with HCI requirements. Our approach of embedding HCI modules within the course for IT managers aimed towards this robust and dynamic learning.

Having made this decision, a survey and analysis of resources available for teaching HCI revealed that there are a rich set of freely available, online and library resources for teaching HCI. This was particularly important because it enables casting of HCI in modules that do not require a separate textbook expense, this helping us limit the cost for students. Furthermore, it is another opportunity for students to learn lifelong learning skills by doing web research and selecting quality materials on HCI.

As we pursued the continuous curriculum improvement for HCI, the rapid transition to mobile computing changed the fundamental nature of HCI in IT. In response, our project took on a larger set of problems and issues related to the explosion of the importance and complexity of HCI and also the diffusion of traditional HCI methods. As we worked, leverage points to effectively teach HCI in the mobile environment became apparent; these leverage points are identified and evaluated in this paper.

4. LESSONS LEARNED AND OPEN ISSUES

In addition to the improvement results, we identified and assessed possible innovations to better manage teaching and learning HCI in today's mobile computing environment. Here are the top recommendations:

4.1 Mobile users are now often the sole arbiters of good HCI and user experiences

Since computing is now primarily done on mobile, highly personalized devices, the user has gone beyond being the ultimate arbiter of what constitutes good HCI and what is a pleasing user experience; they have now become for all practical purposes, the sole arbiter. The mobile marketplace has many good options: Users can choose from a rich set of user experience platforms, e.g., Android, Apple, Blackberry, Windows, etc. After the platform choice, there are bounteous choices of apps and services. The choices are so rich and easily adopted and replaced that users now configure their own mobile computing experiences much as one pursues a favorite hobby. In essence the mobile environment has matured to the point that users can generally immediately fulfill their requirements in real time without any development lag. If the app or service fits in with the user's chosen platform, HCI and the user's experience is good. If not, the user can abandon it in search for one that does fit. With a massive inventory of apps and services, finding a good one is highly likely.

That mobile users are sole arbiters of HCI becomes leverage in IT education because our students can easily understand and accept it because they are mobile users themselves. Asking them to show how they have configured their own mobile environment brings students long ways in a short time towards understanding configuration, the user experience and HCI.

4.2 The methodology for HCI and user experience design is ever increasingly diffuse in the mobile environment

Similar to mobile users becoming the sole arbiters of good HCI, mobile users are now becoming their own HCI and user experience designers; in that way, user-centered design expertise is diffusing throughout the mobile user community. They are personalizing their mobile computers and developing individually-tuned HCI and user experiences through self-customization using devices as platforms and apps and services as components. The highly exclusive and elite HCI design expertise is quickly spreading into the user community.

This commoditization of HCI design provides IT educators with additional leverage points. In the mobile environment, a high level of HCI design capability can be acquired relatively quickly. This means the time spent on HCI education can be compressed with little loss of quality or effectiveness.

4.3 For HCI, adopt a pervasive "Teach the Teachers" approach

Since HCI is now woven throughout IT, the success of IT education depends upon every participant learning HCI. Indeed the 2008 curriculum guidelines called for a solid foundation in HCI. Because of its ubiquity, mobile computing demands that users also understand and use HCI principles. So, for effective HCI education, first all IT teachers should learn the fundamentals of HCI and keep applying them in all opportunities that arise in their classes. Students should be taught to do the same, so that when they are in practice, they likewise can keep teaching their users good HCI. A good goal is to have at least part of the foundational 20% of HCI taught in 80% of the IT courses; realizing that it will take some time to achieve this goal, a good place to start is with cross-functional professional development delivered through, e.g., "lunch and learn" workshops.

This is a leverage point for administrators to facilitate increasing the capability of a department to effectively teach HCI in the mobile environment. Furthermore, this leverage point can be amplified because for HCI education, there are many free, open sources of educational materials that are directly suitable or easily adapted to the mobile environment. Thus, there is dual leverage in teaching HCI in a way that is suitable to be taught by the learner.

4.4 IT professionals should guide users to do "Point-of-Sale" HCI evaluation

Since the mobile device provides a platform for HCI and the user experience, an important HCI function of the IT professional is to guide users to evaluate the HCI of devices as they consider buying them. Here, traditional ergonomics can play a major role. For example, if one-handed operation is required, that will limit the device size. Device mass and torque characteristics will have an influence on rate of fatigue in holding and using the device. Display size will have a significant effect on visual and task performance. In the sum, there are many HCI factors that need to be considered at the point mobile devices are purchased; this is true regardless of whether the purchaser is buying one for individual use or procuring many for corporate use.

Because good information to guide a major purchase is generally seen as a positive, this provides leverage in teaching good HCI within IT. The one who is the "go-to-person" for mobile purchases is seen as having great value. It is also a major link in successful management of the "bring your own device" (BYOD) wave within IT. Teaching students how to evaluate HCI and ergonomics of mobile devices will provide a valuable capability for our IT graduates.

4.5 In IT procurement, especially in the mobile area, always consider a "HCI pilot"

Related to the need for HCI evaluations at the point of sale, IT educators can leverage HCI by teaching students to always give serious consideration to a HCI pilot in any IT procurement, and especially those involving mobile computing and in particular those involving BYOD. In short, the HCI pilot should become as commonplace in IT procurement as is testing a web site across all major browsers.

This is a leverage point for both good HCI and good IT. It brings about good HCI, because there is a systematic test of the HCI in the new or updated IT system before it is completely rolled out. It brings about good IT procurement, because it is a significant test of the effective value as perceived by users of the new or updated system performed prior to system rollout.

4.6 Teaching IT professionals to do research and "fish for good HCI" will keep good HCI in IT systems

Similar to the adage, "Give someone a fish and they can eat a meal; teach someone to fish and they can eat the rest of their lives," a leverage point is to teach IT professionals to do research to keep up to date in the latest tools, techniques and methods for HCI. Indeed in the mobile environment they will have to keep current as it is changing rapidly now with no slow down in sight. This leverage point is amplified as it also teaches the professional responsibility of keeping current, which is present in all professions. For example, point 2.2 of the ACM Code of Ethics and Professional Conduct [9] states that computing professionals should "acquire and maintain professional competence."

4.7 Preliminary results show positive effects

In the first few terms of implementation, we have seen indicators of positive outcomes where students have shown, e.g., an increased awareness of the importance of HCI in information technology and an increased desire to follow HCI research and trends. In a recent term, about half of the students explicitly stated in assignment solutions that they were previously not aware of HCI in IT and that they would continue to use approaches, e.g., user-centered design and accessibility, in their IT practice. One student, who is specializing in information security, adopted a focus on research in the newly forming HCI security (HCISec) area as a result of the course. Granted these results are anecdotal, but they clearly indicate our approach is replacing ignorance of HCI with capable awareness and also prompting interest in advanced research topics of HCI for our students. In the new, minimalist and embedded format, our main stakeholders, students (and their employers), have quit questioning the inclusion of HCI in the curriculum and are now embracing its importance and value in effective information technology.

4.8 Develop and deploy curriculum at the module or learning object level of granularity

The typical level of granularity at which programs of study are analyzed is at the level of a course. Thus, an undergraduate program will typically be seen as consisting of say 40 courses. This level of analysis has certain advantages, including making it easier to track student progress towards graduation, allowing students to transfer courses between institutions, and making it easier for faculty and publishers to determine which textbooks to write or publish. However, the course based model also has certain drawbacks. For example, since we typically like courses to be coherent in the sense that they cover related concepts and skills, it is not always straightforward to include material that is necessary but that does not require a full 3 credit hour course. Moreover, the fact that many faculty prefer to use established textbooks to support their students often makes courses less responsive to the changing needs of students and potential employers as they might be.

None of the issues are of course insurmountable. For example, we were able to find space for a 1 hour HCI module within the existing course structure of our IT program, and publishers are increasingly using custom publications, which allow faculty to assemble a textbook for their course from smaller units.

However, we would at least like to offer the thought that it might be feasible to redesign academic programs at a lower level of granularity, for example as consisting of a larger number of modules (on the order of around 1 credit hour each), or as consisting of an even larger number of learning objects. We are currently doing an analysis of certain areas crucial to IT, including programming, project management, and web technologies, to determine what a program structured around learning objects would look like.

5. CONCLUSIONS/ RECOMMENDATIONS

Overall, our results show that embedding HCI education into an IT course is possible and straight forward when working from defined curriculum outcomes. It is effective in that it embodies the HCI material in the IT model curriculum [7, pgs 71-75] for information technology baccalaureate degrees. Embedding also shows learning outcomes indicating students are effectively learning and employing sound HCI principles and practices. Students realize both the importance and dynamic nature of HCI because they tend to do research to identify current best practices for HCI in their exercise and project work.

Furthermore, we have identified and analyzed significant points of leverage for effectively teaching and learning HCI in the new IT environment of mobile computing. We are using these leverage points to improve teaching of HCI in our IT curricula and recommend them to you also.

Our main findings indicate that this approach of embedding HCI in IT courses is effective in attaining the required curriculum outcomes. Our students effectively applied HCI methods in completing an IT management project. Embedding HCI within existing IT courses works well with both major directions of HCI and HCI education and curriculum design and implementation constraints for small colleges and universities: Required outcomes can be achieved through using solid, freely available HCI materials from, e.g., the web or our university's online library.

Our approach of embedding minimalist HCI in the IT curriculum is in its preliminary stage, yet it appears to have made progress with both the historical difficulties surrounding HCI within computing education and the rapidly changing (mobile) environment of HCI as well. We conjecture that the historical difficulties have been reduced because the embedded approach does a better job of "connecting the dots" between HCI issues as IT issues and HCI solutions as valuable IT solutions as well. Furthermore, the new, mobile environment has changed computing and IT fundamentally, and made HCI a foundational requirement of any successful IT system. So, from our perspective embedding HCI within IT education is a key approach to success.

Finally, we are convinced that the embedding approach can be generalized to teaching and training other topics across the curriculum and within industry. It works well within the ever-expanding educational resources and delivery options of today. We also strongly believe that the practice of embedding material where it is required, rather than in a single course will help student learning.

6. REFERENCES

1. Churchill, E.F., Bowser, A., Preece, J., Teaching and Learning Human-Computer Interaction: Past, Present, and Future, *Interactions*, 20 (2), 44-53, 2013.

2. Evans, B. Smart Phones Are Eating the World, *MIT Technology Review March 15, 2013*, retrieved on 4/4/3013 from http://www.technologyreview.com/photoessay/511791/smart phones-are-eating-the-world/

3. Aguilar, M. The World Now Buys More Smart Phones than Computers, *Gizmodo.com February 3, 2012*, retrieved on 4/4/2013 from http://gizmodo.com/5882172/the-world-now-buys-more-smartphones-than-computers

4. New Internationalist March 2013, Computers and Cell Phones in the Developing World. Retrieved on 4/4/2013 from http://newint.org/books/reference/world-development/case-studies/2013/03/14/computers-cellphones-in-developing-world/

5. Cisco White Paper, Cisco Visual Networking Index: Global Mobile Data Traffic Forecast Update, 2012-2017, Retrieved on 4/4/2013 from http://www.cisco.com/en/US/solutions/collateral/ns341/ns525/ns537/ns705/ns827/white_paper_c11-520862.pdf

6. Manaris, B. Editorial on Human-Computer Interaction. *Computer Science Education*, 13(3), 173-176, 2003.

7. ACM/IEEE, 2008 IT Curriculum, Retrieved on 4/4/2013 from http://www.acm.org/education/curricula/IT2008%20Curriculum.pdf

8. U.S. DOL OSHA. Installing Cables, Retrieved on 4/4/2013 from http://www.osha.gov/SLTC/etools/electricalcontractors/installation/pulling.html

9. ACM Code of Ethics and Professional Practices, Retrieved on 5/29/13 from http://www.acm.org/about/code-of-ethics

Flipping the Classroom - Is It For You?

Rebecca H. Rutherfoord
Southern Polytechnic State University
1100 S. Marietta Parkway
Marietta, GA 30060
(001) 678-915-7400
brutherf@spsu.edu

James K. Rutherfoord
Chattahoochee Technical College
980 S. Cobb Drive
Marietta, GA 30060
(001) 770-310-4322
jrutherfoord@chattahoocheetech.edu

ABSTRACT

Technology is being used to enhance all types of educational experiences. Several new pedagogical methods have been developed that use technology to assist students in learning. This paper will discuss one of these methods –the flipped classroom. The flipped classroom is not necessarily a new idea, in fact, it developed from such things as hybrid or blended classrooms. But flipping the classroom does have different pedagogical implications for student learning. The paper will describe the history of the flipped classroom, mechanisms of flipping the classroom, pros and cons for this method, give examples of how this has worked, and discuss how to get started creating a flipped classroom environment.

Categories and Subject Descriptors

DK.3.2 [**Computer and Information Science Education**]: Information Systems Education – accreditation, organization, curriculum.

Keywords

Flipped classroom, blended classroom, hybrid, virtual education

1. INTRODUCTION

The outcome of this paper is to start a discussion on the merits of using a flipped classroom for IT courses. As IT and STEM educators we need to be aware of how to use technology to enhance student learning and support delivery of classroom material. One of the original methods of using technology is the blended or hybrid classroom. The concept of blended learning involves a student learning ,in part, through online delivery of content and instruction. This methodology also gives students some control over their time, effort, location and pace of delivery. The blended classroom also uses the traditional method of face-to-face classroom participation. [1] The Sloan Consortium defines hybrid courses as those that "integrate online with traditional face-to-face class activities in a planned, pedagogically valuable manner. [2] Part of the difficulty in the blended classroom is that most educators just use the technology to assist in the regular classroom lecture format. The technology is used primarily for reinforcement or drilling of material. Educators don't consider how this methodology can be used in a different way to enhance

SIGITE'13, October 10–12, 2013, Orlando, Florida, USA.
Copyright © 2013 ACM 978-1-4503-2239-3/13/10...$15.00.
http://dx.doi.org/10.1145/2512276.2512299

student learning. The authors believe that a better method that incorporates the ideas of the blended classroom is using the "flipped classroom" method.

2. THE FLIPPED CLASSROOM

The flipped classroom involves flipping the traditional in-class lecture first and using outside supporting technology second to reinforce the lecture. The flipped classroom assigns web-based content (lecture material) as homework FIRST, making time and space available in the face-to-face classroom for more inquiry-based projects and questions. The Khan Academy actually brought this concept to secondary education beginning in 2004 with a series of videos showing how this methodology can be used. There is still a lot of controversy among educators on the merits of flipping the classroom – particularly at the high school level. However, the merits of this methodology and the more mature student lends itself to better use at the university/college level.

The following is a diagram of the flipped classroom.

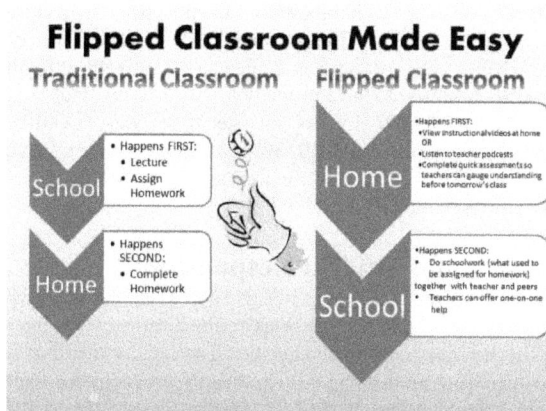

2.1 The History of the Flipped Classroom

Some of the earliest work began with peer instruction in the 1990s done by Eric Mazur at Harvard. Professor Mazur found that by using computer aided instruction he had more time to coach instead of lecture. [10] In 1993, Alison King published the article called "From Sage on the Stage to Guide on the Side", published in College Teaching, Vol. 41, No. 1 (Winter, 1993), pp. 30-35. In 2000, Maureen Lage, Glenn Platt and Michael Treglia published the paper "Inverting the Classroom: A Gateway to Creating an Inclusive Learning Environment". [11] They talked about creating an inverted classroom in order to accommodate many different student learning styles. In other places in 2000, the University of Wisconsin-Madison began using eTeach software to replace lectures with streaming video presentations (voice with power point). In 2004 Salman Khan began recording videos to help a younger cousin with classwork. The Khan Academy grew from this original concept. There are now over 2400 Khan Academy online video lessons available – and they are free of charge! There have been many articles, workshops and presentations about flipping the classroom made over the last several years.

For K-12 instruction, in 2007, Jonathan Bergman and Aaron Sams, who were teachers at Woodland Park High School in Woodland, Colorado began using a new software that allowed them to synchronize voice over power point slides. They began recording and posting their live lectures online for students who were missing class. They were asked to speak around their county to other educators about this teaching method. Soon online videos and podcasts were being used across the county. Other K-12 educators began sharing this method and this caught on quickly across the country. This was the beginning of the blended classroom in the K-12 arena. An example of the K-12 success occurred in Clintondale High School near Detroit, Michigan. Teachers created 3 videos a week to start the pilot. Students watched at home or at school. Each video was only 5-7 minutes – covering a specific topic. Class time was then used for labs or other interactive activities. Students received instant feedback on their classroom activities. They didn't become as frustrated because they actually worked on homework in the class and could get instructor support. Prior to the flipped classroom pilot, 50% of freshman failed English, 44% of freshman failed math and there were 736 discipline cases in one semester. After adopting the flipped classroom, 19% of freshmen failed English, 13% of freshman failed math, and there were 249 discipline cases in one semester. This was a remarkable improvement for the students.

The method of using technology to actually present lecture material caught on quickly. The prevalence of online technology based knowledge delivery systems helped to support the growth of this model. Adults who have viewed online education videos is also expanding. In 2007 15% of internet users viewed online education videos, while in 2010 30% of internet users have viewed online videos. Can we use this same methodology for university/college courses?

2.1 Faculty and Student Responsibility

The flipped classroom concept is not as easy as it first appears. The faculty member's role in the classroom drastically changes with the flipped classroom methodology. The faculty member is no longer the "sage on the stage". The faculty must change their focus from being the purveyor of knowledge to students as the receptacle of that knowledge, to a focus as one who is a facilitator to students and allows the students to take responsibility for much of their learning and knowledge attainment. The faculty member becomes a "guide on the side". This requires a change in the faculty member's concept of what it means to "teach". Many faculty have difficulty with this new concept.

One reason the flipped classroom has become popular is the overall performance of students attaining learning outcomes in a course. The traditional classroom is a one-size-fits-all model and has a limited concept of engagement with the students. The faculty member is actually the one taking the responsibility for the students' learning. Currently, only 69% of students who start high school finish 4 years later. 7,200 students drop out of high school EACH day – 1.3 million per year. Success rates and retention rates at many colleges and universities are abysmal.

The flipped classroom model allows for the student to take responsibility for his/her learning. The faculty member can create classroom experiences that allow for more analysis and synthesis of material. Students can explore additional material in support of the topic being covered. The learning curve for both faculty and students can't be taken for granted with this method. Faculty have to create their lectures and get them posted online – through podcasts, power point with voice, video, etc. They need to have discussions and other interactions that allow students to interact with each other and the faculty member during the reading of the content material. The in-class activities need to address expanding the knowledge of the student and giving students an opportunity for more creative and higher-level critical thinking activities.

3. What the Flipped Classroom Is and What It Is Not

It is important to realize that creating a flipped classroom is not just putting lectures on videos. The pieces of the flipped classroom include: [6]

- Creating videos to take the place of face-to-face instruction
- Providing activities for students to work with peers and faculty out of the classroom to assist in learning
- Freeing up class time for students to work with faculty on other learning activities to reinforce learning
- Allowing the student to take responsibility for much of their learning

Therefore, when examining this model the flipped classroom allows for:

- Increasing interaction and personalized content time between students and faculty
- Creating an environment where students take responsibility for their own learning
- Blending of direct instruction with constructivist learning
- For students who are absent to keep current with their work
- Archiving content for review and study
- Engaged students
- More personalized education for students

The flipped classroom is not:

- Just online videos
- About replacing faculty with videos
- An online course
- A classroom with no structure
- Students in class staring at a computer screen
- Students working in isolation

2.3 Why Does This Work?

There is strong research evidence that supports the flipped classroom methodology. In the book, *How People Learn*, John Bransford, Ann Brown and Rodney Cocking report key findings on how people learn. Two of their theories support the flipped classroom method. Bransford, Brown and Cocking state that:

"To develop competence in an area of inquiry, students must: a) have a deep foundation of factual knowledge, b) understand facts and ideas in the context of a conceptual framework, and c)

organize knowledge in ways that facilitate retrieval and application" (p. 16). [8]

When students work at home watching videos and taking part in peer and faculty interaction immediately, they can correct misconceptions, and begin to build frameworks for organizing the material themselves. In addition, the authors state that:

"A 'metacognitive' approach to instruction can help students learn to take control of their own learning by defining learning goals and monitoring their progress in achieving them" (p. 18).

When the students are able to use higher cognitive functions in the classroom with the faculty member as their guide, accompanying by the peer and instructor interaction outside of the classroom, allows the metacognition to take place in learning.

2.4 What the Flipped Classroom Supports
The flipped classroom supports many positive aspects to support student learning. [7]
1. Provide an opportunity for students to gain first exposure prior to class

There are many methods to introduce new concepts/ideas to students – such as textbook readings, power point lectures, lecture videos, podcasts, screen captures, etc. These methods all allow the students before class to be exposed to the material they are learning.

2. Provide an incentive for students to prepare for class

By providing some sort of task for the students to complete with their outside work, they can also get additional "points" for grades. This also allows for more absorption of the knowledge by providing various methods of completing tasks.

3. Provide a mechanism to assess student understanding

All of the pre-class work, including assignments help with assessing how much the student has "understood" of the topic. It allows the student to then come to class with the questions about the material they didn't understand or comprehend. This allows for immediate feedback if the faculty member uses automatic graded tasks/assignments.

4. Provide in-class activities that focus on high level cognitive activities

As students gain basic knowledge of a topic prior to class, then the faculty member can spend more time helping students achieve a deeper learning of the subject matter. Classroom activities should include types of active learning that assist in higher levels of cognitive learning. These include analysis and synthesis activities. The main point is to have students using class time to achieve higher levels of learning and deepen their understanding and increase skills.

3. HOW TO START AND BENEFITS
3.1 Starting the Flipped Classroom
The flipped classroom has gained popularity both at the K-12 and now the college/university setting. Each faculty member needs to understand this method and how it affects both teaching and learning. Author Ramsey Musallam in his eduTopia article

"Should You Flip Your Classroom" believes in carefully approaching creating a flipped classroom environment. He advocates the following steps: [9]

Step 1 – Identify your current or desired teaching style

Step 2 – Ask yourself this question: Given my style, do I currently use class time to teach any low level, procedural, algorithmic concepts?

Step 3 – If yes, begin by creating opportunities for students to obtain this information outside of the classroom (primarily through videos)

Step 4 – Include a system that encourages reflection and synthesis of homework-based instruction

We would also add to begin looking at creating higher-order learning activities for the classroom following the pre-class learning.

The following shows the comparison of the tradition classroom to the flipped classroom.

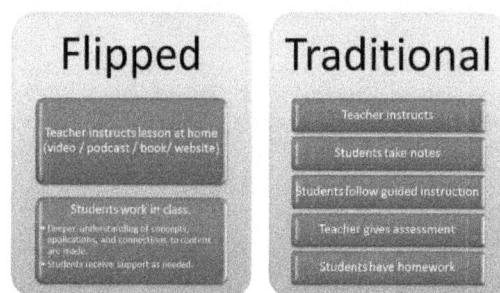

3.2 Benefits of the Flipped Classroom
The flipped classroom allow for benefits for both students and faculty. Some examples are: [4]
- Student-led discussions, tutoring and collaborative learning
- Critical thinking by students
- Problem-based learning
- Collaboration – between student-to-student, and student-to-faculty
- Student ownership of learning
- Student exploration
- Student engagement
- Transformative learning
- Faculty having time to assist students on things they couldn't learning by themselves
- Faculty using technology to assist in teaching/learning
- Faculty having more time to interact with students on one-to-one

4.0 CONCLUSION
The flipped classroom has proven successful in many areas of education. As IT and STEM educators we can embrace the

technology and pedagogy for this new method of teaching/learning. This will require a change of attitude for each of us, but the benefits to the students and faculty outweigh the time involved for creating this new learning environment.

The following is an example of the author's math classroom. It shows how the flipped classroom changes the amount of type of learning that takes place.

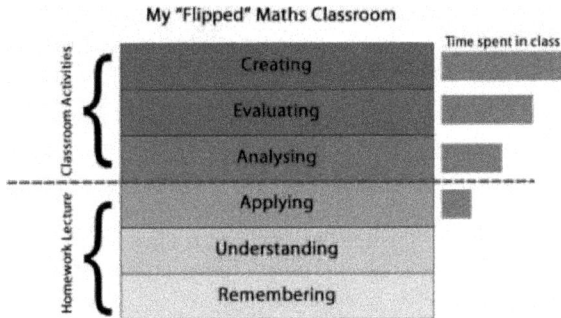

My "Flipped" Maths Classroom

5.0 RESOURCES

[1] *"Blended Learning"*, Retrieved May 31, 2013, from http://en.wikipedia.org/wiki/Blended_learning/

[2] *"the Definition of Blended Learning"*, Retrieved May 31, 2013, from www.teachthought.com/blended-learning-2/the-definition-of-blended-learning/

[3] *"Flipping the Classroom"*, Educational Technology for School Leaders, Retrieved May 31, 2013, from https://sites/google.com/site/adms647summer12/tutorials/flippingtheclassroom/

[4] Bruder, Patricia, *"The Flipped Classroom: Reversing the Way We Teach"*, New Jersey Education Association, Retrieved May 31, 2013, from www.jnew.org/news-and-publications/njea-review/february-2012/the-flipped-classroom-reversing-the-way-we-teach

[5] *"Flip Teaching"*, Retrieved May 31, 2013, from http://en/wikipedia/org/wiki/Flip-teaching

[6] *"The Flipped Class: Myths and Reality"*, The Daily Riff, Retrieved May 31, 2013, from www.thedailyriff.com/articles/the-flipped-class-conversation-689.php

[7] Brame, Cynthia J., *"Flipping the Classroom"*, Center for Teaching Vanderbilt University, Retrieved May 31, 2013, from http://cft.vanderbilt.edu/teaching-guides/teaching-activities/flipping-the-classroom/

[8] Bransford, J.D., Brown, A.L., and Cocking, R.R., *How People Learn: Brain, Mind, Experience, and School,* Washington, D.C.: National Academy Press, 2000

[9] *"Should You Flip Your Classroom"*, eduTopia, The George Lucas Educational Foundation, Retrieved May 31, 2013, from www.edutopia.org/blog/flipped-c;assroom-ramsey-musallam

[10] Mazur, Eric, Feb. 1991, *"Can We Teach Computers to Teach?"*, Retrieved May 31, 2013, from http://mazur.harvard.edu/sentFiles/Mazur_256459.pdf

[11] Lage, Maureen, Platt, Glenn, Treglia, Michael, (2000), *"Inverting the Classroom: A gateway to Creating an Inclusive Learning Environment"*, Journal of Economic Education, Retrieved May 31, 2013, from http://dl.dropbox.com/u/249331/Inverted_Classroom_Paper.pdf

Student Perspective on an Online Asynchronous Introduction to Linux based on User-First Pedagogy

Alessio Gaspar, Sarah Langevin
University of South Florida in Lakeland
3433 Winter Lake Road
Lakeland, FL 33803-9807
863-667-7088
alessio@usf.edu

Naomi Boyer
Polk State College
999 Ave. H. NE.
Winter Haven, Fl. 33881
863-298-6854
NBoyer@polk.edu

Cliff Bennett
Polk State College
3425 Winter Lake Rd
Lakeland, FL 33803-9715
863-669-2837
cbennett@polk.edu

CEReAL group – http://CEReAL.forest.usf.edu/

ABSTRACT

An introduction to Linux is used to survey students' perception of required effort levels, suitability of tools, pedagogies of contents / instruction. Their perception of the relevance of various cognitive skills taught, along with their evaluation of how well the teaching material supports their acquisition, supplements previous findings on the educational nature of an introduction to Linux.

Survey results are interpreted in terms of the impact on student's motivation of the misalignment of their perceptions about the relevance of specific cognitive skills with both academic and industry perspectives. We also review what results teach us about the appropriateness of both pedagogies of contents and instruction. We then discuss observations regarding potential issues and how we might address them in the future.

Categories and Subject Descriptors

K.3.2 [**Computers and Education**]: Computer and Information Science Education – *computer science education, curriculum.*

General Terms

Measurement, Human Factors.

Keywords

Linux, online learning, Bloom Taxonomy, attitude surveys.

1. INTRODUCTION

1.1 Motivation & Previous Work

Computing education researchers have devoted significant efforts investigating the learning barriers encountered by undergraduates in both introductory – e.g. CS0 – and programming offerings.

Proportionally, significantly less work has been devoted to studying such barriers in system administration offerings despite their relevance to Information Technology. The Bloom taxonomies' [2][3] relevance to computing education has already been suggested by multiple studies focused on undergraduate programming pedagogy; see [3-8] for examples.

The application of the Revised Bloom's Taxonomy to an introduction to Linux system administration, revealed that the cognitive skills required from students on graded assignments, along with those desired by their future employers, spread over a spectrum similar to that of programming activities [9-12].

1.2 Objectives

Students' appreciation of higher order skills was found to be sometimes at odds with both academic and industry perspectives [10]. This motivated a more detailed study of the student perspective on various aspects of an introduction to Linux. We use an online anonymous survey to better understand students' attitude with respect to; the suitability of tools, the required effort levels, the pedagogy of contents / instruction, the value of skills being taught and efficacy of the teaching methods.

1.3 Organization

Section 2 establishes the context of this study; specificities of our offering, student population's characteristics, detailed pedagogy of contents and of instruction used. Section 3 discusses how our attitude survey captured the student perspective on the tools we used, required effort level, pedagogies of content and instructions, and their relevance to an established educational taxonomy. Section 4 presents survey results while section 5 discusses them.

2. BACKGROUND

2.1 User-Level Intro to Linux

The main innovation of "User Level Intro to Linux", aka ULIL, is to not start with system administration topics but, instead, aim at preparing IT students for working in a Linux environment as developers, web designers…. The focus is roughly equivalent to that of CompTIA Linux+ certification exam LX0-101.

This strategy has so far attracted a broader range of students, including non IT majors. Informal feedback underlined its relevance to prepare students for upper-level offerings which require them to work with Linux; e.g. IT Networks, IT Security.

ULIL is taught over 15 weeks as an online asynchronous offering. As such, there is no mandatory class meeting. Videos and assignments are made available via a Learning Management System – LMS – also used to turn in assignments. Students meet the TA and instructor using "Blackboard Collaborate" web-conferencing software. These sessions are one-on-one or with small groups. Formative feedback is provided to students for every weekly assignment and exams. Quiz solutions are released after their respective deadline. Non-graded material is available at http://cereal.forest.usf.edu/linux/L1/.

2.2 Student Population

Surveyed students are Junior-standing undergraduates from the University of South Florida who were enrolled in COP3931 User-Level Intro to Linux in spring 2011, fall 2011 or spring 2013.They were not necessarily majoring in Information Technology.

Additional demographic information gathered in fall 2011 and spring 2013 revealed that the average student is 30 years old, employed 26 hours every week, enrolled in 3 other 3-credit courses and spent about 4.5 years employed in IT. Out of the 34 respondents, 85% (29) were males, and15% (5) were females.

Assuming 12 hours of work per week for every 3-credit course, these students have committed to 48 hours of academic workload on top of being employed on average 26 hours per week. The label *overcommitted adult learner* has been used by our team to describe such students. There is high pressure on them to spend as little time as possible on each course. From an instructional perspective, this exacerbates compliant learner tendencies, e.g. "no time to try ungraded exercises", "no time to just explore this topic if it's not on the exam". These are detrimental to the acquisition of a long-term education vs. a short-term training.

It is essential to keep the characteristics of our student population in mind throughout this paper. First, it will explain some of the pedagogical design decisions; e.g. weekly assignments worth a few points. Second, they will allow the reader to interpret our findings in the specific context from which they arose.

2.3 Tools

Students' learning, along with their overall interest in working with Linux, might be hindered by the use of poor tools.

ULIL requires students to work on *Ubuntu Desktop LTS 12.04.* A desktop version was selected to enable us to teach both command line interface tools (CLI) and graphic user interface usage (GUI). Since most students come from Windows or Mac environments, it is expected they will do better in a user-friendly desktop as they progressively learn CLI tools. We favored the Long Term Support edition in order to prevent the need for the instructor to re-record videos featuring GUI elements every semester.

Similarly, students are required to use Virtual Box. Its availability on any platform allows students to keep their preferred OS while working on easy to snapshot / restore virtual Linux images.

2.4 Pedagogy of Contents

Whereas pedagogy of instruction is concerned with how the subject matter is taught, pedagogy of content is focused on which specific topics are taught and in what order. An example of this would be the object first versus fundamentals first dilemma in programming pedagogy.

Table 1 – Topics taught in User-Level Intro to Linux

#	Topic	#	Topic
1	Using Virtual Box	9	Other Distributions
2	Installing Ubuntu	10	Shell Initialization
3	Ubuntu Desktop	11	Redirections
4	Linux Terminals	12	Filters
5	Getting Help	13	Regular Expressions
6	Software Packages	14	File System
7	Shell Quoting	15	Processes
8	User Management		

ULIL's pedagogy of contents diverges from Linux system administration introductions. Our focus is on fostering a deep understanding of the tools available on Linux platforms.

Table 1 lists the topics taught. Most leverage reading assignments from the textbook [1]. Others are presented with videos or hands-on exploration assignments.

2.5 Pedagogies of Instruction

ULIL is delivered as an online asynchronous offering; i.e. no mandatory weekly class meetings, either face-to-face or online. Students appreciate this flexibility due to being full-time employees already, or being geographically unable to attend face-to-face sessions; e.g. deployed military personnel.

Every Monday, one of the 12 online modules is released. Assignments are due the following Monday. This regularity has proven essential to keep students engaged and prevent them from falling behind. Skipping a week, results in losing enough points to deter students, while not irreparably damaging their grade.

Each module covers one or more topics listed in Table 1. Textbook reading assignments and videos provide students with a lecture-like passive learning experience. A support forum is available for students to post questions anytime.

We observed that students often find themselves unable to understand what it is they are missing in such lectures. To remedy this, PQ – Practice Quizzes – are provided. They allow students to test their own understanding, spot topics they missed in the readings, generate questions, without grade penalty.

To ensure students' commitment to understanding this material, 30 minutes long GQ – graded quiz – are administered via Blackboard with limited time and single attempt enforced. There are 12 such quizzes, worth 36% of the students' grades.

Most modules also feature a PA – practice assignment – for students to apply what they learned. These are meant to take most of the student's weekly study time. They guide them to go beyond the readings to explore new topics, or simply apply them in more in-depth. PAs are also meant to reinforce the students' ability to search for new information in technical references; e.g. manpages.

PAs are graded in order to motivate students to turn them in. There are 8 PAs representing 8% of the students' grade. The amount of points is kept low to not penalize explorative learning. Students download the PA's instructions PDF, work on it for about a week, then upload the result by a set deadline.

During the week, they are allowed to work with the instructor / TA to get help solving the PA. During these help sessions, we are careful to not provide solutions but rather identify what students misunderstand in order to provide tailored on-demand lecturing. Feedback is provided the week following the PA's submission in order to help students understand what they missed.

Three exams are administered over the semester. These are equivalent to a PA and represent 45% of the student's grades.

Some modules have DF – discussion forums – which require students to research a simple topic, post a synthesis of their readings, and read other students posts. There are 6 DFs worth 6% of the grade. Grades are mostly participation based.

Table 2 – Learning Activities used in User-Level Intro to Linux

#	Learning Activity	#	Learning Activity
1	Reading Textbook	6	GQ – Graded Quiz
2	Watching Videos	7	PA – Practice Assignments
3	DF – Reading Posts	8	Exams
4	DF – Participating	9	PL – Participating
5	PQ – Practice Quiz		

Forums are also used for 2 PL – Peer Learning – activities which require students to post a few challenges based on what they felt was the most difficult aspect of a module. They then attempt to solve other students' challenges. These activities are used for difficult modules, e.g. regular expressions, in order to help students revisit the material explicitly looking for the most difficult notions which are usually missed on initial readings. These two PL assignments are worth 5% of students' grades.

3. METHODS

We used an anonymous online survey hosted on Survey Monkey to gather students' attitudes and perspectives. The link to take the survey was provided to students via LMS announcement.

Participation was optional but rewarded with extra credit. In order to keep the survey anonymous, a key was provided on the last page of the survey. Students were invited to email it to their instructor so they would be assigned the extra points.

The last version of the survey was administrated with an option to skip to the last page in order to discourage participants from responding randomly just to get to the end of the survey.

Respective response rates were approximately 19/28 (67%) for spring 2011, 19/24 (79%) for fall 2011 and 15/22 (68%) for fall 2013. Estimates are based on best response rate since respondents were allowed to skip any questions.

Over the three offerings of this course, a module has been removed – bash scripting – and survey questions have undergone minor adjustments. Our analysis will mainly focus on the questions related to invariants. When differences affect responses, we will discuss the specifics and how they affect interpretations.

3.1 Tools

A "rate your agreement level with the following statements" question was used to capture the students' attitude toward the usage of Virtual Box and Ubuntu. The relevant statements were;

T1 *Virtual Box was easy to use*
T2 *Virtual Box provided me with the features I needed to support my learning*
T3 *Ubuntu Linux was easy to use*
T4 *Ubuntu Linux provided me with the features I needed to support my learning*

For each statement, students were able to respond using a 5 points Likert scale labeled; "Strongly Disagree", "Disagree", "Neutral Opinion", "Agree", "Strongly Agree".

In addition, "N/A" and "Didn't use it" options were available. Only a few students reported not using virtual box in spring 2011.

3.2 Effort

We used the following question to measure the amount of efforts students perceived devoting to this offering;

E1 *How many hours did you spend every week working on this offering? Provide an average value, round up to the next integer.*

We also used open-ended questions to identify learning activities perceived as most time-consuming and the hardest topics.

E2 *What were the most time-consuming learning activities?*
E3 *Which topics were the hardest to learn about?*

3.3 Pedagogy of Contents

Due to the ever-evolving nature of IT, it is often easy to not expose students to all aspects of the technology being studied. We polled students to provide feedback on the following questions;

PC1 *Which of the topics we studied should have been studied in more depth?*

PC2 *Which of the topics we studied should have been studied in less depth?*
PC3 *Which topics do you think were missing from this user-level intro to Linux*

For the first two questions, we mapped students' responses to the topics listed in Table 1. For the last question, we took note of the responses pointing to something not already taught in the material, thus removing responses such as "more GUI", "more regex"…

3.4 Pedagogy of Instruction

Question PI-1 was formulated to indirectly identify which of the 3 following pedagogies our students preferred;

If given a choice between several good things, it's natural to want them all :) Reality is that students and instructors' time is at a premium and priorities need to be given. Assuming you have only N hours available each week to spend with your instructor. Assuming also that you have a textbook presenting the information that has to be studied this week, which of the following options would you prefer;

#1 Constructivist *Reading the material on your own, then using the time with your instructor to have him address your questions*
#2 Instructivist *Having the instructor lecture based on the textbook's material, then figure out what is still not understood on your own.*
#3 Constructivist hands-on *Reading the material on your own, then using the time with your instructor to have him help you apply this knowledge to exercises.*

Option #2 is instructivist in nature and represents the traditional lecturing model. Option #1 relies on students to engage in active learning via formulating questions to the instructor. The instructor is free to then leverage constructivist pedagogies, based on students' personal learning barriers. Option #3 involves a similar approach but relies more heavily on hands-on learning; rather than asking questions about the material, students and instructors address learning barriers while engaged in a specific project.

Question PI-2 and PI-3 respectively focused on assessing the students' enjoyment of the various learning activities along with their perception of how much each supported their learning.

PI-2 *Rate the degree to which you enjoyed engaging in the following activities, regardless of their ability to support your learning.*

PI-3 *Rate the usefulness of the following learning activities to support your learning, regardless of how much you did or did not enjoy engaging in them. Keep in mind that different activities aim at supporting you with respect to different learning objectives e.g. technical proficiency is different than just discovering open sources possibilities.*

For both questions, students were provided with the list of learning activities outlined in Table 2. They were able to express their opinion using two separate 5-point Liker-scales.

- PI-2's labels were "didn't enjoy at all", "didn't enjoy it much", "neutral", "enjoyed it somewhat" and "enjoyed it very much".

- PI-3's labels were "not useful at all", "not really useful", "neutral", "somewhat useful", "very useful".

Last but not least, we also wanted to validate the usefulness of enforcing strict weekly deadlines in an online asynchronous offering. Question PI-4 specifically targeted this;

PI-4 *It supports my learning to have assignments due every week rather than being left to structure my own learning over several weeks in between graded exams*

Students were invited to rate their agreement with the above-statement using a 5-points Likert-Scale with labels "Strongly Disagree", "Disagree", "Neutral", "Agree", "Strongly Agree".

3.5 Bloom Taxonomy Levels

Previous work established the academic, industry, and student perspectives on the relevance of the Revised Bloom Taxonomy – RBT – levels to Linux system administration education [9][12].

Our first question, RBT-1, was used to assess our students' attitude toward the relevance of these higher-order skills;

> **RBT-1** *Indicate how important you see the following cognitive skills for someone working as a Linux system administrator;*
> - *Remembering technical knowledge*
> - *Remembering conceptual knowledge*
> - *Applying procedural knowledge*
> - *Evaluating or validating alternative solutions*
> - *Troubleshooting*

Responses were on a 3-point Likert Scale with labels "useless", "somewhat important", "very important".

Next, we sought to establish the students' perspective on how well our interventions supported the acquisition of such higher level skills. They were asked to respond to the following question;

> **RBT-2** *Indicate how much the learning activities in this offering helped you develop the following skills;*
> *<list of skills follows>*

The response was provided on a 3-point Likert-Scale with labels "no learning activities helped me develop this skill", "few did", "many did". These items were phrased to be directly relevant to the learning outcomes. They map to the skills, remembering, applying, evaluating, analyze, synthesize RBT levels [3].

4. OBSERVATIONS

4.1 Tools

For the purpose of identifying the overall students' attitudes, we grouped responses falling into "Strongly Disagree" and "Disagree" groups vs. those falling into "Strongly Agree" and "Agree" groups. We labeled them "disagree" and "agree".

Table 3 – Student Perspective on Ubuntu and Virtual Box.

Q	Not used	Disagree	Neutral	Agree	N
T1	12%(6)	6%(3)	6%(3)	78%(41)	50
T2	12%(6)	6%(3)	8%(4)	76%(40)	50
T3		4%(2)	4%(2)	93%(49)	50
T4			4%(2)	97%(50)	49

Aggregated responses for spring 2011, fall 2011 and fall 2013, show strong agreement with statements about "ease of use" (T1), and "learning support" (T2), for virtual box. Agreement is even stronger for analog questions about Ubuntu (T3, T4).

4.2 Effort

Responses to E1, E2 and E3 were aggregated for spring 2011, fall 2011 and spring 2013. A total of 48 responses were reviewed for question E1, providing an average of 9 hours per week devoted to this offering. The minimum was 2 hours and the maximum 25. An outlier who responded 80 hours per week during fall 2011 was removed since he/she also reported a 50 hours a week employment while being enrolled in 2 more offerings. This strongly suggested a typo.

A total of 44 responses were reviewed for question E2. Responses were matched to a specific learning activity; e.g. "hands-on exercises" would be matched to our PAs. Responses which could not be matched, e.g. "homework", or which focused on a topic rather than a learning activity, e.g. "regexp", were removed.

Results show that the PAs are the primary focus for students' time as they are mentioned in 63% (30) of responses. Reading the

assigned textbook sections is second, mentioned in 42% (20) of responses. Forums-based activities, mostly the two peer learning exercises, are the third most mentioned with 5% (2).

Table 4 – Student Perspective on Most Difficult Topics

Topic	2011 only	2011 & 2013
Bash Scripting	49%(17)	38%(17)
Regular Expressions	32%(11)	40%(18)
Bash Init. Files	9%(3)	7%(3)
# respondents	35	45

Question E3 was influenced by the fact this offering was modified during the spring 2013 semester. Bash scripting was introduced in a one week module during the first two times the course was offered; however this topic was moved to another course to make more room for the extension of other topics. As a result, Table 4 lists the most often mentioned topics with their frequency first during both 2011 semesters, then during spring 2013.

4.3 Pedagogy of Contents

Table 5 lists the most mentioned topics for questions PC-1 and PC-2; i.e. topics which students felt should have been studied in more depth and the ones they felt should have been studied in less depth. The total number of respondents was 45 for PC-1, 40 for PC-2. Data is aggregated from spring 2011, fall 2011 and spring 2013.

Table 5 – Student Perspective on Contents

PC-1 more depth	Frequency N=45	PC-2 less depth	Frequency N=40
Bash Scripting	32%(14)	File Systems	15%(6)
Regular Exp.	13%(6)	Regular Exp.	8%(3)
Users / Groups	7%(3)	Bash Scripting	5%(2)
File systems	5%(2)	GUI	5%(2)

For question PC-3, 38 students provided suggestions. We removed the ones overlapping with already taught topics or mentions that the offering was already balanced as is.

The remaining suggestions indicated that some students felt that more system administration would be relevant; e.g. network configuration / monitoring, troubleshooting, mounting drives from windows systems & other basic system administration operations. However, there was no consensus. Many students opposed these suggestions, mentioning they would prefer reducing the command line aspects to remain at a more user-friendly GUI level. Other students mentioned a bit more involved user-level tasks; e.g. setting SSH private / public key pairs, using Emacs / Vi.

4.4 Pedagogy of Instruction

Table 6 shows responses for PI-1 aggregated from spring 2011, fall 2011 and spring 2013; over 50% of students favor a constructivist hands-on pedagogy. The results are rather split between the two other pedagogies thus suggesting that students do not perceive the traditional lecture model as inherently inefficient.

Table 6 – Student Perspective on Pedagogy Preferences

	Options	Frequency
#1	constructivist / active learning / questions	23%(12)
#2	instructivist	25%(13)
#3	constructivist / active learning / hands-on	53%(28)

Questions PI-2 / PI-3 were used with the full list of learning activities only during fall 2011 then spring 2013. Responses are summarized in Table 7. We assigned integer values 0 to 4 to each Likert-scale item, starting with "Strongly Disagree". We then averaged this rating for each learning activity.

Table 7 presents these average ratings along with how each activity ranks; #1 being highest rating. Reading assignments were perceived as both the most enjoyable & relevant activities.

From the usefulness perspective, students then valued the remaining activities in a manner which seems proportional to how many points they were worth; exams / graded assignments first, then practice assignments, then graded quizzes, then the non-graded practice quizzes / study guides.

From the enjoyment perspective, students were not quite as easy to interpret. Results suggest that forum-based activities were among the least enjoyable, e.g. PL / DF, while the reading assignments, graded assignments, practice quizzes ranked highly.

Average for enjoyment / usefulness are respectively 2.36 / 3.02 suggesting that students, despite not necessarily enjoying the activities, were able to recognize their relevance.

We grouped agreement and disagreement responses to question PI-4, as we did in section 4.1.The results suggest that the majority of students 81% (43) agreed with this approach, 12% (6) were neutral, only 8% (4) disagreed out of 53 respondents. These results confirm the benefits of regular, small value, graded assignments in online asynchronous offerings.

Table 7 – Student Perspective on Learning Activities

Learning Activity	PI-2 Enjoyment		PI-3 Usefulness	
	rating	rank	rating	rank
Reading Textbook	2.76	First	3.71	First
Watching Videos	2.65	#2	2.76	#6
DF – Reading	2.12	#7	2.35	Last
DF – Participating	2.21	#5	2.53	#7
Quiz –Practice	2.52	#3	3.12	#5
Quiz – Graded	2.15	#6	3.26	#4
Practice Assignments	2.32	#4	3.48	#3
Graded Assignments	2.62	#2	3.56	#2
PL – Participating	1.94	Last	2.38	#8
Average Ratings	2.36		3.02	

4.5 Bloom Taxonomy Levels
Data on RBT-1 and RBT-2 was aggregated from spring 2011, fall 2011, and spring 2013.

Table 8 shows RBT-1 responses. Based on the number of "Very Important" ratings, troubleshooting ranks first, followed by remembering conceptual knowledge. Applying procedural knowledge is third, followed by remembering technical knowledge & evaluating / validating alternative solutions.

It is interesting to compare this ranking to the ranking, established in a previous study [10], of the relevance of Linux introduction's learning outcomes by educators, industry partners, and students.

Three of the above learning activities map exactly to learning outcomes from [10]; "Apply procedural" maps to "SK1", "Evaluate / Validate" maps to "SK4" & "Troubleshooting" maps to "SK5". Our ranking confirms students' ranking from [10]. Therefore, the same misalignment of the perceptions expressed by students vs. industry partners vs. educators also exists here.

In both studies, troubleshooting is top ranked by students. Educators ranked it 3rd out of 4 in terms of cognitive difficulty while surveyed industry partners ranked it 3rd based on relevance. Applying procedural knowledge is similarly top ranked by students while it is ranked last by both educators & industry. Comparatively, surveyed industry partners ranked higher the ability to evaluate alternative solutions to a given problem. This

skill, while ranked similarly by students & industry partners alike in [10], appears here as the least important for our students.

Alignment of the educator / industry perspectives is necessary to ensure students are taught relevant skills. Alignment of the student / industry perspectives is necessary to ensure proper motivation.

Table 9 shows the responses provided by students to question RBT-2. Results suggest that learning activities are perceived as supportive of the acquisition of lower-level cognitive skills, e.g. remembering & applying. There is a significant drop in the number of students feeling that they were supportive of the development of evaluation & troubleshooting skills.

Table 8 – Student Perspective on higher-skills relevance

Learning Activity	Useless	Somewhat important	Very important
Remember Technical	0%(0)	28%(9)	73%(24)
Remember Conceptual	0%(0)	16%(5)	85%(28)
Apply Procedural	0%(0)	22%(7)	79%(26)
Evaluate / Validate	3%(1)	28%(9)	70%(23)
Troubleshoot issues	6%(2)	6%(2)	88%(29)

Table 9 – Student Perspective on higher-skills support

Learning Activity	None	Few	many
Remember Technical	0%(0)	39%(20)	62%(32)
Remember Conceptual	0%(0)	33%(17)	68%(35)
Apply Procedural Knowledge	0%(0)	31%(16)	70%(36)
Evaluate / Validate Solutions	4%(2)	43%(22)	54%(28)
Troubleshoot issues	13%(7)	45%(23)	43%(22)

5. DISCUSSION & FURTHER WORK
This section proposes interpretations for the results presented. Hypotheses are formulated & future research efforts outlined.

5.1 Improving Motivation
Rankings of Bloom levels, based on Table 8's "very important" ratings, confirm the student's perspective on the relevance of their corresponding learning outcomes as published in [10]. Given the difference in pedagogies of contents & instruction between the introductions to Linux used in this study and [10], these results should reflect students' attitudes on Linux technologies in general.

The fact that student view "evaluating / validating alternative solutions" as being the least important skill to develop, needs to be addressed. This is especially true since they see other moderately important skills, e.g. "troubleshooting" / "apply procedural knowledge", as more important contrary to industry's perspective. Addressing this misalignment is essential to motivate students; skills which are both difficult to learn and perceived as not useful are generally under-studied.

In addition, we believe that such misperceptions may have a long-term insidious impact on the quality of the educational process. A student receiving poor grades on learning outcomes which he or she deems irrelevant is more likely to provide negative feedback. This feedback is blind to the pedagogy of contents, instruction or even their long-term positive impact. As such, it might discourage instructors from persevering in providing appropriate preparation. This is especially plausible in institutions which base teaching evaluations on superficial measures of customer satisfaction.

5.2 Supporting Learning
Results in Table 7 suggest that students' perceived usefulness of learning activities is proportional to the points assigned. Such results corroborate the hypothesis that, given limited time to work on offerings every week, our specific student population reverts to compliant-learner behaviors. This motivates further studies;

[1] Establishing, through a multi-institutional study whether such perceptions exist among full-time students

[2] Establishing the industry perspective on the usefulness of our learning activities in order to rule out a coincidental situation whereby the point value indeed matches both industry & students perceptions of usefulness.

These results might also simply show the need for more efforts in explaining the relevance of low-ranked learning activities. Establishing whether we are dealing with a side-effect of the *overcommitted adult learners* profile will be our next priority.

5.3 Teaching Strategies

Table 6 suggests that, students prefer hands-on constructivism, but do not prefer other forms of constructivism over instructivism. This is in stark contrast with computing education research literature which seems to favor constructivism & active learning.

Additional feedback left by students in open ended questions suggests that their affinity for a lecture model might be due to difficulties with reading assignments. While grades show that the material is not trivial, students do not post or email questions about their readings. This hypothesis is also supported by the success of reading comprehension remedial interventions on marketing students from the same campus [13].

If proven valid, this hypothesis might shed new light on the reasons behind students' appreciation for lectures. Using those to summarize readings might not be the best pedagogical approach, see Table 6, but it might be perceived as necessary to remediate difficulties in acquiring baseline knowledge from written material.

This hypothesis also suggests that developing remedial reading comprehension activities, adapted to IT students' needs, might be much more beneficial than lectures or videos allowing them to bypass acquiring skills which are essential to any IT professional.

5.4 ULIL pedagogy

Results in Table 3 suggest that the use of Virtual Box & Ubuntu was suitable both in terms of learning support & ease of use.

While no consensus was reached on the pedagogy of content, no major problem was identified. Effort level & list of most demanding topics align with expectations; see Table 4.

From the pedagogy of instruction perspective, efforts need to be invested in making the social activities, e.g. forum-based, more enjoyable; see Table 7. This might be a challenge if our students are indeed compliant learners since the notion of an enjoyable learning activity is almost incompatible with investing only the minimal time needed to achieve passing grades. In such situations, increasing the points rewarded or making requirements more explicit – e.g. "Your post should be at least 200 words" – only further refines the parameters to which students will comply without necessarily fostering genuine engagement.

Last but not least, the relevance of focusing on user-level topics rather than system administration ones is difficult to establish. However, a few students mentioned, in unsolicited email feedback, that they found this offering useful to prepare them for subsequent IT offerings which require working with Linux; e.g. IT Networks, IT Operating Systems, IT Security… For such endeavors, a system administration focused version might not be as directly relevant. In addition, during spring 2013, students were offered opportunities to take free certification exams. About a third of students, 7 out of 22, expressed interest. The majority of our students, 15 out of 22, therefore match our target audience; i.e. no interest in specializing in system administration.

6. ACKNOWLEDGMENTS

This material is based in part upon work supported by the National Science Foundation under award #0802551 Any opinions, findings, and conclusions or recommendations expressed in this publication are those of the author(s) and do not necessarily reflect the views of the National Science Foundation.

7. REFERENCES

[1] Harley Hahn, Guide to Unix & Linux. McGraw Hill, ISBN 978-0-07-313361-4

[2] Anderson, L.W., et al. 2001. *A taxonomy for learning and teaching and assessing: a revision of bloom's taxonomy of educational objectives.* Addison Wesley Longman.

[3] Bloom B. S. 1956. Taxonomy of Educational Objectives, Handbook I: The Cognitive Domain. New York: David McKay Co Inc.

[4] Lister, R. and Leaney, J. 2003. Introductory programming, criterion-referencing, and bloom. In *Proceedings of the 34th SIGCSE technical symposium on Computer science education.* ACM, New York, NY, USA, 143-147.

[5] Oliver, D., Dobele, T., Greber, M. and Roberts, T. 2004. This course has a Bloom Rating of 3.9. *6th Australasian Conference on Computing Education* - Vol30 227-231.

[6] Gluga, R., Kay, J., Lister, R., Kleitman, S., and Lever, T. 2012. Over-confidence and confusion in using bloom for programming fundamentals assessment. In *Proceedings of the 43rd ACM technical symposium on Computer Science Education* (SIGCSE '12). ACM, New York, NY, 147-152.

[7] Shuhidan, S., Hamilton, M., and D'Souza, D. 2009. A taxonomic study of novice programming summative assessment. *11th Australasian Conference on Computing Education* - Vol95. Darlinghurst, Australia, 147-156.

[8] Thompson, E., Luxton-Reilly, A., Jacqueline Whalley, J., Hu, M., and Robbins, P. 2008. Bloom's taxonomy for CS assessment. *10th conference on Australasian computing education* - Vol78. Darlinghurst, Australia, 155-161.

[9] Gaspar A., Armitage W., Boyer N., Bennett C., Johnson G.. A Preliminary Validation of Linux System Administration Learning Outcomes, Journal of Computing Sciences in Colleges, JCSC, 28:2, 179-187, 2012.

[10] A. Gaspar, W. Armitage, N. Boyer, G. Johnson, C. Bennett. Designing Linux System Administration Learning Outcomes – Educational, Industry & Student Perspectives. CCSC Rocky Mountain Conference 2012, Metropolitan State University of Denver, Denver, CO. October 12-13, 2012

[11] G. Johnson, A. Gaspar, N. Boyer, C. Bennett, W. Armitage. Applying the Revised Bloom Taxonomy of the Cognitive Domain to Linux System Administration Assignments. J. of Computing Sciences in Colleges, 28:2, 238-247, 2012.

[12] G. Johnson, W. Armitage, A. Gaspar, N. Boyer, C. Bennett. Multi-perspectives Survey of the Relevance of the Revised Bloom Taxonomy to an Introduction to Linux Course. ACM Special Interest Group in Information Technology Education's annual symposium. SIGITE 2012

[13] A. Artis. Improving Marketing Students' Reading Comprehension with the SQ3R Method. Journal of Marketing Education 30:2 p130-137 2008. Sage publisher

The Changing Face of Information Technology

Stephen J. Zilora
Rochester Institute of Technology
152 Lomb Memorial Drive
Rochester, NY 14623
585-475-7643

Stephen.Zilora@rit.edu

Daniel S. Bogaard
Rochester Institute of Technology
152 Lomb Memorial Drive
Rochester, NY 14623
585-475-5231

Dan.Bogaard@rit.edu

Jim Leone
Rochester Institute of Technology
152 Lomb Memorial Drive
Rochester, NY 14623
585-475-6451

Jim.Leone@rit.edu

ABSTRACT

Information technology as an academic discipline began in the early 90's. Since then, there have been many changes in how industry views the discipline. Today, information technology is about large-scale operations. This may be manifested as supporting enterprise services, working with big data, or supporting massive multi-user systems. In this paper, we describe a new curriculum that is based upon the original work in the "2008 Curriculum Guidelines for Undergraduate Degree Programs in Information Technology" document, but addresses modern information technology demands. We discuss a new curricular model for teaching information technology and also the addition of analytics as an overarching theme for the curriculum.

Categories and Subject Descriptors

K.3.2 [**Computers and Education**]: Computer and Information Science Education – *curriculum, information systems education, accreditation*.

Keywords

Information Technology, curriculum, programming, networking, human computer interaction, database, web technologies, analytics.

1. INTRODUCTION

1.1 Background

The emergence of Information Technology as an academic discipline first began in 1992 with the Rochester Institute of Technology leading the way. Lunt, et al. provide an excellent review of the curriculum development and accreditation that followed [8]. In particular, they point out that the discipline "emerged in response to a specific educational need rather than as result of the emergence of a set of research questions that were not covered sufficiently by existing disciplines." That need, as described by Lunt and others [1, 13, 7], is for software and hardware infrastructure for the delivery of information. It is

distinct from the computer science emphasis on theory or information systems emphasis on application. Information technology does not exclude theory or application development, it focuses on the delivery of information.

The Curriculum Guidelines for Undergraduate Degree Programs in Information Technology (hereinafter referred to as "Model Curriculum Document") [9] that evolved from this early work reflected the information technology needs of that time. Five pillars were defined: programming, networking, human-computer interaction, databases, and web systems. These pillars were capped by the topics of information assurance and security, and professionalism.

The Model Curriculum Document also suggested two curricular approaches; pillars-first and integration-first. The pillars-first approach provides foundation and depth in the five key areas. Once skills and knowledge in these areas have been established, a small number of integrative courses are offered that allow students to see how all the pieces fit together. The integration-first approach begins with courses that cut across the five key areas with a focus on establishing context and broad themes. These courses are then followed by in-depth study of each of the areas.

1.2 Industry Demands

In 2011, a Gartner report identified four groups of technology trends [11]:

- **The Connected World:** These technologies support the links between objects in the real (physical) world to enhance their visibility in the virtual (digital) world.
- **Interface Trends:** These technologies create richer links between the physical world and the digital world (or vice versa), and enable the collection or presentation of increasing volumes of data.
- **Analytical Advances:** These technologies support the storage and manipulation of that raw data to derive greater value and insight.
- **New Digital Frontiers:** These trends from outside the traditional boundaries of IT are now "crossing the line" to deliver new capabilities or make existing capabilities significantly more accessible, affordable or available.

The report provides several examples of technologies that fit into these categories such as Near Field Communication that supplements Bluetooth and RFID technologies. But the report's key recommendation is that if businesses are to "deliver new revenue, growth and innovation, then these trends should form the starting point."

A more recent Gartner report describes "Everyone's IT" as a concept of "Bring Your Own Device" to a new level. [10] The report states "What makes Everyone's IT stand out is its mind-set: Widely dispersed and varied uses and applications of information, technology, services and devices should be encouraged and coordinated to empower and rev up ideas, innovation, and team productivity across businesses and boundaries."

Both of these reports strongly emphasize the distributed and ubiquitous nature of information technology today and for the foreseeable future. The reports also emphasize the need for integration--not integration of applications, but integration of IT with business (and personal) operations. IT is becoming intertwined with our daily lives.

Employment organizations such as Robert Half are reporting [14] that technologies such as cloud, virtualization, mobile application development, data warehousing, business intelligence, and business analysis are in very high demand.

The common theme in all these reports is that information technology is transforming from the department to the enterprise. Information technology is about delivering information anytime, anywhere, in any format, and doing that in a robust, secure manner.

2. NEW FACE OF INFORMATION TECHNOLOGY

As Lunt noted, the original IT curriculum grew out of an educational need [8]. The information technology industry has changed over the past 20 years and so has the educational need. This is not to say there needs to be a change in the original 5 pillars. Rather, how those pillars are implemented has evolved over time. The information technology discipline has matured and with that maturity comes a broader perspective. Information technology is no longer about satisfying the needs of department or workgroup personnel. It is about handling corporate information in a way that makes that information available to appropriate users at the appropriate time in the appropriate way. That information is likely stored in multiple data stores across the country or even the world. Similarly, the users who'll be consuming that information are likely spread across the country or the world. The maturation of information technology has brought with it a scale, ubiquity, and constancy of information that few even dreamed of 20 years ago.

Today, an IT professional might have to deal with accessing unstructured information stored in the cloud and deliver it using RESTful services to a variety of platforms including smartphones and iPads. Of course, that same professional also has to be concerned with doing this in a safe and secure manner. The underlying principles are no different than the original concept of the IT curriculum. What is different is the scale. Today's IT professional is not dealing with a locally stored relational database and integrating that with some end-user application. Today's IT professional is dealing with big data, software as a service, asynchronous communications, the enterprise service bus, and other technologies that are critical to the corporation's day-to-day functions and long-term success. It is not just the scale of the technologies that has grown, but also the scale of the IT professional's impact on business operations. [12]

Our users have also changed over the past 20 years. Today's young professionals have grown up in a digital world. We no longer need to train IT professionals to be holding the hands of users, teaching the optimal way to utilize an application. Instead, they will be working to develop intuitive interfaces and robust infrastructures to allow access to more specific information on a larger scale, anywhere and anytime, from diverse applications and devices [6].

Another change over the past 20 years is the emphasis on information as opposed to data. While data consists of facts, information adds context [4]. Converting data to information is a primary concern among researchers and corporate executives. In the academic world we typically referred this subject as analytics, while in industry is more commonly referred to as business intelligence. Sifting through petabytes of data, trying to find recognizable patterns (knowledge discovery) or applying patterns to the existing data (data mining), is a task that requires the assistance of an IT professional. One can argue whether analytics should be included in the IT curriculum as a pillar or an overarching theme. While there are specific skills associated with analytics, we believe that the concept of extracting information from data and working with that information is pervasive and should fit alongside the other overarching topics of professionalism, and information assurance and security. This is represented in Figure 1, a modification to "Figure 3-2. The Information Technology Discipline" presented in the Model Curriculum Document [9].

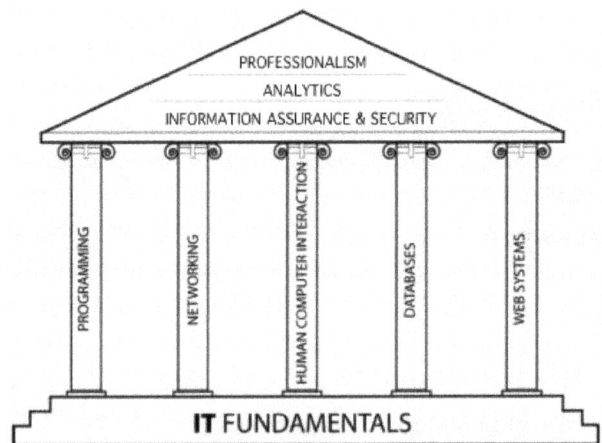

Figure 1. The Information Technology Discipline

3. A NEW CURRICULUM

3.1 Courses vs. Themes

We have used a "traditional" information technology curriculum for years in which students take courses on the various IT aspects. A pillars-first approach allowed achievement of depth, but created the problem of "bringing it all together". Some of the advanced courses attempted to deal with this, but it was often difficult due to varying student background.

In the new curriculum was designed to coincide with the University's change from a quarter system to a semester-based schedule in September, 2013. We have chosen an approach that is neither pillars-first nor integration-first. We are using a hybrid where students start with courses that provide foundational knowledge in each of the pillars and then move on to the topic courses that take a more integrated approach. The topic courses cover a particular aspect of information technology, but are not pillar-specific. For example, once students have learned the basics of web, programming and HCI they take a course in Client Programming that covers the appropriate development of user interfaces in web, mobile and desktop environments. In this course, they use C# to create a desktop user interface as well as JavaScript to create a browser user interface. The interfaces must support the principles they learned in their foundational HCI course and also apply the technologies they learned in their foundational web and programming courses.

In addition to emphasizing the integration of the pillars, this approach also keeps all the concepts in the forefront of the students' minds. It allows us to eliminate the often-experienced problem of students being "rusty" in a particular skill because they had not used it within the recent past.

3.2 Curriculum Overview

The new curriculum exhibits a balance that is consistent with RIT standards. Of the 40 required courses, 21 are within the information technology department. An additional 5 courses are in math, statistics and software engineering. Per institute standards, 25% of the curriculum (10 courses) is reserved for liberal arts and laboratory science courses. Finally, students are allowed to take 4 additional electives in any areas they wish. Figure 2 presents a visual representation of the course distribution. A working layout of the curriculum can be found on our website here: http://ist.rit.edu/degrees/undergraduate/bs-in-it/courses.php

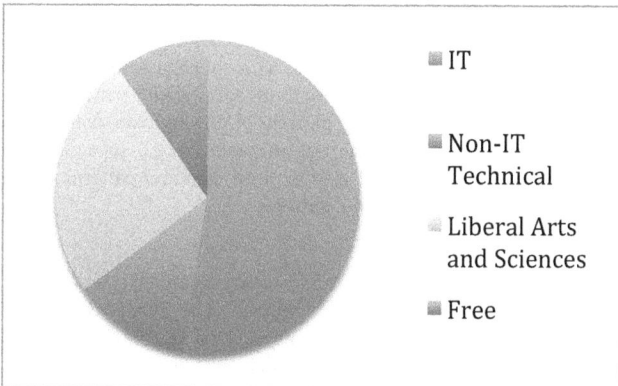

Figure 2. Distribution of Courses

3.3 Pillars

In our new curriculum, we have made no change to the historical pillars of information technology: programming, networking, human computer interaction, databases, and web systems. However, in the new curriculum, the focus on the interpretation of what can be done with the pillars has been augmented. The overarching themes throughout the pillars had been professionalism and information assurance & security, to which we have added analytics.

The changes within the industry's use of the web pillar have been rapidly evolving. Instead of dealing with web pages or even sites, the new curricular approach is about scale and creating/supporting applications. The changes that were made to the landscape of the web with the widespread acceptance of the XMLHTTPRequest object (AJAX) were quick and far reaching. With this we had the ability to maintain state within a single html page. The future adoption of HTML5 and WebSockets will cement this new reality

of actual applications within web pages. (As an example of this, the authors composed this paper entirely on Google Docs where they were able to simultaneously and remotely work on a single copy of the document--an excellent example of the future web applications we want our students to be able to build).

In the new curriculum, the databases pillar also deals with matters of scale. Students learn not only how to construct basic relational database systems but how to work with NoSQL systems, object oriented database systems, and geospatial database systems. Furthermore, students learn how to programmatically connect to a variety of these systems from a variety of programming languages. While they are learning this they are also instructed in proper data security and integrity practices, how to analyze the data in these disparate data stores, and the ethics of working with private information.

Our HCI curriculum has always included both human interaction with an application and working with users as a whole in terms of gathering requirements and facilitating adoption. We experienced problems, however, due to teaching of these principles in isolation. Specifically, students learned how to design a user interface but without consideration for factors such as maintainability, performance, and form factor. In our new topic-oriented approach, students learn principles of usability, but now they are also implementing these interfaces at the same time. For example, when designing an interface that calls for the display of large amounts of data, students get actual hands-on experience working with their interfaces in both desktop and mobile environments.

While students are still able to take courses that focus on hardware and the physical layer, the emphasis in our networking pillar has been shifted to the delivery of services. After completing a foundational course in networking basics (particularly in transport protocols and security) students learn about cloud computing, virtualization, and network management in a service-oriented environment.

3.4 Core Curriculum

The students begin their core studies in the first semester of their freshmen year and conclude the majority of these courses by the middle of their junior year. One core course occurs in the spring of their junior year and there is a full-year senior project. Technical electives are taken in both semesters of the junior and the senior year. For the Senior Project course, the students form project teams and work with external sponsors to experience the entire development lifecycle. Table 1 shows the schedule of topic coverage throughout the core courses. Each checkmark means that the pillar subject is covered in one or more courses.

Table 1 Schedule of Topic Coverage

	Year 1		Year 2		Year 3		Year 4	
	Fall	Spr	Fall	Spr	Fall	Spr	Fall	Spr
Programming	✓	✓		✓	✓		✓	✓
Networking				✓	✓		✓	✓
Web		✓	✓	✓	✓		✓	✓
Database				✓	✓	✓	✓	✓
HCI		✓	✓	✓		✓	✓	✓
Analytics	✓			✓	✓	✓		✓

3.4.1 Foundational Courses

Several courses make up the core's foundation. As you read across each row in Table 1, the first checkmark (also indicated with a blue background) represents a foundational course that is dedicated to that particular pillar. For the Programming pillar, a 2-semester introductory programming course is offered. In this course students learn the basics of object-oriented programming, writing code according to specifications, and the syntax of the Java programming language.

The Networking pillar begins with a course that focuses on data transmission. Students learn the OSI ISO model with emphasis on the transport layer. This allows them to work with web applications and other technologies that require data transmission.

A course in basic website design serves as the foundation for the Web pillar. Students learn how to use CSS, simple JavaScript, and other technologies necessary to create and upload static web pages.

The Databases pillar begins with a course dedicated to designing and implementing a database. Students learn how to create Entity-Relationship diagrams, how to normalize a database, and how to utilize a large set of DDL, DML, and DCL SQL commands using MySQL as the DBMS.

The HCI pillar begins with an examination of the user experience. Topics in this course also include gathering requirements from users, defining user personas, and the psychological factors that enter into robust design of the user experience.

While not a pillar, the Analytics curriculum begins very early where students are exposed to the concepts of big data, data mining, business intelligence, and the difference between information and data. The intent of this course is to set the stage and get them to start thinking like an information specialist.

Also core to the curriculum but not part of any particular pillar is an Ethics course. This course serves the dual purpose of an early introduction to the ethical considerations of dealing with personal and private information and also as an intensive writing course. Industry and professional societies such as the Association for Computing Machinery, the Association for Information technology Professionals, and the British Computer Society have expressed the need for increased emphasis on ethics in information technology curricula. [5] Including ethics as a first year course supports this need and permits later courses to build upon the foundational concepts.

3.4.2 Topic Courses

Other than the seven foundational courses, students will never study a skill in isolation. For example, in their sophomore year students take their second "web" course where they learn how to create dynamic web sites. But in this course students are designing and accessing databases to drive the web site and designing user interfaces that are consistent with sound user experience design principles.

Later in their sophomore year students take two other topic courses. A Data Analytics course builds on the Analytics foundational course and a prior statistics course to teach the students robust data analysis techniques. The course examples will work with databases, but also introduce other data stores. In this same semester students take a client-side programming course. Here they learn how to build web, mobile, and desktop front-ends from diverse data sources. Differences and similarities are pointed out, there is a great deal of discussion regarding form factors and bandwidth, and the students learn JavaScript and C#.

This pattern continues throughout the core with courses such as Server Programming (covering server security, programming a middle layer, and developing and deploying Web services), and Database Connectivity (covering the development of the data layer, administration of connection pooling, and working in the cloud).

3.4.3 Non-IT Technical Courses

The non-IT technical courses consist of two areas: mathematics and software engineering.

3.4.3.1 Mathematics

Mathematics is a cornerstone of any engineering or technical education. Students first take a course in discrete mathematics to solidify their understanding and learn skills for working with logic operations and set theory. Later, they take a course in calculus to help them with their analytical thinking and algorithm development abilities. Students also take a 2-course sequence in statistics. These courses serve as a foundation for their data mining and analysis work.

3.4.3.2 Software Engineering

With the evolution of the need for scalable application solutions, the need for students to have the ability to create reusable code and work within maintainable structures is becoming paramount. To fulfill these needs, the students will be completing a Software Engineering course in software patterns and architectures specifically aimed at enabling them to participate in the software development lifecycle as a contributor instead of an inhibitor. Students will learn common architecture patterns (e.g., SOA, MVC), common coding patterns (e.g., singleton, controller), and basic software engineering principles (e.g., separation of concerns). The course will also explore common patterns in the design of user interfaces and databases.

3.4.3.3 Senior Project

As a culminating experience, all students will take a yearlong, team based, capstone project course. The teams will have representative members from all aspects of IT. Each team will work with an external sponsor and deliver a small-medium scale system together with documentation sufficient to support operation and maintenance. This course includes class time where instructors will fine tune the students' knowledge and practices and align them with the technologies of the day. For example, a first step will be for students to gather and analyze requirements. Instructors will work with students to ensure they are properly applying the skills they learned earlier in their education. This course will also serve as an opportunity for the students to learn and employ Software Development Lifecycle methodologies and project management skills including development of work breakdown structures, scheduling, and resource allocation.

3.5 Concentrations

Once students have completed their core courses they begin their concentration work during their 3rd and 4th years of study. The concentrations address the need for students to think more broadly and to work with real-world scenarios. The concentrations also maintain the cross-pillar design while still providing advanced study. For example, the Enterprise Web Application Development concentration is designed to teach student how to build large integrated web applications. A great deal of the material is focused on browser issues, customization of libraries, and other "front-end" issues, but the concentration also includes courses that cover database application issues such as contention, performance and locking, application and network security, application architecture and server administration.

Students can choose from one of the following possible concentrations or, with the help of an advisor, design their own:

- Enterprise Web Application Development
- Enterprise Application Development
- Enterprise Database Development
- Mobile Application Development

3.5.1 Enterprise Concentrations

The curriculum includes four different enterprise concentrations. Each focuses specifically on different parts of an enterprise scope issue: web application development, application development, and database development. There is overlap across the concentrations. Database Application Development is a required course for the Enterprise Database Development, Enterprise Application Development and Enterprise Web Application Development concentrations. Application Development Practices is a course that Enterprise Web Application and Enterprise Application Development both require. Each of these courses deal with larger issues while allowing the students to focus on their specific domain.

The Enterprise Web Application Development concentration, like all of the other concentrations, is made up of 4 courses (used here as an example of how all of the Enterprise Concentrations would be built):

- Web Server Development and Administration
- Application Development Practices
- Database Application Development
- Web Application Development

After completion of the Web Server Development and Administration course, a student would be able to demonstrate practical knowledge and experience in developing, configuring and administering servers, including understanding issues of platform selection, scalability, security and auditing. Beyond simple administration for common server applications, students would be given tasks designed for building specific use servers as well as future looking event--driven servers.

In the Application Development Practices course, students would gain experience with the process, practices and tools professional developers use to deliver robust maintainable applications. The students will apply these practices and tools to build smaller-scale production-quality applications and systems incorporating development life cycles, version control, test bed development, build utilities, error handling, deployment tools, and documentation.

The Database Application Development course would give students the ability to demonstrate the ability to design and build a database for large-scale systems. The student will have explored topics such as concurrent processing, scalability, performance, and security within the context of developing scalable database information processing systems.

The Web Application Development course provides students with experience building larger-scale web applications with an eye towards performance, optimization, framework and architecture selection, and security. These applications integrate and consume information served from one or many information sources and present the information in an intuitive and usable form.

3.5.2 Mobile Application Development

There has been an explosion in student demand for a diverse set of mobile platform development skills to go along with their other IT studies. To meet this need, we added a Mobile Application Development concentration that covers the full range of mobile delivery--from web applications designed to run specifically on the form factor of a phone to native code applications that running directly on the device operating system.

The Mobile Application Development concentration is made up of 4 courses:

- Foundations of Mobile Design
- Database Application Development
- Mobile Application Development I
- Mobile Application Development II

The Foundations of Mobile Design course introduces the design, prototyping, and creation of applications and Web Sites for mobile devices. Such devices have a unique set of hardware and communication capabilities, incorporate novel interfaces, are location aware, and provide persistent connectivity. This course covers the use of development tools that can be used to push applications to different hardware platforms.

The Database Application Development course is described above in 3.5.1.

The Mobile Application Development courses focus on writing applications natively for these small form factor devices. Students are instructed in the SDKs and programming environments, currently iOS (I), Android (II), and Windows Phone (II). Attention is paid to mobile media, mobile data acquisition and storage, interface conventions, as well as security, privacy and ethics.

4. Future Assessment

The success of this program depends largely on how well the graduating students are received by the workforce and can demonstrate their value to employers. Of course, with the program having just been launched, it is too early to judge. None-the-less, judge it we will. And to accomplish that, we turn to the gold standard of program reviews, the ABET accreditation process. Currently, ABET accredits over 3,100 programs at more than 600 colleges and universities worldwide. Each year, over 2,000 volunteers from 31 Member Societies contribute to ABET's goals of leadership and quality assurance in computing, applied science, engineering and engineering technology education, serving as program evaluators, committee and council members, commissioners, and members of the Board of Directors. [3]

The Bachelor's of Science in Information Technology at RIT was one of the very first IT programs to receive ABET accreditation in 2004 under initial pilot criteria. The RIT IT program was used as an exemplar during those early years and continues to lead with innovative curricular changes. And so too will the program outlined here be subjected to the scrutiny of the ABET accreditation process. [2] Among the criteria reviewed include the student outcomes (knowledge and skills upon graduation), program educational objectives (broad statements that describe what graduates are expected to attain within a few years) and continuous improvement (use of appropriate, documented processes for assessing and evaluating the extent to which both the program educational objectives and the student outcomes are being attained). The results of these evaluations must be systematically used as input for the continuous improvement of the program. At the heart of continuous improvement, is the assessment process designed to ensure the high quality of the program meets the needs of its constituencies.

5. CONCLUSION

The information technology academic discipline originally grew from a demand for a skillset not available in other computing disciplines. Keeping with that spirit and recognizing the change in demands that has occurred over the past 20 years, we have designed a curriculum that meets the needs of IT professionals in the early 21st century. The curriculum still embraces the five pillars of IT, but it also embraces the modern needs for scale, ubiquity, and depth of information.

We are also proposing a third curricular model that is a hybrid of the two models put forth in the Model Curriculum Document. This hybrid model utilizes "short" pillars to establish a foundation and "deep" integration courses that further the students' knowledge in several pillar areas simultaneously.

Finally, we are also proposing adding analytics to the curriculum as an overarching theme. It is commonly said that we are living in the Information Age, but the reality is that we are living in the Data Age. We have petabytes of data at our fingertips, but extracting useful information is non-trivial. Industry and academia recognize the value in this process (referring to the field as analytics and business intelligence, respectively) and the need for us to move from a Data Age to a true Information Age.

6. ACKNOWLEDGMENTS

The development of this curriculum was a joint effort of all members of the Rochester Institute of Technology Information Technology Department. The authors wish to acknowledge the creativity and dedication of their department colleagues.

7. REFERENCES

[1] Abernethy, K., Gabbert, P., Treu, K., Piegari, G., Reichgelt, H. 2005. Impact of the emerging discipline of information technology on computing curricula: some experiences. *Journal of Computing Sciences in Colleges*. 21, 2 (December 2005), 237-243.

[2] ABET - During the Accreditation Process. http://www.abet.org/during-accreditation-process/

[3] ABET – History. http://www.abet.org/History/

[4] Ackoff, R. 1989. From Data to Wisdom. *Journal of Applied Systems Analysis* 16 (1989): 3-9.

[5] Badamas, M. and Ejiaku, S. 2013. Computer Professional Education: The Relevance of Ethics in Information Technology. International Journal of Strategic Management. 13.1 (Feb. 2013), p123.

[6] Hiner, J. 2012. Cloud, iPad, and the end of the geek era. Retrieved May 31, 2012 from http://www.techrepublic.com/blog/hiner/cloud-ipad-and-the-end-of-the-geek-era/10334?tag=nl.e101.

[7] Hislop, G., Kaplan, R., Leitner, L. 2005. Extending an Information Systems Curriculum to Address Information Technology. In *Proceedings of the SIGITE '05 Conference* (Newark, NJ, October 20-22, 2005).

[8] Lunt, B., Ekstrom, J., Reichgelt, H. Bailey, M., LeBlanc, R. 2010. IT 2008: The History of a New Computing Discipline. *Communications of the ACM*. 53, 12 (December 2010), 133-141.

[9] Lunt, B., et al. 2008. Curriculum Guidelines for Undergraduate Degree Programs in Information Technology. Retrieved May 31, 2012 from www.acm.org/education/curricula/IT2008 Curriculum.pdf.

[10] Mahoney, J., Morello, D., Roberts, J. 2012. *Exploring the Future: Everyone's IT*. Retrieved from Gartner Database.

[11] Prentice, S. 2011. *Technology Trends That Matter*. Retrieved from Gartner Database.

[12] Ranganathan, P. and Jouppi, N. 2005. Enterprise IT Trends and Implications on System Architecture Research. In Proceedings of the International Conference on High-Performance Computer Architecture, IEEE CS Press, 2005, pp. 253-256.

[13] Reynolds, C. and Fox, C. 1996. Requirements for a Computer Science Curriculum Emphasizing Information Technology. In *Proceedings of the SIGCSE '96 Conference* (Philadelphia, PA, February, 1996).

[14] RobertHalfTechnology.com. 2012. IT Hiring: The Hot List. Retrieved May 31, 2012 from http://www.roberthalftechnology.com/Positions-In-Demand

Correlation of Grade Prediction Performance and Validity of Self-Evaluation Comments

Kazumasa Goda
Kyushu Institute of Information Science
Dazaifu, Fukuoka 818-0117, Japan
gouda@kiis.ac.jp

Sachio Hirokawa
Kyushu University
Hakozaki, Fukuoka 812-8581, Japan
hirokawa@cc.kyushu-u.ac.jp

Tsunenori Mine
Kyushu University
Motooka, Fukuoka 819-0395, Japan
mine@ait.kyushu-u.ac.jp

ABSTRACT

To grasp a student's lesson attitude and learning situation and to give a feed back to each student are educational foundations. Goda et al. proposed the PCN method to estimate a learning situation from a comment freely written by students[6, 7]. The PCN method categorizes comments into three items of P(previous), C(current) and N(next).

They pointed out a correlation between the student's final results and the validity of a descriptive content of item C, that is something related to understanding of the lesson and learning attitudes to the lesson. However, a problem left in their work is the badness of performance in prediction for upper grade students.

This paper proposes two manners of utilization of PCN scores: the validity level determination for assessment, and for prediction performance of students' final grades.

In order to validate the proposed manners of utilization, we conducted two experiments. First, we employed multiple regression analysis to calculate PCN scores that determine the validity level with respect to each viewpoint. Students who wrote comments with a high PCN score are considered as those who describe their learning attitude appropriately. We also applied a machine learning method SVM (support vector machine) to students' comments for predicting their final results in five grades of S, A, B, C and D.

Experimental results illustrated that as comments of students get higher PCN scores, the prediction performance of the students' grades becomes higher.

Categories and Subject Descriptors

K.3.1 [**Computer Uses in Education**]: Self-Assessment; I.5.1 [**Models**]: Statistical—*Regression Analysis, Support Vector Machine, Text Processing*

General Terms

Education, Learning

Keywords

Learning Activity, User Model, Free-style Comments, PCN Method

1. INTRODUCTION

We have been studying a mechanism to give individualized feedback to students so as to improve their learning activities. To this end, we ask students to freely describe their learning attitudes and behaviors to each lesson. We collect the students' descriptions just after every lesson. While describing comments, the students can reflect on their learning attitudes or behaviors. Therefore, we call the students' comments as free-style comments with their self-reflection or self-evaluation comments. Such the free-style comments, described by students, collected after every lesson are very useful for a teacher to know their learning situations.

The comments tell a lot of things related to the lesson such as their understanding of subjects in the lesson, learning activities they made before the lesson, learning attitudes or behaviors to the lesson. Even some students hesitate to tell the teacher their impression or attitude directly, they can write their thinking in their comment sheets. In other words, comment sheets help students to communicate with their teacher indirectly. Investigating their comments tells the teacher a lot of clues or hints to improve his/her lessons, and those to give the students individualized feedback that help to improve their learning activities.

We ask students to describe three items: P(previous), C(current), and N(next) into their comment sheets. Item P is learning activities for preparation of a lesson. Item C is understanding of the lesson and learning attitudes to the lesson. Item N is the learning plan and goal by the next lesson.

One of the authors subjectively assigned a point to each self-evaluation comment, especially for Item C of the comment. We made sure that the correlation are high between points manually assessed to self-evaluation comments and final grades of the students who described the comments. At the same time, however, it was not easy to distinguish higher grades: S, A, and B. The reasons we assumed are following two: one is that manually assessed points are not fine enough for classifying higher grades, and the other is that students sometimes do not clearly describe their learning activities.

To validate such assumptions, in this paper, we conduct two experiments that evaluate the correlation between self-evaluation comments and the final grade of the students who wrote the comments. The first experiment was conducted to estimate how likely student comments suit for P, C, N items because students sometimes do not describe their learning activities well due to their poor performance of document creation or insincere descriptions. We applied multiple linear regression analysis to students' comments.

We used the occurrence frequency of words appeared in the comments as explanatory variables. As objective variables, we adopted the likelihood of P, C, or N items. The experimental results illustrated that our method has sufficient performance to detect whether or not students' comments are likely as P, C, or N items.

The second experiment was conducted to estimate students' final grades. We applied SVM[8] to students' comments and made it learned the relationships between self-evaluation comments and the final grade of the students. We calculated F-measure and accuracy for estimating the final grades. Experimental results showed that as the self-evaluation comments included expressions more likely as P, C, or N items, estimation accuracy of students' final grades became greater.

In summary, the contributions of this work are the following:

- We propose a students' grade estimation method based on the PCN method that utilizes self-evaluation comments freely described by the students.

- We propose PCN scores that determine the validity level with respect to each viewpoint: P, C, or N. The PCN scores was calculated by multiple regression analysis. The multiple correlation coefficient between each P, C, or N score and self-evaluation comments are over 0.8; that illustrates sufficient performance to detect whether or not students' comments are likely as P, C, or N items.

- We evaluate our grade estimation method with SVM. The experimental results clearly illustrate strong correlation between PCN scores and F-measure or Prediction Accuracy of students' grades.

The rest of the paper is organized as follows. Section 2 describes related work. Section 3 describes the PCN method briefly and shows the comment data we analyzed. Then we introduce the likeliness level of a document as P, C or N item. Section 4 describes how we predict the student's final grade using SVM. Section 5 discusses some of highlighted experimental results. Lastly, we conclude and describe our future work.

2. RELATED WORK

In order to improve a learning process and to enhance a learning effect, it is indispensable to grasp a learning situation. Computers are commonly used in offering teaching materials and in analyzing student's learning behaviors. Research on Educational Data Mining (EDM) is becoming a hot topic [4, 13]. Indeed, a conference focused on EDM has been held since 2008[1]. In such a situation, the research which sets the viewpoint on the student attracts attention. [14] analyzes the effect of student's characters and experiences on the learning behavior pattern. For individualization of a learning process, [12] has proposed a student's modeling. In order to measure an education effect more concretely, [5, 15] applied machine learning methods in predicting student learning performance.

In these researches, analysis is conducted by the teacher in charge, or the administrator of an education system. On the other hand, [11, 10, 3] proposed systems to help students grasping their learning situation. Not only the analysis for research, but also the proposals are made which use the information acquired for advice or support.

Common problems in these researches are collection of the data for analyzing a learning situation and validity verification of the analytical methods or analysis results. A questionnaire with an easy selection branch and the access log to a learning system are easy and efficient tools which require few labors. However, it is difficult to extract the awareness of the issues which students hold and to estimate their willingness in learning from those data. In order to understand individual students more deeply, the detailed observation by a teacher and a direct interview are required. It is difficult, however, to do such enforcement of those activities to the class of a large number of students. We only can make such efforts at most once or twice in a semester.

In order to grasp the learning situation, it is necessary to decide the time particle size before quantifying a learning situation. [6, 7] used a class as unit of time particle size for their analysis. Then they proposed the PCN method where students are asked to describe their self-evaluation of their learning activities from three viewpoints of P(previous to a lesson), C(current in a lesson) and N(for next lesson). [6, 7] reported that there is a correlation between a student's result and the level of likeliness, which we refer as PCN score in the present paper, of their comments with respect to three viewpoints.

There are two tasks left in [6, 7] as further worof the PCN method. The first task is to get rid of the human labor to measure the validity of the free-style comments with respect to three viewpoints. Another task is to clarify the range where a strong correlation holds between the student's results and the PCN scores. In fact, the correlation was not so clear for the students with good results.

The present paper solves the first task by applying multiple regression analysis. The second task is clarified by applying SVM in predicting five grades of student results. It is confirmed that there is a tight correlation between PCN score and the prediction performance. In other word, the more precisely written the comments are, the more accurately the grade can be predicted.

3. PCN SENTENCE AND PCN SCORE

The first author collected the free-style comments of students who attended his programming exercise course. There were two classes and 123 students. The course had 15 lessons. The free-style comments were collected for the last half, that is, from the 7th to 15th lessons.

Each student analyzed his behavior and comprehension concerning to each lesson. We prepared the fill-in forms for comments divided into four items of the prior activity (P) before an exercise, the activity (C) in an exercise, the activity (N) after an exercise and other (O). In these four viewpoints, each student analyzed his study attitude and described freely as short sentences. As a result, we collected 4086 short documents from the students. Each document are assigned with the id of student who wrote the comment and with the category (P, C, N or O) on which the comment was written.

Table 1 summarizes the four viewpoints to classify sentences.

Table 1: Classification of Sentences

Viewpoint	Meaning
P(Previous)	the learning activity before the class time such as review of previous class and preparation for the coming class
C(Current)	the understanding and achievements of class subjects during the class time
N(Next)	the learning activity plan until the next class
O(Other)	other

The analysis of a student's own participating attitude to an exercise was divided and analyzed on a time-axis as four categories of P, C, N and O. We asked the students to write their comments in an appropriate field of the form with respect to P, C, N and O.

However, when we checked the submitted texts, it was not always the case that the content of a comment matches the viewpoints of P, C and N.

This paper introduces the P, C, N and O scores showing whether the self evaluation of students are appropriate with respect to each viewpoint. For example, we evaluate a sentence whether the content of the sentence is really concerned to the viewpoint P, i.e., prior study, by analyzing the words that occur in the sentence. The P score of a student is obtained as the P score of his/her P sentences. The C, N and O scores are calculated similarly.

Each document collected from students is assigned with the category labels P, C, N and O. This category labels are used as observed data. We apply multiple regression analysis using the frequencies of words in the comments as the explanatory variables to predict how appropriate is a sentence as P, C, N and sentence.

More precise description of the method can be written as follows.

First, a sentence s_i is extracted from the comments of a student. The sentence s_i is represented as a vector whose components consist of the values $x_{i,j}$, which is defined as follows:

$$x_{i,j} = \frac{freq(w_j, s_i)}{freq(w_j)}$$

where $freq(X, w_j)$ represents the number of occurrences of a word w_j in a sentence X and $freq(w_j)$ represents the total number of occurrences of the word w_j in all sentences. Then we applied the multiple regression analysis with the following equation:

$$sign(s_i, P) = \Sigma a_j x_{i,j} + \beta,$$

considering $x_{i,j}$ as an explanatory variable and $sign(s_i, P)$ as a response variable, where $sign(s_i, P)$ is 1 if the sentence s_i is determined as a P sentence by human, 0 otherwise.

As the result, we obtained a_j, the weight of words w_j, and the constant β.

Next, the P score of each student u_k is calculated by using the student u_k's P sentences by summating estimated values with the following equation.

$$P(u_k) = \Sigma_{i=1}^{m} \Sigma_{w_j \in s_{u_k,i}} a_j \widehat{x_{i,j}} + \beta,$$

where, m is the number of u_k's P sentences and

$$\widehat{x_{i,j}} = \frac{freq(w_j, s_{u_k,i})}{freq(w_j)}$$

We obtained the C, N and O score, similarly.

Table 2 shows the multiple correlation coefficients between each P, C, or N score and self-evaluation comments; the values of the coefficinets are over 0.8, that illustrate sufficient performance to detect whether or not students' comments are likely as P, C, or N items.

Then we can employ the model to evaluate how the document s_i corresponds properly to the viewpoint P. We can also apply the model to the viewpoints C, N, and O, similary.

Table 2: Multiple Correlation Coefficient of PCN scores

p	0.8876
c	0.8756
n	0.8619

4. PREDICTION OF GRADE BY SVM

Next, we considered to predict each student's results from his/her comments. We chose five grades instead of the mark itself as a student's result. Table 3 shows the correspondence between the grades and the mark.

Table 3: Grade

Grade	Mark	# students
S	100–90	21
A	89–80	41
B	79–70	17
C	69–60	23
D	59–50	7
E	below 49	14
Total		123

We use the same vectorization of the documents as that of computing PCN scores. We applied SVM (support vector machine) to document vectors to predict if the student s_i got the grade S,A,B,C or D based on the document vectors.

We want to analyze the effect of PCN score in predicting students' grades. We ran evaluation experiments with the parameter of the grade (S,A,B,C and D) and the viewpoints (P, C, N and O). Moreover, we want to compare the prediction performance for the students with high and low PCN scores. We made exhaustive evaluation experiments with those parameters. The results are explained in the next section.

In this section, we explain how we evaluate the prediction performance of a grade, by taking S grade as an example, based on comments of students with top 10 C scores.

The ID of a student has a form C-N, where C stands for a class number 1 or 2, and N is the number of the student assigned from 1 in sequence.

The IDs of the top 10 C score students are 2-25, 2-59, 1-4, 2-42, 2-39, 2-18, 1-39, 1-27, 1-25 and 1-46.

To apply SVM-light, we prepared 100 lines of data, which may contain repetition, as shown in Fig. 1. A line represents the comments of a student.

```
-1 1:0.0076 2:0.0085 ... 1149:0.1000 1152:0.1000 # i:2-25
-1 1:0.0076 2:0.0099 ... 1147:0.1000 1150:0.2000 # i:2-59
-1 1:0.0087 2:0.0099 ... 1151:0.1000 1156:0.1000 # i:1-4
-1 1:0.0087 2:0.0113 ... 1144:0.1000 1157:0.1000 # i:2-42
-1 1:0.0087 2:0.0113 ... 1123:0.1000 1143:0.1000 # i:2-39
-1 1:0.0087 2:0.0127 ... 1141:0.1000 1152:0.1000 # i:2-18
-1 1:0.0098 2:0.0113 ... 1143:0.2000 1147:0.2000 # i:1-39
 1 1:0.0076 2:0.0113 ... 1125:0.1000 1127:0.2000 # i:1-27
 1 1:0.0087 2:0.0057 ... 1138:0.1000 1139:0.1000 # i:1-25
 1 1:0.0087 2:0.0127 ... 1151:0.1000 1155:0.1000 # i:1-46
```

Figure 1: Vectorization of Comments for SVM-light

The first column of a line represents whether the student is in S grade or not. If the student is in S grade, the value of the first column is 1, -1 otherwise. The rest of the line represents a list of pairs of word ID and word score. We use the same scores in the previous section. Each word ID has corresponding to a word as follows:

1 do, 2 can, 3 N:do, 4 think, 1123 N:spend,
1125 N:prepare, 1127 N:after, 1138 O:sort,
1139 O:usage, 1141 O:information, 1143 O:uneasy,
1144 O:variable, 1147 P:very much, 1149 P:complete,
1150 P:create, 1151P:expression, 1152 P:in advance,
1155 P:input, 1156 P:toward, 1157 P:term

The tagged words, such as "P:complete", indicate that the word "complete" occurred in a P sentence. The word ID of "P:complete" is 1149. We see "1149:0.1000" in the first line of Fig. 1 that corresponds to the comment of the student "2-25". It implies the student's some comments in P sentence with the word.

We evaluated the prediction performance by 5 fold cross validation. We randomly separated the above 100 lines data into 5 classes. We used 80% of them as training data and constructed a model. Then we applied the model to the rest 20% data and compared a predicted value with corresponding observed data. The total performance is obtained as the average of 5 times trials.

Let $obs(s_i)$ denote if the grade of a student s_i is in S or not, and let $pred(s_i)$ denotes the predicted value for S grade. We calculate the precision, recall, F-measure and accuracy as usual:

$$True = \{s_i | obs(s_i) = 1\}$$
$$False = \{s_i | obs(s_i) = 0\}$$
$$Positive = \{s_i | pred(s_i) = 1\}$$
$$Negative = \{s_i | pred(s_i) = 0\}$$
$$Precision = |True \cap Positive| / |Positive|$$
$$Recall = |True \cap Positive| / |True|$$
$$F-measure = \frac{2 * Precision * Recall}{(Precision + Recall)}$$
$$Accuracy = \frac{|True \cap Positive| + |False \cap Negative|}{100}$$

5. CORRELATION OF PCN SCORE AND GRADE PREDICTION PERFORMANCE

Fig. 2 displays the correlation between C score and the F-measure of predicting S grade of students. The C scores are obtained from C sentences. Fig. 2, 4, 5, 6, 7, and 8 display the plots of correlation for 15 combinations of 5 grades S, A, B, C, and D with 3 viewpoints P, C, and N.

Fig. 2 contains 123 red plus (+) points and 123 green cross (x) points. A red plus point represents the F-measure obtained as the average F-measures of 5 fold cross validation with respect to the set of students whose C scores are in top N (N=1, 2, ..., 123). Green cross points represent accuracy. Precisely, an F-measure is obtained as follows. Firstly, we selected, as the target of analysis, the students whose C scores are in top N. Then we selected 100 data admitting overlap. We applied SVM-light with 5 fold cross validation to this 100 data. As a result, we calculated the average F-measure from the 5 experiments. Finally, we plotted 123 red points where x-axis is the Nth C score and y-axis is the average F-measure. The green points are for the accuracy obtained similarly. We see a strong correlation between the C score and F-measure and between the C score and accuracy.

Next, we calculated the correlation coefficients of the PCN scores and the prediction performance. Table 4 and Fig. 3 display the correlation coefficients.

We see that there are some points at the lower and upper right region in Fig. 2, which are separated far from the regression line.

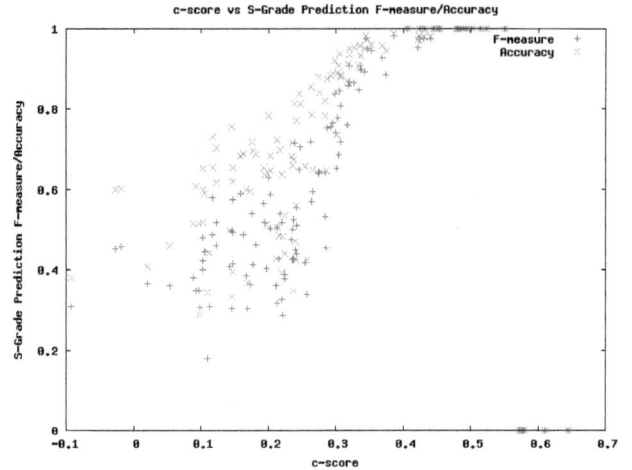

Figure 2: Prediction F-measure of S-grade by C-sentence

We eliminated those points as outliers. We checked students who correspond to those points. We confirmed that those students, who correspond to the points in lower right region, got zero as their result. It may be because they attended the lessons and wrote the comments, but did not take the final exam. The points in upper right region correspond to those student who wrote their comments very properly as C sentence. The C score of those comments is above 0.5. However, the prediction performance is at most 1.0. Therefore, those points do not on the regression line.

We see, in Fig. 2, a strong correlation between the C score and the prediction performance. A close analysis of Fig. 3 tells a delicate difference in correlation coefficients. The correlation coefficients of the viewpoint of C score are the best ones among 3 viewpoints P, C, and N. We can say that C sentences are most reliable to predict students' result. Particularly, the correlation coefficients of C score for the upper grades S, A and B are over 0.8. On the other hand, the correlation coefficients of P score for the grade S and A are lower than 0.4. This implies that the P sentences are useless in predicting good students. However, the P score have high coefficients for lower grades B, C and D. This means that the P sentence is useful to find students who have any trouble or difficulty.

Table 4: Correlation Coefficient of PCN-Score and F-measure

	P	C	N
S	0.3356	0.7956	0.6700
A	0.2647	0.8624	0.7829
B	0.7465	0.8263	0.7076
C	0.7631	0.6602	0.5380
D	0.7355	0.4955	0.2079

6. CONCLUSION AND FUTURE WORK

This paper discussed a realization of the PCN method for analyzing a student's free-style comments from the 3 viewpoints of P, C and N. 4086 comments of 123 students were used to model the PCN score based on multiple regression analysis. The model gave an automated method to calculate the PCN scores of students' comments. The scores measure whether the comments are appropriate to the viewpoints. Another model of predicting students' result is

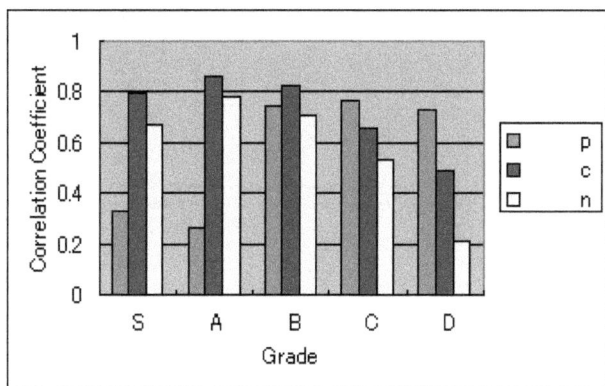

Figure 3: Correlation Coefficient of PCN-Score and F-measure

constructed based on SVM using the same documents when calculating the PCN scores. The students' results are classified into 5 grades. The SVM generates a model to tell if a students is in a given grade or not. It is confirmed that the grade prediction performance and the PCN score have a strong correlation. The interpretation of this result is that the result of students who properly wrote their comments in viewpoints can be estimated with high accuracy.

This result is directly applicable to an everyday student's instruction. The models we obtained in this paper can be used to evaluate how students' comments are written appropriately for the 3 viewpoints. If the scores of comments of some student are very low, we can advice them to rewrite the comments. The automatic feedback will be practical for improve the self-observation capability. Once most students write their comments appropriately, the accuracy of final estimated results will improve. Individual advices will be possible depending on the comprehension level of each student.

It is necessary to improve the prediction performance of students' result as well as PCN score from their comments. Other machine learning methods, such as, neural network, will be candidates of improvement to compare with the present method. Another further work is how to utilize the PCN scores so as to provide useful advice to students.

We also have to investigate what influences are caused by different lectures, subjects or classes. To this end, we need to collect much more students' free-style comments from various kinds of lectures.

One of the difficulty of the PCN method is in collecting free-style comments of students. The quality of the comments matters the performance of the analysis and the prediction. Indeed, only 10 percent students wrote the self-evaluation description when we asked them as volunteer cooperation. In order to get a student to submit a self-valuation descriptive sentence, a certain compulsion would be needed. At least, some sort of system is necessary to be used in submitting the comments. SNS and online bulletin board are efficient to collect opinions and comments. However, not all student would respond if they are left in their will. Particularly, the students with some difficulty or trouble would not answer. Collecting comments that reflects students study situation is crucial to comprehend their learning status. Further research is necessary to realize an environment where they are willing to cooperate to respond.

7. ACKNOWLEDGMENTS

This work was partially supported by JSPS KAKENHI Grant Number 24500176 and 25350311.

8. REFERENCES

[1] R.S.J.d. Baker, T. Barnes, J. E. Beck(Eds.), Educational Data Mining 2008: 1st International Conference on Educational Data Mining, Proceedings. Montreal, Quebec, Canada. June 20-21, 2008.

[2] J. Millis Barbara and J. Zubizarreta, The Learning Portfolio: Reflective Practice for Improving Student Learning. Jossey-Bass publisher, 2009.

[3] P. Brusilovsky, Adaptive Hypermedia for Education and Training. In: P. Durlach and A. Lesgold (eds.): Adaptive Technologies for Training and Education. Cambridge: Cambridge University Press, pp. 46–68, 2012.

[4] T. Calders and M. Pechenizkiy, Introduction to the special section on educational data mining. ACM SIGKDD Explorations Newsletter archive, Volume 13 Issue 2, pp. 3–6, 2011, December 2011

[5] L. V. Fausett and W. Elwasif, Predicting performance from test scores using back-propagation and counter-propagation. In Proc. IEEE World Congr. Comput. Intell., pp. 3398–3402, 1994.

[6] K. Goda and T. Mine, PCN: Qualifying Learning Activity for Assessment Based on Time-series Comments. Proc. CSEdu2011, pp.419-424, 2011.

[7] K.Goda and T. Mine, Analysis of Students' Learning Activities through Quantifying Time-Series Comments, Proc. KES 2011, Part II (LNAI 6882),pp.154–164, 2011.

[8] T. Joachims, Making large-Scale SVM Learning Practical. Advances in Kernel Methods - Support Vector Learning, B. Scho"lkopf and C. Burges and A. Smola (ed.), MIT-Press, 1999

[9] Tsuneo Kuwabara et al., Support Functions for Stalled Students and Their Effect in a Multi-Media Assisted Education System with Individual Advance (MESIA). Transaction of IEICE D-I, Vol. J83-D-I, No.9, pp. 1013–1024, 2000.

[10] Keizo Nagaoka, Development of a Response Analyzer-based Classroom Instruction Support System. Japan Journal of Educational Technology, Vol. 10, No. 3, pp.10–18, 1986. (in Japanese)

[11] Takumi Nishitani et al., e-Learning System Which Help a Teacher to Send Advices to Students' Error Answers in Real-Time. Transaction of IEICE D-I, Vol. J91-D-I, No.6, pp. 1538–1549, 2008. (in Japanese)

[12] P. Elvira, Diagnosing Students' Learning Style in an Educational Hypermedia System, Constantinos Mourlas. Nikos Tsianos and Panagiotis Germanakos (Eds): Cognitive and Emotional Processes in Web-based Education: Integrating Human Factors and Personalization, Advances in Web-Based Learning Book Series, IGI Global, ISBN: 978-1-60566-392-0, pp. 187-208, 2009.

[13] C. Romero, S. Ventura, and M. Pechenizkiy, Handbook of educational data mining, RSJ Baker, 2011.

[14] L. Shi, A. I. Cristea, M. Shahzad Awan, C. Stewart, and M. Hendrix, Towards Understanding Learning Behavior Patterns in Social Adaptive Personalized E-Learning Systems. Proc the Nineteenth Americas Conference on In.formation Systems, Chicago, Illinois, August 15-17, 2013.

[15] A. Zafra and S. Ventura, Multi-instance genetic programming for predicting student performance in web based educational environments, Applied Soft Computing, 12, pp.2693-2706, 2012

[16] B.J. Zimmerman, Self-regulated learning and academic achievement: An overview, Educational Psychologist, 25, pp.3–17, 1990.

S grade

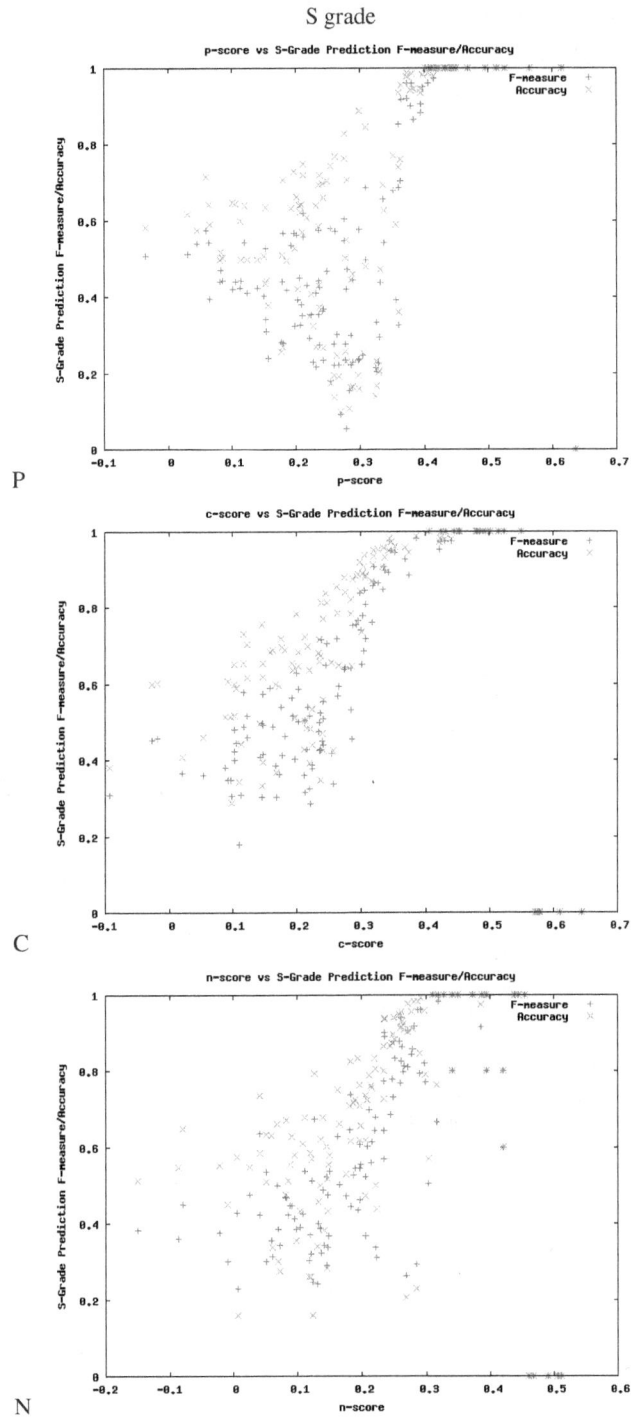

Figure 4: F-measure vs PCN-score (S grade)

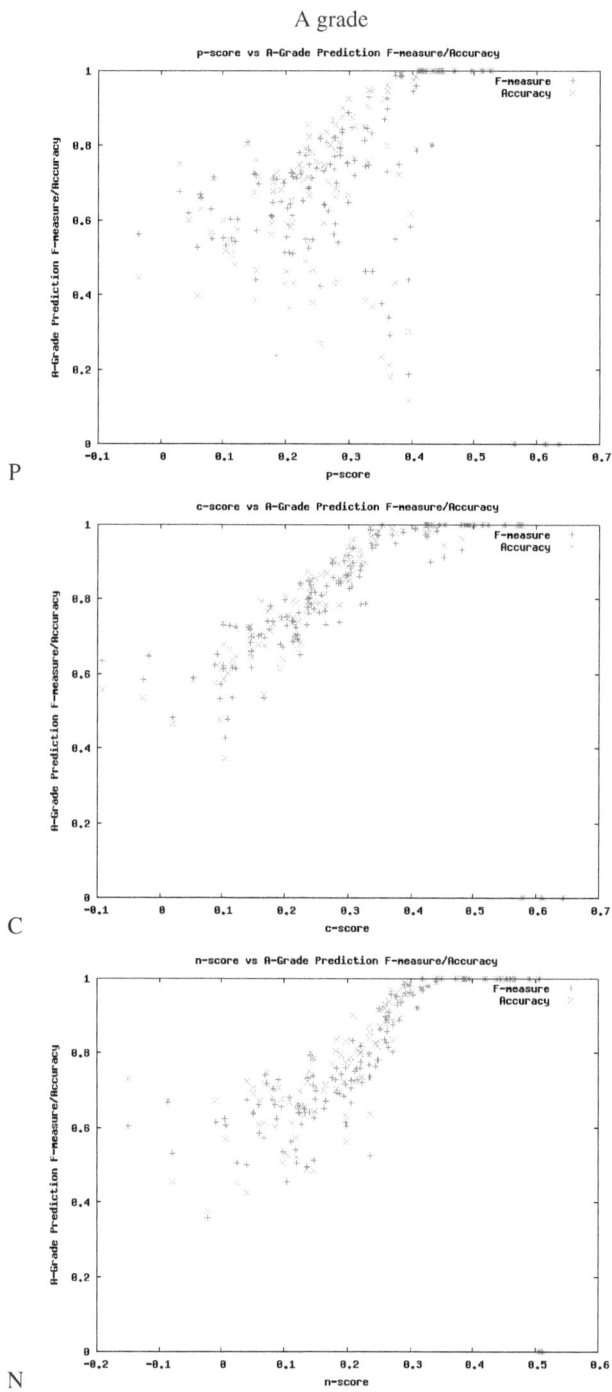

Figure 5: F-measure vs PCN-score (A grade)

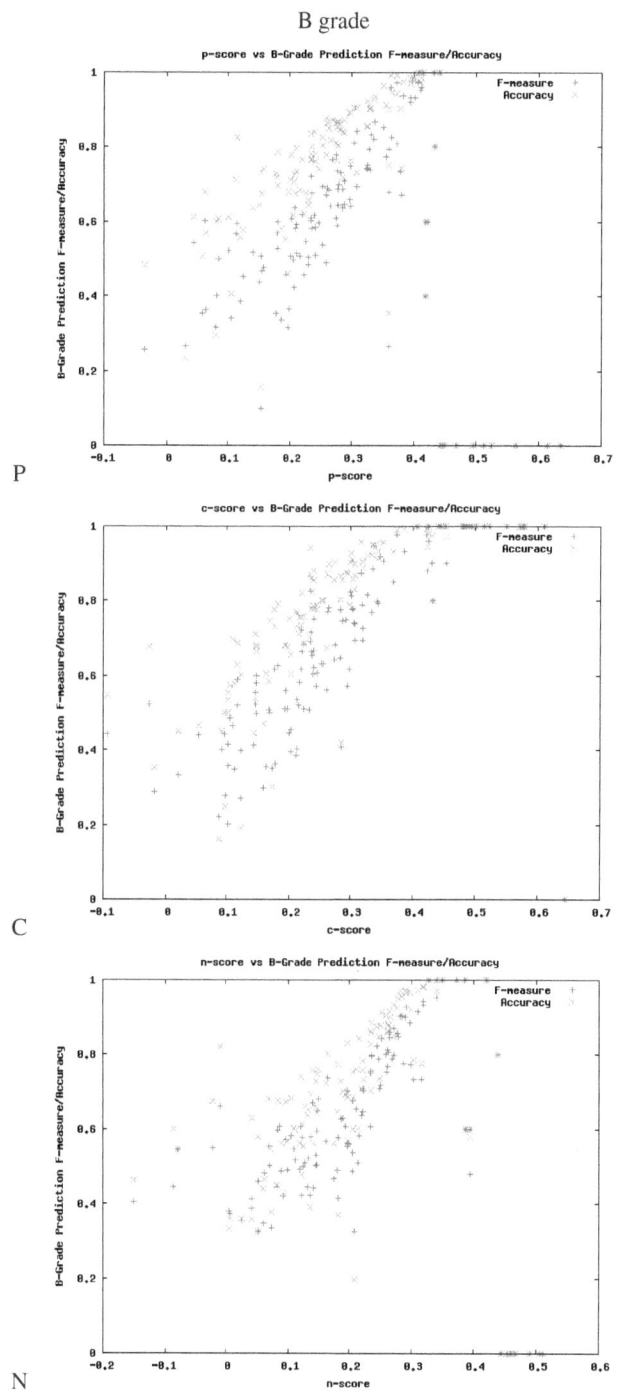

Figure 6: F-measure vs PCN-score (B grade)

C grade

p-score vs C-Grade Prediction F-measure/Accuracy

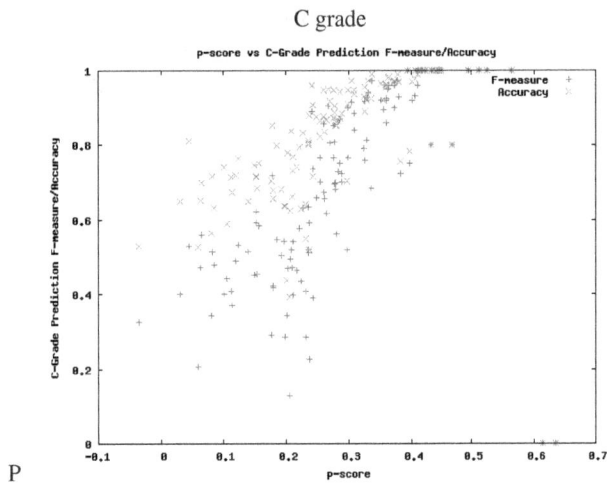

P

c-score vs C-Grade Prediction F-measure/Accuracy

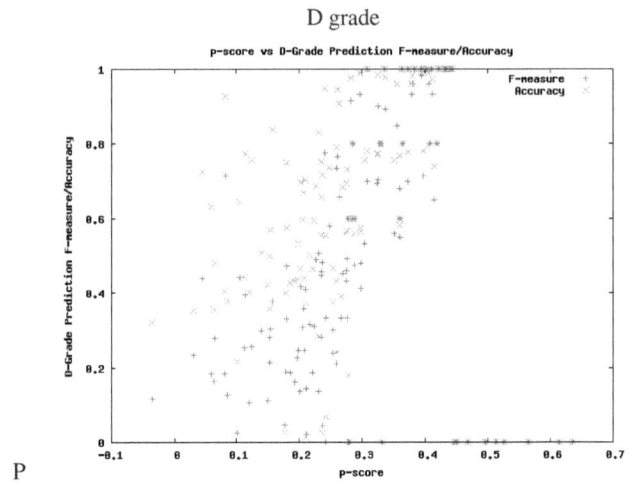

C

n-score vs C-Grade Prediction F-measure/Accuracy

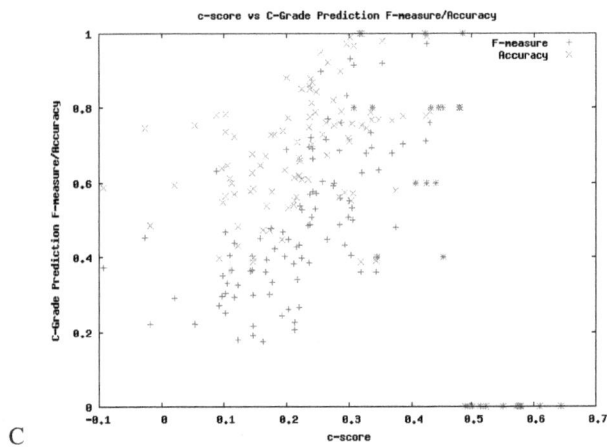

N

Figure 7: F**-measure vs PCN-score (C grade)**

D grade

p-score vs D-Grade Prediction F-measure/Accuracy

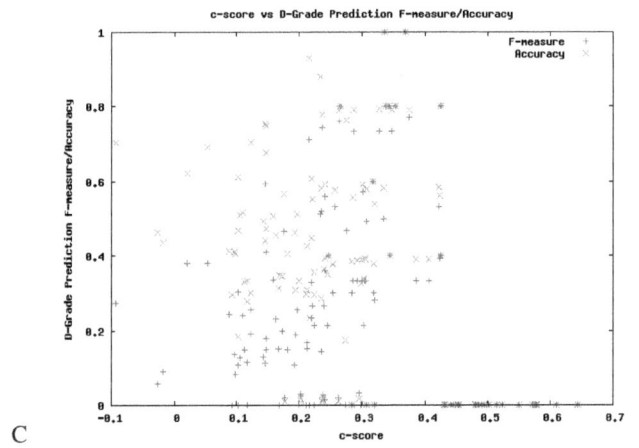

P

c-score vs D-Grade Prediction F-measure/Accuracy

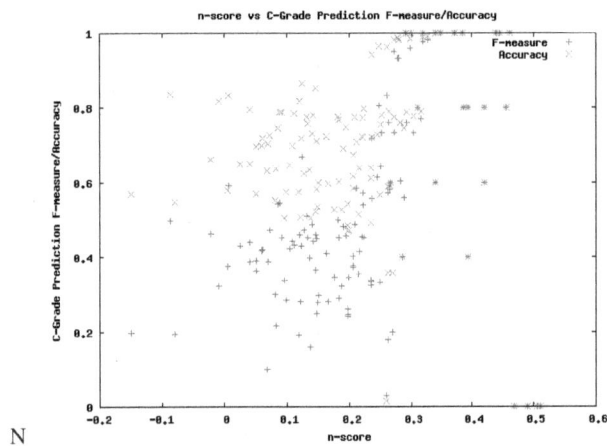

C

n-score vs D-Grade Prediction F-measure/Accuracy

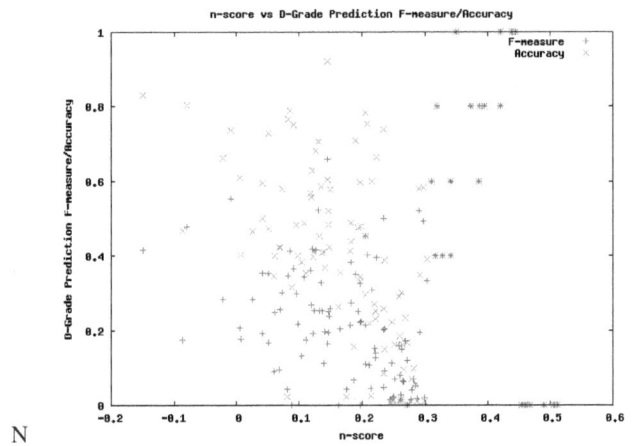

N

Figure 8: F**-measure vs PCN-score (D grade)**

Demographics of Undergraduate Students in Game Degree Programs in the U.S. and UK

Monica M. McGill
Bradley University
Peoria, IL
(309) 677-4148
mmcgill@bradley.edu

Amber Settle
DePaul University
Chicago, IL
(312) 362-5324
asettle@cdm.depaul.edu

Adrienne Decker
Rochester Institute of Technology
Rochester, NY
(585) 475-4653
adrienne.decker@rit.edu

ABSTRACT

Over the last decade, there has been a growth in the video game industry and, at the same time, game degree programs at post-secondary institutions worldwide have grown in quantity and quality. Representation of gender and race in games and in the game industry workforce is an important issue. We explore this topic in our research, providing an overview of the demographics of undergraduate students in game degree programs in the United States and the United Kingdom. We include race, gender, ethnicity, political preferences, sexual orientation and more. Gender results indicate that males make up the significant majority in undergraduate game programs. Women are significantly more likely to think that the gaming industry, programs at the university, and project teams at the university are not as diverse as men think they are. Women are also significantly more likely to report that their programs would benefit from more diversity than men.

Categories and Subject Descriptors

K.3.2 (Computer and Information System Education), K.8.0 (General)

Keywords

Games, demographics, undergraduate students, gender, diversity, curriculum

1. INTRODUCTION

Over the last decade, there has been general agreement that a lack of diversity exists in the game industry workforce. The International Game Developers Association (IGDA) has conducted two industry surveys on the topic [12, 13]. Recent topics on industry sites such as Gamasutra have indicated that this topic is being taken even more seriously, with diversity and representation in games being considered one of the top 5 trends of the game industry in 2012 [10].

Student demographics have been gathered in multiple disciplines and for groups of students at universities in general, with one of the largest being the CIRP Freshman Survey [11]. Studying

student demographics is important for post-secondary institutions. For example, understanding what types of subjects students prefer in high school can provide insight into marketing strategies when recruiting so student interests and strengths are matched with prospective fields of study.

Individuals can break into the game industry in various ways, but all of these require the development of skills, knowledge, and dispositions that relate to the position being sought [2]. Game degree programs at post-secondary institutions have been created to provide a pathway to these skills. These programs have been on the rise worldwide and the number of programs recently hitting an all-time high [7]. They offer one potential pipeline into the game industry, and given the concern over the lack of diversity in the game industry workforce, it is natural to consider student demographics not only for issues related to diversity, but also whether students are properly matched for the field of study.

To date, no systematic studies of undergraduate game student demographics and perspectives on diversity exist. This paper presents the results of our study undertaken to begin this process. Specifically, our research considers the demographics of undergraduate students studying games at universities in the UK and US as well as their general attitudes about diversity in the game industry. We describe the study methodology, present the data collected on diversity within programs in both the US and UK, and briefly explore what the results mean for the game industry.

2. BACKGROUND

While there has been some research into the study of demographics in the game industry, there is little previous work on demographics among undergraduate game students. We provide some insight into the relevance of demographics studies here.

2.1 Game Industry Workforce Demographics

Members of the game industry have studied the workforce to determine the demographics of employees within the industry and have recognized that diversity is important in the field. The IGDA implemented its second survey on diversity in the industry to establish a benchmark on issues of diversity in November 2011 [13]. This survey was a follow up to results of a 2005 survey that showed that the typical game development professional is "white, male, heterosexual, not disabled, [...] and agrees that workforce diversity is important to the future success of the game industry" [12, pp. 9-10].

Because the 2005 IDGA survey was crucial in the development of our study, it is worth considering it in more detail. Due to low response rates elsewhere, only responses from those living in the USA, Canada, the UK, and Australia were considered, giving a sample size of 3,128. Of the responses 66% were from the U.S.,

18% from Canada, 12% from the UK, and 4% from Australia. There was little ethnic diversity in the respondents, with 83.3% identifying as white, 7.5% as Asian, 2.5% as Hispanic/Latino, 2.0% as black, and 4.7% as other. The gender balance among respondents was overwhelmingly male, with only 11.5% of respondents identifying as female.

The 2005 survey also asked about sexual orientation, and 92% of respondents identified as heterosexual, with 2.7% identifying as lesbian/gay, 2.7% as bisexual, and 2.6% refusing to answer. Only 0.96% of respondents identified as transgender. Bisexuals, lesbians, and gays both think that the game industry currently lacks diversity and believe that diversity is important. When asked about disabilities, 87% reported that they did not have any. Of the remaining 13%, the most commonly reported disabilities were mental and cognitive. Cognitive disabilities were reported by 30%, mental disabilities by 31%, sight 9%, hearing 6%, mobility 4%, other 11%, and 9% declined to specify.

Women who responded to the 2005 survey strongly believed that diversity was important for the future of the industry and that diversity impacts the games that are produced. Interestingly, the study found that "non-whites seem to believe strongly that the industry is diverse and teams are diverse more often than whites". Overall, the IGDA concludes by recognizing the importance of diversity in the field both for a broader base of recruiting talent to the industry as well as the ability to create products to appeal to larger audiences.

2.2 Demographics in Games

There have been several important studies on gender and race representations in games and the impact this has on players. After analyzing representation of women in 33 games, Dietz [4] concluded that women in games were hypersexualized in graphical representation, and often had insignificant or stereotypical roles. A more recent study by Downs and Smith [5] concluded that women are still hypersexualized in games more so than men, which is consistent with other research performed on this topic [14, 16].

Other research has examined video games in context to race and offer consistent evidence of the lack of people of color and the reinforcement of racial stereotypes [9, 17, 18]. Leonard [15] goes as far as stating that video games such as the "racist racial project" Grand Theft Auto III "…reveal white supremacy in the form of both content and desire." (p. 6), also noting that racialized images in video games affirm our society's dominant ideas about various subgroups and these are framed through the lens of the dominant group producing such games.

Not only are demographics an issue, but also girls appear to be aware of this imbalance. Schott and Horrell noted in their study that not only were their study participants (all girls) aware of sexism in games, they "…claimed to desire a more balanced portrayal of males and females in games, as well as greater flexibility in character choice." [19, p. 50] They also conclude that several factors influence the amount of time girls play games, including the presence and dominance of male gamers.

The research by Williams, et al shows a correlation between the game industry workforce and the representation of race in games [21]. This is further supported by Everett and Watkins [8], both media critics, who believe that there should be "…broader debates about the rise and diffusion of digital media technologies and the educational pathways" for success in these domains, particularly as they pertain to race and ethnicity. They state that "…if high degrees of learning and education are essential for gaining meaningful employment in the video game industry, the future prospects of black and Latino talent finding a secure place among programmers, design artists, writers, and designers are limited." (p. 160)

2.3 Previous Study of Game Students

To date, the demographics and motivations of game students have been studied far less systematically and thoroughly. Bayliss and Bierre [1] performed a study comparing their game students to the student in other computing degree programs. They found that 10% of the students in their program were females and 90% male. They found that 25% of them want to focus on design and become game designers rather than game software developers. Many of them (31%) had no prior programming experience before coming into the program. With regards to motivation for study, they found that 35% chose their major because they liked to program, with 2% choosing it because they liked problem solving, and 27% because they liked to express their creativity. One of their conclusions was that students who chose to pursue games as a major were more interested in expressing their creativity than their computing peers in other majors.

At University of California Santa Cruz, a large undergraduate course in games was offered to all students at the university that could have counted towards general education credit in the natural sciences area. Since all students need to complete a course in this area to graduate, the course was uniquely positioned to attract from all parts of the student body. The course did succeed in attracting more students from non-engineering majors; however, it still attracted a much larger proportion of males than females, affirming the trends that already exist in technical and engineering courses [20].

3. METHODOLOGY

To explore the research questions, we created the Game Industry Employee Pipeline Survey. Many of these questions were taken directly from the 2005 IGDA survey "Game Developer Demographics: An Exploration of Workforce Diversity" and the 2011 IGDA Industry Survey with permission. The survey consisted of nine demographic questions, one question about favorite high school subjects, four questions about religious preferences, sexual preferences, and political views, and two questions about disabilities (see the appendix for the survey questions). In addition, the survey elicited information about student perceptions of diversity in the game industry. This particular analysis examines the demographics of respondents from the US and the UK against results of the 2005 IGDA survey.

The initial population for this cross-sectional study included undergraduate students in game degree programs in the U.S., UK, and Canada. The institutions initially contacted included public, not-for-profit private, and for-profit private institutions that offered undergraduate degrees in games and included institutions of various sizes and locations with the specific intention of having data from students at a variety of institutions. Faculty at post-secondary institutions in the U.S., UK, and Canada were contacted to participate in the study and act as conduits for disseminating the study to their students. Due to this, faculty were required to receive Institutional Review Board/ethics committee approval at their respective institutions.

As a result, faculty at four institutions in the U.S., two institutions in the UK, and one institution in Canada completed this step. Upon their IRB approval, the surveys were distributed to students within participating institutions between March 1, 2012 and

September 20, 2012. Not enough responses were received from students in Canada to include in the summary. Of the four institutions in the US, three were private institutions and one was public. Both of the institutions in the UK were public institutions.

Two emails were sent to participants on behalf of the faculty researcher, the first announcing the survey and inviting participation. A survey reminder was sent one week after the first. In Canada, the local researcher solicited student participation.

The data collection followed techniques that were previously approved by the researcher's committees on research of human subjects. To gather the data, an electronic form of the survey instrument was created using the Qualtrics online survey tool. Only participants who agreed to the letter of consent that appeared on the first page of the survey were able to complete the survey. As an incentive, participants in the UK and U.S. were offered a chance to enter a prize drawing for a tablet computer upon completion of the survey. To enter the drawing, participants followed a link to a second survey in order to keep the demographic data for the survey separate from the drawing survey that required participants to enter the contact information. Upon completion of data collection, the drawing was held and the prize was awarded. The data from the drawing survey was then destroyed.

Once the data was collected, it was analyzed with the SPSS software tool. Descriptive statistics, specifically frequency counts and percentages were used to answer the questions pertaining to the demographics of students in game degree programs. T-tests were performed on male versus female and white versus non-white responses to understand statistically significant differences in these populations. To ensure internal consistency among the diversity perspectives questions, a Cronbach's Alpha test was performed.

4. RESULTS

There were a total of 315 responses to the surveys from U.S. and UK institutions from the 1240 students emailed. With only one response from Canada, the response was removed from data analysis. Of the U.S. and UK respondents, two were not undergraduates and were eliminated from the data set, bringing the total to 313, a 25.2% response rate. In this section we first present student demographics for the 313 undergraduate respondents, including general demographic data (including age, sex, ethnicity), areas of study within games and career interests, religious and political leanings, sexual orientation, and medically diagnosed disabilities. Following this we present a general summary of perceptions of diversity, and then discuss differences between responses for male versus female and white versus non-white participants.

4.1 Demographic Data

Nearly all respondents were fulltime undergraduate students (98.1%) with the remaining students attending part-time. Participants from each year of study responded, though it should be noted that the US system requires four years of study and UK programs often only require three. 94.9% of participants were in the 18-24 age range, 4.5% in the 25-30 range, and 0.6% in the 31-50 range.

The majority of students (96.8%) were enrolled in a Bachelors Degree in games (i.e. Game Design, Game Development, Game Art, etc.). Only 2.9% indicated that they were enrolled in a Bachelors Degree in a related field, with a concentration in games.

A majority of students studying games are male (87.2%) compared to female (12.8%). The respondents were primarily native English speakers (92.0%) and white (73.5%). Other ethnicities are reported in Table 1.

TABLE I.   ETHNICITY

Categories	Count	%
White	227	72.3%
Black	19	6.1%
Chinese	10	3.2%
Hispanic/Latino	7	2.2%
South Asian (eg East Indian, Sri Lankan, etc.)	5	1.6%
Filipino	4	1.3%
Southeast Asian (eg., Vietnamese, Camobidan)	4	1.3%
Japanese	3	1.0%
Korean	3	1.0%
West Asian (e.g., Iranian, Afghan, etc.)	2	0.6%
Arab	1	0.3%
Other	11	3.5%
Decline to Answer	13	4.1%

4.1.1 Areas of Study and Career Interests

All 313 participants responded to questions in the survey identifying each student's area of study within games. Participants could choose multiple areas of study. Fourteen participants selected "other". Respondents indicating "other" who also selected a listed area were classified according to that area, and respondents who did not select another area were counted in the area closest to the text provided, with game culture counting as game design. The respondent who selected everything was added to each of the other categories.

TABLE II.   AREAS OF STUDY

Areas of Study	Count	%
Game Design	265	84.7%
Game Software Development	198	63.3%
Game Production	117	37.4%
Game Art	68	21.7%
Game Sound	27	8.6%
Undecided	2	0.6%

For interest in careers in games, all 313 participants responded. Only one career interest could be selected. Several participants (12.1%) stated that they were undecided, while 4 participants (1.3%) indicated that they do not intend to pursue a career in the game industry. Twenty-four participants selected "other" and each provided text to describe their interests. They were classified in the listed area that best matched their text response.

TABLE III.   CAREER INTERESTS

Career Interests	Count	%
Software Development (Programming, Software Analysis, Software Engineering, etc.)	126	40.2%
Level Designer	43	13.7%
Undecided	38	12.1%
Artist	36	11.5%
Producer	25	8.0%
Design	10	3.2%
Administrative	7	2.2%
Writer	6	2.0%
Business Management	5	1.6%
Testing	5	1.6%
I do not indent to pursue a career in the game industry	4	1.3%
Quality Assurance	3	1.0%
Audio	3	1.0%
Consultant	1	0.3%
Marketing/PR	1	0.3%

4.1.2 Favorite High School Subject

Participants were asked to identify their favorite subject in high school. Only one subject could be chosen, and there were only 309 responses to this question which was the value used to compute the percentages in the table below. As might be expected, the most popular favorite subjects include technology courses, art, and mathematics. The full set of responses for the favorite subjects is provided in the table below.

TABLE IV.   FAVORITE HIGH SCHOOL SUBJECT

Subject	#	%
Technology courses (computer science, multimedia)	85	27.5%
Art (drawing, sculpting, graphic design, etc.)	60	19.4%
Mathematics	56	18.1%
Social Studies (civics, history, geography, etc.)	24	7.8%
Physics	20	6.5%
English	19	6.2%
Music (orchestra, band, choir)	17	5.5%
Science (chemistry, biology)	10	3.2%
Foreign language	8	2.6%
Other	6	1.9%
Engineering	4	1.3%

4.1.3 Religious and Political Leanings

A total of 306 participants responded to the religious preferences question, with 34 (11.1%) declining to specify their religion (Table V). The majority (44.9%) of participants did not have a religious preference. 12.1% identified as Roman Catholic while 9.5% identified as Other Christian.

For political preferences, 306 participants responded, with most identifying as not caring about politics (28.4%) or being liberal (25.5%). Another large percentage (21.2%) identified with middle-of-the-road ideologies. 8.5% specified other and 7.5% declined to specify. Among those who selected other, 7 (2.3%)

specified Libertarian beliefs, 7 (2.3%) indicated that it depended on the issue, and 1 (0.3%) each indicated Democrat and Labour.

The remaining respondents provided colorful commentary, noting among other things that "rent is too damn high", that "our political system is a circus of idiocy run by sadistic clowns", that they identified with "whoever is not saying crazy things" or those who support "gun rights", that they "disagree with the entire system" or that "all of them are thieves."

TABLE V.   RELIGIOUS PREFERENCE

Preference	Count	%
None	141	46.1%
Roman Catholic	37	12.1%
Decline to specify	34	11.1%
Other Christian	29	9.5%
Other Religion	12	3.9%
Baptist	10	3.3%
Church of Christ	9	2.9%
Muslim	7	2.3%
Jewish	6	2.0%
Methodist	5	1.6%
Presbyterian	4	1.3%
Lutheran	4	1.3%
Episcopaleon	3	1.0%
Eastern Orthodox	2	0.7%
Buddhist	2	0.7%
Hindu	1	0.3%

TABLE VI.   POLITICAL PREFERENCES

Preference	Count	%
Don't care	87	28.4%
Liberal	78	25.5%
Middle of the road	65	21.2%
Other	26	8.5%
Decline to specify	23	7.5%
Conservative	19	6.2%
Far left	6	2.0%
Far right	2	0.7%

4.1.4 Sexual Orientation

A total of 305 participants responded to the question about sexual orientation, with the majority reporting that they are heterosexual (262 or 83.4%). 21 (6.7%) reported being bisexual, 18 (5.7%) declined to specify, and 4 (1.3%) reported being lesbian or gay, as shown in Table VII.

TABLE VII.   SEXUAL ORIENTATION

Orientation	Count	%
Heterosexual	262	83.4%
Bisexual	21	6.7%
Decline to specify	18	5.7%
Lesbian/gay	4	1.3%

A total of 304 respondents responded to the question asking whether they were transgender, with 297 (97.7%) reporting no, 5 (1.6%) declining to specify, and 2 (0.7%) reporting yes (Table VIII).

TABLE VIII.   TRANSGENDER STATUS

Status	Count	%
No	297	97.7%
Decline to specify	5	1.6%
Yes	2	0.7%

4.1.5 Disabilities

Participants were asked to identify one or more medically diagnosed disabilities. The majority (67.5%) of participants stated that they did not have a disability (Table IX). The remaining responses are summarized below with the 5 (1.6%) indicating another disability, reporting dyslexia, diverticulitis, lazy eye, hemophilia, and color blindness.

TABLE IX.   DISABILITIES

Disability	Count	%
None	212	67.5%
Mental illness (e.g. anxiety, obsessive compulsive disorder, post-traumatic stress disorder, bipolar, depressions, schizophrenia, etc.)	28	8.9%
Cognitive disorder (e.g. dyslexia, ADD/HD, specific learning disability, autism, Asperger's, etc.)	26	8.3%
Blind or partially sighted	9	2.9%
Decline to answer	8	2.5%
Yes, decline to specify	5	1.6%
Other	5	1.6%
Deaf or hard of hearing	3	1.0%
Mobility impaired (e.g. paraplegia, quadraplegia, cerebral palsy, ALS, etc.)	1	0.3%

A second question was posed to respondents who indicated that they had a cognitive disability (Table X). Of these, ADD/HD was the most common following by dyslexia and Asperger's.

The one respondent who specified "other" under disabilities but reported dyslexia was added to the total for that specific learning disability. One respondent answered "other" to the question about

cognitive disorders, specifying OCD for Obsessive Compulsive Disorder. This response was classified under mental illness in the table above and not counted here.

TABLE X.   COGNITIVE DISABILITIES

Disability	Count	%
ADD/HD	16	5.1%
Dyslexia	6	1.9%
Asperger's	5	1.6%
Learning disability	3	1.0%
Austism	1	0.3%

4.2 Perceptions on Diversity

The survey included several questions on issues related to diversity both in the game industry and the institution in which the participants were studying. These survey items were similar to items presented on the 2005 IGDA survey with the same Likert responses. Participants were asked to rate diversity-related questions on a Likert scale where 1 = Strongly Disagree, 2 = Disagree, 3 = Agree, and 4 = Strongly Agree. Cronbach's alpha was performed on internal reliability and was deemed to be reliable (α=0.73).

In general students agreed that the game industry was diverse, that a diverse workforce has an impact on the games produced, and that workforce diversity is important to the future success of the game industry (Table XI). They agreed less strongly about diversity in their programs.

TABLE XI.   DIVERSITY PERSPECTIVES

Q	Diversity Statement	N	M	SD
1	The game industry workforce is diverse.	306	3.06	0.751
2	My program at my university is diverse.	306	2.96	0.730
3	Project teams in my game degree program are diverse.	305	2.83	0.686
4	In one or more of my courses, we have discussed diversity.	306	2.55	0.883
5	A diverse workforce has a direct impact (broad appeal, quality, etc.) on the games produced.	305	3.03	0.819
6	My program would benefit from more diverse students.	305	2.90	0.766
7	Workforce diversity is important to the future success of the game industry.	306	3.08	0.772

We considered differences between populations regarding diversity. An independent-samples t-test was performed comparing male and female respondents. The responses for two of the questions were found to be significantly different ($p < .05$). Male respondents indicated higher agreement for "My program at my university is diverse," and female respondents indicated higher agreement for "My program would benefit from more diverse students." Table XII shows the results.

TABLE XII.   DIVERSITY PERSPECTIVES BY GENDER

Q #	Female			Male			p	t
	N	M	SD	N	M	SD		
1	40	2.65	.66	266	3.12	.75	0.00	t(304) = -3.74
2	40	2.55	.85	266	3.03	.69	0.00	t(304) = -3.94
3	40	2.53	.64	265	2.88	.68	0.00	t(303) = -3.05
4	40	2.38	.81	265	2.57	.89	0.19	t(304) = -1.31
5	39	2.90	.88	266	3.05	.81	0.27	t(303) = -1.11
6	40	3.10	.59	265	2.88	.79	0.04	t(303) = 1.73
7	40	3.25	.67	266	3.06	.78	0.14	t(304) = 1.45

We performed an independent-samples t-test comparing white and non-white responses. There were no significant differences between the two groups on any of the questions. The information for each is presented in the table below.

TABLE XIII.   DIVERSITY PERSPECTIVES BY ETHNICITY

Q #	White			Non-white			p	t
	N	M	SD	N	M	SD		
1	224	3.08	.73	69	3.00	.82	0.41	t(291)= 0.82
2	224	2.97	.71	69	2.90	.83	0.46	t(291)= 0.74
3	224	2.85	.67	69	2.74	.78	0.24	t(291)= 1.18
4	224	2.53	.89	69	2.59	.91	0.61	t(291)= -0.51
5	223	3.00	.80	69	3.16	.89	0.15	t(290)= -1.45
6	223	2.83	.77	69	3.12	.74	0.00	t(290)= -2.69
7	224	3.03	.76	69	3.25	.81	0.04	t(291)= -2.02

5. DISCUSSION

This study provided important information about demographics and perceptions of diversity among game students in the U.S. and UK. Like a previous study of game students [1], our work found 87.2% of these students are male and that a large percentage (84.7%) of students are studying game design. Like many other technology-focused fields, a large majority of students (72.3%) are white, with Asians (10%) as the second largest ethnic group. Similar to the IGDA study, our results found that a large majority of students (83.4%) identify as heterosexual. Our work found a similar percentage of transgender game students (0.7%) as found in the industry as a whole (0.96%). Like the game industry as a whole, mental illness and cognitive disabilities are the most commonly reported disabilities.

Unlike a previous study of game students [1], our results show that many students (63.3%) are studying software development with large percentages learning production (37.4%) and game art (21.7%). Again, contrary to previous work [1] only 16.9% of students plan to want to focus on game design after graduation. A much higher percentage (40.2%) intends to focus on software development, and a reasonable percentage (11.5%) intends to focus on art after graduation. Students who study games named technology classes (27.5%), art (19.4%), and mathematics (18.1%) as their favorite high school subjects.

Many game students (46.1%) do not identify with any religion, and among those who do identify with a religion Roman Catholics (12.1%) and other Christians (9.5%) are the most common. Game students are split on their political preferences with the largest group (28.4%) indicating that they don't care about politics. Among those who specified a political preference, the majority

(25.5%) is liberal or middle of the road (21.2%). Conservatives are uncommon (6.2%) among the respondents to this survey.

Our results show a larger percentage of bisexual students (6.7%) and a lower percentage of lesbian/gay students (1.3%) than found in the IGDA survey in 2005. Our work found a larger percentage of students with disabilities (24.6%) than in the IGDA survey (13%). We also provided detailed information about the specific cognitive disabilities among students, the most common of which was ADD/HD.

Students agreed that the game industry workforce is diverse, that a diverse workforce has a direct impact on the games produced, and that workforce diversity is important to the future success of the game industry. The agreement was less conclusive that the programs and project teams in academic are diverse, and it appeared that discussions of diversity were not uniform in game programs. Our results indicate that women are significantly more likely to think that the gaming industry workforce, programs at the university, and project teams at the university are not as diverse as men think they are. Women are also significantly more likely to report that their programs would benefit from more diversity than men.

6. LIMITATIONS

Even with this demographic study, both internal and external threats to its validity exist. The instrument was developed based on previous studies, including the IGDA Diversity study, and has not been validated. Participants from the six institutions may not be representative of the entire population of game students in the US and UK. Students in their first year of studies had a higher participation rate than for each of the other years of study, and this may influence the outcomes of the study as well, since first-year students are more likely to change majors than students in their later years of study.

Some of the questions posed are sensitive in nature. Participants may or may not choose to respond to these truthfully or may have chosen the "Decline to Answer" or "Decline to Specify" choice available on several of the required response questions. The entire study is based on self-reports provided by participants, and care must be taken when interpreting the results. Additionally, though care was taken in choosing survey questions and choices that are unambiguous, there is a risk that the participant may have misinterpreted the questions or choices.

7. CONCLUSION

Though this paper examined the role of diversity perceptions with an emphasis on gender and race, continuation of this research and data analysis is ongoing. Additional planned analysis includes how the data compares specifically to the results of both IGDA surveys as well as the general population and how marginalized groups like black women and persons with disabilities compare to in-game characterizations.

This study answers the question of what types of students study games, while at the same time raises the question about what this data implies. If the game industry believes that workforce diversity is important and their goal is to make their workforce more diverse, then some of the demographics should raise serious concerns. For example, one of the most glaring results of this research is the gender imbalance. For those that are concerned with this issue as either a moral imperative or as a pathway for potentially reaching more consumers, this issue should be examined more closely and in context of industry goals. As noted by Everett and Watkins [8], if the industry is serious about making changes, then the university pipeline may be a potentially powerful place to start addressing the imbalances and providing better opportunities for minorities. In other technology-focused disciplines, much of the focus on recruitment has extended back into secondary and middle school [3], with the recognition that many students have made up their mind about their choice of major prior to entering college or university. It may be benefit for those who are interested in diversifying the gaming industry to consider a similar approach.

8. ACKNOWLEDGEMENTS

We would like to thank the following people for their time and resources in shepherding the IRB process at their respective institutions and recruiting students for participation: Briana Morrison, Southern Polytechnic State University; Jacques Carette, McMaster University; Mark Eyles, University of Portsmouth; and Siobhan Thomas, London South Bank University.

9. REFERENCES

[1] Bayliss, J. D. and Bierre, K. 2008. Game design and development students: who are they? In *Proceedings of the 3rd international conference on Game development in computer science education* (GDCSE '08). ACM, New York, NY, USA, 6-10. DOI=10.1145/1463673.1463675

[2] Braithwaite, B. and Schreiber, I. 2011. Breaking into the game industry. Course Technology PTR. Boston, MA, USA.

[3] Craig, M. and Horton, D. 2009. Gr8 Designs for Gr8 Girls: A Middle-School Program and its Evaluation. In SIGCSE 2009: The 40th ACM Technical Symposium on Computer Science Education, Chattanooga, TN.

[4] Dietz, T. L. 1998. An examination of violence and gender role portrayals in video games: Implications for gender socialization and aggressive behavior. Sex Roles, 38, 425-442.

[5] Dill, K. and Thill, K. 2007. Video game characters and the socialization of gender roles: Young people's perceptions mirror sexist media depictions. Sex Roles. 57:851-864.

[6] Downs, Edward, and Stacy L. Smith. "Keeping abreast of hypersexuality: A video game character content analysis." Sex Roles 62, no. 11 (2010): 721-733.

[7] Entertainment Software Association. (2012). Video Game Courses and Degree Programs Hit All-Time High at U.S. Colleges in All 50 States. Retrieved October 19, 2012 from http://www.theesa.com/newsroom/release_detail.asp?releaseID=179

[8] Everett, A. and Watkins, C. 2007. The power of play: The portrayal and performance of race in video games. The John D. and Catherine T. MacArthur Foundation Series on Digital Media and Learning (2007): 141-164.

[9] Glaubke, C., Miller, P., Parker, M., Espejo, E. (2001). Fair Play? Violence, gender and race in video games. Report from ChildrenNow. Retrieved December 7, 2012 from http://www.childrennow.org/index.php/learn/reports_and_research/article/219

[10] Graft, K. December 2012. The 5 trends that defined the game industry in 2012. Gamustra. Retrieved December 7, 2012 from http://www.gamasutra.com/view/news/182954/The_5_trends_that_defined_the_game_industry_in_2012.php#.UMIYneOe_5g

[11] Higher Education Research Institute. 2012. CIRP Freshman Survey. Retrieved December 2012 from http://www.heri.ucla.edu/cirpoverview.php

[12] IGDA International Game Developers Association. 2005. Game Developer Demographics: An Exploration of Workforce Diversity. Retrieved October 15, 2011 from http:// www.igda.org/game-developer-demographics-report

[13] IGDA International Game Developers Association. 2011. Game Industry Survey 2011. Retrieved December, 2011 from http://www.research.net/s/IGDA_Industry_Survey_M2Research

[14] Jansz, J, and Martis, R.G. 2007. The Lara phenomenon: Powerful female characters in video games. Sex Roles 56, no. 3 (2007): 141-148.

[15] Leonard, D. 2003. "Live in Your World, Play in Ours": Race, Video Games, and Consuming the Other." SIMILE: Studies in Media and Information Literacy Education 3(4), pp. 1-9.

[16] Martins, N, Williams, D.C., Harrison, K., Ratan, R.A. 2009. A content analysis of female body imagery in video games. Sex roles 61(11), pp. 824-836.

[17] Media Education Foundation. 2000. Game Over: Gender, Race, and Violence in Video Games. Available at http://www.mediaed.org/cgi-bin/commerce.cgi?preadd=action&key=205

[18] Packwood, D. 2011. Hispanics and Blacks Missing in Gaming Industry. News America Media. Retrieved December 7, 2012 from http://newamericamedia.org/2011/09/gamer-to-game-makers-wheres-the-diversity.php

[19] Schott, G. and Horrell, K. 2000. Girl Gamers and their relationship with the gaming culture. Convergence, 6(4), 36-54. Retreived on December 7, 2011 from http://con.sagepub.com/content/6/4/36.full.pdf

[20] Whitehead, J. 2008. Introduction to game design in the large classroom. In *Proceedings of the 3rd international conference on Game development in computer science education* (GDCSE '08). ACM, New York, NY, USA, 61-65. DOI=10.1145/1463673.1463686

[21] Williams, D., Martins, N., Consalvo, M., and Ivory, J. 2009. The virtual census: representations of gender, race and age in video games. New Media & Society, 11:815. Retrieved December 7, 2012 from http://nms.sagepub.com/content/11/5/815.full.pdf+html

New Educational Learning Environments: Riding the Wave of Change Instead of Having It Crash Upon Us

Jon Preston, Han Reichgelt, Rebecca Rutherfoord, Chi Zhang, Jack Zheng (Moderator)
Southern Polytechnic State University
1100 South Marietta Parkway
Marietta, GA 30060
(001) 678-915-7399
{jpreston, hreichge, brutherf, chizhang, jackzheng}@spsu.edu

SUMMARY
The environment of higher education is changing; we have new challenges and opportunities created by social media, streaming technology, access to learning materials, and pathways of acquiring and assessing knowledge and skills. This panel discusses forces of change and disruption to existing models of higher education and suggests means by which IT departments can leverage these changes. Each panel participant addresses a specific area, including technology-mediated learning, learning management systems, learning object repositories, ensuring quality control and accreditation, and how to successfully administer and manage these suggested changes.

Categories and Subject Descriptors
DK.3.2 [**Computer and Information Science Education**]: Information Systems Educations – *accreditation, organization, curriculum*

Keywords
Disruption, change, learning management system, massive open online courses, learning objects.

1. INTRODUCTION
The outcome of this panel is to form an extended dialog between IT/computing faculty across the nation to formally explore changes to education and how to best capitalize on these opportunities. This panel will be the springboard for future work, and we believe this will be the first in a multi-year panel at SIGITE; future years will report on formal research and work among this group.

Since this panel consists of five panelists (rather than the typical four), we will present rapid position statements within two to three minutes for each participant and leave no less than 15 minutes for audience engagement and response. Since the goal is to spur discussion during the panel and create a formal ongoing dialog after the panel, the positions serve merely as a brief introduction to avenues of ongoing conversation.

2. POSITION: CHI ZHANG
Students of new generations are using media and technologies to communicate with new people and learn new things in new ways. It is commonly agreed that simulations, digital gaming, and social

networking technologies provide powerful learning opportunities and advantages [3].

To better understand the challenges and opportunities that the educational institutions are facing, in addition to learning success mediated by technology, we may want to focus on the five essential components of learning powered by technology: *learning, assessment, teaching, infrastructure*, and *productivity*, as the National Education Technology Plan 2010 – "Learning Powered by Technology" calls [4].

Learning: Educators want to investigate how we teach to match what students need to know and how they learn. The state-of-the-art technology can be used to "enable, motivate, and inspire all students to achieve, regardless of background, languages, or disabilities" [4, p.x].

Assessment: Technology-based assessment can be formatively used to analyze and modify the instructional practices while collecting evidence of students' knowledge and problem-solving abilities to determine what students have learned from work.

Teaching: The teaching model is shifted to a "connected teaching model". Educators are well connected to the content and resources, to data and information for assessing engaging and relevant learning experience, and peers and experts for improving their instructional practices.

Infrastructure: Infrastructure includes "people, processes, learning resources, policies, and sustainable models for continuous improvement" [4, p. xiii]. An infrastructure for learning is always available to students, educators, and administrators regardless of their location or the time.

Productivity: Technology must be applied to implement personalized learning which empower students to take control of their own learning by providing flexibility on several dimensions, such as need-based learning objectives, content, different learning method and pace, and tailored learning preferences[4].

3. POSITION: JACK ZHENG
Traditional LMSs mainly support formal and organization-centered learning environments. With the advancement of Web 2.0 particularly on open content sharing and social networking services, a new generation of systems is emerging to facilitate teaching and learning. The new systems (or new features added to current systems) are expected to support newer teaching and learning environments as well as to impact the traditional administration and business models. What features of these systems are desired, and how will they impact higher education? The following are some of the features I see of most importance.

Open: the traditional LMS is a relatively closed environment with restrictions on registration, access control, resource sharing, and long term availability. A more open environment is expected to interact with external resources and applications easily, and it should provide easy and flexible access and lifelong support.

Social: a social learning network is an open online learning community for learning, discussion, resource sharing, and collaboration. The new system incorporates common social networking features such as learner profile, learning progress update, cross-course forum, study group, special interest group, public learning material review, etc.

Flexible learning organization: traditional way of learning in higher education institutions is organized by rigid courses and semesters. The new system may need to support more non-formal and informal learning, and to provide corresponding recognition and assessment systems. Some features may include flexible learning units of various levels and lengths, knowledge map or learning path, and gamification which somewhat complements the formal credit system. This flexibility can greatly increase subject coverage and number of learning tracks, which is particularly true in the ever growing IT industry.

Personal learning environment: a personal learning environment is learner-centered. The system is expected to provide adequate self-service in a personal space where learners can store and manage their own learning materials, monitor learning progress, build resources and knowledge repository, all with lifelong access.

Some pilot systems and services have emerged to build more open, social, flexible, and personal learning environments, including CourseSites, OpenClass, einztein.com, OpenLearning, CodeAcademy, etc. Most of these systems do not yet share a common understanding of open and social learning, and they vary greatly in features and structures. The evolution of the system also requires, and probably as a driving factor for, the change of the current higher education business model. It's a challenge as well as an opportunity for the development and adoption of such systems in higher education.

4. POSITION: JON PRESTON

Modern students are immersed in digital content outside the classroom and are entertained by and learn from online videos outside the classroom. We propose that IT learning can be improved by leveraging smaller, more focused learning objects that take advantage of the best practices of engaging online media. Our pilot/beta learning objects heretofore consist of 5-15 minute videos that are very focused on one particular topic; the learning object also consists of pre-requisite requirements (linking it to previous topics to ensure learners are adequately prepared for the content) and assessment tasks to ensure the learner has mastered the content before proceeding to later topics. In the past, it was possible for a learner to pass a course without mastering all the topics; with this learning object-centered approach, each topic is mastered and we ensure a deeper understanding of all topics.

5. POSITION: BECKY RUTHERFOORD

Some of the newer problems dealing with the new ideas and concept for education lie in how these newer concepts can be recognized and evaluated as "learning". Phil Hodkinson, 2003 [2], states that "The challenge is not to, somehow, combine informal and formal learning, for informal and formal attributes are present and inter-related, whether we will it so or not. The challenge is to recognize and identify them and understand the implications". The challenge to traditional formal learning

involves understanding and evaluating of other types of student learning.

Prior Learning Assessment [1] addresses how possible college-level credit may be given to students who can show the achievement of student learning outcomes for a course. Other challenges include MOOCs (massive open online courses), military credit, certifications and similar types of learning. As educators in the IT field, we need to understand how these newer types of learning may be incorporated into our programs.

The other difficulty with the new informal, disruptive types of student learning involves how the accreditation community will view these types of learning. Whether it involves regional accreditation or program accreditation, such as ABET, we as educators need to be addressing these new ways of learning.

6. POSITION: HAN REICHGELT

Undergraduate programs have traditionally been structured as consisting of around 40 courses. This organization has a number of advantages. For example, it is easy to track student progress towards a degree. Also, limiting the number of times a course is offered creates economies of scale. Finally, it becomes relatively straightforward to give student credit for learning that took place at another institution through course transfer.

However, the course-centric organization also has a number of drawbacks. For example, students often learn at different rates and courses typically do not allow for this. So, a student who needs a little more time to master a concept early in a course is often lost when the course moves on to a subsequent concept that relies on the earlier concept. Also, courses typically have a number of different learning outcomes. When a student does not completely master all learning outcomes, we face one of two bad possibilities: Either we fail the student and force him or her to retake the course, including the material that he or she has already mastered, or we pass the student but then run the risk that he or she is not prepared in a later course as it relies on the learning outcome(s) from the earlier course that the student did not master. Finally, courses often require one to package up material that is not needed until much later in the curriculum. For example, many computing programs contain a course in discrete mathematics early in the program of study, even though some of the material is not really needed until much later in the program.

So, can we reorganize programs of study around a large collection of learning outcomes that a student has to master, rather than as a very small collection of courses that a student has to pass?

7. REFERENCES

[1] Fiddler, Morry; Marienau, Catherine; and Whitaker, Urban (2006). *Assessing Learning: Standards, Principles, and Procedures*, 2nd edition, Chicago, Kendall Hunt Publishing

[2] Hodkinson, P., Colley, H. and Malcolm, J. (2003). "The Interrelationships Between Informal and Formal Learning". *Journal of Workplace Learning* 15: 313-318.

[3] Klopfer, E., Osterweil, S., Groff, J., & Haas, J. (2009). Using the technology of today, in the classroom today. *The Education arcade*.

[4] U.S. Department of Education (2010). Transforming American Education – Learning Powered by Technology, *National Education Technology Plan 2010*, Retrieved May 22, 2013, from www.ed.gov/sites/default/files/netp2010.pdf

Should IT2008 be Revised?

Bill Paterson (Moderator)
Mount Royal University
Computer Science & Info. Systems
Calgary, AB, Canada T3E 6K6
+1 403-440-7086
bpaterson@mtroyal.ca

Mary Granger
George Washington University
Information Systems and Technology
Management Department
Washington, DC 20052
+1 202 994 7159
granger@gwu.edu

John Impagliazzo
Emeritus, Hofstra University
Computer Science Department
Hempstead, New York 11549 USA
+1 631-513-2833
John.Impagliazzo@Hofstra.edu

Edward Sobiesk
United States Military Academy
West Point, NY 10996
USA
1-845-446-2611
edward.sobiesk@usma.edu

Mark Stockman
University of Cincinnati
2610 McMicken Circle
Cincinnati, OH 45221-0002
(513) 556-4227
mark.stockman@uc.edu

Ming Zhang
School of EECS, Peking University
No.5 Yiheyuan Road, Beijing
P.R. China
+86-10-62765825
mzhang@net.pku.edu.cn

ABSTRACT
Five years have passed since the final publication of the ACM-IEEE information technology (IT) four-year curricula guidelines (IT2008) [1]. In September of 2012, the ACM Education Board initiated an exploratory invitation to Special Interest Group for Information Technology Education (SIGITE) to determine the efficacy of the current IT curricula guidelines and to suggest recommendations, if any. In this panel the group members will report on its current progress and will solicit input from participants on what aspects of the model curriculum need to be revisited.

Categories and Subject Descriptors
K.3.2 [Computer and Information Science Education] Curriculum

Keywords
IT2008, Model Curriculum, Information Technology Education, IT BoK

1. INTRODUCTION
The Association for Computing Machinery (ACM), through its Education Board and in cooperation with representatives from relevant societies such as the Institute for Electrical and Electronic Engineers (IEEE) [2] and the Association for Information Systems (AIS) [3], has supported for decades the development and evolution of computing curricula models. Examples of such curricula models in addition to IT2008 [1] include computer engineering (CE2004) [4], information systems (IS2010) [5], and, currently in development, computer science (CS2013) [6]. Because of the dynamic nature of the computing disciplines, computing curricula require periodic examination and analysis to determine whether they need modification or enhancement to maintain their currency, relevancy, and usability.

2. Task Group Creation
In an effort to accelerate the ongoing effort to retain currency in its curricula guidelines, the ACM Education Board decided to establish an exploratory Review Task Group for Information Technology (RTGIT) to review the IT2008 document. Dr. John Impagliazzo will serve on the RTGIT as the Education Board representative. Additionally, the ACM Education Board requested that Special Interest Group for Information Technology Education (SIGITE) [7] recommend eight individuals from which the Education Board will select at least two participants. The result being that the RTGIT will consist of at least four, but not more than six individuals appointed by the Education Board who will represent diverse interests in the area of information technology. In addition, the Education Board requested that the RTGIT include cross discipline participation with an international perspective. Following this process the above group members were selected.

3. The Task Group's Mandate
The ACM Education Board gave the RTGIT the following mandate:

1. Conduct a "consultation process" to collect information and opinion from the principal curriculum stakeholders (industry and academia) regarding the need for modification of the IT2008 curriculum model to include elements such as its

SIGITE'13, Oct 10-12 2013, Orlando, Florida, USA.
ACM 978-1-4503-2239-3/13/10.
http://dx.doi.org/10.1145/2512276.2512308

body of knowledge, curriculum architecture, pedagogy, and infrastructure. The Education Board recommends that the RTGIT use a variety of methods for this consultation such as web/email communication, academic and industry surveys, and comments from academic individuals and industrial contacts.

2. Analyze and assess the results of the consultation process to determine whether the document needs modification and if so, describe the type and extent of the changes needed.

3. Prepare and submit a brief report to the ACM Education Board. The report should describe the consultation process used and present an analysis, assessment, and evaluation of the information collected. … (There are further instructions for the task force should we decide to recommend that the model curriculum be revised).

4. Panel Activities

The task group members will report on their findings so far. The major part of the panel session will be collecting feedback from the attendees as to what aspects, if any, of the model curriculum need to be updated. This session will be a part of the consultation process identified in the task group's mandate.

In addition, discussions and questions will be encouraged throughout the session. The major topics to be covered are:

☐ The definition and meaning of information technology in an academic setting and the many overlapping degree titles in the discipline

☐ Background, goals, and timeline of the revisions effort

☐ Current body of knowledge (BoK) structure and its value in today's world

☐ Overview of non-technical areas needed for a useful degree in information technology

☐ Ways to involve more people should IT2008 require significant updating

☐ Public access current RTGIT activities

☐ Additional discussion of items of audience interest

5. Panel Presenters

A brief background for RTGIT members follows.

Bill Paterson (Mount Royal University) is past department chair of Computer Science and Information Systems. He has been a member of Canada's Information Systems Technology Accreditation Council (ISTAC) [8] for five years and is its current chair. He is chair of RTGIT.

Mary Granger (George Washington University) is a member of ACM SIGSCE and AIS SIGED. Mary was AIS Vice President of Education and Director of the Masters of Science in Information Systems at GWU. She is an ABET Program Evaluator for Information Systems.

John Impagliazzo (Hofstra University) is a member of the ACM Education Board and he represents this board on the RTGIT. John was a member and principal co-author of CE2004 committee and currently leads the ACM initiative addressing the revision of CE2004. In addition to participating on the panel, John will present a brief history of computing curricula evolution, provide a brief overview of the IT2008 body of knowledge, and contrast parallel curricula activities related to the current effort for information technology.

Edward Sobiesk (United State Military Academy) is an associate professor in the Department of Electrical Engineering and Computer Science where he has directed both the IT and Core IT Programs. He has a PhD in Computer and Information Sciences from the University of Minnesota. His research interests include electronic privacy, computer science & information technology education, computing ethical and legal considerations, and artificial intelligence.

Mark Stockman (University of Cincinnati) is a long time member of ACM SIGITE and currently serves on its Executive Committee, having previously held the positions of Chair, Vice Chair, Regional Representative, and General Conference Chair. Mark is also a member of the Criteria Committee for CSAB, the lead society within ABET for accreditation of degree programs in computer science, information systems, software engineering, and information technology.

Ming Zhang (Peking University) is a member of the ACM Education Council and a senior member of China Computer Federation. Prof. Zhang has been a member of the Advisory committee of Computing Education, the Ministry of Education in China for more than 13 years. Prof. Zhang will introduce the Computing Curricula in China, named CCC 2006 and the ongoing education reform, especially the big tent of IT undergraduate education in China

6. References

[1] http://www.acm.org/education/curricula/IT2008%20Curriculum.pdf accessed on 2013-05-28
[2] http://www.ieee.org/index.html
[3] http://home.aisnet.org/
[4] http://www.acm.org/education/education/curric_vols/CE-Final-Report.pdf accessed on 2013-05-28
[5] http://www.acm.org/education/curricula/IS%202010%20ACM%20final.pdf accessed on 2013-05-28
[6] http://ai.stanford.edu/users/sahami/CS2013/ accessed on 2013-05-28
[7] http://www.sigite.org/
[8] http://www.cips.ca/ISTAC accessed on 2013-05-28

Identifying Information Technology Graduate-Level Programs

Barry M. Lunt
Brigham Young University
Information Technology
Provo, Utah
luntb@byu.edu

Michael Q. Adams
Brigham Young University
Exercise Science
Provo, Utah
m3adams3@gmail.com

Abstract

This paper follows up on a previous paper identifying four-year IT programs in the USA, and identifies graduate-level programs in IT within the four-year IT programs identified. The entrance requirements are also given.

Categories and Subject Descriptors

K.2.3 [Information systems education]

Keywords

Information Technology; Graduate Programs

Introduction

This paper presents the results of additional study in Information Technology educational programs, specifically in identifying master's level programs available.

In the previous study entitled "Identifying and Evaluating Information Technology Bachelor's Degree Programs"[1], presented at SIGITE 2012, a complete list was obtained showing that 909 academic institutions across the country had bachelor's degree computing programs. It is essential to mention as well that all of the 18 ABET-accredited IT programs were also included in this list.

Once this list was obtained, each institution's program requirements were studied to find potential IT related programs. Then those programs that were potentially IT programs were further evaluated to determine whether they wereIT programs, as defined in the IT model curriculum[2]. Due to possible evaluation bias, an identification procedure was established to determine a program's compliance factor, according to the assessment framework established in proceedings of SIGITE 2011 . The end result showed that of the 909 institutions, 220 had potential bachelor's programs in Information Technology. Each of these

220 programs were fully evaluated and were given a compliance factor, where 4.0 indicated full compliance with the IT model curriculum. There were 173 programs with compliance factor scores ≥ 2.0.

In this current study, the 220 institutions having bachelor's programs in Information Technology were searched for master's degree programs also in Information Technology. In order to determine whether a master's degree program in Information Technology was available, the information on computing programs from each school's webpage was evaluated and sorted into four different categories (Information Technology, Information Systems, Computer Science, and Software Engineering). The results from this new study will provide increased knowledge about more advanced education opportunities in Information Technology, increase opportunities for specialization, and expand employment opportunities.

Method

Because not all of the 220 schools have master's level programs in Information Technology, a spreadsheet was created to store information from each school for evaluation purposes. After all of the necessary information was gathered, potential master's programs from each school were evaluated to determine whether they fit the Information Technology criteria. The following shows the process used and how information was accessed:

- Information on master's level programs obtained from each university/college online webpage
  - Master's level programs were located through an online university catalog, or through "Academics" sections and available lists of all programs offered. (**Figure 1** – catalog example)

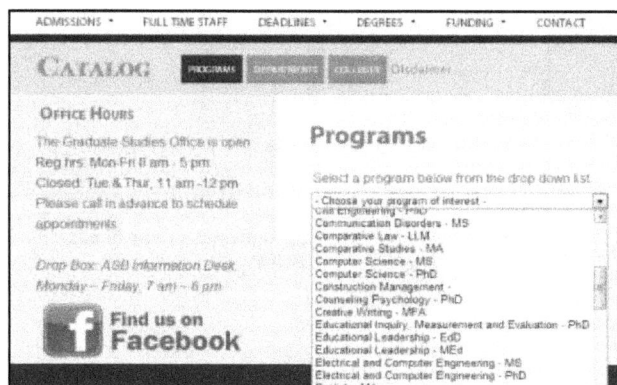

Figure 1

- If possible the following data was collected for each program:
  - Core curriculum (courses, credit weight per course)
  - Program elective courses (and credit weight per course)
  - Open elective courses (and credit weight per course)
  - Program prerequisites (GPA, previous experience, courses, etc.)
  - Whether GRE scores are required or not
  - Degrees beyond master's level available
  - Other certifications offered
  - Source URL's for each page where information was found
- IT-related programs were determined through curriculum/coursework.

Courses in a selected program were compared to the "Pillars of Information Technology" (as established in the SIGITE 2011 paper[3].)

If courses leaned more heavily on areas other than those related to the "Pillars of Information Technology", they were identified accordingly (generally as closely related fields: Computer Science, Computer Engineering, Software Engineering, and Information Systems)

Results

The findings are summarized in a table which is too large to be included in this paper, but which can be found at: http://www.et.byu.edu/~luntb/SIGITE/index.html, in the file, "IT Graduate Programs". Several things are worth noting:

1. 165 (75%) of the 220 schools did not have an Information Technology related program at the master's level.
2. 38 of the 220 schools given compliance factor scores in the 2012 study (17.2%) had Information Technology master's level programs.
3. 14 (6.4 %) schools with related master's level programs were identified as Information Systems programs.
4. 3 (1.4%) schools with related master's level programs were identified as Computer Science programs.
5. There was a very wide range in the number of semester credit hours required for these MS programs, as seen in Figure 2, far beyond what would be expected. We do not know how to account for this very wide range.

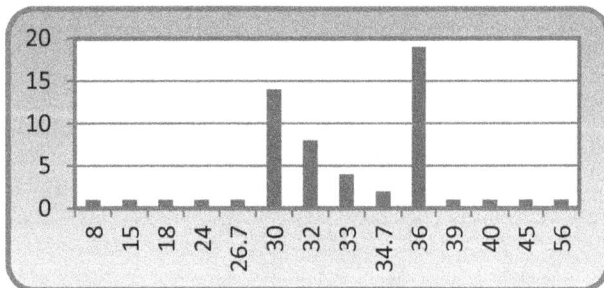

Figure 2: A histogram of the semester credit hours required for the MS-IT programs.

6. There was a great deal of variation in the entrance requirements for these MS programs. As seen in Figure 3, the minimum GPA entrance requirement ranged from 2.0 to 3.0, but was only required by 35 of the 56 programs (62.5%). The

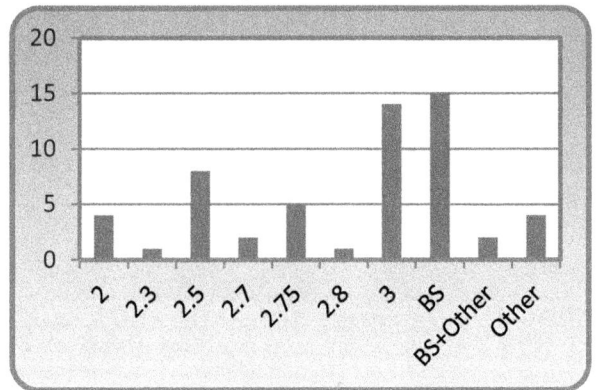

Figure 3: A histogram of the GPA entrance requirements.

remaining 21 programs had no minimum GPA requirement, but did have other entrance requirements such as a completed BS, a completed BS plus other requirements, or had other requirements specific to that institution.

7. There was a great deal of variation in the use of standardized admission tests, as seen in Table 1. Over half (57.1%) of the MS programs did not require a standardized test for admission. Of those that did require the GRE (a few also accepted the GMAT), well over half (62.5%) did not have any minimum score requirements. The remaining 9 programs had varied test score requirements. Only one program had percentile-based score requirements.

Table 1: Standardized Test Entrance Requirements

Test Requirements	#
None	32
GRE – no minimum	15
GRE – with a dept. review	1
GRE – index-based	1
GRE – 140 combined (new scoring)	1
GRE – 290 combined (new scoring)	1
GRE – 450 (old scoring)	1
GRE – 450-450-2.5 (old scoring)	1
GRE – 450-630-4 (old scoring)	1
GRE – 550 (old scoring)	1
GRE – 55%ile (Q, V); 45%ile (W)	1

8. Of the 55 institutions with MS programs in this study, the great majority (48) did not have a doctorate-level program. The seven institutions that did have a doctorate-level program (or programs) are summarized in Table 2.

Table 2: Doctorate-Level Programs at Institutions in This Study

Institution	Doctorate-Level Program(s)
Capella Univ.	Ph.D.-Information Assurance & Security; PhD.-Information Technology Education; Ph.D.-Information Technology Management; DBA-Information Technology Management
Dakota State Univ.	D.Sc.-Information Systems
Eastern Michigan Univ.	Ph.D. - Technology
Purdue Univ.	Ph.D.-Computer & Information Technology
George Mason Univ.	Ph.D.-Information Technology
Nova Southeastern Univ.	Ph.D.-Information Systems
Rochester Institute of Technology	Ph.D.-Computing & Information Sciences

Additionally, as the information from each school was reviewed and stored in the project spreadsheet, there were several recurring points, aside from those outlined previously, which helped distinguish the program types from each other:

1. Information Technology programs usually had one or more of the following:
   a. Curriculum coinciding with the "Pillars of Information Technology"
   b. Various areas and/or courses for specialization
2. Information Systems programs usually included:
   a. Large amounts of business related courses
   b. Focus on management
3. Computer Science programs were usually characterized by a programming-based curriculum.

Discussion

Most of the information we needed for this study was available on each school's webpage. As computing programs were found, their information was collected in a spreadsheet and analyzed. As each school's program information was evaluated we were able to place it in one of the three categories as mentioned above and discover an accurate figure about the Information Technology master's degree programs available across the United States. Since only about 17.7% of the programs encountered fell into the Information *Technology category we can draw a few conclusions:*

- The low percentage could be due to a lack of understanding of Information Technology, or of its availability in advanced education, and if a university sees little demand for such a program, then it will likely not be made available.
- Second, there may be fewer graduate students who desire to pursue further knowledge into the program, and are satisfied with the experience and information they have and wish to pursue their careers instead of further education.
- Third, students who pursued an Information Technology undergraduate degree may have desires to pursue more management type careers and pursue a master's program with such an emphasis.

Conclusion

Of the 220 4-year IT programs given compliance scores in the paper presented at SIGITE 2012[1], 38 of them also have a master's program in an IT-related area. Additionally, seven of them have doctorate programs in an IT-related area. We believe this is strong evidence of the maturing state of IT education in the USA.

References

[1] Lunt, Barry M., Andrew Hansen, Bikalpa Neupane, Richard Ofori, Identifying and Evaluating Information Technology Bachelor's Degree Programs, *Proceedings of SIGITE 2012*, Calgary, Canada, Oct 2012

[2] Lunt, Barry M., Joseph J. Ekstrom, Sandra Gorka, Reza Kamali, Eydie Lawson, Jacob Miller, Han Reichgelt, Computing Curricula: IT Volume, www.acm.org//education/curricula/IT2008%20Curriculum.pdf

[3] Rowe, Dale C., Barry M. Lunt, C. Richard G. Helps, An Assessment Framework for Identifying Information Technology Bachelor Programs, *Proceedings of SIGITE 2011*, West Point, NY, Oct 2011

Keeping Up with Web Development Trends

Craig S. Miller (moderator)
DePaul University
Chicago, IL USA 60604
1 312 362-5085
cmiller@cdm.depaul.edu

Jack Zheng
Southern Polytechnic State University
Marietta, GA USA 30060
1 678 915-5036
jackzheng@spsu.edu

Randy Connolly
Mount Royal University
Calgary, Alberta, Canada T3E 6K6
1 403 440-6061
rconnolly@mtroyal.ca

Amos Olagunju
St Cloud State University
St Cloud, MN USA 56301
1 320 308-5696
aoolagunju@stcloudstate.edu

Categories and Subject Descriptors

K.3.2 [**Computers and Education**]: Computer and Information Science Education

Keywords

Web development, IT curriculum.

1. SUMMARY

Web use continues its remarkable growth, not just in the diversity of applications and the devices that deliver them, but also in the technologies for developing new applications. Most notable is the proliferation of new development methodologies and frameworks. Major trends include stricter adherence to Model-View-Controller (MVC) architecture, object-relational mapping (ORM) for database access, and increased use of client-side technologies and libraries.

IT curriculum models acknowledge the importance of web development [3]. But how well have IT programs kept pace with the emerging trends and requirements of web applications? Do current IT learning outcomes address the needed web development skills? Which development methodologies and frameworks are best for achieving the IT web development learning goals?

This panel addresses these questions by presenting experiences with diverse goals and constraints of web development in IT curriculums. Each panel member has taught web development courses within an IT program under a variety of conditions. In the presentations, each panel member addresses a selection of the following:

1. Role of web development curriculum in alternative models of IT programs.

SIGITE'13, October 10–12, 2013, Orlando, Florida, USA.
ACM 978-1-4503-2239-3/13/10.
DOI http://dx.doi.org/10.1145/2512276.2512309

2. Primary learning outcomes and choice of possible technologies for realizing web development goals.

3. Projects and essential topics for accomplishing web development goals.

4. Challenges and solutions for preparing future web development professionals.

With participation from the audience, the panel session pursues the following objectives:

1. Explore the space of what web development is and how it will be taught.

2. Identify common solutions for addressing learning goals.

3. Engage educators with similar goals and using similar approaches.

The remainder of this paper summarizes the experiences of the panel members and their main contributions to web development issues and solutions.

2. JACK ZHENG

Keeping up with the Real World

Web development courses offered by the IT department at Southern Polytechnic State University (SPSU) have evolved with the advancement of web technologies and development practices. The department monitors industry trends closely to offer more relevant and up-to-date topics that address market and student needs. At both undergraduate and graduate levels, the web development area consists of two major courses. The first one is a required introductory course covering the basics of web development (HTML, CSS, JavaScript, XML, and PHP). The second one is an elective advanced course covering more specific areas that can be adjusted as web technologies advance. Past subjects include ASP.Net, CMS, Web 2.0, and more recently, AJAX, jQuery, and HTML5. The rising trend in mobile computing has also motivated us to develop a new senior technical track (Bachelor of Science) on Mobile and Web.

With increasing number of skills and technologies used in web application development, we are facing a dilemma: on one end, the industry seems to welcome students with experience of newer technologies and practices; on the other end, students need to graduate on time. How can we prepare our students to be ready for their web development career within a limited time frame?

How can we achieve a balance of breadth and depth in web development training? These questions are discussed by the panelists.

3. CRAIG MILLER
Early Emphasis on Architecture

Web development involves core elements in model IT programs including databases, user-centered design, networking and security. The IT program at DePaul University draws upon these elements using web development as the main vehicle for teaching them. Of the five required courses specific to web development, the core two-course sequence emphasizes the role of software architecture and interoperability, an emphasis endorsed in previous work [4,5].

IT majors at DePaul are presented with the "big picture" of a web application early in the program. After one quarter of learning HTML, CSS and elementary programming with JavaScript, they develop comprehensive web applications using the Ruby on Rails framework. Strictly adhering to an MVC architecture, the Rails framework provides scaffold generation, a means for creating a complete application with a few commands. This approach has its tradeoffs. The ability to build whatever application must come later as students learn required programming fundamentals. In the meantime, complexity must be managed by instructors as student develop applications with limited yet meaningful functionality.

4. AMOS OLAGUNJU
Secure Web Design and Implementation

St Cloud State University (SCSU) offers a Bachelor of Science degree in Information Technology Security (BS-ITS). All BS-ITS majors are required to take a course on Web Authoring and Administration (WAA). The students have completed a senior level course on computer networking and have been exposed to JavaScript, Python, C++, etc., prior to taking the WAA. Students who take the WAA learn how to: create tables, frames and collect data with forms on web pages; use JavaScript interactivity capability and embedded objects to vitalize a web; build style sheets and use dynamic HTML to publish web pages; configure resources and implement a web server configuration; provide security for and manage web servers. In the last five years, students in the WAA have used PHP/MySQL for server-side scripting. Students have worked with IIS and Apache web servers. They have implemented database-enabled web applications equipped with protections from Cross-Site Scripting and server-side script attacks for supermarkets, hospitals, a celebrated soft-skills assessment system [6], departments at SCSU, small business companies in Minnesota, etc.

5. RANDY CONNOLLY
Future(s) of Web Development

Mount Royal University offers a Bachelor of Information Systems (BIS) based on IT2008. The BIS has two mandatory web systems courses and an optional upper-level course; the nature of these courses has been previously described in [2]. Yet even with three courses, it is difficult to cover all the necessary content. Many instructors teaching web development have been struggling to catch up to the state of web development circa 2008, and as a consequence, may not have realized that the nature of real-world web development has shifted considerably since 2010, a shift detailed in [1]. The typical server-side development as the staple of most web development courses is becoming less representative of real-world practice because of the increasingly need to integrate rich JavaScript front-ends with server template systems.

This shift provides an opportunity to reassess the role of web development in IT curriculum. Should the web development in IT curriculum be reflective of real-world practice? Or do certain aspects of web development, even if not reflective of current practice, teach essential skills and concepts? If so, what are those essential skills and concepts of web development? The panelists explore these questions.

6. REFERENCES

[1] Connolly, R. 2011. Awakening Rip Van Winkle: Modernizing the Computer Science Web Curriculum, in *Proceedings of the 16th Conference on Innovation and Technology in Computer Science Education*, ITiCSE'11, pages 18-22, New York, NY, USA, 2011. ACM.

[2] Connolly, R. 2010. No longer partying like it's 1999: designing a modern web stream using the it2008 curriculum guidelines. In *Proceedings of the 10th Conference on Information Technology Education*, SIGITE'09, pages 74-79, New York, NY, USA, 2009. ACM.

[3] Lunt, B. M., Ekstrom, J. J., Gorka, S., et al., Information Technology 2008: Curriculum Guidelines for Undergraduate Degree Programs in Information Technology. Association for Computing Machinery (ACM); IEEE Computer Society, November 2008.

[4] Miller, C. S. and Dettori, L. 2008. Employers' perspectives on IT learning outcomes. In *Proceedings of the 9th ACM SIGITE conference on Information technology education*, SIGITE '08, pages 213–218, New York, NY, USA, 2008. ACM.

[5] Morneau, K. A. and Talley, S. Architecture: an emerging core competence for it professionals. In *Proceedings of the 8th ACM SIGITE conference on Information technology education*, SIGITE '07, pages 9–12, New York, NY, USA, 2007. ACM.

[6] Olagunju, A. O. and Soenneker, J. A framework for soft skills training in science and engineering. In *Proceedings of 3nd International Conference on Society and Information Technologies*, Orlando, Florida, pages 122-127, 2011.

Girls in IT: How to Develop Talent and Leverage Support

Mihaela Sabin (moderator)
University of New Hampshire
Manchester, NH 03101
603 641 4144
mihaela.sabin@unh.edu

Deborah LaBelle
Nazareth College
Rochester, NY 14618
585 389 2563
dlabell1@naz.edu

Hiranya Mir
Embry-Riddle Aeronautical University
Daytona Beach, FL 32114
786 545 6650
hiranya.mir@my.erau.edu

Karen Patten
University of South Carolina
Columbia, SC 29201
803 777 2937
pattenk@sc.edu

Suzanne Poirier
Skillsoft
Nashua, NH 03062
603 111 2222
Suzanne_Poirier@skillsoft.com

Seth Reichelson
Lake Brantely High School
Altamonte Springs, FL 32714
407 746 3450
seth_reichelson@scps.k12.fl.us

SUMMARY

The objectives of this panel are to inform the audience about national and regional initiatives developed by the National Center for Women & Information Technology (NCWIT) to reach out to middle and high school girls; learn from promising experiences in which the panelists have been directly involved; and discuss venues to scale and sustain efforts to increase women's participation in technology careers. Panelists will describe their particular experiences, and discuss ways to utilize the Aspirations in Computing program to increase enrollment and retention of females in computing. A minimum of 30 minutes will be set aside for question and answer.

Categories and Subject Descriptors

K.3.2 [**Computer and Information Science Education**]: Computer science education; K.7.1 [**The Computing Profession**]: Occupations

Keywords

Women in Computing, K-12 Education, Community Outreach, Industry-Education Relationships

1. OVERVIEW

Aspirations in Computing is a talent-development pipeline initiative of the National Center for Women & Information Technology (NCWIT). Currently, not enough high-achieving young women in math and science are entering the fields of engineering and computer science. In 2011, just 18% of undergraduate Computing and Information Sciences degrees were awarded to women; in 1985, women earned 37% of these degrees. Young women make up 56% of all college graduates, yet only 18% of computer science graduates [1, 2]. Aspirations in Computing is harnessing this untapped talent source by providing encouragement and visibility, and recognizing technically-inclined young women regionally and nationally. In fall 2009, NCWIT piloted local Affiliate Aspirations in Computing programs in three states, Illinois, Texas, and Florida. In 2013, there were 54 local affiliates serving all 50 states, the District of Columbia, Puerto Rico and the U.S. Virgin Islands. This year, Aspirations Award Affiliates recognized over 1,000 winners and runner-ups. The Aspirations in Computing program has proven successful in retaining women in STEM fields. Participants are surveyed annually to ascertain persistence in the field, college enrollment, and other levels of participation. Of 295 respondents, 193 were in college, and 61% of those students reported a computer science or computer engineering major or minor. Eighty-eight percent of respondents reported a major/minor in a traditionally male-dominated STEM field (Math & Biology are not included in this percentage because women are not under-represented in those disciplines) [2].

2. MIHAELA SABIN

University of New Hampshire at Manchester (UNH Manchester) has joined the NCWIT Academic Alliance in September 2013. Membership in the NCWIT Academic Alliance is free for participating academic institutions and has been benefitting the college with free access to leading-edge best practices for recruiting and retaining women; opportunity for faculty to attend the NCWIT Summit's workshops and round table discussions; access to member-only funding opportunities to involve and support young women in computing-related activities; and exemplary support to establish a regional tri-state affiliate - Maine, New Hampshire and Vermont, for the Aspirations in Computing Award competition.

The New Hampshire Tri-State affiliate recognized ten high school girls and held the award ceremony event at UNH Manchester on April 26, 2013, jointly with the UNH Undergraduate Research Conference – Computing and Engineering Technology Day Senior Projects and Poster Presentations. The event included a hands-on workshop on creating a mobile app on Android phones using the App Inventor platform; panel of women professionals from Manchester and Nashua technology companies; tour of the Computing and Engineering Technology facility and participation in poster presentations; and award presentations ceremony. The Aspirations in Computing Educator award was presented to Ken

SIGITE'13, October 10–12, 2013, Orlando, Florida, USA.
ACM 978-1-4503-2239-3/13/10.
http://dx.doi.org/10.1145/2512276.2512310

Franson, teacher at the Lakes Region Technology Center, Wolfeboro, NH.

3. DEBORAH LABELLE

NCWIT offers the Aspirations in Computing national award each Spring to women of high school age. The award application process asks applicants to explain their current activity and future plans to study in a technical field. National winners of the award receive a small cash award, a new computer, and a trophy for herself and one for her school. More importantly, this award is a way to give needed visibility to the fact that young women are interested in technology and are doing great things at the high school level. In addition, it is a way for women to connect with each other locally and around the nation.

Volunteering to review applications for this award is one way to get involved in NCWIT's initiatives without having to commit a lot of time. The review process is all online, and well organized. The volunteer can choose which areas he or she wishes to review. The volunteers are also invited to attend the award ceremony. Deborah found that being an application reviewer gave her the opportunity to see what sort of technical expertise these young women are developing, where they plan to use their expertise in the future, and how their interest in technology began. Reading the applications of these young women is inspiring and gives the volunteer an avenue to promote women in computing.

4. HIRANYA MIR

Hiranya is a 2011 National Award winner and a 2012 & 2011 Southern Florida Affiliate Award winner. She is interested in a variety of technology related projects, including robotics, networking, and programming. Hiranya is involved in Women of Tomorrow, where she encourages young girls to explore IT and become professionals. She is Vice President of SECME, and head of the Robotic Hand team where she is working on creating and programming a bionic hand.

Because of her dedication and accomplishments, Hiranya received the I.T. Essentials Award, and became CompTIA A+ Certified. Her enthusiasm for learning computer systems runs deep, and she is currently enrolled in Cisco's NetRiders and NetRiders Security competitions. Hiranya attends Embry-Riddle Aeronautical University with a scholarship she received in part because of her accomplishments as an NCWIT Award for Aspirations in Computing award winner.

5. KAREN PATTEN

The Integrated Information Technology (iIT) Program Undergraduate at the University of South Carolina is a founding member of IT-oLogy, along with IBM and Blue Cross Blue Shield – South Carolina. IT-oLogy is a non-profit collaboration of business, academic institutions, and organizations dedicated to growing the IT talent, fostering economic development, and advancing the IT profession. IT-oLogy has three main initiatives: Promote IT (for K-12); Teach IT (for Higher Education); and Grow IT (for Professionals). Students within the iIT Program are actively involved in promoting IT to high school girls and programs through several different activities. Each year a student project team coordinates and delivers a "Create IT" Day for

freshmen and sophomore high school students. These students build laptops, develop games, and use IT to solve problems. Students within the student chapter of the Association of IT Professionals also work jointly with students from the Society of Women Engineers student chapter to sponsor, together with IT-oLogy, a high school Tech Day for Women, which invites women IT professionals and faculty to share their IT career stories.

6. SUZANNE POIRIER

Today, mangers in software development struggle to find qualified candidates. In a recent hiring push at Skillsoft, many of the applicants were under qualified and, even more surprisingly, there were very few women that applied. Companies can encourage female participation at college job fairs by sending female role models into the field. However, college is far too late to reach out to young women to grab their interest in technology.

Suzanne in her pursuit to find out why women were so underrepresented in her chosen field found local opportunities to participate in various events to capture young women's interest in technology. By participating as a panelist at the NH Tri-State NCWIT affiliate award event for high school girls, and as a teacher's aide in Girls Technology Day state-wide event, it stressed the importance of collaboration between industry and academic institutions to create opportunities to show young women that IT and other STEM-related disciplines can be interesting, fun, creative, and something in which they can excel.

7. SETH REICHELSON

Seth Reichelson is the AP Computer Science teacher at Lake Brantley High School in Orland, Florida. He is the current SECME National Champion (three time champ), IBM's Mainframes North American Teacher of the Year, 2009 Bright House Star Teacher of the Year, 2009 Air Force Teacher of the Year, and 2010 Florida's School Board Innovation in Technology Award winner. He has also won all-Florida ACM high school programming contests for the past three years. He is a passionate advocate for diversity and inclusion in the technology field. Seth initially got involved with NCWIT when he attended a Tapestry Workshop with the goal of recruiting more young women into his AP Computer Science class. Using the NCWIT practices he successfully recruited more young women into his AP CS class and currently almost 50% of his AP CS students are female. In 2011, Seth received the NCWIT Aspirations in Computing Educator Award for his outstanding work recruiting and supporting his female students.

8. REFERENCES

[1] National Science Foundation, National Center for Science and Engineering Statistics. 2013. *Women, Minorities, and Persons with Disabilities in Science and Engineering: 2013*. Special Report NSF 13-304. Arlington, VA.

[2] National Center for Women & Information Technology, 2013. *By the Numbers*. NCWIT, Boulder, CO. Available at http://www.ncwit.org/bythenumbers.

[3] DuBow, W. 2011. NCWIT Internal Evaluation Data. NCWIT, Boulder, CO. Unpublished.

Using a Low-Cost Open Source Hardware Development Platform in Teaching Young Students Programming Skills

Lawrence Hill
Information Sciences and Technologies Department
Golisano College of Computing
and Information Sciences
Rochester Institute of Technology
102 Lomb Memorial Drive
Rochester, NY 14623-5603
(585) 475-7064
Lawrence.Hill@rit.edu

Steven Ciccarelli
Electrical, Computer & Telecommunications
Technology Department
College of Applied Science and Technology
Rochester Institute of Technology
78 Lomb Memorial Drive
Rochester, NY 14623-5604
(585) 475-4736
Steven.Ciccarelli@rit.edu

ABSTRACT

The teaching of programming skills to young students is often described by those educators involved as problematic at best. Student issues like mathematical maturity, readiness for complex thought, basic problem solving skills, short attention span especially related to the boredom of traditional programming teaching methodologies, and the lack of exciting problems and their solutions with respect to programming assignments contribute to the angst of many a programming instructor. A small fraction of students who "were just made for programming" always seem to succeed at whatever programming problem is given to them. However, a majority of students, especially pre-college and college freshmen tend to have difficulty in overcoming these issues. It is with that observation that something new, in terms of programming pedagogy, needed to be investigated by this paper's authors.

An ideal opportunity requiring successful programming instruction for 7-12 graders in the local metropolitan area presented itself in the winter of 2012. The students were involved in a statewide competition where groups of students self-selected into project options offered by various sponsoring institutions.

Under the "Technology" choice heading of the state program, the student team and the instructor agreed to program a microprocessor to send messages in International Morse Code. The object of the exercise was to learn basic programming skills and to apply them to solving a problem. The hook was to do something brand new the students had never engaged in, keeping their attention on the end goal, and to see the immediate real-time results of some programming effort along the development cycle as the completed final program took form.

The effort was a resounding success; the students learned in a few Saturday morning sessions more about programming than the authors have experienced over weeks of effort in traditional programming classes at the college freshman level.

Categories and Subject Descriptors

K.3.2 [**Computers and Information Science Education**]: Curriculum

Keywords

IT education, C programming, young students, open source, Arduino, International Morse Code, IDE

1. INTRODUCTION

This work was done in fulfillment of the requirements of the 2012 New York State STEP (Science and Technology Entry Program)[1]. Ten students participated in the project, "Can computers be programmed to send messages in Morse code?", in the Technology group, and were sponsored by the authors' university, with the team being taught by this paper's first author. This program ran over a three-weekend period where the student teams did their work for three Saturday mornings and presented their results on the third Saturday. The work done by this team happened in a total of just nine hours. That is the equivalent time utilized by three weeks in a typical freshman C programming course in terms of lecture contact hours. During the first three weeks in a traditional programming first course, students learn the basics of programming such as the use of some IDE (integrated development environment) in which they perform their work (typically an ongoing process that is not fully mastered until the middle of the term), simple variables, and basic program syntax and structure. Some methodology is usually included whereby the student can make their program prompt the user of their program for some input value and subsequently obtain that value for use deeper within the program. That is about it; nothing more than bare functionality and, most importantly, nothing exciting and fulfilling on the behalf of the student. The students would often comment, "How boring!", and they were absolutely correct. Keep this in mind as a description of the work done by the STEP students is detailed later.

Three Saturday mornings is not enough time to do much of anything, let alone the programming of a microprocessor to accomplish a task (sending Morse code) in which none of the students had any prior experience, in a language (C) that only two students had some previous exposure, but not to the extent this project needed.

Then again, what is Morse code (or more accurately, International Morse Code)? The first Saturday was spent discussing the problem, and an introduction to communication using the Morse system. Two students had dads that were amateur ("ham") radio operators and even knew a few letters in Morse code. Those two students were asked to send a message for help to one another and one of them shouted, "DOT, DOT, DOT, DASH, DASH, DASH, DOT, DOT, DOT!" to the other. Of course this was "SOS", the international distress signal. Almost immediately, the rest of the students realized that this was in fact the distress call and it then occurred to them that every letter of the alphabet must have Morse code equivalents. Everyone was excited and a long discussion ensued that lasted the remainder of the time on that first Saturday. Homework was assigned. They were to go online and find out any information they could about Morse code. They were to come prepared for the next session with their names encoded in Morse such that they could each send their names verbally to a partner. Every one of the students came prepared the following Saturday!

For the topic in the second session, now that the students understood what the microprocessor needed to do, send Morse code, it was necessary to develop a program skeleton the students understood (no time to teach flowcharting here!). It was decided that to keep things simple, and inexpensive as there was little funding for this program, the microprocessor would send the messages using a blinking light. It was also decided that, for this project, it would be adequate to send a single hard-coded message to further reduce the program's complexity. An appropriate step-by-step outline was developed by the students such that they had an idea what their program would have to perform. In the end, there was enough time to implement prompting a user from the IDE to enter a message to be sent on the host computer's screen/keyboard and send that message to the microprocessor for conversion to Morse and subsequent light-blinking. Being able to take their program to the next level of complexity in the allotted timeframe was an unexpected pleasure!

2. THE OPEN-SOURCE REVOLUTION

Open-source projects are all the rage these days, and there is a wealth of processors, development kits, IDEs, and accessories available today to assist both novices and engineers alike to develop very simple to extremely complex systems. The original intent of development systems/boards, from about 1990 on, was to assist product development engineers to try something new, using a component, like a microprocessor unfamiliar to them, for the first time. Manufacturers literally enjoyed giving those things away gratis to developers in the hopes that once familiar with their operation those developers would specify the component in quantities that would be profitable to the device manufacturer. The true cost of those systems was high and if a common person wished to purchase one of them for personal experimentation the cost could have been in the hundreds of dollars. Some kind of development software solution (system compiler for example) was also required and that needed to be purchased at quite a high cost as well. This high cost relegated the use of these development platforms to real corporate design groups only.

Enter the open-source revolution. Early in the 2000's there was a general revolt on expensive single-sourced proprietary design solutions by the masses. Non-corporate development teams banded together and gave rise to the open-source concept where the end product belonged to everyone, could be shared openly, modified by anyone, and redistributed at will. The domain of the closed and very expensive development platforms was reserved for their original intent, the corporate designer, and all kinds of open-source new and inexpensive hardware and software were

developed and found their way into the hands of experimenters worldwide.

3. THE ARDUINO DEVELOPMENT PLATFORM HARDWARE

One of the most common, widely adopted, and very inexpensive platforms used by thousands of non-commercial entities is the Arduino [2]. Arduino was developed in Italy in the mid-2000's and its hardware is currently in its seventh generation, and its development IDE in its fourth major revision. A variety of small companies have started by providing accessories and hardware for the Arduino platform. Limor Fried, a female electrical engineer, formed Adafruit Industries, a very successful woman-owned business entirely based upon the Arduino platform [3]. She has a very complete Arduino tutorial site for those new to the platform [4]. In April of this year Ms. Fried was featured in the IEEE Spectrum journal as an innovator and entrepreneur [5]. The Arduino community is ever expanding and the platform is being utilized by thousands, from small science fair projects to full-scale robotics and much more. Most importantly, and the overarching reason it was chosen for this STEP project, was its ease of use and intuitive IDE and language structure. The students, by the end of the second session, were programming the system to blink the light on demand (not yet in Morse code). That was no small feat! They had to learn how to hook up the Arduino circuit board to a laptop computer, launch the Arduino development IDE, learn some simple C language syntax, upload the compiled code to the Arduino, and watch the results. All this occurred in a mere three hours. The instructor was ecstatic to say the least. It cannot be overlooked that the students were mesmerized and extremely excited to see a piece of hardware that certainly didn't look like anything they had seen before function at their hands right before their eyes. To them, they were using some kind of electrical engineering research item that grabbed their attention and held it for the next three weeks. They were truly motivated to learn more and complete the project's goals. A few of the students contacted the instructor during the weekday gaps in the schedule with questions and ideas. That was exciting to the instructor as, during a typical college term in a beginning programming class, it was rare to have students visit during open office hours even when it was obvious that some of those students needed extra help.

Figure 1. The Arduino Duemilanove ("2009") board. The USB connector is at the upper left. The external connections are available on the black connectors at the top and bottom edges of the board. [2]

The Arduino platform is a single board computer that uses a typical USB interface to connect to the host computer where the Arduino IDE runs. As a stand-alone system, the board gets its power from that USB connection. Since the power sourcing capability of a standard USB port is limited, the Arduino board also has an external power connector where a plug-in wall adapter can be used to supply any needed additional power. That was not the case in the STEP project as all that was being done by the board was blinking an LED lamp that required minimal current. Another feature of the Arduino was the simplicity in which external devices can be interfaced to the processor. In the case of the LED lamp, all that was needed was to plug its two wire leads into the appropriate socket connections on the board. No complicated design skills are needed to interface many of the available accessories, making the creation of complex projects very easy for the student. The electrical portion of the STEP project was now complete.

Anyone can play with an Arduino and make it do remarkable things after spending a minimal amount of time to learn the basics. The students in the STEP project had their boards and computers running in less than a half-hour and they had their LEDs blinking in a uniform fixed sequence (on-off-on-off, etc.). Best of all, the price of a single Arduino Uno board (the current version as this paper is written; see the Arduino website [6] for all the versions of hardware and software), in unit quantities, is roughly $25.00. A USB A-B cable is roughly $5.00. For an outlay of 30 or so dollars, a single student is accommodated. That is the total cost since all the necessary documentation is available online for free (less expensive than even a very inexpensive programming textbook alone). The faculty at this university is considering using the Arduino (or some other similar platform) in lieu of a traditional programming textbook as a course requirement. Another important advantage to such a scheme is that the students can take the platform home to work on their own without being required to sit in a lab. The hardware piece was done.

4. THE ARDUINO DEVELOPMENT PLATFORM SOFTWARE

No microprocessor development environment is complete without suitable methods for 1) generation of the source code, 2) compiling that source code into the appropriate machine language required by the target processor, and 3) uploading that compiled program to the physical processor on the development board. This is called the IDE. The Arduino system comes with a very capable IDE that is fully open-source and meticulously maintained and updated. This is vital, as the processor used in the Arduino, the Atmel ATMega328 family of processors, fully described at [7] finds itself in many commercial products these days, using code developed on the Arduino platform initially. This is what these development environments are typically used for; using them to teach programming for programming's sake is the unique application described in this paper. All the IDE code, libraries, examples, hints and techniques, errata and bug fixes, in the current and all the prior releases, is available on the main Arduino website [8]. The IDE will operate on most standard PC platforms, and appropriate downloadable versions are on that site.

As with any microprocessor development environment (since these chips come with many and varied capabilities) the IDE must be matched with the target microprocessor. That means there will be little code portability at the microprocessor level. In the processor world that is not a problem, but in programming pedagogy, portable code is usually a desired outcome of a development effort (think about web functionality; the JAVA language was designed specifically for portability). There is no ambiguity here; the students in the STEP project had no need to understand this very high level concept. The purpose in the STEP project was to instruct the students in program operation in a simple problem domain, not prepare them to be professional programmers. As such, the Arduino IDE has libraries with functionality that coincides with the ATMega328. The basis for the Arduino IDE is the C/C++ programming language. The language reference is available from [9]. The entire IDE is itself an effort in open-source development, consisting of modules taken from the Processing Environment [10] and the Wiring Environment [11]. In other words, there is a canned procedure for turning on and off a specific I/O (input/output) pin on the processor. If one can turn an interface pin on and off, then one can simply connect an LED lamp to that pin (and a ground connection), and the LED will illuminate and extinguish on demand. That is exactly the basis for the STEP project. Making that LED blink in Morse code then becomes a simple matter of timing those on-off signals. That became the task for the third and last session.

The students had more homework to do between the second and third sessions. Given the necessary coaching, they explored on their own the timing relationships of the dots and dashes in Morse code and how they might implement those relationships such that instead of blinking their LED lamps in a periodic fashion, they could generate a dot-dash pattern that would eventually be the primary goal of the project.

5. THE STEP PROJECT'S PROGRAM STRUCTURE AND CODE

There are two required modules in any Arduino program (or "sketch", a term from the Processing Environment). The first segment of the code sketch is a one-time stand-alone initialization function named "setup". Any pre-initialization tasks that support the program's primary functionality are performed here. In the case of the STEP project, the setup function established two initializations. This setup function runs only once. It should be noted that the code segments presented in this paper have been edited to fit the two-column paper format. A few global variable initializations are left out for brevity. The complete code listing, ready for downloading into an Arduino, is available by contacting the first author. Here is the setup function's code:

```
void setup() {
  // initialize the digital pin as an output
  // Pin 13 has an LED connected on most
  // Arduino boards
  pinMode(13, OUTPUT);
  //initialize the Serial Monitor in the
  //Arduino IDE
  Serial.begin(9600);
}
```

In the STEP project code, this was the only necessary setup functionality. The I/O pin on the microprocessor used to connect to the LED lamp anode (positive lead) was pin 13, and that pin was designated as having output capability. The other LED lead (cathode or negative) was connected to the Arduino's ground connection. Since the user of the system needs a method to input the message to be sent in Morse code, the IDE's serial monitor is enabled at a speed of 9600 baud.

The second required module in this environment is a function named "loop". The idea here is that once the microprocessor begins code execution, it continuously replays the same loop forever, or until the processor is reset or powered-down. This scheme is taken for granted in high level language programming where the hardware's operations are insulated from the user but, when programming a microprocessor in low-level terms, is a factor that must be considered by the programmer. It is in effect an endless loop that is normally considered a horrible thing in high-level programming. This was another advanced topic the STEP students didn't need to learn nor understand. It just happens as a matter of course since all the Arduino coding tutorials and examples use this main loop construct. It should be noted that there is no "main" function in Arduino code. The "loop" function performs what "main" does in typical C code. Within this loop in the STEP code there are two code blocks. The first is coded to run only on the first iteration of the main loop and its purpose is to get the message string from the user via the IDE's serial interface. Its code follows:

```
void loop() {//the forever main loop

  if(loopCount == 0) { //do this block only
      // one time to get the user's message

    Serial.flush();//clear serial buffer

    //prompt the user
    Serial.print("Enter the text to be sent
                  in the box above.\n");
    Serial.print("Use any non-alphanumeric
                  character for a space
                  between words.\n");
    Serial.print("Then click the \"send\"
                  button.\n");

    //get user's input from serial receive
    //buffer
    do {
      if(Serial.available()) {
        while(Serial.available()) {
          message[messageIndex] =
          (char)Serial.read();//store
            //user's message in the array

          if(!isalnum(message[messageIndex]))
          //store a space in message if char
          //is neither letter nor a number
            message[messageIndex] = ' ';
          messageIndex++;
        }//end while

      message[messageIndex] = '\0'; //append
      //the message array with a terminating
      //null character
      }//end if

      delay(100);//wait for serial monitor
    }
    while(messageIndex == 0);

    messageIndex = 0;//reset array index for
                      // next use
    loopCount = 1;//reset counter so this
                    //block executes only once
  }//end if
```

The main loop continues from here later. The first few lines in this block prompt the user for the message to be sent. Then, a do-while loop gets the bytes from the serial interface and stores them in a null-terminated array. The instructor coached the students in the writing of this, and all the following segments of code, but they understood each and every line by the time the project was finished. The next few lines store a space character in the array if the user had entered any but an alpha or numeric character since, in this version of the project, only letters and numbers were considered valid for sending by Morse code. A very real problem with this kind of coding is that the microprocessor runs very much faster than the serial interface can react, hence the delay(100) line that causes the microprocessor to pause for 100 milliseconds while waiting for the serial port to respond. The explanation of this issue to the students was well received (it made sense to them) since they had never coded anything else before. It is suspected that students with prior programming skills confronted with a STEP-like project might have some issues with the concept. At this point in the code the user's message is ready to be converted to Morse code and sent.

The second block in the main loop reads the characters from the array, converts each character to its sequence of dots and dashes, and sends the Morse message by blinking the LED lamp. Once sent, there is a two second delay and the sending of the same message repeats. To enter a new message, the microprocessor must be reset whereby the first half of the preceding code block executes again. The code for the second half of the main loop follows:

```
while(message[messageIndex] != '\0') {
    character = message[messageIndex];//get
            //the character from the array
    Serial.print((char)character);//send the
            //character to serial I/O
    sendLetter(character);//blink the LED in
            //the Morse code sequence
    messageIndex++;//go to the next
            //character in the array
    delay(charSpace);
}//end while

delay(2000);//repeat message sequence
            //after 2 seconds
messageIndex = 0;//reset array for next
            //loop iteration
Serial.print('\n');

}//end forever main loop
```

In this loop within the main loop, the array is read, followed by sending the characters to the serial port as well as blinking the LED lamp in Morse code.

There are three separate functions used in blinking the LED lamp that were coded by the students. In a first iteration of this program's development all the code was written inline without the three functions. It became very clear to the students that it was very tedious to write a program in that fashion and they inquired about some easier method to handle the repetitive tasks. Here were the students asking for function instruction! Functions are a topic loathed by most programming students and some of them struggle to the bitter end without mastering the concept. Using the Arduino platform and its simplistic code illustrated to the STEP students why and how the use of functions greatly improves the writability and future readability of computer programs. The first two functions perform the repetitive task of sending the dots (writedot) and dashes (writedash). This function code follows:

```
void writeDot() {
  digitalWrite(13,HIGH);
  delay(dot);
  digitalWrite(13,LOW);
  delay(dotDashSpace);
}

void writeDash() {
  digitalWrite(13,HIGH);
  delay(dash);
  digitalWrite(13,LOW);
  delay(dotDashSpace);
}
```

The method by which dots and dashes blink the LED lamp is straightforward. Pin 13, the I/O connection chosen on the microprocessor to energize/deenergize the LED lamp, is turned on (made positive) by the "high" parameter in the digitalwrite function call. That pin remains in that high state until it is commanded to go low (or ground). That is achieved by the "low" parameter in the digitalwrite function call.

The third function is used to send the space character that separates multiple words in Morse code. That self explanatory code follows:

```
void writeSpace() {
  delay(wordSpace);
}
```

This function sends nothing; it simply waits the appropriate inter-word spacing time in Morse code.

Between the high and low commands in the writedot and writedash functions, and in the writespace function, there need to be delays that correspond to the timing relationships in the Morse code standard. These delays determine the "on time" of the LED lamp that makes the dots and dashes different in length and the wait interval between words. The timing relationships were defined by the use of global variables. The use of globals is normally discouraged in programming pedagogy but there was insufficient time in the STEP program to take function instruction to the next level, that of multiple parameter-passing techniques. The variable definition code follows:

```
int dot = 240;//dot length in milliseconds
 //all other timings are based on this value
 //the transmission speed can be
 //changed by altering only the dot length
int dash = dot*3;
int dotDashSpace = dot;
int charSpace = dot*3;
int wordSpace = dot*7;
```

In the code sample above a 240 ms dot interval roughly equates to five Morse code words per minute. A treatise describing these timing relationships is available at [12] and is beyond the scope of this paper. The STEP students needed to review that reference as stated previously in one of their homework assignments.

Finally, there is one more function definition to be considered. In the sendletter function, the tedious task of defining each character's Morse code equivalent is handled. Prior to the designing of this function whereby the STEP students wrote all the code manually, in an inline fashion, there was the ah-ha moment on their part that there must be a more efficient way to write the program, as discussed previously. This sendletter function calls the last three functions described. It also accepts one parameter that, when explained to the students, surprisingly made sense to them. Its code follows:

```
//creates the dot-dash sequences for all
//letters and numbers
//accepts both upper and lower case inputs
//Morse code is not case-sensitive
void sendLetter(char letter) {
    switch(letter) {
      case 'A'://dot, dash
      case 'a':
          writeDot();
          writeDash();
          break;
      case 'B'://dash, dot, dot, dot
      case 'b':
          writeDash();
          writeDot();
          writeDot();
          writeDot();
          break;
      case 'C'://dash, dot, dash, dot
      case 'c':
          writeDash();
          writeDot();
          writeDash();
          writeDot();
          break;
```

The code listing continues on the next page.
The case statements for all the remaining letters and numerals occupy this gap. They were edited out for brevity.

```
      case '9'://dash, dash, dash, dash, dot
          writeDash();
          writeDash();
          writeDash();
          writeDash();
          writeDot();
          break;
      case '0'://dash, dash, dash, dash,dash
          writeDash();
          writeDash();
          writeDash();
          writeDash();
          writeDash();
          break;
      case ' '://make word space
          writeSpace();
          break;
      default:
          break;
    }//end switch
}
```

The code segment is a switch statement that uses the "falling through" concept to accept both upper and lower-case letters, a fairly tough to teach concept in freshman programming classes. The STEP students understood it completely. All 26 letters and the 10 numerals were coded in the switch statement allowing for any text message to be entered and sent by the students. The coding portion of the STEP project was complete.

6. CONCLUSION

The end goal of the STEP project was to use a computing platform to solve a problem. That was certainly accomplished by the STEP students. At the very last minute in the third session they authored a PowerPoint presentation describing what they had accomplished, along with a code listing as described previously. Then, at a celebration lunch and presentation immediately following the last working session, they presented their slides and fully described the code that was produced, much like the previous explanation. The audience and the instructor were amazed at the level of detail and understanding the students had with respect to this fairly complex project. They solved their problem using computing.

From the instructors' viewpoint a very different outcome was experienced. In three short weekends and a few hours on their own outside of the working sessions, these students learned an amazing array of programming skills. Those skills (in no particular order) were:

- Algorithm development
- Arduino IDE operation and interaction
- Arduino language syntax and program structure (very C-like)
- Variable types and initialization (char, int)
- Array declaration and initialization
- Array indexing, writing and reading
- Decision statements (if, switch)
- Loops (while, do-while)
- Conditional operators (case statement fall-through, = =)
- Negation operator (!)
- Function definition and calling
- Basic parameter-passing
- Using built-in library functions
- Timing and delay relationships
- Prompting the user
- Accepting user input
- Basic serial I/O

Successfully teaching, and having the students learn, this depth of material in an elementary (first term) programming class to any first-year students is a difficult undertaking in the best of circumstances. However, these very young students with an enthusiastic instructor did just that in three short weekends.

As mentioned in the abstract there are many obstacles to overcome when teaching young students programming. Three things were learned from this project. The first is that real-world problems need to be addressed to give the programming students a sense of purpose. The second is the introduction of a new methodology in programming pedagogy that keeps the students actively engaged and craving for more. The third is the use of an inexpensive but powerful platform, both in hardware and software, that allows the students to be creative and give them the opportunity to work on their assignments out of class and not be tethered to a particular venue like the classic programming lab. The low cost nature of a platform such as Arduino together with its vast array of support information freely available online, in lieu of a $100.00 textbook and expensive IDE software, is the final "nail in the coffin" in traditional programming education in these authors' opinion. Additional work needs to be done with respect to programming instruction in full-term college level programming courses. That will be the subject of future work.

7. REFERENCES

[1] http://www.highered.nysed.gov/kiap/step/

[2] www.arduino.cc/

[3] http://adafruit.com/

[4] http://learn.adafruit.com/

[5] Kumagai, Jean. *Profile: Limor Fried – The founder of Adafruit Industries champions Do-It-Yourself electronics.* IEEE Spectrum Online. April 22, 2013. http://spectrum.ieee.org/geek-life/profiles/profile-limor-fried

[6] http://arduino.cc/en/Main/Products

[7] http://www.atmel.com/Images/doc8161.pdf

[8] http://arduino.cc/en/Main/Software

[9] http://arduino.cc/en/Reference/HomePage

[10] http://www.processing.org/

[11] http://wiring.org.co/

Both authors are associate professors in their respective departments. In prior careers they were software and electrical design engineers. Both have a deep passion for teaching and pedagogical research. The first author has taught programming at the graduate and undergraduate levels for 17 years.

Reaching the 'Aha!' Moment: Web Development as a Motivator for Recursion

Amber Settle
DePaul University
243 S. Wabash Avenue
Chicago, IL 60604
1-312-362-5324
asettle@cdm.depaul.edu

ABSTRACT

One of the topics within programming that has remained a challenge for both educators and students is recursion. We present an approach to teaching recursion that has the potential to increase the motivation of students to master recursion. The approach is novel in its focus on file system and web search, problems that are directly relevant to all computing students and particularly of interest for those in the area of information technology. Participants in the workshop should bring a laptop with the latest version of Python installed to follow along with the examples discussed.

Categories and Subject Descriptors

K.3.2 [**Computers and Education**]: Computer and Information Science Education: Curriculum

Keywords

Recursion, programming, web development, Python, information technology, computing, motivation

1. INTRODUCTION

One of the most fundamental topics in the computing curriculum is programming, and its centrality has led information technology educators to make programming one of the pillars of the model IT curriculum [6]. As with many areas of study, not every topic in the programming curriculum is equally easy to master for students and recursion has proven to be one of the most difficult [3]. One of the early papers on recursion notes: "Many of the first 'AHA' experiences of students learning about recursion happens when studying applications which are amenable to graphic explanations" [4, pg. 263]. Given the relationship between student motivation and learning to program [1], it is surprising that relatively little attention has been paid to improving student motivation for learning recursion. One study found it had the potential to improve student interest in computing [5], another showed that students were enthusiastic about learning recursion using a game [2], and a third suggested that graphical problems not easily solved iteratively could be motivating for students [8]. These few papers addressing student motivation represent a small fraction of the body of work on teaching recursion.

SIGITE'13, October 10–12, 2013, Orlando, Florida, USA.
ACM 978-1-4503-2239-3/13/10.
http://dx.doi.org/10.1145/2512276.2512325

In this workshop we demonstrate an approach to recursion that culminates with a concrete problem in the area of web development. In his textbook [7], Ljubomir Perković places the chapter on recursion just prior to a chapter on web development foundations. Using the carrot of creating a web crawler, students build their abilities with more fundamental recursion problems. The recursion chapter requires students to write a program that mimics the behavior of a virus-detection program, which leads naturally to the problem of parsing web pages and crawling the web in the following chapter. It also has the benefit of being amenable to graphical explanations and a natural problem for students who have used search engines their entire lives.

2. THE APPROACH

The approach to recursion described here is taken from the textbook *Introduction to Computing Using Python: An Application Development Focus* by Ljubomir Perković [28]. The textbook was developed out of his notes for a two-quarter-long Python programming sequence. The courses in question were designed for students with little or no programming experience, and the early chapters introduce basic syntax including data types, imperative programming, textual data and files, and execution control structures. Because of the simplicity of Python syntax, more advanced topics such as exception handling, containers, and object-oriented programming can be introduced relatively quickly. Later chapters focus on applications for the earlier material including graphical-user interfaces, web application development, and databases and data processing.

The chapter on recursion strategically appears just prior to the chapter on web application development. The chapter begins with a series of simple functions that operate on integers. The first is a straightforward example of printing a sequence of numbers to the screen which is immediately followed by the problem of printing the digits of an integer one per line to the screen. A discussion of recursive function calls and the stack using the digit printing example is presented next. The following section has multiple examples of recursive functions including another pattern printing problem and a function that uses the turtle graphics module in Python to print Koch's curve. The section concludes with a function that simulates a virus-scanning program, introducing the Python os module. A section on run-time analysis follows, including an example that demonstrates repeated halving of exponents in computing the power function to demonstrate the efficiency that recursion can bring and the Fibonacci series example to illustrate how duplicated computations can make recursion inefficient. The next section is on searching, describing first linear search and then binary search. Problems with a similar structure to searching such as uniqueness testing, removal of duplicates, and finding the mode are also discussed. The chapter concludes by discussing the Towers of Hanoi problem.

The exercises at the end of the recursion chapter include a variety of problems with various recursive approaches. There are some additional printing problems. A function to compute the number of ones in the binary representation of a number and a function to print a value in a specified base are listed. Some classic recursive problems are present, such as the greatest common divisor, finding the permutations of a list, and computing Pascal's triangle. A problem considering how to display Levy's curve builds on the graphical work done with Koch's curve. Several problems work toward the web development material that follows including a problem that opens files containing the names of other files and then recursively searches them, a problem that traverses and prints every subfolder and file of a directory, and a problem that requires returning the path to a specified file within a directory or its subdirectories.

A chapter on web application development and web searching immediately follows the recursion chapter. The web development chapter opens with a brief review of the world wide web, including web servers and clients, URLs, and HTTP. The highlights of HTML are presented since students are not assumed to have knowledge of the language. The next section discusses the Python WWW API where three important modules are discussed. The module urllib.request allows HTML files to be opened in much the same way that files are opened. The module html.parser provides a parent class HTMLParser that can be overridden to parse HTML files in various ways, requiring the programmer to write various methods. Some examples are provided, including a parser to print the values of href attributes in anchor tags. The final module is urllib.parse which contains a method urljoin that allows a programmer to construct absolute URLs from relative URLs found in web pages. A section on string pattern matching follows, introducing regular expressions found in the re module. With all of the pieces in place the final section is a case study of the development of a web crawler. Several versions of the web crawler are introduced, starting with one that does not take cycles into account which is then improved into one that maintains a set of URLs that have already been visited to avoid that issue. A brief discussion of breadth-first versus depth-first analysis is provided in the text, with follow-up exercises at the back of the chapter. The chapter concludes with a discussion of web page analysis using text processing concepts introduced in earlier chapters.

3. MOTIVATIONAL ASPECTS

Perković's approach is novel in its use of realistic searching problems as a concluding point for the exercises. Within the chapter on recursion students see searching problems and a program that uses the os.listdir and os.path.join functions from the os module to mimic the behavior of a virus-detection program. In the following chapter an HTML parser that mines URLs from web pages is developed and then used to produce two recursive versions of a web crawler. These problems have two strong benefits. First, the students are amply familiar with them, having navigated directories and used search engines on a nearly daily

basis. But perhaps more importantly these are problems for which recursion is the most natural problem-solving technique. While iterative solutions can be developed for them, the iterative versions are less intuitive and more complex than the recursive ones.

The motivational approach for recursion used in the text is particularly appealing for information technology students. Web development is crucial in the IT model curriculum, constituting a pillar of the curriculum (Web Systems) and appearing in the Programming section of the curriculum under the Integrative Programming Technologies area [6]. If information technology students are to learn recursion, it makes the most sense that they do so in a context that is central to their field.

4. ACKNOWLEDGMENTS

Our thanks to Ljubomir Perković for his support in developing this workshop and for his comments on an earlier draft. Thanks also to André Berthiaume for his comments on an earlier draft.

5. REFERENCES

[1] Carbone, A., Hurst, J., Mitchell, I., and Gunstone, D. 2009. An Exploration of Internal Factors Influencing Student Learning of Programming. In *Proceedings of the 11th Australasian Computing Education Conference*, (Wellington, New Zealand, January 2009).

[2] Chaffin, A., Doran, K., Hicks, D., and Barnes, T. 2009. Experimental Evaluation of Teaching Recursion in a Video Game. In Proceedings of the *2009 ACM SIGGRAPH Symposium on Video Games* (New Orleans, Louisiana, August 2009).

[3] Dale, N.B. 2006. Most Difficult Topics in CS1: Results on an Online Survey of Educators. *ACM SIGCSE Bulletin*, 38:2, pp. 49 – 53.

[4] Elenbogen, B.S. and O'Kennon, M.R. 1988. Teaching Recursion Using Fractals in Prolog. In *Proceedings of the 19th SIGCSE Technical Symposium on Computer Science Education* (Atlanta, Georgia, USA, February 1988).

[5] Gunion, K., Mildford, T., and Stege, U. 2009. Curing Recursion Aversion. In *Proceedings of 14th Annual Conference on Innovation and Technology in Computer Science Education* (Paris, France, July 2009).

[6] Information Technology 2008. Curriculum Guidelines for Undergraduate Degree Programs in Information Technology. Association for Computing Machinery and IEEE Computer Society. http://www.acm.org//education/curricula/IT2008%20Curriculum.pdf, accessed May 2013.

[7] Perković, L. 2012. *Introduction to Computing using Python: An Application Development Focus*. John Wiley & Sons.

[8] Stephenson, B. 2009. Using Graphical Examples to Motivate the Study of Recursion. *Journal of Computing Sciences in Colleges*, 25:1, pp. 42-50.

Using Video Game Development to Engage Undergraduate Students of Assembly Language Programming

Jalal Kawash and Robert Collier
University of Calgary
2500 University Dr. NW
Calgary, Alberta, Canada
+1 (403) 220 6619, +1 (403) 210 8483
jkawash@ucalgary.ca, rdcollie@ucalgary.ca

ABSTRACT

It is widely accepted that the instruction of programming in assembly language is often a challenging and frustrating experience, both to educators and undergraduate students. Although little can be done to simplify the curriculum, it is absolutely crucial that frustration not compel students to abandon the subject. Our use of game development in a second-year course affords a unique opportunity to present this complex subject, without omission, in such a way as to create an experience that most students find entertaining. The results of a class survey indicated that 65% of participants agree or strongly agree that the experience was enjoyable (with only 11% in disagreement). We conclude that this ensures a sufficiently engaging experience that offsets the tedium inherent to the subject. The consensus of most students was that the complexity of video game design does not detract from their enjoyment of the course and contrarily has a positive impact on their learning overall. This position is supported by additional survey results.

Categories and Subject Descriptors

K.3.2 [**Computers and Education**]: Computer and Information Science Education – *Computer Science Education, Curriculum.*

Keywords

Computer Science Education, Game Development, Assembly Language Programming, Hardware/Software Interface

1. INTRODUCTION

With most current computer science students having been introduced to programming through one of the high-level languages, such as Java, assembly language programming is a subject that students typically find tiresome (in the best case) and frustrating (in the worst case). Computer programming in assembly is certainly a tedious process and is often described as "dry" [1], "difficult to learn", and "confusing" [2]. This impression is exaggerated if the course is concerned with

advanced assembly language programming, specifically with programming for the hardware/software interface. Nevertheless, advanced assembly language programming is a necessary evil in many computer science, information technology, and engineering programs. Consequently, post-secondary educators are strongly motivated to make the process both engaging and rewarding for the students.

In this paper, we describe our experience with an advanced course in assembly language programming primarily concerned with programming for the hardware/software interface. In order to engage students and ignite their interest, we have been using interactive video game programming for their project assignments. The creation of a fully functional game is a challenging task in itself, but requesting that students write such a game entirely in assembly language would seem, on the surface, to make an already complex problem even more so. In this paper, we demonstrate otherwise. We show that this approach has many advantages, not the least of which is the introduction of the "fun factor" to a subject that is traditionally considered rather boring. On the technical side, a further advantage is that game design in assembly forces students to work directly with advanced topics such as interrupt stealing. This is a topic that few students will have encountered elsewhere. It is also worth noting that the approach we follow exposes students (as early as second year) to the creation of fully fledged device drivers in assembly.

It was noted by Puhanet *et al.* [6] that since the vast majority of students will have received instruction in a high-level language before taking a course in assembly language programming, many students perceive instruction in assembly language as "a step backward". Consequently, students of assembly language courses are often unmotivated. This undoubtedly contributes to Yehezkel *et al.*'s observation [7] that the cognitive model of the internal operations of a computer (typically imparted by instruction in assembly language) is "often incomplete or erroneous". This has been identified as a critical issue in both computer science and engineering programs. Yehezkel *et al.* also noted that to address the issues with the cognitive model, simulation and visualization are widely applied to enhance student understanding [7]. Unfortunately, simulator development is usually performed ad hoc (leading to a range of disparate simulators), and furthermore, we stress that this approach does nothing to address the formerly noted absence of motivation. Furthermore, although the attempts made by Wolfer and Rababaah [8] to employ a robotics laboratory to provide a hands-on environment for assembly language students might certainly contribute to student engagement and motivation, the cost of such a laboratory cannot be easily dismissed. It should also be noted that the investigation conducted by Fagin and Merkle [9] indicated that test scores in class sections that use robotics were actually lower than sections that did not. Thus, the effective support and instruction of students in assembly language programming remains an open topic, and we believe that directly addressing the problem of student motivation would be a significant step on the path towards the most effective approach.

Although this paper is, to the best of our knowledge, the first to explore the instruction of students in assembly language through the use of game design, it has been noted that many software engineering (and by extension computer science) projects are not sufficiently enjoyable to engage students [3]. This fact can be somewhat remedied through the use of game-centric modules [3]. It has also been noted that game design provides "an ideal framework" for students to develop knowledge in topics of computer graphics, artificial intelligence, networking, and high-level programming language skills [4]. Hence, it was not unreasonable for us to investigate the use of game programming for teaching assembly language at the undergraduate level. Previous results have also indicated that the creation of games can advance the development of computational thinking [5], representing an additional advantage to the approach we present with this paper.

The rest of this document is organized into five sections. Section 2 describes the course upon which this study was conducted, with Section 3 discussing some necessary technical details. Several complete student projects are discussed in Section 4, with the results of a student survey explored in Section 5 and a concluding summary presented in Section 6.

2. THE COURSE

The subject of this paper is Computing Machinery II (CPSC 359) at the University of Calgary. As suggested by the course title this is the second of a pair of early undergraduate courses, both of which are considered mandatory for a Bachelor's degree in Computer Science. In the prerequisite course, students are exposed to assembly language programming and general computer architecture and organization. In CPSC 359 the emphasis is on the hardware/software interface. Students are exposed herein to digital-logic design, microarchitecture design, interrupts and interrupt handling, and hardware I/O. Of these topics, this paper is concerned primarily with interrupts and hardware I/O. At the time this investigation was conducted, the underlying hardware was the Intel x86 architecture [13].

For this part of the course, students are required to develop an interactive video game written entirely in assembly language, by way of a pair of assignments. The fact that they must use a low-level video library, namely the VESA BIOS Extension (VBE) [15] necessitates that the students work with port- and memory-mapped I/O. Since the game must be interactive, the students must also develop specialized PS/2 keyboard and/or mouse drivers, requiring that they program and register their own interrupt handlers. It should also be noted that before students encounter the assignments that lead up to the game development they are given a more "classical" assignment, involving command-line interaction.

The enrollment in the course for the winter semester of 2013 was 97 students, divided into three lab tutorials. Although there is a dedicated lab for this course, most students opted to use DOSBox [16] for the development of their games.

3. TECHNICAL BACKGROUND

In this section we provide some necessary technical background that is relevant to some of the explicit learning objectives of this course:

1) understanding hardware and software interrupt mechanisms,

2) programming and stealing interrupt handlers, and

3) programming with port- and memory-mapped I/O.

The Intel x86 architecture offers three basic modes of operations, and two of these, *real-address* mode and *protected* mode, are relevant to this paper. In the real-address mode a hardware device can be accessed without any protection. However, in the protected mode the access of hardware must be done through the operating system via privileged system calls. The creation of device drivers is a topic that must be addressed by the students in the creation of the game. Hence, it must be done in the real-address mode in order to work with hardware directly.

It must be emphasized that the following extensive and technical treatment demonstrates the complexity of the learning objectives specified by this course.

3.1 Hardware I/O

VBE provides nine software interrupts (INT 10h) that replace or extend the BIOS interrupt library for video handling, and VBE supports a number of different graphics resolutions. In this course, we ask students to work with XGA (i.e., 1024×768 with 256 colors).

The frame-buffer architecture maps a region in video memory to the display, with each byte in memory corresponding to a pixel on the display (assuming XGA). Thus, setting a pixel value simply requires changing the corresponding byte in memory.

In addition to memory-mapped I/O, students are required to work with port-mapped I/O, a task that uses separate memory (i.e., port memory) in order to communicate with various hardware devices. Sending information to a device entails writing a value to a corresponding port for the device. In the Intel x86 architecture, this is accomplished by the OUT instruction. The complementary task of reading from a device is supported through the IN instruction. Unlike memory-mapped I/O, port-mapped I/O is intended for low-volume data movement of a maximum of 4 bytes by each instruction.

The students of CPSC 359 are asked to work with PS/2 keyboards and mice due to the relatively simple mechanism of packet communication through the appropriate ports. A PS/2 keyboard sends up to 2 bytes for each of the make and break events generated by pressing and releasing a key. These bytes are read from the required port and stored in memory for the interrupt handlers. Similarly, a standard PS/2 mouse sends movement and/or button information to the host using a 3-byte packet as shown in Figure 1.

The movement values in the second and third bytes are integers in two's complement. The values that represent the mouse's offset (relative to its previous position) are in units that are determined by the current resolution.

Bit / Byte	7	6	5	4	3	2	1	0
1	Y Overflow	X Overflow	Y Sign Bit	X Sign Bit	Always 1	Middle Button	Right Button	Left Button
2	X Movement							
3	Y Movement							

Figure 1. The structure of a PS/2 mouse packet

3.2 Programming Interrupts

A *hardware interrupt* is an asynchronous signal from hardware indicating the need for immediate attention and is generated by an electrical signal from a hardware device. The students are introduced to the Programmable Interface Card (PIC) architecture and the interrupt vector architecture. Thus, they are exposed to CPU traps that lead to the execution of *Interrupt Service Routines* (ISRs). An appropriate ISR is selected in order to execute and handle or service the interrupt. Students are expected to know how to write an ISR in assembly and how to register it in the vector table. The latter task is known as *interrupt stealing*.

A typical hardware ISR consists of: (1) saving any CPU registers that the ISR uses, (2) performing the steps needed to service the interrupt (example, read data from a port, save it, set/clear flags, etc.), (3) resetting the PIC(s), and finally, (4) restoring any registers saved in step (1). Figure 2 shows an example ISR written in the Intel x86 assembly for hardware interrupt 9 (i.e., the PS/2 keyboard interrupt); the ISR depicted disables the keyboard, except for keys <q>, <escape>, and <right-arrow>.

Once the ISR is written, it must be "installed". This requires its address (segment and offset) to be put into the desired slot in the interrupt vector table. There may be another ISR already installed for the interrupt. Hence, the programmer would normally save the address of the old ISR so that it can be restored at the end of the program. In the real-address mode, this is accomplished by the software interrupt INT 21h. In protected mode this has to be done through the DOS Protected Mode Interface (DPMI) [14].

DPMI is an API that allows DOS programs to execute in protected mode but access advanced hardware features. Equivalently, DPMI allows programs to switch between the real-address and protected modes, depending on whether or not the hardware needs to be accessed directly. The API can be accessed using the assembler with the software interrupt INT 31h. Moreover, since programs running in protected mode may be "paged out", DPMI has services to "lock down" memory. It is essential that the ISR code and data are locked and locking is also provided through the INT 31h services.

The general procedure for installing an ISR under DPMI entails: (1) saving the address (selector/offset) of the old ISR, (2) locking the region of code for the ISR, (3) locking the region(s) of data used by the ISR, (4) placing the address (selector/offset) of the new handler into the interrupt vector table, and (5) reinstalling the old handler before terminating the program. Figure 2 shows an excerpt from a program that installs an ISR for a PS/2 keyboard.

Having thoroughly explored the complex and challenging subject matter that is the objective of this course, it is not unreasonable to suspect that the reader has already recognized that the development of these programs can be exceedingly tedious. This is exceptionally difficult for students at the undergraduate level. Nevertheless, the results described in the following sections clearly indicate that the development of video games is sufficiently entertaining to offset the tiresome nature of the work and make the entire process more engaging and rewarding.

```
[SECTION .text]
newInt9:
        enter 0,0
        push eax ; save register eax;
        ; read from port 60h (keyboard) one
        ; byte into al
        in al, 60h
        ; determine what key is pressed
        cmp al, 10h ; raw code for q
        je storeQuit
        cmp al, 1h ; raw code for escape
        je storeQuit
        cmp al, 4Dh ; raw code for R arrow
        je storeRight
        jmp clearPIC
storeRight:
        mov byte [action], RIGHT
        jmp clearPIC
storeQuit:
        mov byte [action], QUIT
clearPIC:
        mov al, 20h
        out 20h, al ; clear the PIC
        pop eax ; restore eax
        leave
        iret ; end for ISR

[SECTION .bss]
        action resb 1
        endData resb 1
```

Figure 2. Example x86 program defining an ISR

```
[SECTION .text]
mystart:
        push dword newInt9
        push dword endNewInt9
        call lock_mem ; lock code in newInt9
        push dword action
        push dword endData
        ; lock variable action used by newInt9
        call lock_mem
        push dword newInt9
        ; newInt9 is address of new handler
        call install_handler
        call setupXGA
        mov byte [action], 0
nextKey:
        cmp byte [action], RIGHT
        je moveRight
        cmp byte [action], QUIT
        je done
        ; … the rest of case statement goes here
        jmp nextKey
moveRight:
        mov byte [action], 0 ; reset action
        call transRight
        jmp nextKey
        ; … the rest of cases goes here
done:
        call cleanXGA
        call remove_handler
        ret
```

Figure 3. Excerpt from a program for stealing INT 9

4. VIDEO GAME PROJECTS

To meet the objectives of CPSC 359, students were asked to develop a somewhat simplified incarnation of a widely-known video game, written completely in the Intel x86 assembly language. Among the submissions were versions of Space Invaders [11], Tetris [12], and Pac-man [10]. Although a thorough examination of each of these games would exceed the scope of this paper, the reader must certainly recognize the complexity of each of these projects. Figure 4 shows actual screen shots taken from some exemplary games developed by students.

Each of the games depicted in Figure 4 requires overriding the keyboard ISR in order to control the objects on the screen, and some examples might also include mouse functionality, which requires stealing the mouse ISR as well. Furthermore, none of the requested games require extensive video processing, apart from basic drawing, translation, and rotation of objects. This was a conscious decision to ensure that students would not need to expend any considerable effort on the visual elements, since CPSC 359 does not include computer graphics among the learning objectives. These topics are not typically covered by the curriculum until the following year.

5. ASSESSMENT AND DISCUSSION

After completing and submitting their projects, each of the students in class was asked to participate in a survey (reproduced in the appendix), and 58 of these surveys were ultimately received. This section describes the results in explicit detail.

5.1 Quantitative Summary

65% of the respondents agree or strongly agree that they enjoyed working on a video game (Figure 5). Only 11% disagree, with the remaining students noncommittal. Only 20% of students reported that another project (i.e., something other than a video game) would have been more enjoyable (Figure 6). 52% of the students would disagree with this, favoring the video game deliverable, with 28% of the students remaining neutral.

The class is split almost evenly (Figure 7) over whether they could have achieved a better mark if something other than a game was required (32% disagree, 35% neutral, 33% agree).

Finally, when students were surveyed about their learning outcomes (Figure 8), 46% think they learned better by developing an interactive game, while only 23% disagree. Furthermore, 74% of the surveyed students report that they believe they learned a significant amount by developing a video game, and only 7% disagree (Figure 9).

5.2 Qualitative Discussion

The majority of the written comments from students who rated their enjoyment of the development of a video game as neutral still conveyed the feeling that the experience was fun overall. That being said, the fact that these students felt that the development project was "*tedious*", "*a lot of work*", or has "*a lot of details to master*" contributed to the neutral rating they reported. For example, one student (#33) stated that the experience was "*more fun than other boring programs, but a lot of work and time is needed to understand how to implement it.*" Another student (#16) said "*I found it interesting and enjoyable, but because it was a bit frustrating I could say it was a neutral experience (very time consuming)*", and still another student (#49) explained their neutral rating by stating that he or she would have "*liked it more if it wasn't assembly*".

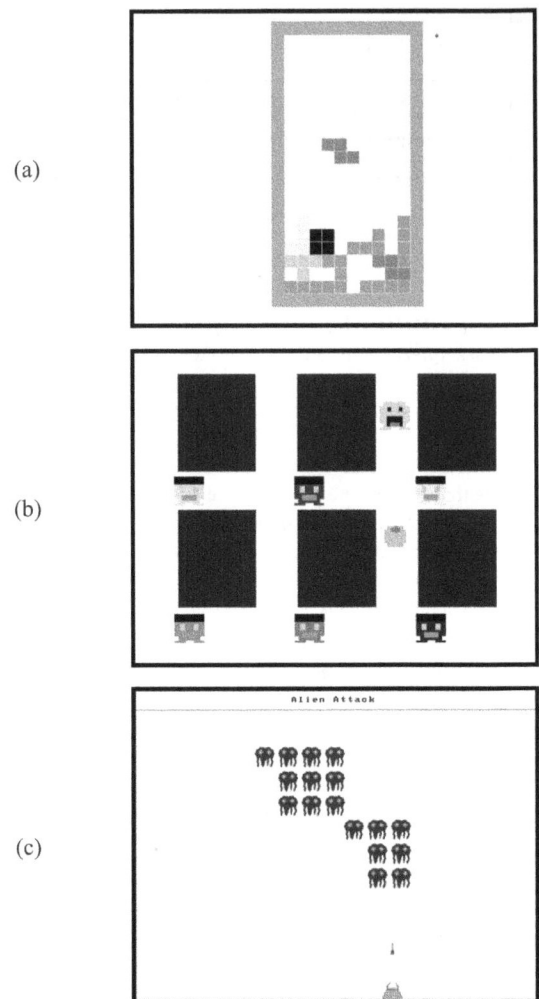

(a)

(b)

(c)

Figure 4. Example student project screenshots for (a) Tetris, (b) Pac-Man, and (c) Space Invaders

Similar statements were also provided by some of the students that *disagreed* with the statement in survey item 3. However, it should be noted that the majority of these students expressed issues either with assembly programming in general or with a perceived lack of time required to complete the project. One such student (#6) stated that "*programming in assembly is hard and programming games is hard too. The errors that came up had no explanation*", while another student (#29) stated that "*working on a game like Pac-Man in assembly is very difficult as the level of the language is low and some things require great detail and tedious work.*" The overwhelming majority of the students who disagreed on this item (i.e., that they enjoyed working on the interactive game) also indicated that they have completed less than 75% of the project. The few who disagreed with item 4 (i.e., a preference for a non-game deliverable) also indicated a completion level of less than 75% of the project.

From these results, it is reasonable to conclude that the entertainment factor was very (but not entirely) effective in combatting the tedious nature of the subject matter without sacrificing any of the difficult-to-achieve learning objectives. In short, an overwhelming majority of students thought that the idea of developing an interactive video game in assembly was an enjoyable experience that resulted in a net improvement to their learning outcomes.

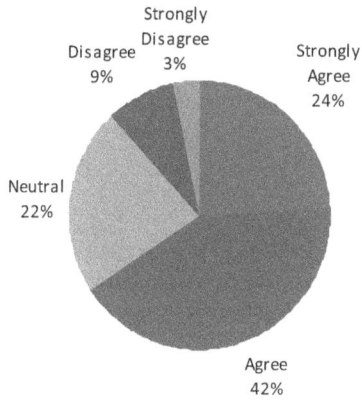

Figure 5. I enjoyed working on the interactive game

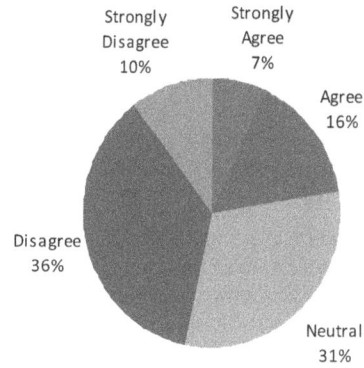

Figure 8. I think I could have learned more from the assignments if something other than an interactive game was required

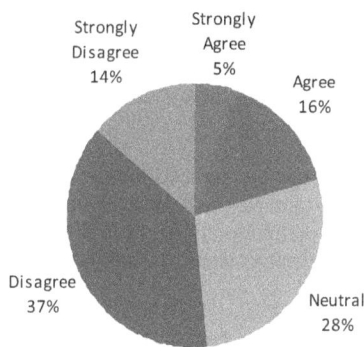

Figure 6. I could have enjoyed the assignments more if something other than an interactive game was required

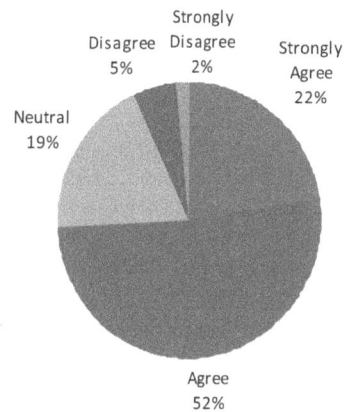

Figure 9. Overall, I think I have learned a lot developing this game

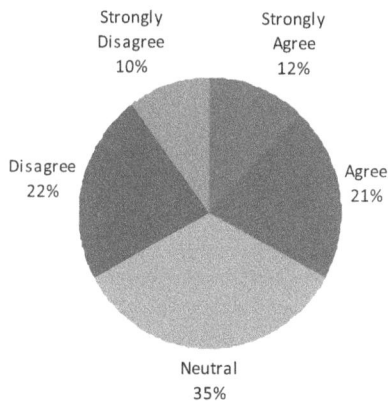

Figure 7. I think I could have done better the assignments more if something other than an interactive game was required

6. SUMMARY

We have described our experience with requiring interactive game development to teaching the hardware/software interface in assembly language. At first, we feared this approach might do more to aggravate the complexity of the subject than to motivate and engage students. However, the results of our student surveys and several exemplary projects demonstrated evidence to the contrary. The development of interactive video games allowed most students to enjoy the subject to a greater extent and the vast majority agreed that the approach improved their learning experience and outcomes.

7. ACKNOWLEDGMENTS

We thank the CPSC 359 students at the University of Calgary that participated in the survey conducted in the Winter 2013 semester. Without their effort and feedback, this work would not have been possible.

8. REFERENCES

[1] C. Zilles (2005). SPIMbot: An Engaging, Problem-Based Approach to Teaching Assembly Language Programming. In Proceedings of the 2005 Workshop on Computer Architecture Education.

[2] D. Crookes (1983). Teaching Assembly-Language Programming: A High-Level Approach. Software Microsystems, vol. 2, no. 2, pp. 40-43.

[3] K. Claypool and M. Claypool (2005). Teaching Software Engineering Through Game Design. In Proceedings of the 10th Annual SIGCSE Conference on Innovation and Technology in Computer Science Education

[4] S. Schaefer and J. Warren (2003). Teaching Computer Game Design and Construction. Computer-Aided Design, vol. 36, pp. 1501-1510.

[5] A. Basawapatna, K. H. Koh, and A. Repenning (2010). Using Scalable Game Design to Teach Computer Science From Middle School to Graduate School. In Proceedings of the 15th Annual Conference on Innovation and Technology in Computer Science Education.

[6] J. Puhan, A. Burmen, T. Tuma, I. Fajfar. (2010). Teaching Assembly and C Language Concurrently. Interational Journal of Electrical Engineering Education, vol. 47, no. 2, pp. 120-131

[7] C. Yehezkel, W. Yurcik, M. Pearson, and D. Armstrong. (2001). Three Simulator Tools for Teaching Computer Architecture: EasyCPU, Little Man Computer, and RTLSim. Journal on Educational Resources in Computing, vol. 1, no. 4, pp. 60-80.

[8] J. Wolfer and H. Rababaah. (2005) Creating a Hands-On Robot Environment for Teaching Assembly Language Programming.

[9] B. Fagin and L. Merkle. (2003). Measuring the Effectiveness of Robots in Teaching Computer Science," In SIGCSE Technical Symposium on Computer Science Education.

[10] Pac-Man History. Retrieved 2013/05/20, from Pac-Man Official English Site: http://pacman.com/en/pac-man-history

[11] Space Invaders. Retrieved 2013/05/20, from Classics Reunited: http://www.classicgaming.cc/classics/spaceinvaders

[12] The History of Tetris. Retrieved 2013/05/20, from Tetris.com: http://www.tetris.com/history/index.aspx

[13] K. Irving. Assembly Language for x86 Processors. 6th Edition. Prentice-Hall (Pearson Education), February 2010.

[14] DOS Protected Mode Interface (DPMI) Specification: Version 0.9 Printed 1990/07/26. Retrieved 2013/05/20 from: http://homer.rice.edu/~sandmann/cwsdpmi/dpmispec.txt

[15] VESA. Retrieved 2013/05/20 from: www.vesa.org

[16] DOSBox, an x86 emulator with DOS. Retrieved 2013/05/20 from www.dosbox.com

9. APPENDIX

This appendix contains the survey questions provided to the students.

CPSC 359 - Winter 2013
Video Game Development in Assembly
Anonymous Survey

This survey aims at assessing certain aspects of your experience with developing the video game in assignments 2 and 3. The results will be used in a pedagogic study.

1. I have worked on the video game (alone, in a team)

2. What rough percentage of the functionality of the game have you completed (If you worked on the assignment as a team, check what the entire team completed)? ($< 25\%$, 25% to 50%, 50% to 75%, 100%)

3. I enjoyed working on the interactive game (strongly agree, agree, neutral, disagree, strongly disagree)

Explain ____

4. I could have enjoyed the assignments more if something other than an interactive game was required (such as something that is more similar to Assignment 1) (strongly agree, agree, neutral, disagree, strongly disagree)

Explain ____

5. I think I could have done better on the assignments if something other than an interactive game was required (such as something that is more similar to Assignment 1)

(strongly agree, agree, neutral, disagree, strongly disagree)

Explain ____

6. I think I could have learned more from the assignments if something other than an interactive game was required (such as something that is more similar to Assignment 1) (strongly agree, agree, neutral, disagree, strongly disagree)

Explain ____

7. Overall, I think I have learned a lot developing this game. (strongly agree, agree, neutral, disagree, strongly disagree)

Explain ____

COR: A New Course Framework Based on Elements of Game Design

Thomas Gibbons
The College of St. Scholastica
1200 Kenwood Avenue
Duluth, MN 55811
tgibbons@css.edu

ABSTRACT

Taking cues from the root causes of anxiety and poor student performance, a new course framework is developed using three key elements of game play. These game play elements are abstracted into an integrated teaching framework that gives students a choice in actions, options for cooperation and competition, and allows for revisions of work.

Two case studies are examined that demonstrate how this framework can be implemented. One shows how this framework can be incorporated in the final project of a systems analysis and design course. The other shows how the framework can be used in a game design course to prepare students for different career paths.

Categories and Subject Descriptors

K.3.2 [**Computer and Information Science Education**]: Computer & Information Science Education – Information Systems Education, Curriculum.

General Terms

Design, Experimentation.

Keywords

Student-centered, gamification, flipped classroom.

1. INTRODUCTION

Concepts from game design have been applied to teaching in many different areas and their use in education has been researched by many. See [1] and [2] for summaries of current research. Much of this research has tended to focus on a few basic techniques from games including the use of points [1], character upgrades [3], and in-game achievements [4]. Researchers have also looked at how certain key elements from games can be used in the classroom including autonomy or self-determination [5] as well as a sense a free will when performing a task and competence through challenges and competitions [6].

The COR framework, defined below, takes three key aspects of game play and abstracts them into a teaching framework. These are 1) Choice in actions, 2) Options for cooperation and competition, and 3) Revisions of work.

These three components are developed from game design theory as primary ways to reduce student anxiety and increase student motivation and performance.

Two case studies are examined using this model. The case studies show how the framework can be applied in different situations. Both quantitative and qualitative results are used to show the effect of this framework.

2. ROOT CAUSES OF ANXIETY

Anxiety has long been known to have a negative effect on student learning [7]. Anxiety tends to decrease the motivation of students. The student that is anxious spends time worrying about an assignment, project, or exam and has less time to focus on class work. Psychologists use Attentional Control Theory to describe how anxiety impacts learning by reducing goal-directed attentional systems [8].

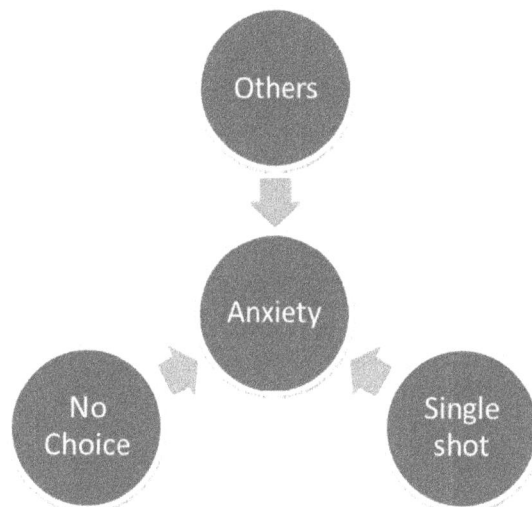

Figure 1: Root Causes of Anxiety

Three root causes of anxiety in the classroom are identified and a framework is defined to manage these root causes of anxiety. The root causes are: 1) Students having no choice in the activities and assessments they must perform. 2) When student's grades are dependent on other students' performance. 3) Students only getting a single chance to succeed on an assignment or exam.

These causes of anxiety are analyzed in detail below and depicted in Figure 1 in a layout which will be mirrored by the framework defined in section 4 below.

2.1 No Choice in Activities or Assessment

The first producer of anxiety is the prescriptive nature of courses. Most classrooms have requirements for learning activities and the student assessments that students must perform.

First, students have little choice of what learning resources they can use. The teacher dictates the use of lectures or hands-on labs, and the student must learn by whatever method the teacher chooses. Best practices suggest teachers employ a variety of learning activities targeted to the different learning styles of the students. This simply guarantees that much of the student's time is spent on learning activities which do not fit their learning style, while waiting for that one activity that will help them learn.

Second, students have little choice in their assessment. They do not get to choose the assignments or exams which will determine their grade. Again, best practices suggest teachers use a variety of assessment measures, but this results in students completing assessments that do not fit their learning style.

Together, this lack of choice in activities and assessments increases the anxiety of students.

2.2 Dependency on Others

The second producer of anxiety is when a student's grade is dependent on other students' performance. This may be seen in two ways.

First, students may compete directly with one another. While some top students are motivated by direct competition, this causes anxiety in many other students. Students feel anxious when their grade on an exam is determined not by their performance alone, but by the one top student who "sets the curve."

Second, many classes require students to cooperate on group projects where the project's grade is based largely on the group's combined work. Many students feel anxious when their grade will depend on the actions of the "slacker" group member.

2.3 Single Shot at Success

Many students suffer impaired performance on difficult tasks including suffering from test anxiety [9]. One of the primary causes of this is the stress of having only a single change to take an exam. While the stress induced by getting just one chance to successfully complete an assignment or exam may induce high performance in top students, it also causes anxiety in many other students and hinders the learning process.

This test anxiety is carried over to all assessment activities where the students have a single attempt to succeed. It is common practice in most assessments that students get only one attempt.

3. GAMIFICATION WITHOUT A GAME

Gamification has been defined as "the use of game design elements in non-game contexts" [10]. There has been extensive work done on gamification, but much of this has focused on the use of the simple game elements of points, badges, and a leader board (Werbach, 2012).

But according to Elizabeth Lawley, "The recent trend toward 'gamifying' applications, however, often reduces the complexity of a well-designed and balanced game to its simplest components, such as badges, levels, points, and leaderboards. The resulting implementations don't just fail to engage players; they can actually damage existing interest or engagement with the service or product" [11].

There have been efforts to incorporate the entire game complexity into the classroom [12]. These efforts have often used the fantasy worlds of role playing games as a backdrop. This tends to decrease the interest of female students, for while the number of females playing video games has increased in recent years, there is still far higher interest among males in these types of games and storylines [13].

The key to why games are engaging and used to reduce our stress and anxiety is not simply ability to earn points, get on the high score board, or playact with dwarves or alien characters. Games are engaging because of three key points:

1. Choice of Actions – we chose what games to play and what our characters do in the games.

2. Options for Competition and Cooperation – we choose who we compete against or cooperate with.

3. Multiple Lives – if we fail, we get to try again with a minimal penalty.

The next three subsections will analyze these three components of game play and how they can be used in a framework for reducing anxiety in the classroom.

3.1 Choice of Actions

It is often hard to define simple concepts like "What is a game?" and "What does it mean to play?" Many of the definitions related to playing games center on the concept of choice. Examples include "Play is free movement within a more rigid structure" and "Play is whatever is done spontaneously and for its own sake" [14].

Research in both economic game theory [15] and video game design [16] reinforce the idea that player choice or autonomy is an important factor in motivating players and making games fun. Jesse Schell makes meaningful choice a central feature in his theory of games and says "I find that about eight out of ten times someone comes to me asking for help on a game prototype that 'just isn't fun,' the game is missing this kind of meaningful choice."

Yet most classes are set up so that all students perform the same set of learning activities in the same order. It is as if all the students are traveling down the same learning path without any choice.

3.2 Options for Competition and Cooperation

Video games typically allow a number of options for how players can compete or cooperate with other players. Game designers have learned that different players are motivated by different types of competition and cooperation. [14] Some people like to compete with friends, while this causes anxiety in other people. Some people like to compete against themselves, while others do not find this motivating.

On many video games today, you will see these different options. Games will include a solo option where a single player tries to complete a set of challenges alone, competing only against the computer or the challenge itself. Games will also include an option to play with others. This might include cooperative play or competitive play with friends or anonymous players on the internet.

Game designers have learned that what motivates one player can make another player anxious and cause them to leave a game.

3.3 Success through Failure

One of the defining characteristics of a video game is the low cost of failure. Early coin operated video games had a relatively high cost of failure; starting the whole game over again and losing a quarter. Today's games save the game state in multiple places during the game. Failure means you only have to try the last level over again or repeat the last section.

The cost of failure is limited to the time spent since the last save state. This is often just a few minutes. Players can attempt a difficult section of the game again and again, until they succeed. The opportunity to reattempt a section of a game after failure is a key attribute of video games. It allows games to challenge players, because players do not have to succeed on the first attempt.

4. The COR Framework

Elements from game design can be abstracted and used in the classroom. The COR framework defines three related elements that are based on the three causes of anxiety outlined in section 2 and combined with the three elements of game design from section 3.

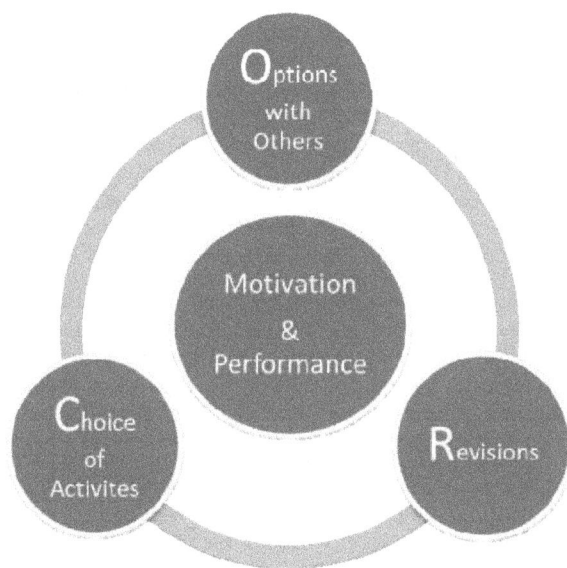

Figure 2: Structure of the COR Framework

4.1 Choice of Activities

The standard classroom gives very little choice to the student, aside from where to sit. Traditional assignments tend to be very prescriptive by design.

Student-centered or learner-centered methods often do introduce some choice to the student. These methods may give students some control over not only how they learn, but what topics they study. In reality, this control is often limited to a few standard techniques including:

- Contract grading which allows student to choose how points are weighted on assignments [17].

- Time Banks which allow students to customize assignment deadlines. [17].

- Allowing the class as a group to decide what topics to concentrate more time on in a course.

While providing some choice, these methods do not allow students to individualize the topics they wish to study or the activities they want to do. Shared lectures require all students to cover the same topics in the same order, since they all attend the same lecture. Teachers have used open ended learning activities that allow some choice in the activities, but not a choice on the topic.

If a teacher is giving a lecture, it is impossible to give two different lectures at the same time; every student is going to hear the same series of lectures in a traditional classroom. But today's technology allows teachers to record multiple lectures and have students choose what lecture to listen to.

By introducing multiple lecture options into a flipped classroom, students can be given a choice in the learning path they want to travel. If students have different career plans, they can choose learning paths that will better lead them to their future career. If students have different skill sets, they can choose learning paths customized to what they already know.

Recent work by Atanas Radenski has shown that using a learning management system to give students "assisted freedom of choice" provides the highest level of motivation [18].

The first component of the COR framework is giving students a choice in activities.

4.2 Options for Competition and Cooperation

Using competition as part of the educational process has been shown to have mixed results [19]. Research has shown that competition is a good motivator for more-abled students, but causes anxiety and discourages less-abled students [20].

This suggests that competition is a useful tool for motivating students, but that students should be given options on how or whether than want to compete. Some students are motivated by direct competition with peers, while others prefer to compete anonymously or only against themselves.

Educational research also suggest that student cooperation, especially when used with active learning activities, can increase student achievement and student satisfaction [21]. But the use of cooperative learning, particularly group projects, presents a number of challenges. Top among these is the challenge of individual assessment of group work [22]. Students should then be given the option to participate in active learning activities and methods should be used to help assess individual students in group work.

Options for competition and cooperation form the second component of the COR framework.

4.3 Revisions and Retrying Work

The third component in the COR framework is allowing students to attempt activities multiple times. By lessening the cost of failure, video games encourage players to fail in many small ways while succeeding in the game.

You may think that allowing multiple attempts at a difficult challenge is limited to video games and not the classroom. Most computer teachers do not allow students multiple attempts at assignments. But allowing multiple attempts is a standard practice in other disciplines. Multiple drafts of papers are a key component of many writing assignments in the English Department [23] and the use of multiple drafts is also seen in writing assignments in the science classroom [24].

Yet, from a game design perspective, multiple drafting is not the same as multiple lives in a video game. The main reason is multiple-drafting is generally required of students, and this is the reason many students dislike multiple-drafts. Rather than allowing students to fail and reattempt an assignment, multiple drafting requires students to fail multiple times.

Game design requires that students can succeed on the first attempt, but allows for failure and reattempts. Current Learning Management Systems (LMS) facilitate multiple attempts and make the challenges of tracking multiple attempts easier. Blackboard version 9.1 allows teachers to enable multiple attempts for assignments and control how many attempts are available to students. It then tracks each attempt a student makes on an assignment.

Allowing students to attempt assignments multiple times provides a number of benefits:

- Teachers can control the stress level in the classroom. Allowing multiple attempts reduces the stress and can make doing assignments more enjoyable.

- Teachers can challenge students more. Most video games design certain challenge levels with the expectation that players will have to attempt them multiple times. Similarly, challenging assignments can be presented to students with the expectation that students will fail on the first attempt.

- Having students repeat assignments makes them more of a teaching tool rather than just an assessment tool, since students pay more attention to what they did wrong on the first attempt in order to correct this on later attempts.

Allowing multiple attempts at assignments requires more work correcting the additional attempts. Traditional ways to address this has been using self or peer grading [25] or utilizing teaching assistants.

Today's Learning Management System (LMS) makes it easier than ever to score and track a student's multiple attempts on an assignment or quiz. A typical LMS will allow the instructor to set the number of times a student can attempt an assignment or quiz. Typical options that are available are the traditional single attempt, unlimited attempts, and a fixed number of attempts. Allowing students to redo activities frees to student to try more activities and experiment with different learning paths.

5. CASE STUDIES
The COR framework has been evaluated for the last two years in a number of courses. Two case studies are presented below to assess how framework can reduce anxiety and motivate students.

5.1 Choice in a Final Project
Over the last two years, the COR framework has been implemented in the author's Junior-level systems analysis and design course. In this course computer majors make up only half of the class, since this course is required by other majors. A large component of the course is the final project, where students implement the techniques from the course.

In the traditional course, each student completed a 100 point final project individually. Over a three week period, students completed activities for the final project corresponding to phases in the system development lifecycle. Since each student was doing every activity of the project, the scope of the activities had to be limited and some activities were left out of the project. Feedback from students showed that they found the final project lackluster and many students wanted more challenges in one area or another.

The course was then modified to incorporate the COR framework in the final project. The scope of the final project was expanded significantly and students worked on the final project in teams of three, rather than individually.

Students' anxiety is often increased when their grade on a group project is based on work of their teammates. It is challenging to evaluate individual work in a group project [26] and even commonly used methods like peer evaluations have been shown to be problematic [22].

The author designed a new project format called the Sum of Parts project which supports the COR framework in a group project. Students were divided into teams of three and the project was explicitly divvied up into set activities.

The choice of activity portion of the COR framework was implemented by giving each student a choice of what activities they wanted to do. While the students worked as a team on the project, students were individually responsible for the activities they chose to complete. The project contained 327 points of activities and any one student could not earn more than 100 points on the project. This meant that there were activities in the project that teams would not choose to complete. Thus students were able to choose activities that supported their future careers and interests, while working with fellow team members.

Group projects force students to cooperate, but this often causes stress among students. By allowing students to submit work independently within a group project and allowing them to choose which activities they complete, they are given more options for cooperation. Students can cooperate closely or more loosely.

The final aspect of COR is allowing students to attempt activities multiple times. Allowing students to try activities multiple times eliminated the fear students had of trying challenging activities. They could try an activity and if they did not successfully complete it, they could either try it again or try a different activity without endangering their grade.

Both quantitative and qualitative feedback was collected from students in the case study. Quantitative feedback was collected using end-of-course surveys. The results of these surveys showed that:

- 83% of the students found the Sum of Parts project was less stressful than other group projects. 17% of the students found the Sum of Parts project just as stressful as other group projects, but no students found Sum of Parts projects more stressful than other group projects.
- Over 95% of the students preferred being graded on individual work rather than receiving a single group grade on the final project.

- Over 95% of the students felt that the Sum of Parts project encourages better group participation than other group projects.

Qualitative feedback supported the quantitative results, showing that even though the challenge level of activities was increased, students experienced less anxiety and were more satisfied with the project. Students were observed spending significantly more time on the project activities and their final reports showed that they were highly motivated by the project as they were able to focus on the activities they enjoyed.

5.2 Choosing a Path to a Career

The COR Framework was originally designed for a Junior and Senior level course in game design. One of the challenges in teaching an undergraduate course in game design is choosing what topics to cover. Some students want to learn advanced game programming while others are more interested in 3D model design, yet the undergraduate computer curriculum generally has room for only one game design course.

In past years, this course was taught as a survey course introducing students to different topics, while not being able to provide a depth of coverage of any one topic. The result was dissatisfied and unmotivated students as measured by the completion rate on assignments and results of student satisfaction surveys.

A partially flipped classroom model allowed the course to be restructured using the COR framework. Topics in the course were grouped into five areas. While students were required to complete activities in all five areas, they were able to choose two of the five areas to focus on and complete advanced work. Students were thus able to choose to do advanced activities in 3D modeling or programming, depending on their future career plans.

For the second component of the COR framework, students were also given options for competing and cooperating with each other. Students could choose if they wanted to be listed with other students on a public scoreboard that showed how many points each student had earned in each of the five areas. Students could also choose whether to compete in weekly challenges. Finally, students could choose between individual and group assignments.

In this early development of the COR framework, students could not resubmit assignments, but instead many more assignments were available that students could choose to do. If a student did not receive full points on one assignment, another assignment could be completed for additional points.

Student performance and motivation were measured in two ways. First, the percent of students completing the needed course assignments showed how motivated students were in the course. Of the 15 students in the updated version of the course, only 2, or 13%, failed to complete the needed assignments. This compared with 58% of the students in the original course who missed at least one required assignment.

Second, in an anonymous student satisfaction survey, 100% of the students in the updated course found the course intellectually motivating and 90% of the students were satisfied with the course objectives.

6. CONCLUSION

The COR framework defines three elements taken from game design that work together to reduce student anxiety and improve student motivation and performance.

A case study applying this framework to group projects shows more than 80% of the students found the project less stressful, even though the project was made more challenging than the traditional project. A second case study applies the COR framework to allow different career paths through a game design course. This case study showed a significant increase student performance measured through assignment completions.

7. REFERENCES

[1] Mekler, E. D., Brühlmann, F., Opwis, K. and Tuch, A. N. Disassembling gamification: the effects of points and meaning on user motivation and performance. In *Proceedings of the CHI '13 Extended Abstracts on Human Factors in Computing Systems* (Paris, France, 2013).

[2] Kapp, K. M. *The Gamification of Learning and Instruction: Game-based Methods and Strategies for Training and Education*. Pfeiffer & Company, 2012.

[3] Raymer, R. Gamification: Using Game Mechanics to Enhance eLearning. *eLearn*, 2011.

[4] Fitz-Walter, Z., Tjondronegoro, D. and Wyeth, P. Orientation Passport: using gamification to engage university students. In *Proceedings of the Proceedings of the 23rd Australian Computer-Human Interaction Conference* (Canberra, Australia, 2011).

[5] Deterding, S. *Situated motivational affordances of game elements: A conceptual model*. In *Proceedings of the ACM CHI Conference on Human Factors in Computing Systems* (Vancouver, BC, 2011).

[6] Aparicio, A. F., Vela, F. L. G., Sánchez, J. L. G. and Montes, J. L. I. Analysis and application of gamification. In *Proceedings of the 13th International Conference on Interacción Persona-Ordenador (INTERACCION '12)*. ACM, New York, NY. DOI=10.1145/2379636.2379653 http://doi.acm.org/10.1145/2379636.2379653

[7] Mandler, G. and Sarason, S. B. A study of anxiety and learning. *The Journal of Abnormal and Social Psychology*, 47, 1952, 166.

[8] Eysenck, M. W., Derakshan, N., Santos, R. and Calvo, M. G. Anxiety and cognitive performance: attentional control theory. *Emotion*, 7, 2 2007, 336.

[9] Eysenck, M. W. and Calvo, M. G. Anxiety and performance: The processing efficiency theory. *Cognition & Emotion*, 6, 6 1992, 409-434.

[10] Deterding, S., Dixon, D., Khaled, R. and Nacke, L. From game design elements to gamefulness: defining "gamification". In *Proceedings of the Proceedings of the 15th International Academic MindTrek Conference: Envisioning Future Media Environments* (Tampere, Finland, 2011). ACM

[11] Deterding, S. Gamification: designing for motivation. *interactions*, 19, 4 2012, 14-17.

[12] Sheldon, L. *The Multiplayer Classroom: Designing Coursework as a Game*. Course Technology Press, 2011.

[13] Jenson, J., Castell, S. d. and Fisher, S. Girls playing games: rethinking stereotypes. In *Proceedings of the 2007 conference on Future Play (Future Play '07)*. ACM, New York, NY, USA, 9-16. DOI=10.1145/1328202.1328205 http://doi.acm.org/10.1145/1328202.1328205

[14] Schell, J. *The Art of Game Design: A book of lenses*. Morgan Kaufmann Pub, 2008.

[15] Sarin, R. and Vahid, F. Predicting how people play games: a simple dynamic model of choice. *Games and Economic Behavior*, 34, 1 2001, 104-122.

[16] Malone, T. *W. 1980. What makes things fun to learn? heuristics for designing instructional computer games. In Proceedings of the 3rd ACM SIGSMALL symposium and the first SIGPC symposium on Small systems (SIGSMALL '80)*. ACM, New York, NY, USA, 162-169. DOI=10.1145/800088.802839 http://doi.acm.org/10.1145/800088.802839

[17] Aycock, J. and Uhl, J. Choice in the classroom. *SIGCSE Bull.*, 37, 4 2005, 84-88.

[18] Radenski, A. 2009. Freedom of choice as motivational factor for active learning. SIGCSE Bull. 41, 3 (July 2009), 21-25. DOI=10.1145/1595496.1562891 http://doi.acm.org/10.1145/1595496.1562891

[19] Wallace, S. A. and Margolis, J. Exploring the use of competetive programming: observations from the classroom. *J. Comput. Sci. Coll.*, 23, 2 2007, 33-39.

[20] Hercy, N. H. C., Winston, M. C. W., Calvin, C. Y. L. and Tak-Wai, C. Equal opportunity tactic: Redesigning and applying competition games in classrooms. *Computers & Education*, 53, 3 2009, 866-876.

[21] Johnson, D. W., Johnson, R. T. and Smith, K. A. Active learning: Cooperation in the college classroom. 1991).

[22] Kennedy, G. J. Peer-assessment in group projects: is it worth it? In *Proceedings of the Proceedings of the 7th Australasian conference on Computing education - Volume 42* (Newcastle, New South Wales, Australia, 2005).

[23] Dicker, S. J. and Sheppard, K. The effect of multiple drafts on structural accuracy in writing. *TESOL Quarterly*, 19, 1985, 168-170.

[24] Sanford, J. *Multiple Drafts of Experimental Laboratory Reports*. Kendall/Hunt, City, 1983.

[25] Nuwar Mawlawi, D. Assessing the relationship between different types of student feedback and the quality of revised writing. *Assessing Writing*, 16, 274-292.

[26] Anewalt, K., Polack-Wahl, J. A., Beidler, J. and Smarkusky, D. L. Group projects across the curriculum. *J. Comput. Small Coll.*, 19, 2, 2003, 232-237.

Embedding Virtual Meeting Technology in Classrooms: Two Case Studies

Ye Diana Wang
Applied Information Technology Department
George Mason University
10900 University Blvd. MS 4F5
Manassas, VA 20110, USA
1-703-993-9288
ywangm@gmu.edu

Seungwon "Shawn" Lee, PhD
Tourism and Event Management
George Mason University
10900 University Blvd. MS 4E5
Manassas, VA 20110, USA
1-703-993-9915
slz@gmu.edu

ABSTRACT

Innovative Internet applications coupled with improved videoconferencing capabilities have led to the proliferation of virtual meeting technology (VMT) in recent years. This paper aims to bring to light VMT as an effective classroom instructional tool, especially for IT education, and the possible ways to embed this technology in classroom settings in the form of two case studies of IT courses. The paper makes a unique contribution to the research by providing empirical evidence and indicative support for the successful application of VMT in different classroom settings and exemplifying the use of VMT as an effective instructional technology and an enabler of active learning.

Categories and Subject Descriptors

K3.2 [**Computers and Education**]: Computer and Information Science Education – *Information Systems Education*

Keywords

Virtual Meeting Technology, Videoconferencing, Classroom Instruction, IT Education

1. INTRODUCTION

We have witnessed tremendous technological advancements in the past ten years; they have fundamentally changed the way we live, communicate, teach and learn [1]. Some of the most important advancements have been the dramatic increase in bandwidth speed, which has facilitated innovative Internet applications, and the significant improvement in video and audio streaming technology, which has made videoconferencing possible. Innovative Internet applications coupled with improved videoconferencing capabilities have led to the proliferation of virtual meeting technology (VMT) [1, 2].

VMT represents the tools for facilitating interactive and synchronous communications that take place over the Internet using features such as audio and video, instant messaging, and

application sharing [3]. Though the technology was originally intended as a low-cost alternative means to business travel for companies, more and more educators are beginning to see its potential benefits by adding real-time interaction in distance education courses as well as offering new opportunities in traditional, face-to-face classrooms. Virtual meetings offer a way to engage students in fully interactive, online learning experiences such as lecture, tutoring, demonstration, office hours, and other activities [3]. In addition to the videoconferencing capability, features, such as electronic white boards, online chat, file or desktop sharing, and audience polling, make the technology increasingly appropriate for education. When used effectively, VMT can enrich the learning process through the integration of new resources, strengthening of knowledge, fostering communication and integration, and facilitating the assessment and monitoring of students [4].

Although VMT is deemed to be suitable for educational purposes, research on the use of synchronous video in education is lacking in the literature [5]. The majority of research focuses on text-heavy, interactive tools (e.g., discussion board, chat room) or asynchronous, one-way videos (e.g., video recording, podcast) as the delivery media for distance education [6, 7] as well as their role in promoting teamwork and collaboration [8, 9]. Some research investigates the use and effectiveness of synchronous videoconferencing tools in distance education courses or e-learning environments [5, 10]; however, there is very little pedagogic evidence providing the practical details of using VMT in classroom instruction.

This paper aims to bring to light VMT as an effective classroom instructional tool, especially for IT education, and the possible ways to embed this technology in classroom settings. The rest of the paper is organized as follows. First, the paper begins with an overview of the advantages of using VMT as a classroom instructional tool and the different types of VMT setup. Next, the paper illustrates how VMT can be integrated into both physical and virtual classrooms in the form of two case studies of IT courses. The paper concludes with a short summary highlighting the contribution of the work and directions for future explorations.

2. ADVANTAGES OF VMT IN CLASSROOMS

VMT enables instructors and students to communicate in real time and is considered advantageous for classroom instruction for at least the following reasons:

SIGITE/RIIT'13, October 10-12, 2013, Orlando, Florida, USA
Copyright 2013 ACM 978-1-4503-2239-3/13/10...$15.00.
http://dx.doi.org/10.1145/2512276.2512279

Synchronous interaction: Videoconferencing has the unique ability to simulate the richest form of human interaction, namely, face to face. Previous studies in the area of human communications show that more than 60% of all communications are derived from nonverbal behaviors using gestures, emotions, body language, etc. [2] Therefore, live instruction via VMT offers opportunities for students to develop a high level of interaction and allows them to become more engaged during lectures, thereby enhancing the quality of learning.

Inclusion of industry professionals: Students can benefit greatly from the experiences of experts in the relevant field or industry professionals; however, inviting full-time, leading industry professionals, who usually have a busy schedule, to a weekday class is a challenging task. VMT can serve as a solution to this challenge by bringing industry professionals to students in their comfort zone and by connecting students to the real world outside of the classroom.

Ease of use and convenience: VMT applications are mostly easy to use, especially for today's students who are comfortable with technology and can learn a new tool quickly. With minimal equipment (e.g., computer, webcam, microphone, Internet connection), a student can log into a live lecture session and fully participate in the discussion from any location. Some VMT applications are sophisticated and cross-platform compatible, allowing users to access using mobile devices, such as smartphones and tablet computers. Using VMT can not only bring convenience to students but also expose them to additional tools that they may use in their continued education and in their professional careers [10].

Green technology: VMT is not just good for students; it is also good for the environment. Since video communications are completely digital and transmitted over the Internet, classes that utilize VMT help the reduction of gasoline consumption and emissions and save time by reducing the number of students, instructors, and experts who have to commute to campus.

3. TYPES OF VMT SETUP

As virtual meetings are gaining popularity in the corporate world, in government, in the nonprofit sector, and at academic institutions, the market begins to abound with software applications, tools, and equipment for facilitating virtual meeting or video conferencing in various forms. The virtual meeting technologies that are commonly used in educational settings can be loosely classified into the following three types of setup, in increasing order of complexity: (1) student computer with software applications, (2) instructor computer connected to projector screens, and (3) telepresence room.

3.1 Student's Computer with Software Applications

In this type of setup, instructors and students are able to connect to a virtual meeting session and speak to and see each other using a personal computing device. This setup requires the fewest hardware requirements—a computer with Internet connection, a webcam (standalone or integrated), a microphone (wireless or wired), and speakers is all that is required. At least one VMT software application must be used and it can range from free to fee-based and support from 1 to as many as over 1000 people:

Small-size session: Free applications, such as Skype[1], Google Hangouts[2], and ooVoo[3], can support group videoconferencing up to 9 ~ 12 people; they are most suitable for small groups or one-on-one instruction [11]. These services are completely free, but they require users to sign up for a new account and download a client program to be installed on their computers. The Group Video Calling feature in Skype was previously available only to paid Skype Premium subscribers; however, starting in March 2013, members of Skype in the Classroom[4] can use the service free of charge [12].

Medium-size session: Fee-based services, such as GoToMeeting[5] or GotoWebinar and WebEx Meetings[6], can support group videoconferencing up to 25 ~ 100 people; they are most suitable for classes of regular size—20~40 students. In virtual meeting sessions facilitated by these services, there needs to be at least a person playing the host or organizer role, who is responsible for initiating and managing the meeting and has more privileges than other attendees, such as inviting participants, changing views, opening polls, etc. Both GotoMeeting and WebEx Meetings are cross-platform compatible (e.g., Windows, Mac) and support mobile access (e.g., iPad, iPhone, BlackBerry, Android device). In particular, WebEx Meetings also support Toll-free phone call-in for audio if the users choose to do so.

Large-size session: Fee-based services, such as Adobe Connect[7] and Microsoft Lync Online[8], can support group videoconferencing up to 8,000 people; they are most suitable for large-scale webcasting or webinars. Both services are considered the leading Web conferencing platforms on the market today. Neither of the services requires the users to download any client program, offering instance access to online meetings via a Web browser. In particular, Adobe Connect leverages Adobe Flash® Player, installed on virtually all Internet-connected computers, and provides some superior functionality across operating systems, including instant desktop sharing, permission-based catalog folder access, customizable URLs, training group management, etc. [13].

3.2 Instructor's Computer Connected to Projector Screens

In this type of setup, an instructor's computer in a physical classroom with some equipment that provides better quality of audio and video capabilities is assumed. This setup requires a computer with high-speed Internet connection, single or dual-panel projector screen (connected to the instructor's computer), a webcam with pan/tilt/zoom capabilities, a microphone (wireless or wired), and speakers with amplifier. This setup is most suitable for videoconferencing with one or more endpoints outside of the

---

[1] http://www.skype.com/en/

[2] http://www.google.com/+/learnmore/hangouts/

[3] http://www.oovoo.com/home.aspx

[4] https://education.skype.com/

[5] http://www.gotomeeting.com/fec/online_meeting

[6] http://www.webex.com/products/web-conferencing.html

[7] http://www.adobe.com/products/adobeconnect.html

[8] http://office.microsoft.com/en-us/lync/lync-online-overview-and-features-online-meetings-and-instant-messaging-FX103789571.aspx

classroom and often takes place in synchronous distance education sessions while there are other students in the classroom.

Because this setup is typical in academic settings, the VMT software application used is usually an integrated component of a learning management system (LMS). Currently, the leader in this area is Blackboard Collaborate[9], which has built on Wimba and Elluminate and provides an interactive web conferencing and virtual classroom environment designed for teaching and learning and real-time collaboration [14]. Using Blackboard Collaborate, instructors can share PowerPoint presentations and other content using a virtual whiteboard. Additional features include multi-person audio and video, screen sharing, chat, and breakout rooms, etc. Another leading LMS, Moodle, can also be enhanced to support videoconferencing by including plugins, such as VideoWhisper[10], or open-source software suite, such as MIST/C[11].

3.3 Telepresence Room

Telepresence is an immersive style of videoconferencing that emulates the experience of having all participants, typically between 5 and 20, in the same room [15]. The difference between telepresence and traditional videoconferencing is that more senses are involved [16]. The technology transmits crystal-clear audio and high-definition video in real life-size between rooms that are designed to match and appear as an extension of each other. Eye contact, facial expressions, and nonverbal cues are experienced the same way as in real life, making telepresence an "immersive, life-like communications experience" and "engaging, rich-media learning environments" [17].

Telepresence rooms require a more advanced and permanent installation, and therefore, have high infrastructure costs. This type of setup requires a telepresence system with built-in touch screen control panel, multiple room-size LCD screens that deliver high-definition images, robotic camera clusters that are placed at eye level, integrated microphones that provide shielding to block audio interference, high-end speakers that are capable of reproducing fine acoustic details, thin light reflectors that provide integrated lighting with reduced glare, as well as furniture (executive desks and chairs). Companies such as Cisco[12] and BrightCom[13] are leading providers for telepresence solutions in today's market and have educational institution customers such as University of Pennsylvania's Wharton School, Duke University, and George Mason University [16].

4. CASE STUDIES

The following section illustrates how VMT can be embedded in classrooms in the form of two case studies of IT courses. The case studies were chosen for two reasons. Firstly, VMT is used in different settings: one in a virtual classroom or a completely online environment, and the other in a physical classroom, for which there are still few empirical studies. This provides an opportunity to reflect on some differences, in practice, between

in-class and online settings. Secondly, the technology setup is very different: Case Study One represents the first type of VMT setup as previously mentioned, where students participated in virtual meetings with the instructor, the trainer, and the students via personal computer installed with a VMT client program; Case Study Two represents the second type of VMT setup as previously mentioned, where students in the classroom participated in videoconferencing with guest speakers via the instructor's computer connected to projector screens. Taken together the case studies illustrate how VMT can support IT education in different ways.

4.1 Case Study One: Embedding VMT in a Virtual Classroom

4.1.1 Course Description

The course is a 3-credit elective course offered to undergraduate students with sophomore or higher standing in the Bachelor of Tourism and Event Management program at GMU. The main objectives of the course are: to introduce hospitality management information systems (HMIS) technology and its application from managerial and strategic perspectives; and to survey computer applications, products and trends in gathering, analyzing, storing and communicating information within hospitality sectors.

The class meets twice per week for 1 hour and 15 minutes with 25 students. The course includes lectures, hands-on training of HMIS applications, and guest speaker lectures from the hospitality IT industry.

4.1.2 Problems

As it is a technology course, the focus of this course is on hands-on training of key applications as well as conceptual understanding. One of the key training sessions happened to be on a day before the university's Thanksgiving break, and many students expressed that they had already made travel arrangements before the semester started. While rescheduling of this training could have been an option, the industry trainer could not reschedule it due to his busy schedule. It is important to note that this training was complimentary as a courtesy of the software company that supports university students, so it was not reasonable to ask the industry trainer to reschedule his work schedule with potential loss of opportunity costs to the company. With the given conditions, the course instructor had to search for a solution to fulfill the goal of hands-on training while accommodating many students who could not be present in the classroom. In addition to that, as the students had little experience in IT content and applications (this course is the only IT course in the program), it was critical to have a real time interactive training session that allowed questions throughout the session. Most of all, providing a sense of face-to-face connection with the trainer was important to keep the students engaged as they were at their own places (e.g. home, airport, campus etc.) without the instructor's supervision.

4.1.3 VMT Selection and Setup

One other key component of this course was the application of meeting technology, which had triggered the course instructor to search for a solution that could fulfill both components (meeting technology and hands-on software training) into one session. VMT was ideal as it can provide web-based real time seminars

---

[9] https://www.blackboard.com/Platforms/Collaborate/overview.aspx

[10] http://www.videowhisper.com/?p=Video+Conference

[11] http://netlab.gmu.edu/MISTC/

[12] http://www.cisco.com/en/US/products/ps7060/index.html

[13] http://www.brightcom.com/main_telepresence.html

with face-to-face video functionality. After careful research and discussion with the trainer in search of the best solution, GoToMeeting was chosen as the best solution.

GoToMeeting is a Web-based VMT application. It comes with two versions: one is GoToMeeting and the other is GoToWebinar. GoToMeeting is a simple but powerful online meeting tool that allows collaboration among up to 25 attendees. It allows easy and instant switching of presenter duties (e.g., keyboard and mouse control, interaction with the shared screen, spotlight and arrow tools, etc.) to any attendee in the meeting. In addition to screen sharing, it also supports virtual face-to-face meeting via its patented, HDFaces® videoconferencing capabilities. HDFaces allows capturing facial expressions and body language of attendees using webcams and can enhance quality of communication. Audio is transferred using an integrated audio conferencing feature (using computer's microphone and speakers or telephone). GoToMeeting has been commonly used for online meeting, sales demo, online presentation, and sharing and reviewing documents.

GoToWebinar is a great tool for company-wide all-hands meetings, supporting up to 1,000 people at the same time. It allows one or more presenters to join a meeting session from their own PC or Mac computers. GoToWebinar also includes the HDFaces videoconferencing feature for up to 100 attendees and provides additional capabilities of sending automated, customizable reminder e-mails to attendees. Through these essential features, GoToWebinar allows attendees to ask questions by typing or chatting and provides hands-on experience by application sharing. More importantly, its recording feature makes recording of a webinar – including all the phone and computer audio – possible for future review and reuse. When a webinar is completed, a webinar organizer can collect feedback by asking attendees to complete a post-session survey.

The HMIS application, for which students needed to receive hands-on training in the class, was called MeetingMatrix. It is a tool that helps meeting and event venues attract and interact with buyers (e.g. meeting /event planners) and help them evaluate, select, and work with venues. The MeetingMatrix room diagramming software enables planners to quickly create accurate event diagrams and easily communicate with their clients and venues.

In order to meet the objectives of the course, the VMT tool used in that lecture must be able to support the following:

- demonstration of the MeetingMatrix by a trainer;
- videoconferencing that shows the face of the trainer (to enhance reality of the training and to stimulate the students' motivation);
- checking attendee list remotely;
- students' hands-on training and application of MeetingMatrix; and
- allowing students to ask questions during the practice

Compared to GoToMeeting, GoToWebinar was a better fit with features that met the aforementioned requirements. Moreover, the company (trainer) of MeetingMatrix already had a license for GoToWebinar, so it was a cost-free option for the instructor and the students. The required setup for the session were: (1) cloud-based GoToWebinar application; (2) cloud-based MeetingMatrix application; (3) Internet connection; (4) computer; (5) speakers and microphone; and (6) Webcam. In regard to the travelling students, they needed a laptop or tablet PC (e.g., iPad), an iPhone or an Android device with a downloaded GoToWebinar app, a Meeting Matrix app and Internet connection.

The course instructor and trainer scheduled the GoToWebinar session and sent webinar invitations to the students by email. The students could access the Webinar session from their laptop or tablet PC and register by clicking the "Register Now" button embedded in the email invitation. Once the students logged in, each student could choose to use their computer's microphone and speakers or call in via telephone to have audio capability. The course instructor facilitated the administrative aspect of the VMT-based training by checking the attendee list, confirming connectivity and delivery of shared screen and audio/video to students, adding comments that could enhance students' understanding, as well as supporting students who might experience difficulties in connecting to the session due to their unstable or slow Internet connection while they were in their home or public space. The trainer led the software demonstration and managed the audio/video functions, the chat module, and the application sharing functionality.

The GoToWebminar window consists of four easy-to-use interface components as shown in Figure 2:

- *Full desktop sharing module:* this area displays the trainer's screen - anything the presenter shares on-screen.
- *Attendance and Audio control module:* this module presents current attendees in a session and allows the trainer to control the audio (microphone) function of students.
- *Chat module*: This module allows live text chat for Q&A.
- *HDFaces video module:* this module displays real time trainer's face via webcam connected to the trainer's computer. It supports two-way video/audio communication; therefore students' faces can be displayed if necessary.

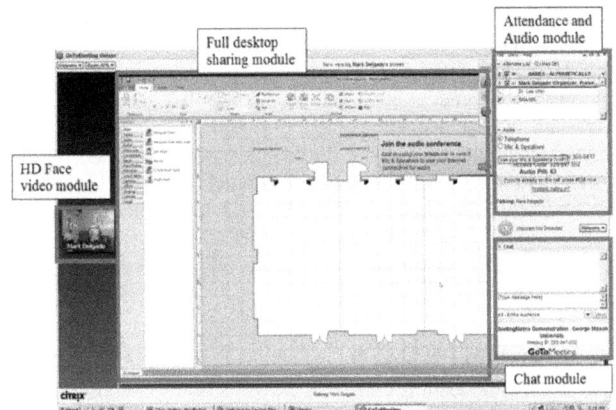

Figure 2. Actual Class Screenshot of MeetingMatrix Training via GoToWebinar with HDFaces Video

4.1.4 Student Feedback

The VMT based software training offered a successful alternative to in-class trainings. With the success of the first VMT based application training session, the same training was offered again in the following semester. The effectiveness of this VMT based hands-on-training is well described in the following students' comments.

I think it was comparable to an in-class presentation.

It was a good presentation; I enjoyed learning about MeetingMatrix in that way.

I really enjoyed the demonstration and benefitted greatly from it.

4.2 Case Study Two: Embedding VMT in a Physical Classroom

4.2.1 Course Description

The course is a 1-credit mandatory junior transition course offered to undergraduate students with sophomore standing in the Bachelor of Science in Applied Information Technology program at George mason University (GMU) [18]. The main objectives of the course are to guide students to make informed decisions when choosing a concentration (i.e., database technology and programming, healthcare IT, information security, networking and telecommunications, and Web development and multimedia) within the program, to bring awareness to the career paths that are available within each concentration area, and to provide insights into the senior design project experience, graduate programs, certifications, and university resources.

The class meets once per week for 2 hours and 45 minutes during the first or last 7 weeks of the semester. The main topics of the course are covered primarily by guest speakers whom are chosen and invited by the course coordinator, both from within the university as well as from the industry. Except for the first and the last classes, two or three guest speakers are assigned to each of the middle five classes. The course is taught in a seminar style, where an average of 30 to 40 students can participate by listening to the guest speakers' presentations, asking relevant questions, and engaging in in-class discussions.

4.2.2 Problems

Because the course is offered in an average of 4 to 6 sections on two campuses each semester, the guest speakers have to present the same materials multiple times in different sections, which are usually scheduled during the day on weekdays, throughout the semester. This is difficult for academic guest speakers from within the university to do; it is even more challenging for industry guest speakers, who are full-time IT professionals (e.g., network engineer, CEO of an IT company, Federal government employee, program alumnus) and have a busy schedule.

In addition, as the students benefit the most by interacting with the guest speakers face-to-face and communicating with them directly, simply playing a recorded video of a guest speaker's previous presentation or demonstrating his or her presentation slides in class is not enough or intellectually stimulating to the students. The coordinator, who is also one of the instructors for the course, was facing scheduling issues as well as the challenge of providing an active and engaging classroom learning environment that facilitates real-time, two-way communications and is comparable to a live seminar with the guest speakers.

4.2.3 VMT Selection and Setup

VMT comes to the rescue as a needed solution to the aforementioned problems; however, the selection of the equipment and setup are constrained by the classroom settings. Because the course does not require students to have access to computers as other computer lab courses, the classrooms assigned

to the course are the Technology Enhanced Classrooms (TEC) intended for lecture-style classes with minimal technology support. Each TEC comes equipped with an instructor station, where there is a computer that can project to a large screen and play audio from multiple speakers in the room; there is no camera, microphone, or any other equipment installed on the computer for conducting a videoconferencing session with a remote location. Also, the instructor's computer is configured to have basic software programs (e.g., Web browsers, Microsoft Office, etc.) and Internet capabilities but not allow installation of any other software application without the proper network administration access. For these reasons, the course coordinator came up with a creative VMT solution that is low-cost, portable, and feasible for the existing classroom settings.

The VMT software application used is Blackboard Collaborate, which is integrated into the university's adopted learning management system, Blackboard Learn. The instructor can create a Collaborate session any time in the Blackboard course folder and have the speaker access a session via a guest link in an email invitation. The guest speaker does not need to be registered on Blackboard and can access the Collaborate session via a Web browser or a mobile device without having to travel to the campus. The Collaborate session window consists of four easy-to-use interface components:

- *Audio & Video Panel:* this panel displays the video of the guest speaker when he or she has a webcam connected to the computer and allows the speaker to speak to a headset connected to the computer. A maximum of six talkers and webcams can be simultaneously supported in two-way communications.
- *Chat Panel:* this panel provides live chat or instant messaging capabilities, allowing another way for the instructor and the guest speaker to communicate, especially before an audio and video session is established.
- *Participants Panel:* the guest speaker is displayed immediately in this panel as he or she logs into the session. As a session moderator, the instructor can easily grant privileges (e.g., a moderator role) to the guest speaker as needed.
- *Content Area:* this area provides several powerful content-sharing features, such as White Board, which enables participants to write, draw, and collaborate on the displayed content simultaneously or load presentations created in other software; Application Sharing, which enables participants to share single, multiple applications or the entire desktop or grant control of any application to other participants; and Web Tour, which enables participants to open any website within the session window or a separate browser.

In order for the students to directly interact with the guest speaker as if they were in the same room, the instructor has used an AKG WMS40 Mini Dual Wireless Microphone System, as shown in Figure 1. The set consists of a dual mini receiver, a clip-on microphone with built-in transmitter, a handheld microphone with built-in transmitter, and a 3-pin mini XLR instrument cable, which is intended for stage performance. To connect the wireless microphones to the computer through the receiver, a dual ¼-inch to 3.5mm stereo adapter cable has been used, where the two ¼-inch connectors are plugged into the receiver supporting two channels of audio and the 3.5mm connector is plugged into the audio input port on the computer. This allows the guest speaker to receive audio from both microphones: the clip-on was used by the instructor and the handheld was passed around and used by the students.

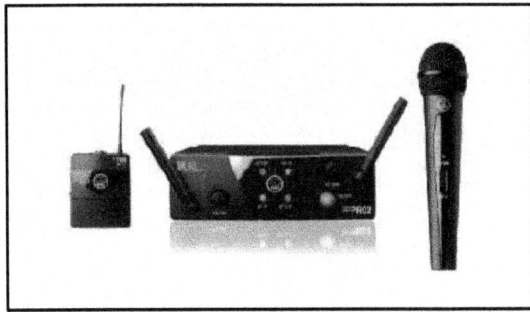

Figure 1. AKG WMS40 Mini Dual Wireless Microphone System (© 2013 Harman International Industries, Inc.)

Although the VMT setup described in this case supports two-way audio communication but one-way video communication (from the guest speaker to the students), it is presently sufficient for the purpose of the course. With the innovative use of the dual wireless microphones, the instructor can quickly turn a regular classroom into a virtual meeting room and create a learning environment that fosters student learning and participation. The VMT software application, namely Blackboard Collaborate, is also intuitive to use, requiring almost no training or experience to get started by the instructors and the guest speakers.

4.2.4 Student Feedback

The option to present remotely has been made available to the guest speakers for the past two semesters, and more than a dozen guest speakers, especially from the industry, has chosen this option. Despite the obvious advantages of in-class presentations given by the guest speakers, more than half of the students think Collaborate sessions are comparable to in-class presentations and appreciate the ability to interact with the guest speakers directly and see their faces. A survey is performed at the end of the semester to measure outcomes from the course and receive suggestions for future improvements. One of the questions on the survey specifically asks students' opinion about the Collaborate sessions. Some positive feedback includes the following:

It was similar to an in-class presentation. Everyone was engaged.

I actually liked the Collaborate sessions.

I think it was nice that we could interact and ask questions just like in-class.

5. CONCLUSIONS
In an era of mobility and flexibility, Virtual Meeting Technology offers an effective, affordable, green solution to many challenges faced by today's IT educators. The paper makes a unique contribution to the research by providing empirical evidence and indicative support for the successful application of VMT in different classroom settings and exemplifying the use of VMT as an effective instructional technology and an enabler of active learning.

In addition to continuously refining the courses illustrated in the case studies, future efforts will focus on creating customized tutorial videos that aim to provide step-by-step instructions to

users (e.g., instructors, experts, students) of the VMT tools and alleviate any possible technical issues prior to a virtual meeting session. Other areas of prospective exploration may include applications of VMT in other domains, such as distance music lessons or K-12 education.

6. REFERENCES
[1] Rollag, K. and Billsberry, J. 2012. Technology as the enabler of a new wave of active learning. *Journal of Management Education, 36*(6), 743-752.

[2] Janitor, J., Fecilak, P., and Jakab, F. 2012. Enabling long distance education with realtime video. In *Proceedings of the 2012 IEEE 10th International Conference on Emerging eLearning Technologies & Applications (ICETA)*, 167-171.

[3] Educause. 2006. *7 Things You should Know about Virtual Meetings*. Retrieved April 27, 2013, from http://net.educause.edu/ir/library/pdf/ELI7011.pdf

[4] Santoveña-Casal, S. M. 2012. Teaching-Learning process by synchronic communication tools: the Elluminate Live case. *Electronic Journal of Research in Educational Psychology, 10*(1), 447-474.

[5] Warden, C. A., Stanworth, J. O., Ren, J. B., and Warden, A. R. 2013. Synchronous learning best practices: An action research study. *Computers & Education, 63*, 197-207.

[6] Cox, B. and Cox, B. 2008. Developing interpersonal and group dynamics through asynchronous threaded discussions: The use of discussion board in collaborative learning. *Education, 128*(4), 553-565.

[7] Hartsell, T. and Yuen, S. C. Y. 2006. Video streaming in online learning. *AACE Journal, 14*(1), 31-43.

[8] Shea, P., Li, C. S., Swan, K., and Pickett, A. 2005. Developing learning community in online asynchronous college courses: The role of teaching presence. *Journal of Asynchronous Learning Networks, 9*(4), 59-82.

[9] Beldarrain, Y. 2006. Distance education trends: Integrating new technologies to foster student interaction and collaboration. *Distance education, 27*(2), 139-153.

[10] Ellingson, D. A. and Notbohm, M. 2012. Synchronous distance education: using web-conferencing in an mba accounting course. *American Journal of Business Education (AJBE), 5*(5), 555-562.

[11] Karabulut, A. and Correia, A. 2008. Skype, Elluminate, Adobe Connect, Ivist: A comparison of web-based video conferencing systems for learning and teaching. In *Proceedings of the Society for Information Technology & Teacher Education International Conference*, 481-484.

[12] Ishizuka, K. 2013. Skype announces free group video calling for teachers. *School LibraryJournal*. Retrieved April 28, 2013, from http://www.thedigitalshift.com/2013/03/k-12/skype-announces-free-group-video-calling-for-teachers-sxswedu/

[13] Adobe. 2013. *White Paper on Adobe Connect and Microsoft Lync Server Meeting Product Comparison*. Retrieved April 29, 2013, from http://www.getconnect.com/wp-content/uploads/Adobe-Connect-vs-MS-Lync-Comparison.pdf

[14] Blackboard. 2013. *Building a 21st Century Teaching, Learning, and Collaborating Enironment*. Retrieved April 29, 2013, from https://www.blackboard.com/CMSPages/GetFile.aspx?guid=09533213-5498-44de-ae13-05c24b0604f5

[15] Lichtman, H. S. 2006. Telepresence, effective visual collaboration and the future of global business at the speed of light. *HPL, Human Productivity Lab Magazine*.

[16] Domonell, K. 2012. Choosing telepresence: When and how to take the plunge. *University Business Magazine*. Retrieved April 29, 2013, from http://www.universitybusiness.com/article/choosing-telepresence

[17] Cisco. 2013. *White Paper on Telepresence in Education*. Retrieved April 29, 2013, from http://www.cisco.com/web/strategy/docs/education/cisco_telepresence_in_education_white_paper_final.pdf

[18] Aksoy, P. 2011. A novel junior transition course for students of applied information technology. In *Proceedings of the 2011 conference on Information technology education*, 49-54.

Using Virtual Machines to Improve Learning and Save Resources in an Introductory IT Course

Geoff Stoker, Todd Arnold, and Paul Maxwell
Department of Electrical Engineering and Computer Science
United States Military Academy
West Point, NY
(845) 938 - 2193
{geoffrey.stoker, todd.arnold, paul.maxwell}@usma.edu

ABSTRACT

Information technology courses often require the use of software and hardware to support classroom learning. These systems can assist in achieving the learning objectives for a course through classroom problems and laboratory exercises. The procurement and maintenance of these systems can be a challenge even for well resourced organizations. In this paper we discuss how virtual machines can relieve organizations of some of their resource burdens while effectively achieving course learning objectives and provide examples of how that is currently done at the United States Military Academy.

Categories and Subject Descriptors

K.3.2 [**Computer and Information Science Education**]: Computer Science Education – *abstract data types*

Keywords

Information technology, virtual machines

1. INTRODUCTION

Teaching Information Technology (IT) often requires the use of software packages (e.g., web page servers, software development kits) and hardware systems (e.g., client computers, network switches) to reinforce learning objectives. To effectively teach IT subjects, the use of multiple operating systems, heterogeneous computers, and networks with various architectures is often required. The procurement, configuration, and maintenance of these packages and systems can present a significant expense in terms of money and personnel hours. In resource constrained organizations, this can be an insurmountable obstacle. Using *virtual machines* (*VM*), course designers can incorporate these important IT systems into their lesson plans while adhering to the resource constraints that are imposed upon them.

In IT courses, it is frequently useful to develop classroom or laboratory environments with a variety of configurations. Those configuration choices include items such as, operating systems, processor/machine architectures, networking architectures, and installed software. Manually configuring a set of machines to meet the needs of an IT course or courses consumes hours of

technician time. Additionally, certain IT learning objectives may not be implementable using standard classroom equipment. Activities such as hacking and experimental networking configurations are often not acceptable to system administrators due to the risks involved for the rest of the network infrastructure. To be able to achieve the learning objectives in these situations, your choice is to have a specially configured and isolated classroom/lab or to use virtual machines. For introductory-level students, tasks such as installing and configuring software can be challenging. Additionally, control over a student's choice of processor and operating system for their personal computer is usually infeasible. If a particular software package is required for classroom learning then there exists the risk that the package will not function properly on the student's hardware platform with their choice of operating system. These two software issues create an extra burden for the instructor and the technical staff as they try to resolve the problem for the student.

One method to overcome many of these obstacles is to use virtual machines such as VMware Workstation and VMware Player [1][1]. Virtual machines provide a flexible and relatively inexpensive way to design and execute classroom and laboratory exercises without the purchase of hardware and the time cost for IT support personnel. Using virtual machines, classroom and laboratory exercises can be developed that have heterogeneous operating systems and processor architectures, relieves the requirement to purchase additional processors, and alleviates the vulnerabilities presented by executing IT lessons on standard machines. Additionally, virtual machines can allow an instructor to quickly reset or change the machine environment in a time constrained setting (e.g., between class hours) in a way that would be infeasible for a technician to reconfigure physical equipment.

In this paper we describe how virtual machines can be used in an entry-level IT course to support the course learning objectives. The use of virtual machines allows for the exploration of various environments found in introductory IT courses ranging from hacking labs to basic web site creation. We compare how the core Information Technology course at the United States Military Academy conducted its lessons prior to the incorporation of virtual machines to the current and future lesson plans. Included is a discussion on the advantages and disadvantages of using virtual machines in the IT classroom.

The remainder of the paper begins with a discussion of other efforts using virtual machines in section II. In section III, we

---

RIIT'13, October 10–12, 2013, Orlando, Florida, USA.
Copyright © 2013 ACM 978-1-4503-2494-6/13/10...$15.00.
http://dx.doi.org/10.1145/2512276.2512287

---

[1] The views expressed in this article are those of the authors and do not reflect the official policy or position of the Department of the Army, Department of Defense, or the U.S. Government.

discuss how virtual machines can be implemented in an entry level IT course. We then provide conclusions and suggestions for future work in section IV.

2. RELATED WORKS

The idea of using virtual machines for IT education is not new. In the last several years, many authors have discussed techniques for incorporating virtual machines into the framework of their courses. In general, these ideas have fallen into two main categories: using virtual machines to allow distance learning and using virtual machines to create networked environments for higher-level (i.e., junior, senior) IT courses.

Examples of work in the first category can be found in [2, 3, 4]. These papers describe using virtual machines to create Virtual Networked Labs (VNL) that students can access remotely using networked client systems. The main focus of these works is to enable students enrolled in distance learning programs to have a similar experience as those on-campus students who have access to a physical lab. The authors describe how they were able to establish virtual labs with similar capabilities as their physical labs and thus facilitate the remote students' learning. Our work does not fall into this category. We are promoting the advantages that can be obtained by using virtual machines in the on-campus environment.

In the work of [5] and [6], the authors describe using virtual machines in an on-campus environment. In their environment, virtual machines were developed to provide a laboratory for advanced courses in IT, such as, system and network administration, and information security and assurance. This virtual lab clearly enables students at the higher levels of IT education the opportunity to learn advanced topics without the need for expensive hardware and software. In our work, we extend this concept into the lower levels of IT education where the majority of students are not IT majors. We seek to leverage the benefits of virtual machines in that domain to conserve resources and augment student learning.

3. VIRTUAL MACHINE IN AN INFORMATION TECHNOLOGY COURSE
3.1 Background

At the United States Military Academy, every student is required to take a set of courses known as the core curriculum. The core curriculum is designed to support the Academy's educational goals of providing students with a breadth of knowledge to draw from after graduation. One of the Academy's goals focuses on educating our graduates to understand information technology and states: "Graduates understand and apply Information Technology concepts to acquire, manage, communicate and defend information, solve problems, and adapt to technological change." [7]

To support the Academy's IT goal, the Department of Electrical Engineering and Computer Science teaches two IT courses within the core curriculum. The first, IT105: Intro to Computing and Information Technology, is taken during freshman year, is taught to 99% of students, and covers basic computer functionality and programming concepts. The second course, IT305: Theory and Practice of Military Information Technology Systems, is most often taken during the students' third year which is after our students choose their major. Those who choose an engineering

major meet the IT goal through courses taken within their major. As a result, IT305 is taken by students who select a non-engineering major, which is about 80% of each graduating class.

The goal of IT305 is to provide these non-engineering students with an understanding of the underlying theory behind the types of hardware and software systems they will see upon graduation. Specifically, upon completing the course the students should be able to:

1. Understand the underlying physical and mathematical concepts relevant to IT
2. Understand the ways in which IT systems function
3. Articulate the methods for successfully employing IT systems
4. Demonstrate the effective use of IT to solve problems and make decisions
5. Understand the importance and implications of IT

To support these outcomes, the students are introduced to Web 2.0, databases, networking, and cyber security, in that order.

3.2 Using Virtualization in the Classroom

Accomplishing the goals of IT305 requires the use of specific software packages and hardware systems. To standardize these tools and teaching methods, we require all of our students to install and use the same development tools. For the web page portion of the course, we use Microsoft Expression Web 4.0.

Expression Web is not part of the standard software package provided to each student, so the first course challenge is getting all of the students to download and properly install the software. Since the population we are targeting is the non-technologically inclined, there are sometimes significant challenges in getting everyone to a stable state where we can begin the course work. Every semester we encounter students who are challenged by the installation process or who experience software or hardware compatibility issues. The result is our instructors and computer support technicians spend numerous hours each semester attempting to resolve these issues so the students can commence with the learning process. One particularly difficult challenge occurred when attempting to install Expression Web on the standard student Windows Vista image and a specific hardware platform (which was issued to the entire cohort group). Expression Web functioned incorrectly on the combination of hardware and operating system. The only way we were able to resolve the issue was when the entire year group was upgraded to Windows 7. The upgrade eliminated the Vista specific issue though the specific cause of the problem was never fully resolved. Avoiding this type of problem would save instructor and computer support technician time and alleviate student frustration.

A way to minimize the impact of introducing additional software to the student computers for each portion of the course would be to virtualize the software. This could be accomplished by the creation of a VM using a tool such as VMware Workstation [1] with the software pre-installed in a stable configuration. Students could then utilize the software regardless of their underlying system using VMWare Player or VirtualBox.

Another method to avoid installation issues is to virtualize the application. Tools such as VMware's ThinApp [8] can create a virtual executable that will run the desired software on a machine yet is more light weight than a full VM. The students simply download an executable package that runs the software. No matter the technique, the students could be provided a course virtual solution at the beginning of the semester that has all of the software packages required for the semester.

In addition to the administrative difficulties of software installation and usage, IT courses are often required to use specialized hardware and software to achieve their learning objectives. For IT305, a major learning experience occurs during the networking block in three hands-on lab periods. In our profession, each of our graduates will experience using or operating a network in a military tactical environment. To simulate this they are required to construct the user portion of a tactical network (Figure 1), that is similar to a small office environment of about 40 employees. The devices include switches, laptops, and Voice over IP (VoIP) phones. We also introduce them to some network monitoring tools (e.g., SNMPc, Solar Winds Orion) they may use on their networks. Errors are purposely introduced into the network during the labs for experience with troubleshooting.

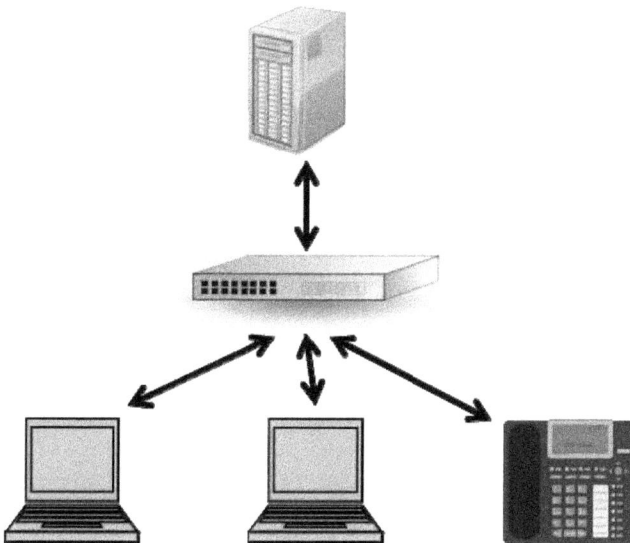

Figure 1. Example configuration of an IT305 networking lab. The lab connects different client systems to a server using network switches.

While valuable as a teaching tool, these hands-on lab experiences are costly, both financially and physically (i.e., scheduling classroom resources). Similar to many institutions, we do not have enough dedicated networking lab space for constructing these networks, so we must reserve eight additional classrooms each semester just for the labs. This means other courses cannot use the spaces during those class hours for the entire semester thus constraining the academy. Additionally, to support the labs, each classroom requires dedicated networking equipment. This is a costly investment, especially because the equipment is used only during these three lab periods each semester.

Instructor time, another constrained resource, is also impacted with this lab configuration. Because the networking equipment is only used a few times each semester, every instructor must construct the lab just as the students will to identify faulty equipment before the lab period. Before each lab hour, the instructors must also place the equipment in the room because the equipment cannot be left unsecured in the classrooms. Furthermore, the lab rooms are often used by other courses during the hours immediately preceding the lab times and thus

unavailable for conducting this set-up procedure. Many times, instructors are only allowed the 15 minutes between classes to set up the entire lab worth of equipment. This constraint can result in lab exercises that do not fully meet their desired learning objectives.

Virtualization of the hardware and software used in these lab exercises could reduce or eliminate many of these issues. The basic networking labs could be taught with a focus on basic functionality, configuration, and connectivity. The clients and servers used in the labs, to include the phones, can be virtualized and run on the students' laptops in their regular classroom thus freeing the institutional resources and requiring fewer pieces of dedicated hardware. Lab preparation can then be as simple as connecting networking cables between student laptops and a classroom switch. Using virtual machines and virtual network simulators, such as Dynamips [9], students would be responsible for configuring network devices during the labs. This virtualization would allow each student to connect, configure, and troubleshoot the entire network while doing so in a less resource intensive environment.

The Cyber security portion of the course is a block of five lessons, with four of the lessons providing hands-on experience. The first block introduces the students to the Army's Blue Force Tracking (BFT) system [10]. Blue Force Tracking is used by the Army to digitally track its assets (e.g., tanks, helicopters) on the battlefield, providing units with real-time location information and messaging capability. This system is fielded Army-wide and is a critical Army IT system to the deployed force.

Rather than just providing the students with an overview of the system, we want experiential learning to occur. However, each system is a stand-alone Linux-based device and is only allowed on a tactical network. We are not authorized to connect the devices to the classroom network. In addition, each of these BFT systems is costly and requires access to a satellite network for proper operation.

To provide the students with access to the system, we created VMs with the BFT software pre-installed and were given an exception to connect the VMs to the network on a temporary basis. Using these virtual machines, each classroom is able to construct a tactical network and simulate a deployed unit as it moves across the battlefield using the virtual BFT interface. The VM provides the same functionality and appearance of the real system without the expensive hardware.

The other three lessons of the cyber security block provide lessons on reconnaissance, defensive, and offensive cyber operations. Based on end of course feedback each semester, the hacking labs really capture the imagination of many of the students and is at least interesting to all of them. The context of the hacking block is designed to illustrate important points about the risks associated with operating personal computing devices on public networks like those found at airports or public restaurants.

Once again, restrictions on connecting either vulnerable systems to the network or on installing 'hacking' tools onto networked computers poses a challenge for IT courses. Institutional network administrators are responsible for the entire network and therefore are rightfully resistant to allowing these types of systems on the network. This reasonable constraint poses a challenge for those attempting to impart IT lessons to students. A solution to this challenge is to virtualize the lab. As a result, we distribute two

VMs to the students that contain virtual attacking and defending machines connected over an isolated virtual network.

In the first lesson of this virtual lab, we familiarize students with the concept of a virtual machine and spend some time emphasizing the difference between applications that are running on an installed operating system, such as Windows 7 which is installed on their individual laptops, and the virtual machines that are complete operating systems running logically within their laptops. Each student makes use of an Attacker machine and a Defender machine, both of which are running an installation of un-patched Windows XP Pro. We use the image in Figure 2 to help them understand abstractly how the three machines co-exist.

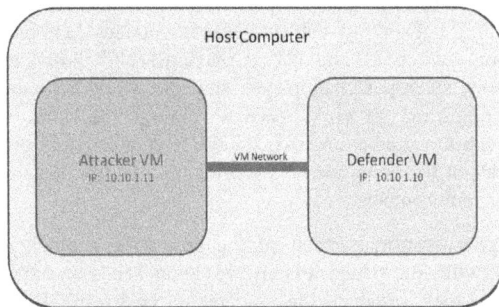

Figure 2. System configuration for IT course hacking laboratory exercise.

Once the students start the VMs, they see something similar to Figure 3. The VM on the left with the red desktop and many shortcut icons is the Attacker and the VM on the right with the blue desktop is the Defender.

During the first hacking lab we expose the students to the concepts of vulnerabilities, threats, and risks and set the stage for a cyber attack with reconnaissance of the defender machine. Because the scenario is of a migrant user temporarily making use of a public network, we stress that whatever protection a user can reasonably rely on must be present on their individual PC. Simple steps, like having a firewall and having it enabled are important ones. We use the specific tools SuperScan v4.0 (McAfee) and Winfingerprint 0.6.2 (available SourceForge) to show students that information about their computer name, the current Windows version and patch level, usernames, open ports, etc., are readily available over the network from any machine that is open to probing. This type of information is covertly collected by the Attacker about the Defender for use in subsequent lessons.

During the second hacking lab lesson we illustrate how the information gathered about a target machine can be used to find an entry point into it. We start with simple ideas like trying to guess a password for one of the accounts we discovered and show how we can leverage the power of computers to automate and accelerate the guessing process. During this task, which uses a batch file and a dictionary file, we are able to expose students to things very few have previously experienced, like using command line tools and MS-DOS commands to gain access across the network to another machine's C: drive. We extend the entry point search to using pwdump and John the Ripper to demonstrate how the process can be quickly expanded once access to a machine is gained. Just prior to this task we direct them to reset a password for one of the Defender machine's accounts to test how easy or hard it is for automated tools to guess students' passwords. We also talk about and demonstrate how tools like Nessus

Vulnerability Scanner are available to help us find weaknesses and focus our defensive efforts.

The third and final lesson of this block is quite successful at exciting and alarming most of the students. Using the tools Sub7 by mobman – sent via Trojan attachment – NetBus, and Metasploit, students are able to have the Attacker machine take total control of the Defender machine. The impact of these three hands-on lessons is immense and would not be nearly as effective, or even possible, without the ability to use VMs to gain exposure to all these tools.

Conservatively, to conduct these hacking labs with real equipment would require 108 computers, 54 cross-over cables, and about 40 person-hours of technician support each semester to properly resource the labs and deal with any failures. These computers could be relatively low-powered ones that cost less than $500 each or be repurposed from life-cycle requirements. The cost in instructor or technician time to deal with student-caused configuration problems, or the loss for subsequent classes in instruction quality due to unusable computers is hard to gauge; we just note that it would be non-zero.

3.3 Implementation Challenges

There are many advantages to using VMs. Virtualizing labs and lessons can reduce the need for additional equipment; the space in which it must be set-up and/or stored; the instructor time required to set it up and tear it down if not permanently set-up; and the technician time needed to configure, maintain, and troubleshoot it. Given the skill-level of our student population, using VMs greatly reduces the complexity of teaching topics like the hacking labs by eliminating the time required for installation and configuration of the necessary software. The use of VMs also reduces the security risks to the primary school network and the risks of students creating problems with the starting configuration of the labs for each subsequent course section.

Of course, use of VMs brings its own challenges. Someone on staff must be competent at building and configuring the baseline VM required for lessons or tools that are being virtualized. The file size of VMs is not small, for example our Attacker machine is about 5 GB and the Defender machine about 3 GB. The issue of software licenses also cannot be ignored. Virtualization methods that rely on network connectivity, such as Citrix, are subject to network availability and throughput. Access to these networked virtual systems can pose a problem when students are off campus and require access to the software.

However, overall the advantages of using VMs greatly outweigh the disadvantages. As we move through the process of reducing and eventually eliminating dedicated computer labs, the ability to use virtualization to present key IT topics will be important in providing our students a very worthwhile hands-on experience while reducing the amount of resources required.

4. CONCLUSIONS AND FUTURE WORK

In conclusion, the use of virtual machines in introductory information technology courses can help students realize the course learning objectives. The virtual machines provide

Figure 3. Screen capture of IT hacking laboratory exercise. Left window shows the attacking machine and the right window shows the defending machine.

educational tools to assist with the students' learning while alleviating some resource requirements, such as, heterogeneous machines, heterogeneous operating systems, and technical support hours. Additionally, the VMs can reduce student stress and save them time by removing issues that arise from incompatible software and hardware combinations. Using the United States Military Academy IT305 course, we have demonstrated how virtual machines can be integrated into the introductory course material. The use of virtual machines in introductory courses can also facilitate their use in advanced IT courses due to student familiarity with the tool.

Future work in this domain could include a detailed comparison of courses using traditional teaching methods versus a virtual machine based course. Additionally, an analysis on which IT topics are best suited for VMs would be useful to allow course designers to focus their efforts in those areas.

5. REFERENCES

[1] VMware, http://www.vmware.com/, accessed 30 April 2013.

[2] C. Border, "The development and deployment of a multi-user, remote access virtualization system for networking, security, and system administration classes," *Proceedings of the 38th SIGCSE Technical Symposium on Computer Science Education* (SIGCSE '07), ACM, New York, NY, pp. 576 – 580.

[3] L. Leitner and J. Cane, "A Virtual Laboratory Environment for Online IT Education," *Proceedings of the 6th conference on Information Technology Education* (SIGITE '05), ACM, New York, NY, pp. 283 – 289.

[4] P. Li, L. Toderick, and P. Lunsford, "Experiencing virtual computing lab in information technology education," *Proceedings of the 10th conference on Information Technology Education* (SIGITE '09), ACM, New York, NY, pp. 55 – 59.

[5] W. Bullers, S. Burd, and A. Seazzu, "Virtual machines – an idea whose time has returned: Application to network, security, and database courses," *Proceedings of the 37th SIGCSE Technical Symposium on Computer Science Education (SIGSCE '06)*, ACM, New York, NY, pp. 102-106, 2006.

[6] M. Stockman, "Creating remotely accessible 'virtual networks' on a single PC to teach computer networking and operating systems," *Proceedings of the 4th conference on Information Technology Curriculum (CITC4 '03)*, ACM, New York, NY, pp. 67 – 71.

[7] Office of the Dean, "Educating Future Army Officers for a Changing World," 3rd ed., West Point, NY.

[8] VMware, *Thinapp User's Guide*, http://pubs.vmware.com/thinapp4/help/wwhelp/wwhimpl/js/html/wwhelp.htm, accessed 24 May 2013.

[9] Graphical Network Simulator, *Dynamips*, http://www.gns3.net/dynamips/, accessed 27 May 2013.

[10] FBCB2 – Blue Force Tracker, http://en.wikipedia.org/wiki/Blue_Force_Tracking, accessed 27 May 2013.

Learning Agile Software Engineering Practices using Coding Dojo

Kenny Heinonen, Kasper Hirvikoski, Matti Luukkainen, Arto Vihavainen
University of Helsinki
Department of Computer Science
P.O. Box 68 (Gustaf Hällströmin katu 2b)
Fi-00014 University of Helsinki
{ kennyhei, khirviko, mluukkai, avihavai }@cs.helsinki.fi

ABSTRACT

Information technology and computer science educators are experiencing an industry-driven change from plan-based software engineering development processes to more people-oriented Agile software engineering approaches. While plan-based software engineering practices have traditionally been taught in lectures, Agile practices can often be best learned by experiencing them in a realistic situation. One approach for bringing Agile practices to the learning community is a coding dojo, where a group of participants solve a programming task together using test-driven development and pair programming. Coding dojo is a form of learning which values concrete experience in a realistic context. In our experiment, we embedded a coding dojo into the Agile practices part of our undergraduate software engineering course. The participating students considered the coding dojo a useful experience, and most of them (82%) would recommend participation in coding dojos for their fellow students, as well.

Categories and Subject Descriptors

K.3.2 [**Computers and Education**]: Computer and Information Science Education *Computer Science Education*

General Terms

Experimentation

Keywords

coding dojo, software engineering, agile methodologies

1. INTRODUCTION

The industry-driven movement towards the use of Agile software engineering practices has caused a stir in higher education. Instructors in software development methodologies need to find a balance between conveying an understanding of the history, traditional plan-based methodologies [12],

and giving enough time to cover Agile methodologies. One of the challenges in introducing Agile methodologies is that higher education is traditionally seen as lecture- and self-study-based, where practical experience plays only a small role, while Agile methodologies are often best learned by truly experiencing them.

For example, the so-called *inspect and adapt* effort, where a team continuously monitors their working processes and adapts them in order to become more efficient, requires deep understanding and practical experience of both the team- and process-specific aspects, as well as an understanding of the problem domain, in which the team acts.

Agile methodologies are a collection of best practices, which are often combined as a development team adapts their practices during a task. For example, the Scrum framework [14] and Kanban method [1] are both often used in combination with best practices from Extreme Programming (XP) [4] such as Pair Programming and Test-Driven Development (TDD) [3].

Teaching Pair programming and TDD in a higher education institution is challenging. Knowing in principle what they mean has only little value since just having abstract, theoretical knowledge about a practice does not imply a deep understanding nor a change in mental processes [5], which should be the purpose of higher education.

We have observed that by asking students to practice pair programming and TDD on their own very rarely leads to success. Especially when students are novice programmers, starting by writing a test first seems to be extremely hard, and proceeding in the small steps that the TDD cycle requires often demands explicit guidance. In order for the instruction focused on Agile practices to have an impact on students' behavior, each student should have the opportunity to truly experience pair programming and TDD in a guided setting. Essentially, an experienced instructor, who provides scaffolding, should be present when pair programming and TDD are practiced by students for the first time.

The work presented in this paper is about how a *coding dojo* [13], a safe learning environment for practising various programming-related skills, can be utilised to convey Agile software engineering best practices as part of a course, and how a dojo is viewed from a student's perspective.

This article is structured as follows. In sections 2 and 3, we explain the pedagogical framework in which we base our instruction, and further detail test-driven development and pair programming. Section 4 discusses various types of coding dojos, and outlines some of the challenges in organizing a dojo in a higher education setting. In section 5, the dojo experiment in our Software Engineering course is explained, and in section 6, the outcome of the dojo experiment is analyzed. Finally, we conclude the experiment, and discuss our ongoing work.

2. PEDAGOGICAL FRAMEWORK

The utilization and creation of a realistic environment for learning Agile software engineering practices is backed up by the theory of situated cognition [5], which emphasises that knowing and doing should not be separated. Having a classical classroom setting, where students listen to a teacher discussing and perhaps demonstrating a technique, may lead to theoretical, abstract knowledge on a topic, but not to deeper understanding that could be easily transferable into practice.

In order for learning of a skill or knowledge to be effective, it should happen in an authentic application context and culture with real tools, where both knowing and doing can be combined. As context, culture and the defined activity all play a part in the learning process, some parts of learning can also be unintentional or unanticipated from the facilitator's point of view. This can be seen in students acquiring potentially harmful working habits, if the situation, in which the students study, does not prevent them.

One way to *situate* the learning in an appropriate context is to apply apprenticeship learning such as cognitive apprenticeship [7]. In cognitive apprenticeship a learner starts by first watching a master, i.e. an instructor, engage a problem. An essential part of the process is that the master explicitly speaks out the mental thought process behind his working process, thus giving a model of the task for the learner. This makes it possible for the learner to start understanding the actual problem-solving process and the tasks that the master performs.

Once the learner has a grasp on the task, she can start performing parts of the task by recalling how the master previously worked. Simply engaging in a problem is not optimal as, despite given a model, the student's behavior is heavily influenced by her confidence on her ability to perform a task [2]. Therefore, at the start, the master scaffolds the student by helping her forward in the task by giving temporary help, ensuring that the student is able to proceed and reaches an optimal working process.

It is important that the student does not become dependent on the scaffolding, and as soon as the student is able to proceed on her own, the scaffolding is dismantled. As the learner proceeds with taking on larger and larger tasks, she also discusses the learning process with the master, i.e. articulates the problem and the domain that they both are engaged in.

3. TEST-DRIVEN DEVELOPMENT AND PAIR PROGRAMMING

Test-driven development (TDD) [3] is a discipline that originates from Extreme Programming [4]. In TDD, the usual software development cycle that starts with design, continues with programming, and ends up in testing, is reversed. The developer starts a programming task by writing a test that specifies a small part of the intended behavior of a component under construction. After the test is done, the developer proceeds to write the code, which makes the test pass. Once the test passes, the developer continues by writing another test, and again the code that makes the test pass. The intention is that the developer does not write code "just in case some feature would be needed in the future", but only if a previously written test requires a feature to be implemented. Writing code only when a test enforces it has a tendency to lead to a codebase that consists of simple and decoupled objects, which have clearly defined interfaces. All of these attributes are usually connected to the extendibility and maintainability of written code [10].

After following the TDD cycle for a while, the developer may notice that the structure of the written code is not optimal, e.g. it may contain redundant parts or lack a needed abstraction. In such a case, the developer must refactor [9] the code to keep its internal quality at a good level. Since refactoring is supposed to be done whenever needed during the TDD-based development, the design of the program evolves as the codebase grows.

TDD is complemented by pair programming [4], where two persons use a single workstation and act together to pursue a goal. The person who possesses the keyboard is often called the *driver* while the other person is called the *navigator*. The driver advances the task by writing the actual code, while the navigator constantly inspects the code that the driver has written and thinks about the problem from a different perspective, perhaps already planning the next step the pair is supposed to take. The driver and the navigator continuously engage in a discussion, where they articulate the next steps and design decisions. Every now and then the persons change roles.

Although pair programming may at first seem overly resource consumptive, it has many benefits. One of the most important benefits is the constant knowledge sharing within the team of programmers that uses pair programming to achieve their goals [6]. In addition, it has been noticed that pair programming produces code that has less defects, and has a more maintainable design than code developed by single developers [6]. Pair programming also improves the discipline of the developers: they become less likely to skip testing, and tend to use their time more efficiently instead of checking email and browsing the web.

Both TDD and test-driven development can be efficiently experienced in a coding dojo, which is a meeting for people willing to practice their coding practices.

4. CODING DOJO

Coding dojo is a meeting where a small group of participants gathers together to practice programming [13]. Its main goal is to act as a safe and non-competitive environment, in which everyone is allowed to learn and make mistakes and share their knowledge so that everyone can improve and become better at their craft. Coding dojos are typically organised by a *dojo master*, whose task is to facilitate the space and time, while the participants engage in solving a problem. Often at least part of the participants acts as an audience, whose task is to monitor the working process of other participants and give feedback and improvement suggestions.

The problem that the participants engage in is usually not too complex and can even be previously unknown to the participants. This way the participants are able to focus more on honing their programming process, and not spend too much time on planning a solution. Another motivation for not giving out too challenging problems is that each group typically contains both novices and experts. However, if the main focus of the session is to practice problem-solving, more challenging problems may be appropriate.

Various types of coding dojo exist. One of the variants is the *randori kata* dojo, in which the participants solve a problem using pair programming and possibly TDD. In randori kata, one of the participants acts as the driver, and one as the navigator. The rest of the participants act as a silent audience, who observe how the driver and the navigator work together towards a solution. After a specific time-interval or via some other mechanism, the driver moves to the audience, the navigator starts to work as the driver, and a member of the audience moves in to act as the navigator.

The driver and the navigator work towards the solution by communicating with each other, making sure they both know what to do next. Although the observers start forming opinions and suggestions about the progress, they must remain quiet. A possible exception is a situation where the driver and the navigator are completely stuck, and indicate that they need help. Naturally, during the switch of navigator and driver, the new navigator can discuss with the previous navigator, who assumes the position of the driver.

In a version where TDD is practiced, the audience can also voice out their thoughts when all tests pass, or if a timeout is deliberately called. During a timeout, the participants revisit their approach and discuss possible alternative strategies.

Another variant of the coding dojo is the *prepared kata* dojo [13], where one or more of the participants have solved a problem previously, and solve it again in the dojo. The rest of the participants review the working process and the solution, and ask questions whenever they have one or do not understand why something was done. The goal is that the audience understands the solution so that they could later attempt to perform it by themselves.

In a coding dojo, the participants are engaged in learning in several ways; the participants can observe and analyze as others work towards a solution, and ask questions or give suggestions. As a participant works towards a solution either as a driver or a navigator, she receives valuable feedback from her pair as well as others, which helps her to reflect on and improve her own working practices.

4.1 Coding Dojos and Higher Education

Coding dojos have been previously organized in a higher education settings as separate sessions, not belonging to any formal courses (see e.g. [13, 16, 8]). Most of the dojos held in universities have been facilitated by outside experts or the students themselves, thus being mostly of self-organizing in nature. In contrast to the previous dojos run in a university setting, our approach was to make dojo part of a mandatory course.

Organizing a coding dojo in a university setting has its challenges. If a coding dojo is embedded within a single course, the availability of the activity is constrained by the course duration. On the other hand, if a dojo is created as an extracurricular activity that does not bring study credits or affect course grades, students may choose not to participate at all, as they often prefer activities that affect course outcomes.

When comparing coding dojos to exercise labs, where students work on problems under the guidance of an instruc-

tor, coding dojos have both advantages and disadvantages. Dojos create an environment, where training and learning agile practices such as TDD and pair programming, which are difficult to practice on your own, can be practiced more easily.

The benefits are not only limited to learning technical skills, but also include practicing highly valued soft skills [11] such as communication. As students work towards a solution, they articulate both the process and the problem, and simultaneously practice voicing out improvements on both domain-specific problem constructs as well as more generic working processes.

Facilitating a coding dojo in University setting can be easier than facilitating a free-for-all coding dojo, as skill-level, tools, and the social context are typically known already beforehand at University.

The disadvantages and challenges of coding dojos are often related to students' self-confidence, values and communication. Students may feel insecure about their own performance, which may make the meeting an uncomfortable situation. Another problem is that some students value the velocity at which a problem is solved more than code quality and maintainability. The more participants there are, the more opinions there are, which makes it harder to form a consensus on what should be done next and how.

In the worst case scenario, some participants take the meeting too seriously, do not participate properly in a bi-directional communication, and get angry at participants who aren't productive enough, while erasing parts of the previous solution as they act as the driver, forcing their own solutions on others. This can typically be prevented by having a dojo master, i.e. the teacher acting as dojo facilitator present, whose task is to remind the participants that mistakes are supposed to happen and that everyone should take it easy. In addition, the dojo master can limit the number of participants to a relatively small number, e.g. between 4 and 6.

However, limiting the group sizes to a small number brings additional demands on the facilities in which the dojos are held, as well as increases the amount of time required from the available instructors.

5. CODING DOJOS AT OUR UNIVERSITY

In our experiment, a randori dojo session was added to our 4th semester undergraduate software engineering course. The goal of the session was to have students practice how TDD and pair programming work in a real-life-like setting, and not just in theory, and also give them the understanding needed to organize coding dojos themselves in the future. Each session lasted two hours, and included roughly 1.5 hours of programming, and a 10 to 20 minute retrospective, during which the participants discussed the overall experience and setting, and considered possible future improvements. Each participant in the course took part in at least one dojo session.

5.1 Test Dojo

Experimenting with adding the dojo content to the course started with a 2-hour *test dojo*, which was held for the course staff and a few voluntary students. In the dojo, the participants worked through a problem, while switching roles to experience all the sides in a dojo.

The test dojo was an invaluable way of discovering some of the pitfalls and difficulties associated with dojos, such as having participants compete in the situation or start dominating the solution. It was also an integral part of the learning process for the course staff so that they could understand and experience what it is like to participate in a dojo, and how a person taking the role of dojo master should behave.

In addition, it was valuable to notice that some of the course staff were in a "lecturing mode", even while acting as dojo masters; they had the feeling that they should be instructing the participants how to proceed. However, as the goal of the dojo is to allow the participants to solve the problem, it was emphasized that the interventions should be kept to a minimum. When advice is needed, instead of giving direct advice, instructors should mostly restrain themselves to posing suitable questions that stimulate the students so that they can come to the right conclusions.

During the test dojos, it was also realised that the dojo masters would need to minimise the stressfulness and competitiveness of the dojos, especially when they would be held for the students.

5.2 Dojo Implementation

Each dojo had 4 to 6 students and a member of course staff as dojo master. The sessions were held in a small room equipped with a laptop and a projector, and the student groups were filled based on the enrollment order. This led to a situation, where participants had varying skill sets and knowledge about programming, testing and TDD. The goal was to make the dojos a fun and relaxed, but educational event, where the students would learn practices that they could also apply in the future.

The coding dojos lasted for 2 hours, applied a 5-minute cycle duration, and the programming task that students were supposed to solve was unveiled step by step by the dojo master. The dojo master emphasized that the goal was to implement the given features in the simplest possible way: this was also to force the need of refactoring the code as the task evolved more complex.

The reason for not letting participants know the full scope of the project already at the start was to simulate the iterative nature of an agile software project where the customer's opinions may evolve during the process. This also gave a concrete example of how the design of the software evolves during an iterative process.

During the coding dojos, the students worked towards building a student registry. The task was designed so that there were easier moments as well as refactoring. The outline of the programming task that the students were working on was as follows:

Task: Student Registry

1. A user is able to list students in a register

2. A user can add a course mark to a student

   (a) A student is identified by her name

   (b) A course is identified by its name

   (c) The course mark includes a grade

3. A user can see the number of students that have passed a course

4. The grade for a course is an integer between 0 and 5, and invalid marks should be ignored

5. A user can see the average grades for a given course

6. A user can see the courses that a student has taken

   (a) For each course, only the best grade is shown

7. A user can see the amount of courses that a student has completed

8. A user can see the grade average for a given student

9. As a course mark is added to a student, an old course mark should be replaced if the new course mark is better for the specific course and student

10. When adding a course mark, the number of credits for the course should also be included

11. A user can see the list of courses that a student has taken

12. A user can see the list of students that have taken a course

The system was developed as a console application, deliberately moving the focus away from UI design towards the internal structure of the application. As the "You aren't gonna need it"-principle was enforced throughout the activity, students were essentially required to start the task by implementing a class that contains a collection of strings; doing the simplest thing that could possibly work. Once the class was implemented, the students proceeded with creating a functionality for adding a course mark. All activities were performed by strictly following TDD, and refactoring was encouraged whenever necessary.

Typically, during the two-hour session, the students were able to finish most of the task. While there was no "perfect solution" during the timeframe, future improvements were also discussed after concluding a session.

6. ANALYSIS

A total of 73 students attended 15 sessions, where they were guided and monitored by the instructors. In addition to facilitating the dojo, instructors also observed outbursts, comments, and working practices, which were later collected to form a coherent view of the students' experiences. In addition, the participants were asked to fill in a survey that studied the applicability of a coding dojo to a higher education context.

6.1 Instructors' Analysis

Although the initial expectation was that the least skillful individuals could feel uncomfortable with the practice, even more talented participants who had previous experience in TDD felt the situation was unnatural at first. As the driver was put into the spotlight, the expectations for her success were high. At first, this caused momentary freezes for some of the drivers, and the navigators on the other hand did not always have a good way of helping the driver.

Once the driver and the navigator got used to their roles and got more familiar with the process, they began to proceed at a more rapid pace. In some dojo sessions this led to the discovery of another pitfall. Some sessions started to see a competitive nature between individuals who were acting as an audience, and those who were acting as the driver and

100

the navigator. Although most of the participants knew each other, some didn't find this competitive situation pleasant or helpful for their coding flow.

As the competitiveness was already experienced in the test dojo, dojo masters were quick to react to the situations, and direct the process back on track.

There was no single typical session. As the proficiency of the students varied considerably, and the students themselves were the primary actors in the sessions, the content and direction was heavily influenced by the skill levels. Depending on the skill level of students, the amount of interaction also varied. In sessions, where most of the students were less proficient in programming, students rarely voiced out their concerns about a specific issue, while in sessions, that had students with existing programming background, e.g. hobby projects or experience from the industry, the students were more active in pointing out improvements and sharing their practices.

Most of the students considered the 5-minute cycle quite short. Sometimes they were spent mostly in understand what the previous pairs had accomplished. Once the tasks got more complex and refactoring was necessary, an intervention was often needed from the dojo master, who advised the pairs to stop tinkering and start to consider and sketch out what changes were needed for the architecture.

6.2 Survey

The survey that the students were asked to fill after the coding dojo contained questions on programming-related background, Likert-scale questions related to the dojo atmosphere, usefulness, learning, and whether the students would suggest participation to their fellow students. In addition, the students were asked to fill in open-ended text questions, where they could assess their learning during the dojo session, and give open feedback and improvement suggestions.

The scale of the Likert-scale questions ranged from "1 = strongly disagree" to "5 = strongly agree". No forced choice method was applied, and the participants also had the option of choosing "3 = neither agree nor disagree".

A total of 50 participants answered the survey (68.5% of the participants), and the answers are summarized in Table 1, from which we have left out the option "3 = neither agree nor disagree".

The results of the survey are displayed in Table 1. Most of the students felt that the dojo situation was not competitive, and that the atmosphere was relaxed. A majority of the students felt that the usefulness of good programming became evident in the dojo, and that a dojo is useful for improving their own programming practices.

Almost one half of the students experienced "Aha!" moments in the dojo, and most of them learned new programming practices and more about how a group works. Over 80% of the students would encourage a fellow student to participate in a dojo, and 70% of them would participate in future coding dojos.

Upon reviewing the textual feedback provided to the open-ended questions, many of the students considered a dojo "A welcome addition to the teaching practices at the department". The most notable objective was that the students felt that they had achieved practical understanding of TDD and pair programming, in addition to avoiding over-engineering of a solution.

Many of the students would have liked to have a clear, textual representation of the problem already at the beginning of the session. We had chosen to reveal the problem step-by-step, which reduces the possibility of over-engineering, forces students to work in small steps and also gave the students a concrete opportunity to experience what the incremental design [15] of software feels like.

Although there were always observers present, the students felt that the situation was relatively relaxing. One of the contributing factors is the relatively fast cycle (5 minutes), which added to the feeling of community, and which some, however, did criticize as being too fast.

Many of the textual comments were also surprising. As the experiment was designed, the goal was to emphasize agile software engineering practices to the students. However, for some students, the dojo introduced them to "life-improving shortcuts and key-combinations", and for some the dojo was the first time they had participated in pair or group programming, and they received positive experiences. As one of the participants put it:

> This was the first time that I participated in any sort of "group programming". The experience definitely lowered the threshold of participating in future events such as hackathlons etc.

6.3 Instructors' Unanticipated Findings

From an instructor's perspective, the dojos worked quite much according to our expectations as a mean of teaching pair programming and TDD. Despite the individual flavour in each dojo session, even the least successful sessions gave the intended experience to the participants.

Dojos gave the instructors a unique opportunity to observe how students act together in an actual problem-solving setting. Through the observations it became evident that the working process of quite a remarkable portion of the students is still somewhat non-optimal, even after nearly two years of studies. Also it became evident that many students used the programming environment in a rather suboptimal way, and did not utilize e.g. the embedded support mechanisms such as shortcuts for automatic code generation, refactoring, and the embedded API-descriptions, which ease programmers' mental burden during repetitive tasks.

The extent to which the suboptimal working habits were observed came as a surprise to the instructors, and gave us a clear indication that we need to take measures against the development of bad habits.

7. CONCLUSIONS AND CURRENT WORK

Coding Dojo is a good addition to teaching Agile software engineering practices because it allows the students to experience practices such as pair programming and TDD in a relatively authentic context. The main benefit over traditional labs is the audience in the coding dojo, whose task is to provide comments and suggestions, which can be used for reflection of the students' own study practices.

A majority of the dojo participants saw the dojo as non-competitive and relaxing, and learned new things about both teamwork and programming. Students in general see a dojo as something that many of them could suggest to others, and many would like to participate in a dojo also in the future.

Table 1: Likert-scale questions of the survey on student perspectives on coding dojo, and the distributions for the student answers.

Question	% s. disagree	% disagree	% agree	% s. agree
atmosphere and usefulness				
The atmosphere in the dojo was relaxed	0%	8%	42%	42%
The atmosphere in the dojo was competitive	36%	36%	2%	2%
Usefulness of good programming practices became evident in the Dojo	2%	18%	46%	10%
Dojo is useful for improving your own programming practices	4%	8%	46%	14%
learning				
I experienced "Aha!" moments in the Dojo	4%	14%	38%	8%
I learned new programming practices in the Dojo	6%	22%	48%	12%
I learned more about how a group works in the Dojo	2%	6%	52%	18%
participation				
I would encourage a fellow student to participate in a coding dojo	2%	0%	54%	28%
I would participate in coding dojos in the future	4%	4%	48%	22%

In our context, the experiment with coding dojos in the software engineering course led to a small-scale student movement that has started to create pop-up coding dojos on campus. As an example, a few of our students that participate in organizing K-12 outreach activities, organized a dojo session for an algorithmics club that is attended by high-school students interested in programming competitions.

During the dojo, many types of learning was observed. One spontaneous outburst after the dojo defines the goal quite well:

> *I had learned about TDD already before, but only now I really understand what it is about.*

In addition to students learning about the intended practices, quite a lot of students indicated that they had learned helpful things such as key combinations and shortcuts, which were not planned as part of the learning objectives beforehand. This is in line with the situated view of learning that stresses that some parts of the learning is also unintentional, as it depends heavily on the context and interaction.

In our current activity, we are supporting the students that wish to organize their own dojos by providing facilities whenever needed. In addition, we are starting to embed the coding dojo in other courses such as our server-side web development course.

8. ACKNOWLEDGEMENTS

The authors would like to thank Juhani Hietikko, Jussi Härkönen, Juho Rautio and Vesa Ylönen from Houston Inc. for hosting a pilot coding dojo, which helped us to smoothen the path for embedding coding dojos into formal education.

9. REFERENCES

[1] D. J. Anderson. *Kanban*. Blue Hole, 2010.
[2] A. Bandura. *Self-efficacy*. Wiley Online Library, 1994.
[3] K. Beck. *Test Driven Development: By Example*. Addison-Wesley, 2002.
[4] K. Beck and C. Andres. *Extreme Programming Explained: Embrace Change (2nd Edition)*. Addison-Wesley Professional, 2004.
[5] J. Brown, A. Collins, and P. Duguid. Situated cognition culture of learning. *Educational Researcher*, 18(1):32, 1989.
[6] A. Cockburn and L. Williams. The costs and benefits of pair programming. In *the First International Conference on Extreme Programming and Flexible Processes in Software Engineering*. ACM, 2000.
[7] A. Collins, J. Brown, and A. Holum. Cognitive apprenticeship: Making thinking visible. *American Educator*, 15(3):6–46, 1991.
[8] Dojo coding day at Durban University of Technology. http://www.pieterg.com/2012/6/dojo-coding-day-at-durban-university-of-techn.
[9] M. Fowler. *Refactoring: improving the design of existing code*. Addison-Wesley Longman Publishing Co., Inc., Boston, MA, USA, 1999.
[10] R. C. Martin. *Clean Code: A Handbook of Agile Software Craftsmanship*. Prentice Hall, 2008.
[11] R. L. Meier, M. R. Williams, and M. A. Humphreys. Refocusing our efforts: Assessing non-technical competency gaps. *Journal of Engineering Education*, 89(3):377–385, 2000.
[12] W. Royce. Managing the development of large software systems. In *Proceedings of IEEE WESCON 26*. TeX Users Group, August 1970.
[13] D. Sato, H. Corbucci, and M. Bravo. Coding dojo: An environment for learning and sharing agile practices. In *Proceedings of AGILE '08*. IEEE, 2008.
[14] K. Schwaber and M. Beedle. *Agile Software Development with SCRUM*. Prentice Hall, 2002.
[15] J. Shore. *The Art of Agile Development*. O'Reilly, 2010.
[16] University of Houston Coding dojo. http://www.codedojo.org/.

QuizPower: A Mobile App with App Inventor and XAMPP Service Integration

David Meehan
University of New Hampshire
88 Commercial Street
Manchester, NH 03101
603 454 6552
david.meehan.unh@gmail.com

Mihaela Sabin
University of New Hampshire
88 Commercial Street
Manchester, NH 03101
603 641 4144
mihaela.sabin@unh.edu

ABSTRACT

This paper details the development of a mobile app for the Android operating system using MIT App Inventor language and development platform. The app, Quiz Power, provides students a way to study course material in an engaging and effective manner. At its current stage the app is intended strictly for use in a mobile app with App Inventor course, although it provides the facility to be adapted for other courses by simply changing the web data store. Development occurred during the spring semester of 2013. Students in the course played a vital role in providing feedback on course material, which would be the basis for the structure of the quiz as well as the questions. The significance of the project is the integration of the MIT App Inventor service with a web service implemented and managed by the department.

Categories and Subject Descriptors

D.1.7 [**Visual Programming**]; D.2.6 [**Programming Environments**]: Graphical environment; H.3.5 [**Online Information Services**]: Data sharing

General Terms

Design, Languages, Experimentation

Keywords

App Inventor, mobile computing, data store, web service

1. MOTIVATION

1.1 Mobile Computing First and For Most

Computing Technology program at University of New Hampshire at Manchester has expanded its computing curricula with an introductory course that satisfies the University's Environment, Technology, and Society general education requirement, CIS 415 Mobile Computing First and For Most. The course teaches computational thinking in the context of solving problems of social and environmental relevance and emphasizes issues of inclusiveness of diverse cultural backgrounds, life experiences, and talents that all students bring to class. Students learn how to create mobile apps for Android operating system with App

SIGITE13, October 10-12, 2013, Orlando, FL, USA
Copyright 2013 ACM 978-1-4503-2239-3/13/10...$15.00.
http://dx.doi.org/10.1145/2512276.2512300

Inventor, a visual blocks-based programming language and development platform. The App Inventor project, led by Hal Abelson from MIT and Mark Friedman from Google was released publicly in 2010. App Inventor codebase, run-time environment, app projects' cloud storage, and community resources are now supported and hosted by the MIT Center for Mobile Learning [1].

COMP 415 was first offered in Spring 2013. The class had fifteen students: ten students in the B.S. Computer Information Systems (CIS) program and five students majoring in History, Communication Arts, Political Science, Biology, and Engineering Technology. Although enrollment sample size is small, gender and race demographic data breakdown of 13% female students (both CIS majors) and 20% underrepresented minorities in computing showed a higher participation from underrepresented groups than gender and race representation percentages in the CIS program (10% females and 5% underrepresented minorities).

The course requirements consisted of eight homework assignments (16% of the final grade), two exams (48%), one 6-week creative project developed by teams of two students (10%), one 6-week creative project developed by teams of five students (20%), and project presentation at the University's Undergraduate Research Conference (6%).

1.2 Guided Practice and Self-Assessment

App Inventor with Android smartphones, coupled with a studio-based teaching and learning model [2], suggests a positive effect on students' motivation, creativity, achievement, and attitudes towards computer science [3]. Class pedagogy of studio-based learning was further inspired by the course textbook [4] and its scaffolding approach to learning from telling the app's user story to creating an original app:

tell $\rightarrow$ build $\rightarrow$customize $\rightarrow$conceptualize $\rightarrow$ create

In this model, when students progress through these five layers, the scope of guidance they receive decreases, while expectation for higher-order cognitive skills increases.

Students in CIS 415 reported more study time out of class than in other classes and were fully engaged in peer learning activities: pair programming lab exercises; structured class forum participation; collaborative project activities during 3-hour weekly class meetings; and further collaboration outside class to share and review artifacts with Google Drive and Google Sites services.

Students became proficient with *building* apps by following tutorial instructions. The use of peer learning helped students meet the *customization* requirements of apps built from tutorials. What remained a challenge was *conceptualizing* programming language constructs and design techniques. These competencies were critical for scaffolding competencies to *create* apps from description of the app's features and user stories.

To help students achieve conceptual learning outcomes, homework assignments and creative project iterations were enhanced with worksheets that required students to practice test questions. Retrieval, as a learning activity, has been found to be a powerful way to enhance conceptual learning in science [5]. To make retrieval practice integral part of the class learning activities, four worksheets with more than 80 questions were assigned over the course of the semester. A CIS senior and student tech consultant in the department (this paper's first author) and the course instructor (paper's second author) developed and refined the worksheets' questions and answer keys.

We had plenty of opportunities to learn about students' struggle with concept comprehension and inferences from in-class activities, tutoring and help sessions, and class forum discussions. Our quest for composing relevant questions and improving the clarity and conciseness of the answers gave us the idea of QuizPower, an app to guide students through a self-directed assessment and practice with test questions.

2. OBJECTIVE

QuizPower research and development project was intended to:
- Guide students in their practice with test questions that assess comprehension and require inferences;
- Be a case study of a creative project with educational relevance for students.

The prototype we developed is an interactive tool with which students:
- (1) Get access to questions organized by topics
- (2) Select topics to study and quiz themselves
- (3) Go through topic questions in a random order
- (4) Enter their answer
- (5) Compare their answer with the tool's answer
- (6) Self-assess quality of answer to remove question from further study if answered adequately
- (7) Receive feedback on progress based on how many questions were answered correctly from those attempted.

Non-functional requirements of the project were that:
- (1) QuizPower be developed primarily in App Inventor
- (2) Questions be stored in a web data store.

3. PROJECT APPROACH AND METHODS

3.1 App Inventor Platform

App Inventor is a free and open source server software that runs in the MIT App Inventor's cloud. Developers need a Google account to access the App Inventor's development service[1]. To design an app's user interface and decide on the structure of its architectural components, developers need to use a browser, in which they run the Component Designer tool. To implement the app's behavior and logic of the component methods, developers use the Blocks Editor, a Java web application that is downloaded on demand from the Component Designer on the developer's client computer.

The App Inventor language has a rich library of component classes[2]. Component classes represent basic user interface facilities (text box, button, canvas, arrangement, etc.), sprites (touch-sensitive objects), and a wealth of built-in, smartphone-specific functional features (texting, phone calling, contact search, sensors, camera, sound player, video player, etc.). Apps developed with App Inventor can be compiled and packaged into an application package file (APK) to be distributed and installed on Android mobile devices. The packaging command, available in the Component Designer, generates the APK file and downloads it to the client computer, a USB-connected phone, or a phone connected over Wi-Fi. The downloading over Wi-Fi option requires the MIT AI Companion app, which establishes a connection between the Android mobile device and client computer over the MIT RendezVous Server.

3.2 Software Development Process

We developed the project in spring 2013 over a ten-week time period using an agile software development approach with weekly sprints. At the beginning of each sprint we chose the sprint backlog items. We held two or three meetings every week to track our progress and update the backlog of work items.

Before we sketched user stories and user interface mockups, we sampled student questions and answers from a variety of sources: class forum, in-class lab activities, student assignment self-evaluations, and help sessions. Our goal was to create practice worksheets that were informed by student common misconceptions. We classified over 80 questions into sixteen topical categories: animation, architecture, components, conditionals, control flow, data types, debugging, events and event handlers, expressions, lists, loops, procedures, sensors, software development process, variables, databases and web services. These questions became the basis of the students self-directed assessment and practice we envisioned for the QuizPower app.

As explained in the following sections, architectural and implementation decisions have changed during development iterations in order to address performance and maintainability issues.

3.3 Quiz Questions Data Store

3.3.1 *App Inventor's Google App Engine Database Service*

Early on in the development process we determined that the use of a data store was necessary to reduce the coupling between the quiz questions and the QuizPower engine. The data store also allowed us to experiment with different branches of the code base independently of acquiring, refining, and encoding quiz questions.

App Inventor library has a database component class called TinyWebDB. This class facilitates communication between the app and a specialized web-based database of (tag, value) pairs, hosted through the Google App Engine. TinyWebDB component has StoreValue( ) and GetValue( ) methods, by which tagged values are placed into and retrieved from the database. When a GetValue( ) server request succeeds, a GotValue event is generated with (tag, value) information that is made available to the app's logic (Figure 1).

---

[1] http://beta.appinventor.mit.edu

[2] http://beta.appinventor.mit.edu/learn/reference/

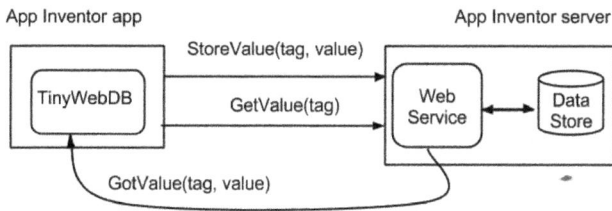

Figure 1: App Inventor communication with Google App Engine web service via TinyWebDB methods and event handler[3].

Data store hosting enabled by the Google App Engine has the advantage of eliminating any administrative overhead, including administration tasks for scaling the service instance. The database administration tasks left to us were to manage entries in the data store (get, store, view, and delete operations), control write access to the data store for testing purposes only, and monitor usage.

By default, TinyWebDB component communicates with a web service[4] that manages a data store shared by all possible App Inventor users. The service limits, however, the number of database entries to 1,000 per user. To create a custom web service for our QuizPower app, we used the Google App Engine Launcher client application to:

- Adapt a custom web service template in the textbook [4] such that it uniquely identifies the QuizPower data web store among Google App Engine web services

- Set QuizPower web service properties (title, URL, and other web service required properties).

The drawbacks with this solution were query performance and ease of data manipulation. We did not want to limit the number of questions per topic that a student would be interested in practicing with. What we observed, however, was that the time to retrieve the questions for a single topic (on average 20 questions/topic) was more than one second (on average 3 seconds) when we run experiments that were using the college's Wi-Fi network. This was not problematic until the interface was refined to include the possibility of a student requesting questions from more than one topic.

We also expected to be able to change quiz question data in the web data store easily and efficiently. Google App Engine data web service has very simple data manipulation operations. There is no facility to store multiple entries from a data file or selectively update or delete multiple entries from the data store based on filtering conditions. Given these restrictions, our focus shifted to a relational database solution that integrates MySQL with App Inventor.

3.3.2 MySQL Service Integration

Google App Engine supports a SQL database instance via Google Cloud SQL. This is a fully managed web service that offers a scalable MySQL database running on Google infrastructure. Although this service met our performance needs, it is not a free and open source software solution, and we did not have the expertise to delve in it right away. The question we were

interested in was whether we can integrate our own instance of a MySQL database with App Inventor.

To establish communication between the QuizPower app and MySQL database instance, we used the App Inventor Web component class. This class has methods that make HTTP GET and POST requests to a given URL to get or post data in text stream format. There are two methods of the Web component class that we used for integration with a relational database:

1. get( ) request - initiates communication with the web app specified in the URL property of the Web component instance. SaveProperty value of the WebService instance determines whether a GotText or GotFile event is triggered. In our implementation, this value is set to false to trigger GotText event. It performs an HTTP GET request.

2. gotText( ) event handler - takes four parameters: URL, response code, response type, and the actual content of the response. Response content is in text stream format and received upon successful completion of the get( ) request.

To bridge the App Inventor communication with a relational database, we configured a run-time environment that had MySQL, PHP, and Apache web server support bundled together. We used a server machine managed by our department and installed a XAMPP[5] stack instance. Next, we created a relational database using MySQL to store quiz questions organized by topics. We then developed a PHP application to retrieve and produce a text stream with quiz questions from the database – all of them or filtered by topics. In the QuizPower app, we created WebService, an instance of the App Inventor's Web component class, and initialized it with the URL of the PHP app.

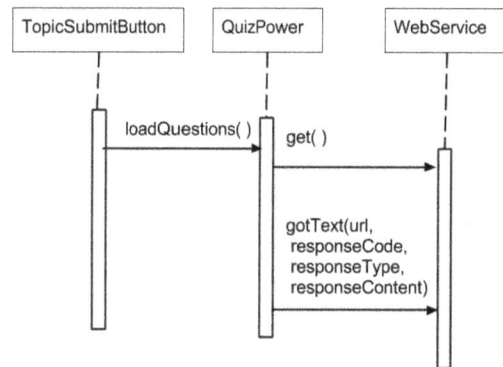

Figure 2 QuizPower interaction with WebService.

In Figure 2, we show the interaction between the user's selection of topics and the WebService operations that perform data store retrieval of topic questions.

---

[3] Figure 1 is adapted from Chapter 10 Persistent Data [4].

[4] http://appinvtinywebdb.appspot.com

[5] Free and open source cross-platform distribution of Apache, HTTP server, MySQL database, and interpreters for scripts in PHP and Perl (www.apachefriends.org/en/xampp.html)

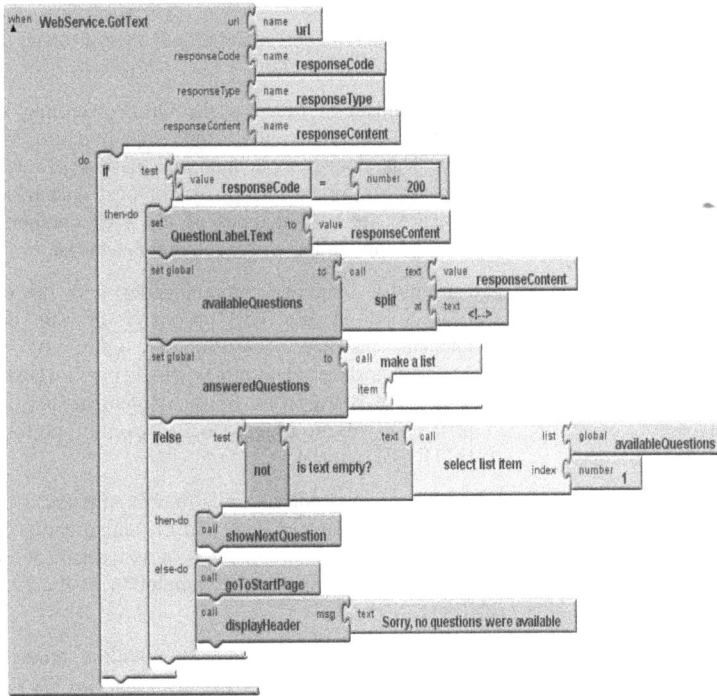

Figure 3. QuizPower Blocks Editor view of the gotText event handler.

Figure 4. QuizPower's Component Designer view.

After a student selects any number of question topics, the QuizPower app calls WebService.get( ) to make a request to the URL of the PHP application. The underlying HTTP GET request carries topic information in the URL query string. The PHP application extracts topic information from the $_GET associative array and communicates with the MySQL database to retrieve a list of corresponding questions and answers. The list is then "echoed" into a dynamic HTML page that is sent back as a text stream captured by the responseContent parameter of the WebService.gotText( ) event handler. Figure 3 illustrates the App Inventor implementation of the GotText( ) event handler.

4. RESULTS

The result at the end of the spring 2013 semester was a mobile application developed with App Inventor for the Android platform. The app maintains a list of questions related to topics the student selects when starting the app. The decisions we made during development have improved the app's performance and usability. The app can be easily scaled to work with any number of quiz questions and topics by simply adding new questions and topics to the database and corresponding selection buttons to the app's interface.

4.1 Components

The foundation for all apps developed in App Inventor is a rich library of component classes. Component instantiations from these classes are objects that perform the app's work. When creating components, the developer initializes the component property values.

Figure 4 has the list of all components used by the Quiz Power app. The object hierarchy shows aggregation associations among QuizPower components, as displayed in the Component Designer tool. Except for the SolutionNotifier and WebService components, all the other components model the app's interface, with buttons, labels, and horizontal and table arrangements.

4.2 User Interface

User interface arrangements are hidden or displayed depending on the user activity. In total, there are three main views: topic selection view modeled by the TopicPage, question view modeled by the QustionPage, and the solution view corresponding to the SolutionPage (Figure 4).

When students first start the app, they are presented with the topic selection view (Figure 5). Upon making their topic selection, they see the question view, in which they answer questions picked at random from the selected topics. Upon submitting an answer to a question, the solution view presents the correct answer. Students self-assess their answer and continue practicing with the remaining questions.

Our initial design had multiple-choice questions. In that scenario, the student answer was checked against a correct choice. Although this version was simple to implement, figuring out meaningful choices to pick from was the difficult part. Literature on peer instruction with concept test questions points to the challenge of writing effective multiple choice questions [6]. We decided to start with short answer questions and gain more insight about student misconceptions before moving to multiple-choice questions.

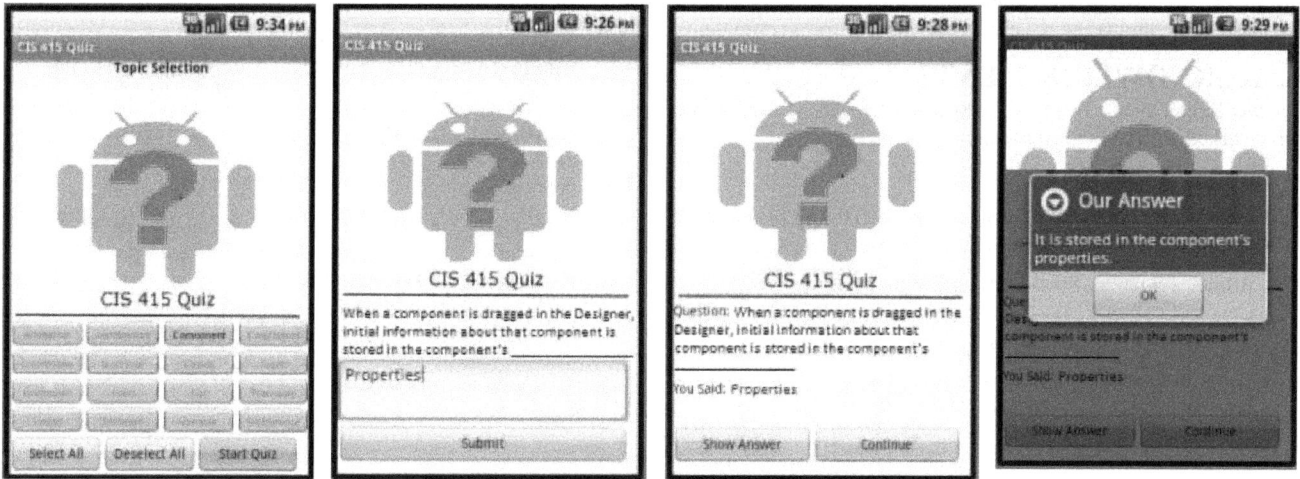
Figure 5. QuizPower user experience sample.

The final result was a simple solution that displays the student answer along with the correct answer. In this case students could use prompt feedback to judge the accuracy of their answers. In Figure 6 we show the activity diagram of the app's user interface.

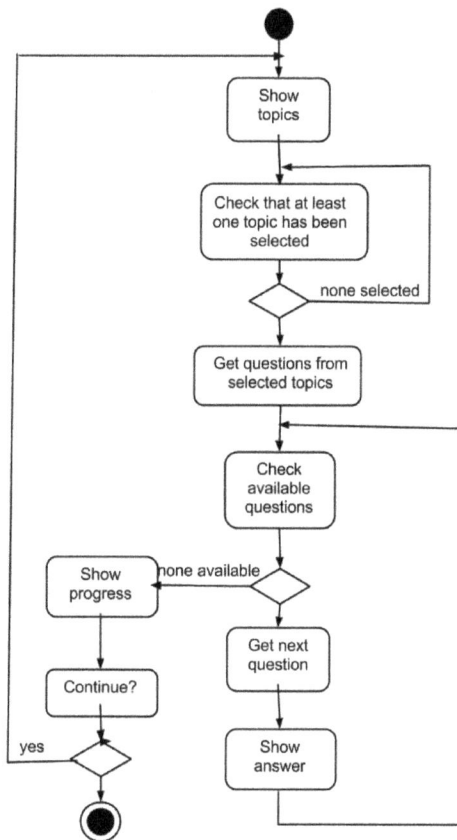

Figure 6. Activity diagram of the QuizPower user interface.

4.3 MySQL Integration
The most important finding of the QuizPower development project was the integration of MIT's App Inventor development services with a web service hosted by the department infrastructure. The MySQL database implementation proved to be successful in reducing query times and simplifying database management operations. The end result was a high performance question and answer retrieval app, which could scale well regardless of the number of topics selected. Using a MySQL database instead of the conventional TinyWebDB service simplified our App Inventor codebase and eliminated tedious data manipulation and encoding schemes imposed by TinyWebDB. MySQL integration with App Inventor via a PHP application opens many opportunities for using App Inventor platform to develop more sophisticated apps with much larger and complex data stores.

5. CONCLUSION
The goal of our project was to develop QuizPower, an app for Android mobile devices using the App Inventor language and MIT App Inventor development and packaging service. Our motivation for creating QuizPower is supported by evidence that retrieval practice is a powerful way to promote meaningful learning of complex concepts commonly found in science education. With QuizPower, students in a general education course for all majors could practice test questions to better learn concepts in a mobile computing course. The project's current product is a working prototype written in App Inventor, PHP, and MySQL. This implementation solution integrates App Inventor development and packaging service with a XAMP-based execution environment.

Further work with this project has multiple directions. First, we plan to deploy the app in a live, production environment for use in the CIS 415 course in our department, as well as similar courses in other STEM disciplines in our college. The goal of making QuizPower publicly available is to improve and expand the collection of test questions. Second, we are interested in converting the app's codebase from App Inventor to Java to gain more control over the app's performance and functionality. We would also like to provide students with a preliminary evaluation of their answers based on the presence of desired keywords. A keyword could be a simple word or grouping of words with similar meaning. Finding keywords indicative of the goodness of an answer would require learning from the app's usage and application of machine learning techniques.

Finally, we plan to develop a MakeQuizPower app for course instructors to manage the topics and questions in MySQL database, thus eliminating the need to do any SQL programming.

6. ACKNOWLEDGMENTS

We would like to acknowledge the Spring 2013 CIS 415 students, who worked with us in the development of this app.

7. REFERENCES

[1] MIT Center for Mobile Learning. 2013. MIT App Inventor. Retrieved from http://appinventor.mit.edu.

[2] Brown, J.S. 2006. New Learning Environment for the 21st Century: Exploring the Edge. *Change* (September/October).

[3] Ahmad, K. and Gestwicki, P. 2013. Studio-based learning and App Inventor for Android in an introductory CS course for non-majors. In *Proceeding of the 44th ACM technical symposium on Computer science education* (SIGCSE '13). ACM, New York, NY, USA, 287-292.

[4] Wolber, D., Abelson, H., Spertus, E., and Looney, L. 2011. App Inventor: Create Your Own Android Apps. O'Reilly Media.

[5] Karpicke, J. D., & Blunt, J. R. 2011. Retrieval practice produces more learning than elaborative studying with concept mapping. *Science*, 331, 772-775.

[6] Grissom, S., Simon, B., Beck, L., and Chizhik, A. 2013. Alternatives to lecture: revealing the power of peer instruction and cooperative learning. In *Proceeding of the 44th ACM technical symposium on Computer science education* (SIGCSE '13). ACM, New York, NY, USA, 283-284.

A Preliminary Review of Undergraduate Programming Students' Perspectives on Writing Tests, Working with Others, & Using Peer Testing

Alessio Gaspar, Sarah Langevin
University of South Florida in Lakeland
3433 Winter Lake Road
Lakeland, FL 33803-9807
863-667-7088
alessio@usf.edu

Naomi Boyer
Polk State College
999 Ave. H. NE.
Winter Haven, Fl. 33881
863-298-6854
nboyer@polk.edu

Ralph Tindell
University of South Florida
4202 E. Fowler Avenue
Tampa, FL 33620
863-914-3032
rtindell@cse.usf.edu

CEReAL group – http://cereal.forest.usf.edu/

ABSTRACT

Techniques such as Pair Programming, or allowing students to run their programs against a reference test harness, have demonstrated their effectiveness in improving grades or retention rates. This paper proposes to supplement the existing literature by investigating students' perceptions of the benefits of writing tests, working with other students and using Peer Testing. Responses to an online anonymous survey cast new light on the relation between testing and programming and confirm previously postulated limitations of collaborative approaches; i.e. the unbalanced nature of contributions and lack of didactic interactions in student groups. We then examine how Peer Testing is perceived and discuss its relation to both collaboration and test-based pedagogies.

Categories and Subject Descriptors

K.3.2 [**Computers and Education**]: Computer and Information Science Education – *computer science education, curriculum.*

General Terms

Measurement, Human Factors.

Keywords

Peer Testing, Novice Programmers, Programming Pedagogy.

1. INTRODUCTION

A significant body of literature exists on the benefits of having novice programmers write tests; refer to [2][3] for examples. Using testing principles to enable students to run their programs against the instructor's reference test harness has also proven helpful [4][5]. Peer Testing, a variant in which students run their programs against other students' tests, has been less studied [6][7]. This idea is based on the assumption, well-grounded in educational theory, that students are more likely to be challenged by tests that are within their zone of proximal development [13] than by tests provided by the instructor. Previous work also highlights the relation between Peer Testing and the introduction of constructivism in pair programming activities [8][9][10][11].

This paper proposes to investigate in more details the specific benefits to students of writing tests, working with others freely, and using Peer Testing. To gain deeper insight, we identify subpopulations of respondents characterized by their affinity for writing tests or working with others. These subpopulations are then compared to one another with respect to attitudes toward all three learning activities.

The remainder of this paper is organized as follows. Section 2 provides background information on this study and details on our methodology. Sections 3, 4 and 5, respectively, analyze students' perspectives on using tests, working with others and using Peer Testing. Section 6 discusses findings and future work.

2. BACKGROUND

This section establishes our study's specifics in terms of the survey population, material taught, and pedagogies used. We also discuss the research methodology for collecting data.

2.1 Research Methodology

An anonymous online survey hosted on Survey Monkey was used to gather students' attitudes and perspectives. A link for the survey was provided to students via announcement on the Learning Management System (Blackboard).

Participation was optional but earned extra credit to reward participants for their time. To keep the survey anonymous, a "key" was provided on the last page of the survey. Students were invited to email that key to their instructor for extra points. To discourage students from providing random responses to get the key, an option was available to obtain the key without responding to the survey.

Most questions allowed respondents to provide feedback using one of the following Likert scales:

- **5-point agreement Likert scale** with labels "Strongly Disagree", "Disagree", "Neutral", "Agree", "Strongly Disagree". Results are presented in terms of labels "Agree" / "Neutral" / "Disagree" by aggregating responses on the 2 first and 2 last labels of the original scale. Sample questions: Q3, Q4, Q5, Q6, Q8, Q12, Q13, Q14, Q15, Q16.
- **5-point frequency Likert scale** with labels "Almost Never", "Seldom", "Sometimes", "Often", "Most of the time". Responses were presented using labels "Rarely" / "Sometimes" / "Often" by aggregating responses on the two first and two last labels of the original scale. Sample questions: Q9, Q10.

- **3-point frequency Likert scale** with labels "Often", "Sometimes", "Never". Sample question: Q7

In addition, average ratings were reported by assigning integer values starting at 1 to each label.

2.2 Surveyed Population

The survey population consisted of junior standing undergraduates, enrolled in IT Program Design during fall 2012. A total of 30 students visited the survey page, 14 opted to obtain the key without responding, 16 opted to answer the questions but only 15 of them actually answered the questions. We refer to the latter group as population P0 since we will identify sub-groups later in the paper.

IT Program Design is the 2nd programming course for IT majors. To gain admittance, students must pass an introductory programming class, which is often taught in Java with a focus on a "fundamentals first", as opposed to an "objects first" pedagogy. IT Program Design focusses on three main learning outcomes.

First, it explicitly teaches the thought process used to deliver programs from requirements. Many students learn in other courses only to work with requirements that fully specify solutions in plain English, which they then translate into Java.

Second, it introduces students to system-level concepts such as execution stacks, pointers, memory allocation.

Third, it prepares students for upper-level system-oriented offerings using the C language [12].

Topics covered map to [1]: fundamentals, functions, arrays, pointers, strings, dynamic memory allocation, user-defined types and elementary data structures. These topics are covered in 7 modules. The material, excluding graded assignments and quizzes, is available at

http://cereal.forest.usf.edu/clue/progdesign/.

2.3 Pedagogy

IT Program Design is taught as an online asynchronous offering. Students work on the various activities in each module on their own schedule as long as they meet set deadlines.

Each module is two weeks long. The first week is devoted to reading assignments; posting questions on forums; meeting on Elluminate to get personalized help; working on apprenticeship exercises; and watching step-by-step solution videos. The latter are implementations of cognitive apprenticeship [8]. By the end of each module's first week students take a time-limited, single attempt allowed, graded quiz online.

During the second week, students work on a mini project. Detailed feedback is provided along with a "satisfactory or not" evaluation, which earns students participation points.

IT Program Design's main pedagogical innovations reside in its use of apprenticeship exercises, testing and peer testing.

The topic of apprenticeship exercises is out of the scope of this paper, but the reader is referred to [8][9][10][11] for details. Writing a test harness is strongly encouraged for non-graded practice assignments (PAs) and required in graded programming assignments (GPAs). Originally, testing was introduced to help address the problem of loss of intentionality in programming [10].

Peer Testing was used in all practice and graded assignments. Students are instructed to post the file or files implementing the test functions in their project on a forum. They may download other students' test files and run their solutions against them.

3. PERSPECTIVES ON TESTING

This section investigates students' perspectives on writing tests for their programs as part of learning to program.

3.1 Survey Questions

Our first question, Q2, focused on establishing the degree to which students used tests out of compliance vs. genuinely appreciating their benefits. The question was as follows:

Q2 *Which of the following describes best your usage of tests this past semester;*
   1. *I wrote tests for all my programs, graded or not*
   2. *I only wrote tests for graded programming assignments, even when they didn't require it*
   3. *I only wrote tests when the graded programming assignments required it*

Students selected one of the three available options. The first one captures positive attitudes toward testing whereby the respondent used tests in all the programs they wrote without external reward. The second is meant to identify respondents who value testing enough to leverage it in graded assignments but who may not see the point in using it in every program they write. The last statement is meant for respondents who only used tests in order not to lose points. This question allowed us to identify two sub-populations:

P1 *Students who adopted testing in all their activities without need for external rewards – Q2 response #1*
P2 *Students who used testing as compliance with mandatory requirements – Q2 response #3*

The next questions, Q3 / Q4 / Q5, evaluated the perceived usefulness of using tests for, respectively, debugging programs, understanding requirements and improving programming skills.

Q3 *Designing tests helped me find errors in my programs.*
Q4 *Designing tests helped me better understand the requirements for my programs*
Q5 *Designing tests helped me learn to program.*

Students were invited to rate their agreement with the above statements using a 5-points agreement Likert scale.

3.2 Observations

Table 1 summarizes responses to Q2. A single student adopted testing only for graded assignments. The majority of others adopted testing for all their programs; thus, suggesting its perceived usefulness. This assessment is in line with other studies on the positive impact of testing e.g. [2][3][4][5].

Table 1 – Q2

Response	#
I wrote tests for all my programs, graded or not	9
I only wrote tests for graded programming assignments, even when they didn't require it	1
I only wrote tests when the graded programming assignments required it	5

Table 1 shows that the sizes of subpopulations P1 and P2 are, respectively, N=9 and N=5. Table 2 shows the levels of agreement of populations P0, P1 and P2 with questions Q3 to Q5. A majority of respondents agreed to the three types of benefits.

Looking at the average rating for P0 instead of the aggregated responses suggests a marginally stronger agreement level for Q3, with Q4 and then Q5. Benefits to students are most obvious as they relate to finding bugs rather than understanding requirements or even learning to program in general. P2 respondents follow the same ranking while P1 respondents equally rate their agreement to all three benefits.

Results suggest that students who do not find a benefit in writing tests also only use tests when required to do so.

Table 2 – Q3 to Q5

Question	P	Disagree	Neutral	Agree	Avg
Q3	P0	1	5	9	3.87
	P1	0	2	7	4.22
	P2	1	3	1	3.00
Q4	P0	3	4	8	3.60
	P1	0	2	7	4.22
	P2	3	2	0	2.40
Q5	P0	3	3	9	3.53
	P1	0	1	8	4.22
	P2	3	2	0	2.20

3.3 Discussions

The initial impression is that P2 students seem to be compliant learners in so far as they used tests only when required to do so in graded assignments. However, most compliant learners should have seized the option described in section 2.3, which allowed them to get the survey key without taking the survey.

It is therefore possible, in contradiction to the available literature [2][3][4][5][9], that writing tests was perceived as genuinely useless by P2 students. Table 2 shows that disagreement levels for P2 respondents are non-uniform. The highest agreement level for P2 was on that writing tests helped in finding bugs. Due to the overall agreement, regardless of subpopulations, this outcome is potentially one of the main agreed-upon benefits of writing tests.

Writing tests to formalize requirements was expected to be helpful by triggering questions that would help students better understand expectations. However, P2 responses suggest that representing requirements in tests was not more helpful than simply implementing them directly in the program. This contrasts the educational benefits of writing tests with those observed by software engineers for whom they represent a more objective formalization of requirements.

Similarly, P2 students felt that writing tests did not help improve programming skills in general. While testing undeniably yields better quality software, the skills involved in writing tests are not necessarily the same as those used in writing programs. As such, tests might help students become better developers in the long term without supporting in the short term their acquisition of more elementary programming skills.

4. PERSPECTIVE ON PROGRAMMING WITH OTHERS

This section establishes the attitude of our students regarding working with others on programming tasks.

4.1 Survey Questions

The first question is meant to identify subpopulations based on whether respondents worked with others.

Q7   *Rate how often you've worked on programming tasks with other students regardless of whether they were graded or non-graded; e.g. programming assignments, group projects, exercises or simply while participating in "study groups."*

Respondents were asked to answer the question two times: "*Before taking this course*" and "*During this course*". Each response used a 3-point Frequency Likert scale. This question allowed us to distinguish two sub-populations:

P3   *Students who actually worked with other students during this course; Q7 responses "Often" or "Sometimes".*

P4   *Students who never worked with other students in this offering;*

Q7 responses "Never".

Question Q8 used a 5-point agreement Likert scale to measure respondents' perspectives on working with other students.

Q8   *Rate your levels of agreement with the following statements. Working with other students on programming tasks...*
- *...is more enjoyable than working alone*
- *... is more beneficial to my grades than working alone*
- *... is more beneficial to improving my individual programming skills than working alone*
- *... is more beneficial to understanding how to apply the lectures than working alone*

Question Q9 used a 5-point frequency Likert scale to measure how often students "take the lead" in terms of efforts or tutoring.

Q9   *How "balanced" are the contributions of the other students working with you?*
- *I end up contributing more toward the end result than others*
- *I end up explaining more to others than they explain to me*

Q10 offered a list of activities for respondents to rate using the same 5-point frequency Likert scale. These activities exemplified leadership (1), responsibility (2), tutoring by explanations (3,4), involvement in others' work (5,6), tutoring by lecturing (7) and constructivist tutoring (8). See Table 6 for activities list.

Q10   *Rate how much of the following types of contributions you provide when working with other students on programming tasks <list of contributions follows – see Table 6 for details>*

4.2 Observations

Table 3 suggests an increase in how often students worked with others from previous semesters and this offering. It also establishes the size of our subpopulations; P3 is N=9, P4 is N=6.

Table 3 – Q7

Responses	Never	Some times	Often	Avg
Before this offering	8	7	0	2.53
During this offering	6	5	4	2.13

Table 4 shows the response distribution for Q8. P0 students agreed in majority to all statements with marginal differences. The average ratings show statements #2 and #3 as being in the lead.

Table 4 – Q8

	Responses	P	Disagree	Neutral	Agree	Avg
1	...is more enjoyable than working alone	P0	2	5	8	3.47
		P3	0	2	7	4.11
		P4	2	3	1	2.50
2	... is more beneficial to my grades than working alone	P0	2	4	9	3.60
		P3	0	1	8	4.22
		P4	2	3	1	2.67
3	... is more beneficial to improving my individual programming skills than working alone	P0	2	4	9	3.60
		P3	0	1	8	4.22
		P4	2	3	1	2.67
4	... is more beneficial to understanding how to apply the lectures than working alone	P0	3	5	7	3.40
		P3	1	2	6	3.89
		P4	2	3	1	2.67

The fact that students rated identically the benefits to their grades and to the improvement of their programming skills suggests they perceive both as equivalent.

When comparing sub-populations P4 & P3 students from the former have more pronounced disagreement / neutral feedback.

Table 5 shows Q9 responses. Most students rarely take the lead in contributing and even more rarely in explaining to others. This suggests that, as could be expected, regardless of whether students work together in a balanced manner [9] their focus is not on helping the other students but on completing the project.

Table 5 – Q9

Responses	P	Rarely	Some times	Often	Avg
I end up contributing more toward the end result than others	P0	7	4	4	
	P3	4	3	2	2.67
	P4	3	1	2	
I end up explaining more to others than they explain to me	P0	8	3	4	2.53
	P3	5	2	2	2.44
	P4	3	2	1	2.67

Table 6 Q10 responses suggest that the majority of respondents rarely engage in the activities we listed when working with others.

Table 6 – Q10

#	Statement	P	Rarely	Some times	Often	Avg
1	Leading by breaking down the problem then assigning tasks to others & myself	P0	8	6	1	2.07
		P3	5	3	1	2.11
		P4	3	3	0	2.00
2	Implementing the parts of the overall project which were assigned to me	P0	5	5	5	2.87
		P3	3	2	4	3.00
		P4	2	3	1	2.67
3	Explaining the parts I implemented to the other students	P0	4	10	1	2.60
		P3	2	6	1	2.78
		P4	2	4	0	2.33
4	Explaining to other students how to implement their parts	P0	7	7	1	2.27
		P3	4	4	1	2.33
		P4	3	3	0	2.17
5	Fixing bugs in other students' parts	P0	10	5		1.93
		P3	7	2	0	1.78
		P4	3	3		2.17
6	Explain their bugs to other students	P0	9	6		2.07
		P3	6	3	0	2.00
		P4	3	3		2.17
7	Helping others improve their programming skills by "lecturing them" or providing advice	P0	8	7		
		P3	5	4	0	2.00
		P4	3	3		
8	Helping others improve their programming skills by understanding what their misconceptions are then providing counter examples	P0	9	5	1	2.07
		P3	5	3	1	2.22
		P4	4	2	0	1.83

Let us look at these responses based on the attitudes they reflect;

Leadership (1) – This activity implies an ability or willingness to organize programming tasks, whether alone or in a group. It was rarely the focus of respondents, regardless of the population. This is not surprising in so far that novice programmers should not be expected to easily take on the role of "developer lead".

Responsibility (2) – Regardless of the subpopulation considered, respondents are split on how often they implement their own parts. This suggests unbalanced contributions in teams.

Instructivist Tutoring (3,4,7) – While respondents were likely to explain what they did to others (3), they were not frequently involved in "explaining" to others how to do their work (4) and even less in tutoring them (7). This suggests that, as was hypothesized before [8][9], the primary goal of students working together on programming projects is to complete the work rather than to help each other improve skills.

Constructivist Tutoring (5,6,8) – Beyond the willingness or ability to help other students, responses suggest an even less frequent involvement in activities which require understanding a partner's mistakes or misconceptions. As partners in a project, students probably perceive investing in understanding the work or thoughts of others as inefficient. This is in sharp contrast with constructivist beliefs that put such understanding of mistakes or previous knowledge at the forefront of effective teaching.

4.3 Discussion

The consensus in the computing education literature is that collaboration among students, e.g. pair programming, is efficient for both individual skills development and retention [16]. However, previous work led us to hypothesizing that the nature of the student-to-student interaction in such collaborations might be improved [8][9]. More specifically, techniques such as Peer Testing might help address the unbalanced nature of students' contributions levels along with the lack of didactic dialog.

While professional programming teams often follow the mentor / apprentice variant [3], each member has already acquired the ability to program. In students groups, differences in skill levels are likely to be much more pronounced. Table 5 confirms that most students see themselves as infrequently contributing more than others. Similarly, Table 6 shows, via responses to item #2, that students are equally split in how often they implement the tasks they were assigned. Respondents who reported working with others – P3 – report implementing their assigned tasks more often than those who reported not working with others, i.e. P4.

Similarly, Table 6 item #1 suggests that few students, regardless of subpopulation, frequently take the lead. This item also captures the ability to break down the task at hand into smaller sub-problems, which is not expected to be wide-spread among novice programmers. These results are consistent with expectations.

Therefore, responses confirm that groups are based on unbalanced contributions: some students contribute more often, others do so sometimes, but the majority lack involvement.

Further, our data provide insight regarding the nature of the didactic exchanges taking place inside such groups. Table 6 reveals that students are even less likely to offer educational help to others than to contribute a fair amount of work. While a good proportion of students are willing to explain, few are interested in lecturing others and even fewer in getting involved with other students' work. This is in stark contrast with the computing education researchers' focus on constructivism vs. instructivism [14][15]. Constructivism requires instructors to "get involved" with students' attempts, understand their misconceptions and build on their previous knowledge, rather than simply state the solution. When students work together, instructivism prevails, thus limiting potential educational benefits.

Together, these observations confirm the two above-mentioned hypotheses that motivated the design of Peer Testing [8][9]. The next section examines whether students' perception of Peer Testing is aligned with its expectations to address the shortcomings confirmed in this section.

5. PERSPECTIVES ON PEER TESTING
This section explores students' perspective on Peer Testing.

5.1 Surveys Questions
The first questions, Q12 / Q13 / Q14, were meant to explore how Peer Testing supported students' learning.

Q12 *Being able to use my classmates' tests helped me improve my own tests.*

Q13 *Being able to use my classmates' tests helped me improve my own programs by identifying missing features in them.*

Q14 *Being able to use my classmates' tests helped me improve my own programs by finding errors in them.*

The next question, Q15, inquired as to whether Peer Testing was successful in allowing students to receive help from others while still requiring them to understand and fix their own bugs.

Q15 *Using classmates' tests forced me to figure out my errors myself instead of letting a classmate do it for me.*

The next question, Q16, went one step further by asking whether students saw this approach as more beneficial to improving their skills than just having someone else fix their bugs.

Q16 *This form of collaboration led me to develop my own programming skills more than if I had only shared programs directly with classmates.*

The last question, Q17, was meant to capture whether the students' experience with Peer Testing was positive.

Q17 *In your next programming-related offering would you like to be offered the option to use peer testing again?*

5.2 Observations
Table 7 summarizes responses for the various subpopulations identified so far. We will focus on P0 first.

The questions aimed at establishing Peer Testing's usefulness, i.e., Q12, Q13, Q14, feature high levels of agreement. This suggests that students perceive benefits from exchanging tests with others not only to improve their own tests, obviously, but also to improve their programs. These perceived benefits are paired with an overall positive experience as illustrated by a majority of students expressing agreement to Q17.

However, students are a bit more divided regarding the idea that Peer Testing is more beneficial than sharing programs; see Q16.

5.3 Relation to group work predisposition
Understanding the general perspective of respondents about working with others is essential to making sense of their attitude toward Peer Testing. Table 7 responses from students who worked with others – P3 – and those who did not – P4 – show that both subpopulations' ratings result in a similar ranking of questions. P4 students saw fewer benefits. Regarding their overall experience, as measured by Q17, P4 students seem split between being neutral and agreeing about whether they would like to use Peer Testing in the future if given the option. The majority of P3 students responded positively. No student opposed being offered the option to use peer testing again.

Table 7 – Q12 to Q17 with P0

Question	P	Disagree	Neutral	Agree	Avg
Q12	P0	2	1	12	4.07
	P1	1	0	8	4.22
	P2	1	1	3	3.60
	P3	0	1	8	4.33
	P4	2	0	4	3.67
Q13	P0	3	0	12	3.93
	P1	1	0	8	4.11
	P2	2	0	3	3.40
	P3	1	0	8	4.22
	P4	2	0	4	3.50
Q14	P0	3	1	11	3.87
	P1	1	1	7	4.00
	P2	2	0	3	3.40
	P3	0	0	9	4.44
	P4	3	1	2	3.00
Q15	P0	3	2	10	3.73
	P1	2	0	7	3.78
	P2	1	2	2	3.40
	P3	1	1	7	4.00
	P4	2	1	3	3.33
Q16	P0	3	5	7	3.40
	P1	1	3	5	3.56
	P2	2	2	1	2.80
	P3	1	3	5	3.67
	P4	2	2	2	3.00
Q17	P0	0	5	10	
	P1	0	2	7	
	P2	0	3	1	n/a
	P3	0	2	7	
	P4	0	3	3	

5.4 Relation to attitude toward testing
Table 7 shows responses from students who used testing – P1 – along with those who only used it when required – P2. Students in subpopulation P2 systematically agreed less to any of the potential benefits. When ranking questions by average rating, both subpopulations kept the same relative levels of agreement.

5.5 Discussion
Table 7 reveals that students' feedback on the benefits of Peer Testing is very positive across all subpopulations.

However, the lowest average agreement rating across all subpopulations is that of question Q16. This suggests that students do not see Peer Testing as better for improving their programming skills than having other students look at their programs and directly point out mistakes. The added requirement for students to resolve their own bugs once they have been pointed out by their peers' tests is the most salient difference between Peer Testing and a method like Pair Programming. There is insufficient data at this point to assess whether the benefits of pair programming regarding individual skill development are equivalent to those achieved by peer testing [16]. Further study will be required to determine whether this difference yields a better or worse impact.

Interestingly, students who did not work with others (P4) or didn't use tests when not required (P2) still supported the idea of using Peer Testing again in Q17. This suggests that Peer Testing might have the potential to affect further these students by:

- Allowing those who are not working with others, hence not using traditional group work methods, to still engage with their peers and benefit from it.
- Allowing those who are not using tests to be exposed to the potential benefits of testing via other students' tests.

6. DISCUSSION& FUTURE WORK

Because Peer Testing requires each student to write his or her own tests, it yields the same potential benefits as other testing-focused pedagogies. However, its originality lies in its ties to both collaborative pedagogies, e.g. pair programming [16], and situations where an instructor-provided test harness is available for students to test their solutions [4][5].

The main difference between Peer Testing and having students work together lies in limiting "help" to exchanging tests. This allows students to receive help in identifying bugs while still having to design and troubleshoot their own implementations. While students acknowledged the usefulness of Peer Testing to find bugs, they also communicated a preference for having other students directly point out problems in their programs. From an educator's perspective, it is essential to go beyond preferences that might be influenced by the fact that some students would systematically opt for the easiest approach even though it might fail to help them in developing more thoroughly their own skills. Therefore, our next step will be to quantify whether Peer Testing leads students to develop stronger individual programming skills than, for instance, pair programming.

Peer Testing is very similar to having students run their programs against the instructor's reference test harnesses, as done with most automatic grading systems. In both situations, students get additional feedback on how close their programs are to fulfilling requirements. However, Peer Testing provides students with tests that should not be blindly trusted since they have been designed by peers. We believe Peer Testing requires that students devote more thought to understanding tests rather than simply using them as an automatically produced check list. Therefore, while the results of applying tests to a student program doesn't provide feedback on the programming process itself, it is less likely that a student would be able to arbitrarily modify his or her program until it pass the tests [8] when using Peer Testing rather than using instructor tests. Establishing this requires further exploration about how students make use of the results of tests in general, and how they leverage the results of tests provided by an instructor versus other students (peers). Qualitative research designs will be explored to do so.

7. ACKNOWLEDGMENTS

This material is based in part upon work supported by the National Science Foundation under award #0836863 Any opinions, findings, and conclusions or recommendations expressed in this publication are those of the author(s) and do not necessarily reflect the views of the National Science Foundation.

8. REFERENCES

[1] Deitel P., Deitel H.. C How to Program. 7/e. Prentice Hall, 2012. ISBN-10: 0-13-299044-X

[2] Will Marrero and Amber Settle. 2005. Testing first: emphasizing testing in early programming courses. SIGCSE Bull. 37, 3 (June 2005), 4-8. DOI=10.1145/1151954.1067451

[3] Chetan Desai, David Janzen, and Kyle Savage. 2008. A survey of evidence for test-driven development in academia. SIGCSE Bull. 40, 2 (June 2008), 97-101.

[4] Stephen H. Edwards. Using software testing to move students from trial-and-error to reflection-in-action. In Proc. 35th SIGCSE Technical Symp. Computer Science Education, ACM, 2004, pp. 26-30.

[5] Stephen H. Edwards. Improving student performance by evaluating how well students test their own programs. Journal of Educational Resources in Computing, 3(3):1-24, September 2003.

[6] M. H. Goldwasser, "A gimmick to integrate software testing throughout the curriculum," presented at the Proceedings of the 33rd SIGCSE Technical Symposium on Computer Science Education, ACM, New York, NY, pp. 271-275, 2002

[7] S.H. Edwards, Z. Shams, M. Cogswell, and R.C. Senkbeil. Running students' software tests against each other's code: New life for an old "gimmick." In Proceedings of the 43rd ACM Technical Symposium on Computer Science Education (SIGCSE '12), ACM, New York, NY, 2012, pp. 221-226.

[8] A. Gaspar, S. Langevin, N. Boyer. Constructivist Apprenticeship through Antagonistic Programming Activities, Encyclopedia of Information Science and Technology, 2/e, 2007, Volume 2.

[9] A. Gaspar, S. Langevin. An Experience Report on Improving Constructive Alignment in an Introduction to Programming. Journal of Computing Sciences in Colleges, December 2012, volume 28, issue 2, pp. 132-140

[10] A. Gaspar, S. Langevin. Restoring Coding with Intention in Introductory Programming Courses, Proceedings of the ACM Special Interest Group in IT Education Conference, Oct 18-20, Sandestin, FL, 2007

[11] A. Gaspar, S. Langevin. Active learning in introductory programming courses through student-led "live coding" and test-driven pair programming, EISTA 2007, Education and Information Systems, Technologies and Applications, July 12-15, Orlando, FL

[12] A. Gaspar, A. Ejnioui, N. Boyer. The Role of the C Language in Modern Computing Curricula: Part 1 – survey analysis, The Journal of Computing Sciences in Colleges, Vol. 23 issue 2, pp. 120—127, CCSC Publisher (Consortium for Computing Sciences in Colleges, USA), 2007

[13] Vygotsky, L.S. (1978). Mind and society: The development of higher psychological processes. Cambridge, MA: Harvard University Press.

[14] Tom Wulf. 2005. Constructivist approaches for teaching computer programming. In Proceedings of the 6th conference on Information technology education (SIGITE '05). ACM, New York, NY, USA, 245-248.

[15] Andrew K Lui, Reggie Kwan, Maria Poon, and Yannie H. Y. Cheung. 2004. Saving weak programming students: applying constructivism in a first programming course. SIGCSE Bull. 36, 2 (June 2004), 72-76.

[16] Grant Braught, Tim Wahls, and L. Marlin Eby. 2011. The Case for Pair Programming in the Computer Science Classroom. Trans. Comput. Educ. 11, 1, Article 2 (February 2011), 21 pages.

Computing is Not a Rock Band:
Student Understanding of the Computing Disciplines

Faith-Michael Uzoka
Dept. Computer Science &
Information Systems
Mount Royal University
4825 Mount Royal Gate SW
Calgary, AB, T3E 6K6
403-440-6674
fuzoka@mtroyal.ca

Randy Connolly
rconnolly@mtroyal.ca

Namrata Khemka
nkhemka@mtroyal.ca

Marc Schroeder
mschroeder@mtroyal.ca

Janet Miller
Dept. Student Counselling
jbmiller@mtroyal.ca

ABSTRACT
This paper reports the initial findings of a multi-year study that is surveying major and non-major students' understanding of the different computing disciplines. This study is based on work originally conducted by Courte and Bishop-Clark from 2009 [7] and then repeated by Battig and Shariq in 2011 [3], but which uses a broadened study instrument that provided additional forms of analysis. Data was collected from 199 students from a single institution who were computer science, information systems/information technology and non-major students taking a variety of introductory computing courses. Results show that undergraduate computing students are more likely to rate tasks as being better fits to computer disciplines than are their non-major (NM) peers. Uncertainty among respondents did play a large role in the results and is discussed alongside implications for teaching and further research.

Categories and Subject Descriptors
K.3.2 [Computers and Education]: Computer & Information Science Education – information systems education.

Keywords
Information technology, computer science, information systems, software engineering, computer engineering

1. INTRODUCTION
One of the most important achievements in computing education has been the recognition and elaboration of at least five different computing disciplines, namely computer science (CS), information systems (IS), software engineering (SE), computer engineering (CE), and information technology (IT). These different disciplines are carefully articulated in, for instance, the ACM Computing Curricula Overview Report of 2005 [1]. The authors of the Overview Report crafted a series of area charts to indicate not only the relative focus of the five disciplines but also to show that there is topic overlap in all the disciplines. The title of this paper refers to the fact that the computing disciplines should be understood to be quite unlike the distinct roles in a typical rock band. That is, few people would confuse the sound of drums from the sound of someone singing in that they are playing very different and distinct roles and instruments. The computing disciplines, by contrast, have considerable overlap between them, a fact recognized as well by [2] and [7].

Despite the overlap between the computing disciplines, universities have to offer distinct computing degrees that typically do not blend curricula between the different disciplines (for an exception, see [4]). For students, their initial understanding of the different computing disciplines may play a large role in how they decide which (if any) computing program to register in. This paper reports the initial findings of a multi-year study that is examining major and non-major students' understanding of the different computing disciplines. This study is an extension of work originally conducted by Courte and Bishop-Clark (C&BC) [7]. Like the C&BC study, this study examines student knowledge of the five different computing disciplines; unlike C&BC, this study tried to also capture the overlap between the computing disciplines in the design of its survey.

2. RELATED WORK
In 2009, C&BC [7] surveyed undergraduate students' understanding of the differences between the five ACM-identified computing disciplines. Students from a variety of computing majors, as well as non-majors, were asked to associate job task descriptions with the best disciplinary fit. Their results suggest that students do not always have a clear understanding of disciplinary scopes (especially SE and IT), even in many cases among majors – though major students unsurprisingly knew their discipline better than non-majors. These findings were validated by a subsequent study by Battig and Shariq [3], who also found that disciplinary differences were better understood by students at small, liberal arts-based institutions. Earlier work by Courte and Bishop-Clark [8] also deals in part with understanding of disciplinary differences (although between CS, IS and IT only).

Other studies of perceptions about computing tend to focus solely on CS, or on "computing" generally, with no differentiation between the ACM-identified disciplines. An exception is a study by Helps, Jackson and Romney [11] which surveyed CS, IS, IT and non-computing majors at Brigham Young University regarding, among other things, their understanding of disciplinary differences between CS, IS and IT. It is interesting to note that a significant number of students from different computing majors often laid claim to disciplinary responsibility for tasks involving keywords such as "networking". As was observed in the paper, respondents may have been reacting to different aspects of networking (for example, programming network protocols versus configuring LANs). It is important to anticipate multiple interpretations of broad terms when designing such surveys.

Other studies of perceptions among undergraduate students tend to focus primarily on attitudes and beliefs about CS (or "computing" generally) as an intellectual or academic discipline, or on personality traits and attitudes of computer scientists, instead of on task descriptions for practitioners. In [12], Hewner and Guzdial surveyed attitudes about the computing discipline among students close to graduation. Lewis, Jackson and Waite [13] surveyed students' attitudes about CS as an accomplishment and as an intellectual discipline, both early and late in the curriculum, and compared them against faculty responses from the same department. Among other results, the researchers concluded that beginning CS students display a more varied range of views than students closer to graduation, suggesting that understanding of the field is incomplete among incoming students. Similarly, Perrenet [15] tracks the evolving attitudes and beliefs of CS majors in years 1, 2 and 3, and compares these with those held by faculty. A small number of survey questions (5 out of 27) dealt with the view of the working CS professional. Biggers, Brauer and Yilmaz [4] compared perceptions of CS held by graduating students versus those who had left the major. Their survey dealt in part with respondents' understanding of the nature of CS, and they found that "leavers" had an overwhelming tendency to characterize the profession negatively, as an "asocial, coding-only field with little connection to the outside world". Note that many leavers had left the major after a freshman year which included programming-heavy courses. By contrast, a significant number of graduating students, in their characterization of CS, specifically indicated that it is not purely coding, and does *not* involve tasks they perceived at being part of IT, such as "fixing hardware".

Fidoten and Spacco [10] surveyed faculty who advise undergraduates in course selection, in part to determine how well they distinguish CS from IT. Their results showed that a large minority of non-CS faculty advisors appear to have an inaccurate understanding of how these disciplines differ.

Studies of high school students have focused primarily on reasons why students in advanced mathematics and computing courses choose not to major in CS. This includes work by Carter [5], as well as Moorman and Johnson [14], both of which included an analysis of responses by gender. Lack of knowledge about CS is not listed in the top three reasons for rejecting the major in Carter's paper, although roughly half the respondents listed that as a factor. A greater proportion of female respondents cited this as a reason, however. Carter also found that 80% of respondents indicated no understanding of what CS majors learn.

Computing educators are not alone in their concern that prospective students and incoming majors display insufficient understanding of the distinct focuses of the disciplines. A strikingly similar issue was raised by Elrod and Cox with respect to the Engineering disciplines [9]. Their results showed lack of understanding of the Engineering profession (generally) among high school students. And, of the 16 Engineering disciplines they dealt with in their study, the mean understanding of Computer Engineering fell below the average mean understanding across disciplines. As in much of the computing literature, these authors called for better career advising and recruiting information.

3. METHODOLOGY

In both the C&BC and B&S studies, students were given 15 task descriptions and for each task they had to indicate which of the five disciplines was the best fit for that task. The main drawback to these two studies is that the students had to choose a single discipline for a task, which does not capture the possibility of

overlap between the disciplines. To address that drawback, our study allowed the participants to choose how much each task fit with each of the five disciplines using a five-point Likert scale, with 1 being "No Fit" and 5 being "Best Fit". Participants were also able to answer with "Don't Know", in response to the task overall. As well, many participants did not supply any answer (not even the No Fit option) for some disciplines on some task questions. These were coded as zeros and statistical analysis was run with and without the zero data. Figure 1 illustrates a sample question as it appeared in the questionnaire.

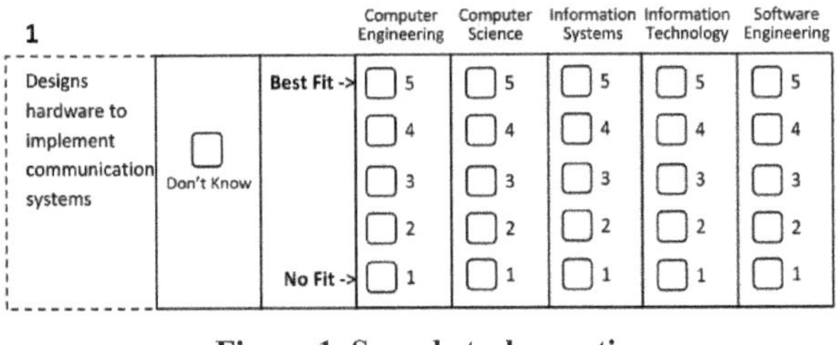

Figure 1. Sample task question

The 31 job-related tasks used in this questionnaire included the 15 tasks identified by C&BC, plus fifteen new tasks added by the authors and an additional task that is not typically associated with the computing field. This task (number 24) was taken from the ACM's descriptions of duties typically performed by an electronics engineer (EE), and does not emphasize a software component. The essence of adding the additional task was to find out if the students could distinguish between a task performed by a computer engineer and a closely related non-computing discipline. A complete list of the tasks contained in the questionnaire is presented in Table 1.

The first 15 tasks in Table 1 are those from the C&BC study. The last five tasks were purposely unclear – they were five typical "real-world" computing job tasks that lacked the obvious signal words (i.e., "business", "system", "hardware", "theory", and "technology") of the C&BC tasks. The intent was to find out if relatively-inexperienced students understood the tasks associated with different computing disciplines, prior to enrolment in computing courses/program. At a future stage, we intend to survey students who are in their final years in the university and also faculty, and then do a multi-group comparison.

4. RESULTS
4.1 Participants

Questionnaires were provided across ten sections of six introductory computing classes at a mid-sized Canadian university in the Fall 2012 semester. Note that there are two computing programs at the host university: a computer science program and a blended IS/IT program. 250 questionnaires were distributed, out of which 199 questionnaires were properly filled and returned for analysis. This represents a response rate of 79.6%. Of those who completed the survey, 28% were female and 72% were male. Table 2 lists some of the gathered demographic data.

Table 1. Tasks Considered

#	Best Fit	Description
1	CE	Designs hardware to implement communication systems
2	CS	Uses new theories to create cutting edge software
3	CE	Builds hardware devices such as iPods
4	IS	Is business oriented
5	SE	Focuses on large-scale systems development
6	CE	Integrates computer hardware and software
7	IT	Troubleshoots and designs practical technical applications
8	CS	Focuses on the theoretical aspects of technology
9	IS	Combines knowledge of business and technology
10	IT	Applies technology to solve practical problems
11	SE	Designs testing procedures for large-scale systems
12	IS, IT	Selects computer systems to improve business processes
13	IT	Applies technical knowledge for product support
14	CS	Utilizes theory to research and design software solutions
15	SE	Manages large scale technological projects
16	SE	Develops software systems that are maintainable, reliable, efficient, and satisfy customer requirements
17	IS	Focuses on information, and views technology as a tool for generating, processing and distributing it
18	SE	Utilizes sound engineering practices to create computer applications
19	IT	Provides a support role, within an organization, to help others make the best use of its technical and information resources
20	CS	Uses a wide range of foundational knowledge to adapt to new technologies and ideas
21	IS	Uses technology to give a business a competitive advantage
22	CE	Develops devices that have hardware and software in them
23	CS	Applies mathematical and theoretical knowledge in order to compare and produce computational solutions and choose the best one
24	NA (EE)	Focuses exclusively on hardware design, including digital electronics, with little or no involvement in software design
25	IT	Understands both technology and business, but with a focus more on the technical side
26	SE	Uses programming skills to create or modify business solutions
27	IT	Develops or maintains web sites
28	SE, IS	Manages a team of software developers
29	IS, IT	Manages a company's computing department
30	SE	Evaluates and improves the usability (user experience) of computing systems
31	IS, IT	Works with an organization's data assets

Table 2. Partial Demographic Data

Variable	Options	%
Program of Study	IS/IT	25.1
	CS	23.1
	Non-Major	51.8
Level of Study	Year 1	58.6
	Year 2	17.2
	Year 3	11.6
	Year 4	8.6
	Other	4.0
Prior Computing Experience	None	81.3
	< 2 Years	11.1
	2-5 Years	4.5
	More than 5	3.0

4.2 Rank Order Analysis

Rank order analysis was utilized in determining the students' ranking of the disciplinary tasks relative to the five computing disciplines. A further analysis was carried out to determine the levels of match between students' task rankings and the disciplinary best fit. The task-disciplinary best fits were based on the works of C&BC and the researchers' analysis of the ACM's disciplinary task descriptions. We note that there were some task overlaps between disciplines (tasks 12, 28, 29, and 31). Such overlaps have been recognized in our match analysis.

Table 3 shows a partial summary of our rank analysis. The results indicate that 100% of tasks relating to computer engineering were "very accurately" matched by the students (that is, in that they were all ranked number 1 according to the technique shown in Table 4), 60% were very accurately matched for computer science, 87.5% for information systems, 66.7% for information technology, and only 37.5% for software engineering. The poor to ok matches were mostly associated with tasks 15, 26, 27, and 30.

Table 3. Discipline Match Distributions

Match Level	CE	CS	IS	IT	SE
Very Accurate (5)	4(100.0%)	3(60.0%)	7(87.5%)	6(66.7%)	3(37.5%)
Accurate (4)	0 (0.0%)	2(40.0%)	1(12.5%)	2(22.2%)	2(25.0%)
Ok (3)	0(0.0%)	0(0.0%)	0(0.0%)	1(11.1%)	1(12.5%)
Fair(2)	0(0.0%)	0(0.0%)	0(0.0%)	0(0.0%)	1(12.5%)
Poor (1)	0(0.0%)	0(0.0%)	0(0.0%)	0(0.0%)	1(12.5%)
Total Tasks	4	5	8	9	8

Due to space constraints, we are unable to completely describe the methodology and results of our rank order analysis. As an illustration of our rank order methodology, consider Table 4, which shows the percentage responses for Task 1 along with the rankings. CS and IT are tied in terms of the mean, median and mode. IT has a lower percent of those who were not sure if Task 1 had a fit with the discipline. IT is therefore ranked before CS.

Table 4. Example Rank Ordering

Don't Know % for this question	Level of Fit	CE	CS	IS	IT	SE
15.6	No Answer	19.6	26.1	25.1	25.1	24.1
	1(No Fit)	2.0	7.0	9.5	9.5	20.6
	2	1.0	10.6	18.6	15.1	11.1
	3	7.5	23.6	21.1	16.1	11.1
	4	20.1	23.1	14.1	20.1	13.6
	5(Best Fit)	49.7	9.5	11.6	14.1	19.6
Mean		3.56	2.39	2.24	2.39	2.28
Median		4.00	3.00	2.00	3.00	2.00
Mode		5	0	0	0	0
Rank		1	3	5	2	4

4.3 Differences between Program Groups

Analyses were conducted to determine if there were any clear differences between the three groups of respondents, that is, between IS/IT, CS, and NM (non-major) students. Responses to individual tasks were analyzed using one-way ANOVAs. Non-responses were included as zeros. Statistically significant differences ($p < 0.05$) were found between program groups on 19 of the 31 questions, with most differences occurring between the IS/IT and NM groups. In general, the IS/IT students were more likely to rank the real-world tasks as better fits to the IS and IT disciplines.

4.4 Task and Discipline Uncertainty

A significant percentage of respondents either answered "Don't Know" for a task or didn't provide a response for a discipline on a task, as can be seen in Table 5. A full 20% of the 199 respondents rating 31 different tasks answered "Don't Know" on a given task. Also, within each task, some respondents did not supply a rating for a given discipline (e.g. how CS fits with Task 1). NM students answered DK more frequently, on average 7.5 times, in comparison to 4.2 for the IS/IT group and 5.7 for the CS group. However, based on our ANOVA cutoff this difference between groups was not significant.

Table 5. Task and Discipline Uncertainty

Task 'Don't Know' Percent	Discipline Non-Responses (Relative to Task) Percent				
	CE	CS	IS	IT	SE
20.0	31.4	30.9	31.2	30.9	31.6

Our suspicion is that many of the non-response answers were due to respondents leaving discipline choices blank rather than choosing the No Fit option (as shown in Figure 1). Regardless, our respondents were uncertain about one out over every five task which is a significant finding.

4.5 Discipline Cluster Scores

Since each discipline was associated with specific tasks, these scores were combined and averaged to create Discipline Cluster Scores. Figure 2 shows the discipline results using all of the data. Due to the significant uncertain percentages shown in Table 5, we also compared the cluster scores with the non-responses removed, which is shown in Figure 3.

The data in Figure 2 was subjected to a one-way analysis of variance that revealed only three significant differences between

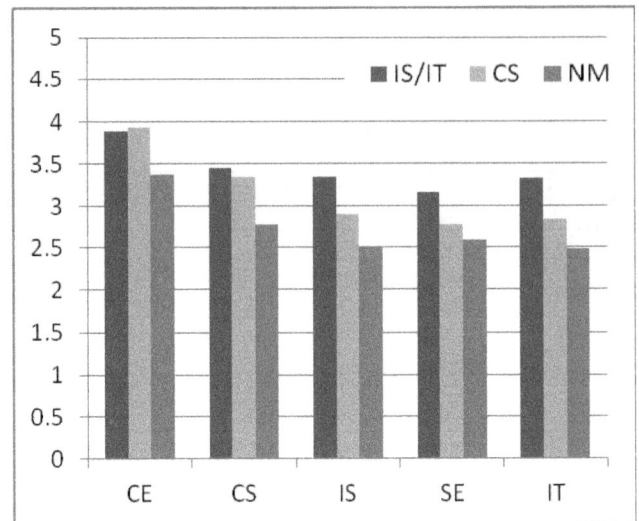

Figure 2. Discipline Cluster Scores

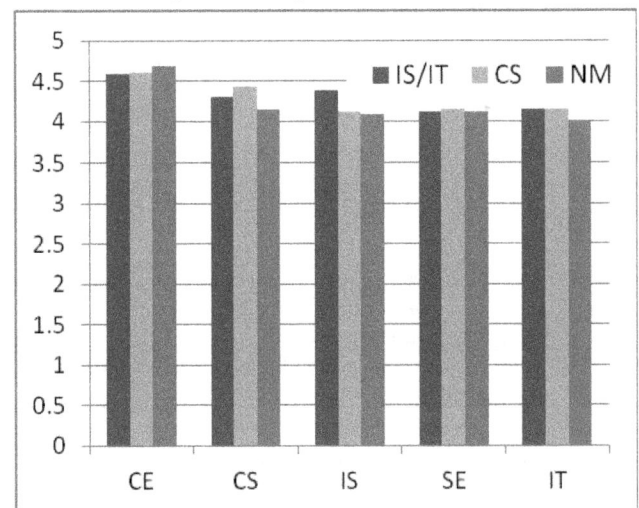

Figure 3. Discipline Cluster Scores (non-responses removed)

groups. The IS/IT students were found to make significantly better matches on three of the cluster scores compared to their NM peers – for cluster CS, IS and IT. There were no other significant findings between groups. When non-responses were left out of the analysis, only one significant difference emerged – on the IT discipline cluster score, where again IS/IT students out-performed their NM peers.

4.6 Non-Computing Task Performance

Since Task 24 was not associated with any of the computer disciplines under study (and in fact was an engineering-related task), all Task 24 answers were combined for each student and results were averaged for each program group, as shown in Table 6. Results were then analyzed using a one-way analysis of variance which found no significant differences between groups. Average scores on Task 24 were then compared to average scores overall, and to average discipline cluster scores. Results showed that Task 24 responses were significantly lower than those for the other tasks.

Table 6. Task 24 Performance

	IS/IT	CS	NM
Task 24 Average Scores	2.08	2.10	1.89

5. DISCUSSION

The intention of the researchers in this first phase of the study was to survey students who had little or no experience in computing. This was achieved by focusing on students who were taking an introductory computing course, thus providing insight into whether students who enroll in computing programs have a clear understanding of disciplinary outcomes of the respective programs. Participation in this study was high (79.6%), and computer-specific programs showed demographics typical of enrolment, and thus likely reflects our population of interest. Similarly, the demographic breakdown of the students in non-computing majors was reflective of the general university population, and likely results can be considered generalizable. Of the students who participated, most were first year students, and it is hoped that the findings here will reflect how first-year students typically perceive discipline-specific tasks and activities relating to computing fields.

With respect to ranking analyses, our results show that the best matching occurred for tasks that related to CE(100.0%), followed by IS (87.5%), IT (66.7%), CS (60.0%), and SE (37.5%) These results are reasonably close to that encountered by C&BC in that they found 82% of CE tasks were correctly identified which contrasts quite favorably to the 13% of SE tasks.

Looking at task-by-task questions for each of the five disciplines, and including missing data as reflecting uncertainty (as shown in Table 5), results show significant differences between the three program of study groups (IS/IT, CS, and NM) on 19 of the 31 items. Generally NM students tended to rank tasks as having lower fit with each discipline, and generally IS/IT students tended to rank tasks as having higher fit. At best this means the IS/IT students were more likely to be correct in their matchings, but at worst, it might suggest a response bias where computing students were more likely to assume that there is a higher fit for all tasks. However, if there had been a response bias in place, we would have seen similar scores associated with Task 24, and this was actually not the case. All students were successful in recognizing that Task 24 was a low-fit with the five computer disciplines. This reveals a certain amount of positive discernment capabilities among our participants, and suggests that a response bias wasn't at work.

Moving from individual items to discipline-level analysis provided more information about how students understand these five computer disciplines. Like the earlier C&BC study, our results show that students are not always clear about the disciplinary "fit" of different computing tasks. However, by allowing students to specify a degree of disciplinary fit, our study showed that by and large students are able to get their discipline matches close despite being inexperienced with computing. This could be construed as more encouraging than the results reported in C&BC and in [3]. Furthermore when non-responses are left out (that is, when participants didn't specify any value for a discipline), then Discipline Cluster Scores were quite high across all three groups (with NMs only falling slightly behind in matching the IT discipline correctly). In other words, when a student had an opinion about a disciplinary match, it was usually accurate.

Also like the earlier studies, our data showed that the CE tasks had higher fits across all three student groups compared to the other discipline cluster scores. Whether this was due to students having a clearer understanding of computer engineering than of other disciplines or simply due to the CE tasks in the study being more fortuitously worded is unclear. Future studies will add additional CE task questions to help clarify this uncertainty.

Another important result shown is the lower likelihood of correct identification with the IS/SE/IT tasks. This highlights how important it is for faculty in these fields to better articulate what these fields encompass, and to better communicate this information to prospective and current students alike. The better performance of the IS/IT student group on the IS/SE/IT tasks (when taking non-responses in account, as shown in Figure 2) is also noteworthy and in need of explanation, especially given that all three student groups had similar demographics. One hypothesis is that since the IS/IT students were more "open" to a non-standard (i.e., non-computer science) computing program, they had examined the different computing disciplines as part of their research on choosing a degree program.

Our data also showed that the most "confusion" about what discipline a task belonged to were those tasks connected to larger/real-world technological/software projects (tasks 15, 26, 27, and 30). Given that these larger projects often involve a variety of different skills and abilities, this uncertainty could even be construed as a positive sign.

There is however a rain cloud in this seeming sunny picture of student knowledge. The very significant percentages of task and discipline uncertainty across all five sub-disciplines as shown in Table 5 does indicate that all three student groups (IS/IT,CS,NM) have large gaps in their knowledge about the disciplines. This ignorance was quite likely masked in the C&BC approach since it did not provide an option for specifying uncertainty. Further analysis is being performed to determine if uncertainty varied in a statistically significant way between the three groups and/or across years of study.

6. LIMITATIONS

The main limitation of our study is similar to that of the C&BC study that inspired it: namely, if the task descriptions were too clear or too vague, then this would compromise the statistics and any conclusions drawn from them. As well, the five disciplines did not have the same number of tasks for which the discipline was the best fit. It might be possible in the future to equalize ambiguity across task descriptions, and/or to ask students to provide their own explanations or definitions of the computing fields through open ended questions.

Another limitation was that we did not have any CE or SE students in our study due to our university not having a CE or SE program. This meant that we were not able to do a comprehensive comparative analysis of task perceptions of students enrolled in the five computing disciplines in order to have a comprehensive cross-disciplinary analysis of task/skills understanding. This limitation could conceivably be addressed in the future if data was obtained from universities that have a CE and SE programs.

7. CONCLUSION

Over the last two decades, computing has undergone a reasonable level of differentiation into five sub-disciplines. This has generated some level of sub-disciplinary task ambiguity. This ambiguity resides in the minds of students, faculty, and even employers. Over the years, ACM has made conscious efforts to define the sub-disciplines in terms of suggested program contents/ expected outcomes and skills required to prepare the student for the dynamic labor market. ACM suggests the need for a clear understanding of these disciplines by the academic community (including students).

A few studies have been conducted on task understanding of these disciplines. Our study adds to the literature on disciplinary task/skill identification by enhancing an instrument initially developed by C&BC [7] by identifying an additional 15 skills from the ACM sub-discipline descriptions and by allowing participants to specify a degree of disciplinary fit.

Our results show that the computing disciplines do not have the clarity of the division of labor in a rock band: students are not always clear about the disciplinary "fit" of different computing tasks. This corroborates previous findings [3,7,8]. But, when students provided an opinion about fit, major and non-major students alike were actually often close to correctly identifying the correct discipline. This result is a new finding and by-product of our revised survey design in comparison to C&BC.

We found that task ambiguity was mostly associated with tasks connected to larger/real-world technological/software projects. A previous study [11] found task ambiguity in tasks related to 'networking'. Our study also shows that when including non-responses, IS/IT students had a better task understanding that those enrolled in the computer science program. This is supported by [13] who found beginning CS students to display a more varied range of views on task-discipline relationship.

Disciplinary task/skill ambiguity is not peculiar to computing. Even long-established disciplines such as engineering grapple with task/skill understanding by students and faculty [9]. Educational institutions and other relevant agencies that advertise programs need to make conscious efforts to provide proper discipline task/skill specifications for potential students. There is also a need for some ternary collaboration between post-secondary institutions and professional organizations (such as ACM) on one hand, and between post-secondary and secondary institutions on the other hand, to constantly define and agree on program expectations/outcomes and make such definitions and agreement are known to students prior to career choice.

8. ACKNOWLEDGMENTS

Our thanks to Courte and Bishop-Clark [7] for kindly sharing their original task questions.

9. REFERENCES

[1] ACM (2005) Computing Curricula 2005 – The Overview Report. (http://www.acm.org/education/education/curric_vols/CC2005-March06Final.pdf).

[2] Anthony, E. (2003). Computing Education in academia: toward differentiating the disciplines. Conference on Information Technology Education.

[3] Battig, M. and Shariq, M. 2011. A Validation Study of Student Differentiation Between Computing Disciplines. In *Information Systems Education Journal.* 9, 5 (October 2011), 105-115.

[4] Biggers, M., Brauer, A. and Yilmaz, T. 2008. Student perceptions of computer science: a retention study comparing graduating seniors with cs leavers. In *Proceedings of the 39th SIGCSE technical symposium on Computer science education*

(SIGCSE '08). ACM, New York, NY, USA, 402-406. DOI=10.1145/1352135.1352274 http://doi.org/10.1145/1352135.1352274

[5] Carter, L. 2006. Why students with an apparent aptitude for computer science don't choose to major in computer science. In *Proceedings of the 37th SIGCSE technical symposium on Computer science education* (SIGCSE '06). ACM, New York, NY, USA, 27-31. DOI=10.1145/1121341.1121352 http://doi.acm.org/10.1145/1121341.1121352

[6] Connolly, R. and Paterson, B. (2012). Even so with the pieces borrowed from others: Dressing an IS program in IT clothing. SIGITE'13.

[7] Courte, J. and Bishop-Clark, C. 2009. Do students differentiate between computing disciplines?. In *Proceedings of the 40th ACM technical symposium on Computer science education* (SIGCSE '09). ACM, New York, NY, USA, 29-33. DOI=10.1145/1508865.1508877 http://doi.acm.org/10.1145/1508865.1508877

[8] Courte, J. and Bishop-Clark, C. 2007. Student perceptions of computing majors and professionals. *J. Comput. Sci. Coll.* 23, 1 (October 2007), 21-27.

[9] Elrod C., Cox, L. 2006. Perceptions of Engineering Disciplines among High School Students. In *2006 American Society for Engineering Education National Conference Proceedings.*

[10] Fidoten, H. and Spacco, J. 2012. What do computer scientists do?: a survey of CS and non-CS liberal arts faculty. In *Proceedings of the 17th ACM annual conference on Innovation and technology in computer science education* (ITiCSE '12). ACM, New York, NY, USA, 279-284. DOI=10.1145/2325296.2325362 http://doi.acm.org/10.1145/2325296.2325362

[11] Helps, R., Jackson, R. and Romney, M. 2005. Student expectations of computing majors. In *Proceedings of the 6th conference on Information technology education* (SIGITE '05). ACM, New York, NY, USA, 101-106. DOI=10.1145/1095714.1095739 http://doi.acm.org/10.1145/1095714.1095739

[12] Hewner, M. and Guzdial, M. 2008. Attitudes about computing in postsecondary graduates. In *Proceedings of the Fourth international Workshop on Computing Education Research* (ICER '08). ACM, New York, NY, USA, 71-78. DOI=10.1145/1404520.1404528 http://doi.acm.org/10.1145/1404520.1404528

[13] Lewis, C., Jackson, M. and Waite, W. 2010. Student and faculty attitudes and beliefs about computer science. *Commun. ACM* 53, 5 (May 2010), 78-85. DOI=10.1145/1735223.1735244 http://doi.acm.org/10.1145/1735223.1735244

[14] Moorman, P. and Johnson, E. 2003. Still a stranger here: attitudes among secondary school students towards computer science. In *Proceedings of the 8th annual conference on Innovation and technology in computer science education* (ITiCSE '03), David Finkel (Ed.). ACM, New York, NY, USA, 193-197. DOI=10.1145/961511.961564 http://doi.acm.org/10.1145/961511.961564

[15] Perrenet, J. 2009. Differences in beliefs and attitudes about computer science among students and faculty of the bachelor program. In *Proceedings of the 14th annual ACM SIGCSE conference on Innovation and technology in computer science education* (ITiCSE '09). ACM, New York, NY, USA, 129-133. DOI=10.1145/1562877.1562920 http://doi.acm.org/10.1145/1562877.1562920

Infusing Social Science into Cybersecurity Education

Mark Stockman
University of Cincinnati
Cincinnati, OH 45221
(513) 556-4227
mark.stockman@uc.edu

ABSTRACT

Cybersecurity, while definitively categorized as a sub-discipline of computing, is widely considered multidisciplinary in nature. This paper documents two attempts to adopt non-computing ideas and approaches in undergraduate cybersecurity courses for information technology majors. Specifically, the author uses the social sciences (criminal justice and political science) to elicit a deeper understanding of cybersecurity problems and to present interdisciplinary methodological approaches to students who, in their careers, will be tasked with defending against cyberthreats.

Categories and Subject Descriptors

K.3.2 [**Computers and Education**]: Computer and Information Science Education – *curriculum.*

General Terms

Management, Measurement, Documentation, Design, Security.

Keywords

Cybersecurity; Information Technology; Pedagogy; Criminology; Political Science; Crime Prevention; Interdisciplinary; Cybercrime; Network Security.

1. INTRODUCTION

Most who study and teach in the field of cybersecurity recognize its place as a sub discipline of computing. Crowly, in 2003, was one of the first to attempt compiling a body of knowledge for cybersecurity referencing NIST (National Institute of Standards and Technology) and ISC2 (International Information Systems Security Certification) [1]. While there were some policy and law areas addressed, the burgeoning body of knowledge consisted almost entirely of computing topics.

Rowe, Lunt, and Ekstrom make a case that more specifically this new field falls under the information technology umbrella of computing [2]. They connect the information assurance and security element listed in the IT 2008 Model Curriculum to the current concept of cybersecurity [3]. Again, the focus is solely on technical computing topics of the discipline.

Perez, et al. document existing information assurance and security programs, targeting NSA centers of excellence [4]. They found only one of 73 baccalaureate-degree programs located (or co-located) outside a traditional academic computing department. In their study of these programs, the authors call for an effort of curricular uniformity with "meaningful curricular guidelines" for cybersecurity degree programs.

The recent literature recognizes that cybersecurity education should include skills outside the traditional computing space to best prepare the workforce for current and future challenges faced by government and industry. Kallberg and Thuraisingham begin to redefine the discipline as cyber operations rather than information assurance or cybersecurity [5]. They too evaluate the NSA designated schools/programs, though primarily those designated for cyber research. This new look at security takes a more holistic view investigating not only defensive measures of security but introducing an offensive posture, the "active defense" necessary for national interests. As such, they point out that cybersecurity should require elements of social science.

In perhaps the clearest indication of the changing needs of cybersecurity education, in 2010 an NSF supported effort brought together educators, cybersecurity professionals, government officials, and other experts to discuss the state of cybersecurity education. The report from this gathering addressed the United States government's past funding of cybersecurity education and makes recommendations for future efforts [6]. The three-day workshop established "cross-cutting principles for addressing cyber security education and training." Of the six principles laid out, the first three are of note for this paper.

- Cyber security is an international issue. Strategic planning should go beyond the federal level, taking into account needs, concerns, and opportunities at the national and international levels.

- Cyber security requires a multi-disciplinary approach. Efforts should be made to educate and partner with disciplines not always thought of as related to cyber security.

- Curative-not palliative-approaches are needed to address causes rather than symptoms of the continuing security breaches in computer systems.

The courses described in this paper attempt to address on a micro curricular level these principals. The last of these principals is perhaps the most significant and can begin by using the recommendations set forth in the first two. Cybersecurity professionals can continue to chase the incidents that come their way, but it will become more beneficial to begin looking for the root of the problems faced.

Harknett, Callaghan, and Kauffman use the term cyberagression "to capture the range of activities associated with disruptive computer hacking, cybercrime, cyberespionage, cyberconflict, and cyberwar recognizing that each of those terms provides greater precision to specific realms of aggression." [7] The traditional forms of aggression associated of these acts continue to be studied primarily by those in the disciplines of criminal justice and political science. Each of these disciplines contains a wealth of empirical data about prevention of and response to acts of aggression. These data are turned into techniques and strategies to educate future practitioners in their respective fields.

Because nearly all acts of cyberaggression have a correlate in the physical world, the research and techniques for prevention/response should be passed on to cybersecurity professionals. Even prevention research into those acts that seemingly have limited correlation to anything physical, like disruptive computer hacking, may benefit from strategies to prevent physical acts of aggression.

2. METHODS

With these two social sciences in mind (criminal justice and political science) for interdisciplinary infusion into cybersecurity education, the author and his institution offered two new undergraduate level information technology courses. The first, a special topics offering, dealt with bringing the knowledge of criminal justice, Cybercriminology. The second course, a university sponsored interdisciplinary course, was lead by a pair of faculty from political science and information technology to merge the technical with the behavioral aspects of cybersecurity, Cyberattack Red Team Collaborative Seminar.

2.1 Criminal Justice - Cybercriminology

Within the networking/systems track of the undergraduate information technology degree at the author's university, the students' final track course is Special Topics in Network/Systems. The class is taken in the fall semester of the senior year. The content of this course often changes from year to year, based on new technologies or the work of the faculty member assigned to teach the course.

Students in the class have already taken several applied technical courses within their chosen specialty, several of them security specific. The course prerequisites for the Special Topics course include System Administration, Information Security and Assurance, Network Infrastructure Administration, Enterprise System Administration, Network Security, and Computer and Network Forensics. The students had also all completed several terms of full-time work experience through cooperative education work assignments and other IT coursework outside networking/systems. Details of the program and track requirements have been detailed in prior work [8,9].

With a recent research focus into traditional criminal justice, specifically criminology and crime prevention, the author used the special topics course as a way to educate these soon to be information technology professionals about the nature of traditional crime/criminals and prevention of crime. More specifically, the author was inspired by the work of John Eck's research on place managers' affect on the reduction of crime [10]. Property owners can take steps in how they manage their properties to positively impact on the reduction of crime. The author postulates that information technology professionals, specifically system and network administrators, are in essence place managers of systems, networks, and data.

The information technology undergraduate degree program at the author's institution is uniquely offered out of the College of Education, Criminal Justice, and Human Services. The author used this relationship to engage doctoral students from the university's highly regarded School of Criminal Justice to participate in the course's development and offering.

In the first of three class meetings each week, students were presented with a traditional criminological or crime prevention theory, along with its associated research findings. Techniques developed for the use of these theories by practitioners (law enforcement, place managers) were also presented. These weekly presentations were delivered by the author or doctoral students from the School of Criminal Justice. There was little to no mention of cyberaggression in these initial talks.

For the second class meeting, students were put into groups to discuss the presentations in light of their knowledge of the potential existing cyberthreats and the implementation and management of information technologies. The author and doctoral students were present to answer any questions about the theory.

The students were asked to put the theories in the context of cyberagression. Could the information they learned that week be used in their work as information technology professionals, specifically cybersecurity? Do any existing strategies or technologies used in computer and network security pull from the theories of traditional criminology or crime prevention? How would this knowledge affect their future work as information technology professionals?

Finally, in the final meeting of the week each group presented their ideas about the applicability of the criminological or crime prevention theory to cybersecurity. The class, as a whole, then discussed their findings. As a weekly assignment, each student performed more research on the theory presented and integrated their personal ideas for its applicability to cybersecurity into a two page paper. At the end of the semester, students were tasked with diving deeper into one of the theories to write a more substantial paper on its applicability to cybersecurity.

2.2 Political Science - Cyberattack

As part of an effort to encourage interdisciplinary education to solving real world problems, the author's university instituted a teaching and learning initiative called UC Forward. One part of this initiative is to provide funding for courses that adopt such an interdisciplinary focus. The author, a faculty member in the information technology (IT) degree program, partnered with a faculty member from the political science (POL) program to teach such a course centered on cybersecurity, Cyberattack Red Team Collaborative Seminar. The course is cross-listed as both an information technology and political science offering.

The Cyberattack class is officially listed as a senior level course (though being a senior is not a pre-requisite) under both the IT and the POL sections and is open to be taken by students from any major within the university. While there is no official pre-requisite yet for the course, the instructors asked interested students to first apply to participate before being officially admitted.

The intent of the screening was to assure for some level of disciplinary diversity and commitment by the students participating in the class. While the instructors sought and obtained some diversity in the course, a plurality of those applying came from IT. Ultimately, nine out of the twenty students in the first offering were IT majors. Other registered students came from political science, criminal justice, and business.

The major project of the Cyberattack course was for cross-disciplinary teams to research and plan a potential cyberattack. The teams were to take on the role of the attackers and systematically plan a full digital attack against a specific target with some goal in mind such as cyberterrorism, financial gain, or militaristic action. The pedagogy being that by working towards planning an attack, students would become prepared to also defend such attacks. Additionally, their findings could be shared with industry partners as research for their future cybersecurity efforts.

The cyberattack research and exercise consumed the last half of the semester. Preparing for this work, it became necessary to provide enough instruction on the behavioral and technical sides of cybersecurity so all students developed a shared understanding of the cyberthreat environment.

As such, students read documents associated with policy, militaristic strategy, international relations then participated in lectures/discussions lead by the political science instructor about such topics. The author also contributed by discussing with the class and creating online videos about the basics of computers, networks, current cyberthreats, and how information technology professionals currently defend against potential attacks.

Students were also given access to partners external to the university who provided their perspective on the cyberthreat landscape. These external partners included cybersecurity professionals from federal agencies (Department of Homeland Security and US Central Command), local law enforcement, a large corporation sensitive to international based theft of its intellectual property, and a consulting firm that performs penetration testing for financial clients.

The student teams were quite creative in their identities and attack vectors chosen to exploit their targets. One team took on the identity of an anarchist group of college students out to wreak havoc by attacking the SCADA systems of a water treatment facility. Two teams formulated attacks against financial institutions; one a Ukrainian mafia out to steal money and another a team of hackers out to punish a crime family by stealing their money and redistributing it to global humanitarian organizations. The final team formed themselves as a drug cartel aiming to steal research on chemical compounds and the corresponding manufacturing procedures from a university research center to create synthetic illicit drugs.

Using publicly available information, each team formulated a plan of attack against their target from start to finish using both social and technical methodologies. Ultimately, each team was also assigned the identity of one of the other team's target to defend during a tabletop role-play scenario. In preparation for the tabletop scenarios, each team consulted with both instructors about their attacks. Like the Cybercriminology course, IT students were provided with input from non-technical sources to inform their decision-making.

3. RESULTS
While difficult to quantify, anecdotally the author saw benefits from infusing the social sciences into cybersecurity education within the courses described here. Students identify that they will use what they learned in their careers and the student deliverables in both courses were impressive for undergraduate students.

3.1 Criminal Justice - Cybercriminology
The author was impressed with the ability of students to quickly grasp the criminological concepts introduced to them in the Cybercriminology course then apply the new knowledge to cybersecurity. The doctoral students from the School of Criminal Justice also noted the maturity of analysis by the students.

Even after intensive study and thought about such applications, the undergraduates found connections new to the author that have since affected his own research trajectory. One example of this was the author's initial hypothesis about the age of entry into hacking activities. Initially thinking it would come at a later age than traditional crime due to skills required to participate in cybercriminal activities, the undergraduates observed instead that entry would be earlier than traditional crime based on social control theories. Parents will not allow their pre-adolescent children to roam the streets where they might participate in crime but freely allow them to spend time on the computer unsupervised where cybercrime can be allowed to occur. A study is currently underway to test the revised hypothesis.

In an informal survey of the 18 students enrolled in the class, all but one thought the course should be offered again. All but two believed they would be able to apply what they learned to their future careers as IT professionals. All but two felt that if a cybersecurity track were being created, this course should be a requirement. Finally, half of the students stated that their career interests have changed to some degree after haven taken the class.

3.2 Political Science - Cyberattack
The IT students obtained a perspective on cybersecurity from a political science perspective because of the Cyberattack course. Readings, lectures, and discussion with non-IT students provided them with insight about the landscape in which they will be tasked with protecting digital assets. Students were sensitized to the international realities based on cyberthreats and their likelihood of coming to fruition. Discussions about the economic ties to the United States of countries like China verses other countries provided a measure of awareness that many young IT professionals will not appreciate or fully understand.

The deliverables by the student teams were outstanding. One motivated team provided several hundred pages of analysis about their target and attack. Each team's analysis included real vulnerabilities found using only public sources of information. One team included a sophisticated spear-phishing attack on a high ranking IT official of their target's organization. The team leveraged public information from his social media profiles to craft a legitimate looking invitation to his local golf club. Another team found a front facing web vulnerability that might have been the same information used in the initial stages of a recent $45 million ATM heist. A publicly advertised corporate retreat was the timing for one team's initial attack, recognizing that there would be confusion trying to get in contact with key personnel during that time.

The defense scenarios too showed awareness beyond the technical nature of cybersecurity. Students learned from the non-technical peers as well as the research compiled during their attacks. This was infused into their defense strategies.

In an informal survey administered by the Provost's office students commented with high praise about the course and its interdisciplinary nature.

"A UC forward class takes a multidisciplinary approach to learning. Instead of having a class comprised solely by one major, you have a class filled with students from a variety of majors. Due to this diversity, it is possible to leverage the unique strengths of every major in the class when working on a team project."

"Outstanding. An eye opener, not just the subject matter, but how other disciplines work together."

"A mixture of students from different backgrounds working together on a mutual problem, with the goal of learning from the problem and the students outside your major."

"A lot of my other classes this semester have been pretty dry and boring, but this class is fantastic! I actually look forward to go to this class, vs. my other classes. My other classes I don't enjoy them, I'm reluctant to attend them and look forward to leaving; however I do have great a attendance record in all of my classes."

"I would strongly suggest that UC Forward be expanded to many disciplines and problems across UC! This model is changing the way that we view education and has been one of the most outstanding experiences that I have had during the last five years!"

"I wish there were more classes like this!"

The success of this class has lead to the creation and approval for an interdisciplinary certificate that undergraduates at the author's institution can now obtain, Fundamentals of Cybersecurity. The certificate includes courses in information technology, political science, and criminal justice, concluding with the Cyberattack course as its capstone.

4. ACKNOWLDEGEMENTS

Richard Harknett co-taught the Cyberattack course and continues to broaden my understanding of the nature and prevention of acts of cyberaggression. Michael Holiday and Nicole Lasky, doctoral students from the University of Cincinnati's School of Criminal Justice, volunteered their time to create and deliver lectures for the Cybercriminology course. Hazem Said invited me to be part of the initial Cyberattack course proposal, and the University of Cincinnati's Provost's office funded the initial offering of the Cyberattack course.

5. REFERENCES

[1] Crowley, E. 2003. Information system security curricula development. In *Proceedings of the 4th conference on Information technology curriculum* (Lafayette, Indiana, October 16-18, 2003). ACM, New York, NY, 249-255.

[2] Rowe, D. C., Lunt, B. M., & Ekstrom, J. J. 2011. The role of cyber-security in information technology education. In *Proceedings of the 2011 conference on Information technology education* (West Point, New York, October 20-22, 2011). ACM, New York, NY, 113-122

[3] Lunt, B. M., Ekstrom, J. J., Gorka, S., et al., Information Technology 2008: Curriculum Guidelines for Undergraduate Degree Programs in Information Technology. Association for Computing Machinery (ACM); IEEE Computer Society, November 2008.

[4] Pérez, L. C., Cooper, S., Hawthorne, E. K., et al. 2011. Information assurance education in two-and four-year institutions. In *Proceedings of the 16th annual conference reports on Innovation and technology in computer science education-working group reports* (Darmstadt, Germany, June, 2011). ACM, New York, NY, 39-53.

[5] Kallberg, J., & Thuraisingham, B. 2012. Towards Cyber Operations The New Role of Academic Cyber Security Research and Education. In *Proceedings from the 2012 IEEE International Conference on Intelligence and Security Informatics* (Washington, D.C., June 11-14, 2012). IEEE, New York, NY, 132-134.

[6] Hoffman, L. 2010. Building the Cyber Security Workforce of the 21st Century: Report of a Workshop on Cyber Security Education and Workforce Development. *GW Cyber Security Research and Policy Institute Report# GW-CSPRI-2010-3, December 15, 2010.*

[7] Harknett, R. J., Callaghan, J. P., & Kauffman, R. 2010. Leaving Deterrence Behind: War-Fighting and National Cybersecurity. *Journal of Homeland Security and Emergency Management*, 7(1), 22 (2010), 1-24.

[8] Said, H., Stockman, M., Leung, S., et al. 2004. An implementation of a core curriculum in an information technology degree program. In *Proceedings of the 5th conference on Information technology education* (Salt Lake City, Utah, October 28-30, 2004). ACM, New York, NY, 138-143.

[9] Stockman, M., Said, H., Leung, S., et al. 2004. An implementation of a networking track in an information technology degree program. In *Proceedings of the 5th conference on Information technology education* (Salt Lake City, Utah, October 28-30, 2004). ACM, New York, NY, 94-100.

[10] Eck, J. E., & Wartell, J. 1998. Improving the management of rental properties with drug problems: A randomized experiment. *Crime Prevention Studies*, 9, 161-185.

Performing Robots: Innovative Interdisciplinary Projects

Debra L. Smarkusky
dls102@psu.edu

Sharon A. Toman
sat11@psu.edu

Peter Sutor, Jr.
pws5164@psu.edu

Christopher Hunt
cxh5200@psu.edu

Penn State Worthington Scranton
120 Ridge View Drive
Dunmore, PA 18512

ABSTRACT

By challenging and engaging students in interdisciplinary projects, we provide a learning platform to enhance creativity, critical thinking and problem-solving skills, while promoting an innovation-oriented culture in academia. In this paper, we summarize interdisciplinary and undergraduate research projects in music and animation that integrate technologies from both disciplines to create unique and innovative projects. Iterative development coupled with various forms of visual and audio feedback enhanced the student learning experience with positive feedback from students. These efforts have resulted in the awarding of internal grant funding, interest in additional undergraduate research projects, and enhanced awareness of the application of technology to other disciplines.

Categories and Subject Descriptors

J.5 [**Computer Applications**] *Arts and Humanities,* K.3.2 [**Computer and Information Science Education**] *Computer Science and Information Systems Education*

General Terms

Design, Experimentation

Keywords

Interdisciplinary Projects, Java, Music, LEGO Mindstorms, leJOS NXJ, Sibelius

1. MOTIVATION AND RELATED WORKS

Interdisciplinary teaching and interpretation of technology for various applications provides a means to maintain a computer workforce for the nation's economic, cultural, and democratic vitality. The use of robotics allows one to achieve this goal by integrating technology and software development with art, physics, mathematics, and cognitive science [13]. The leJOS NXJ [8] and LEGO® MINDSTORMS® [6] were utilized in an advanced software engineering project to provide experiences with remote device interfaces, multi-threading and network communications [9]. Within academia, faculty are using interdisciplinary projects to build bridges between academic areas to encourage students to explore, build hypotheses, experiment, and development critical thinking skills for problem solving [3].

Because many of the most pressing problems of the day are best solved using interdisciplinary approaches, it is important that students be well educated in their own disciplines and at the same time be prepared to engage in interdisciplinary projects [1].

To enhance design (creativity) and development (computational thinking), an introductory computer science course in the curriculum was replaced with an interdisciplinary and "connected" pair of courses in creative arts, humanities, history, math, computer science, natural sciences, and social sciences, which resulted in an increase in female enrollments, retention in computing, and new energy for interdisciplinary research opportunities [5]. Utilizing active-learning exercises to expose students to a variety of programming, animation and music theory components, students developed software applications and music compositions that followed a similar development process to include requirements definition, design, implementation, and test/debug phases [11].

Students should have opportunities to engage in interdisciplinary undergraduate research projects where they can build confidence and enhance their learning [2]. The creation of a multi-disciplinary capstone design and integration course required faculty to collaborate across disciplines and participate in multi-disciplinary teams. During this experience faculty became familiar with the challenges of learning and integrating knowledge among disciplines, which is similar to the same experience students will face after graduation [12]. Barker completed an interview study of both faculty research mentors and undergraduates that analyzed the organizational, social and intellectual conditions under which undergraduate research was being conducted, and observed that undergraduate research projects in science, technology, engineering, and mathematics (STEM) have benefits such as "improved retention in both the major and discipline-related careers; ability to work independently and to communicate well with a team; increased confidence in academic knowledge and technical skill; broader awareness of the discipline; and awareness of career opportunities and support for making career choices" [2].

In the remaining sections of this paper, we specify the technologies that were selected for the completion of the music and animation components of our projects which include Sibelius, LEGO Mindstorms NXT, leJOS, and Bluetooth. We then describe the expected goals, scaffolding of knowledge and specifications for each of our interdisciplinary (Amazing Bots and Choreography) and undergraduate research projects (Row Bots, Streaming Performers, and Symphony in "R"). We conclude with a summary and future works.

2. MUSIC/ANIMATION TECHNOLOGIES

2.1 Sibelius

Sibelius (www.avid.com/US/products/Sibelius7) is sophisticated music notation software for composers and arrangers that can be utilized by beginners and students with a small learning curve. Its user interface is task-oriented and allows users to have the ability to create and edit a musical score, as shown in Figure 1. Sibelius uses point-and-click interface which enables users to insert notes,

Figure 1. Musical Score in Sibelius.

instruments, musical symbols, nuances, lyrics, as well as a professional digital sound library. Sibelius allows users to develop professional quality musical scores and is equipped with a high-quality, integrated playback screen which displays bar numbers, as well as the timeframe of the music and provides audio and visual feedback to the user.

2.2 LEGO MINDSTORMS NXT

We decided to utilize the LEGO MINDSTORMS NXT, shown in Figure 2, for our project due to the extensible nature of the

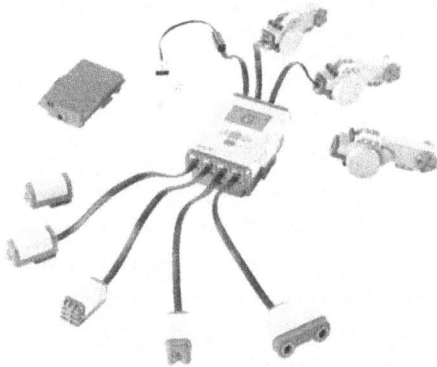

Figure 2. LEGO® MINDSTORMS® NXT.

platform, abundance of documentation that is available, and the less expensive nature of these robots compared to other robot kits [6]. The NXT brick includes four sensor ports ('1', '2', '3', and '4') and three input ports ('A', 'B', and 'C'). LEGO offers a wide variety of sensors to include a Sound Sensor, Light Sensor, NXT Color Sensor and Ultrasonic Sensor. Communication between the computer and the NXT brick can be realized with a USB cable connection or programmed to use the Bluetooth® (www.bluetooth.com) wireless communications.

2.3 LeJOS NXJ

LeJOS NXJ is a Java programming environment for the NXT that was originally created from the TinyVM project, which was an implementation of a Java Virtual Machine for LEGO MINDSTORMS RCX system [8]. We utilized the leJOS firmware to replace the NXT MINDSTORMS factory-loaded software and provide access to a Java Virtual Machine, a library of classes that implement the NXJ Application Programming Interface (API) for execution on the brick, a library of Java classes for computer programs that communicate with the brick via USB or Bluetooth, PC tools for debugging and flashing the firmware, and the capability to compile, link and upload programs and other files to the NXT brick. The original firmware can be reloaded at any time using the supplied LEGO software.

The benefits of using leJOS NXJ was that it utilizes the high-level Java programming language, supports object-oriented programming, provides students with an opportunity to use open source software, can be developed using the NetBeans (www.netbeans.org) or Eclipse (www.eclipse.org) Integrated Development Environment (IDE), and has associated plugins for both environments. For more advanced Java development, listeners, event-handling, conversion and playing of 8-bit WAVE files, and multi-threading are supported to provide opportunities for challenging, multimedia-based and problem-solving projects.

3. INTERDISCIPLINARY PROJECTS

When we first started experimenting with the concept of music and animation with LEGO Mindstorms, our goal was to create a LEGO Orchestra. We checked the literature but could not find any references to the creation of original musical scores or the streaming of music using LEGO Mindstorms. We discovered that there were built-in sound clips (e.g. buzz, beep, chirp, etc.) within the NXT brick that could be played via the leJOS software, and there seemed to be project templates to create a very small song playing note by note from the NXT, but there was not a manner in which an entire sound file with a fuller sound quality or one that included multiple instruments could be played. Given the general size of an audio file, we were challenged with finding a way to store the music file on the NXT brick as well as ensure that when a music file was played that is was continuous and without interruption.

The music and animation projects that we present in this section were successful in many ways. In addition to providing collaborative research and learning opportunities between the Information Sciences and Technology (IST) and Music Departments at our campus, these projects can be further developed and utilized in advanced computing projects for multimedia, or utilized as a platform for interdisciplinary projects between technical and general education courses. These projects are presented in a scaffolding manner in that we build on knowledge learned from one project (completed as a course requirement or part of undergraduate research efforts) to gain insight and ideas for additional projects. Each of these projects present opportunities for students from IST, Computer Science, and/or Music Theory to be excited about the use of technology and participate in the project definition, choreography, musical selection, or programming of the robot to include the development of code for the streaming of movements and audio to LEGO Mindstorms.

3.1 Amazing Bots

This project was assigned in a Distributed Computing course to allow students an opportunity to experience LEGO Mindstorms NXT robots and complete Java applications using the leJOS software. Their goal was to develop an application that would enable a robot to complete the specified maze, as shown in Figure 3, using the sound, ultrasonic and color sensors. This project would utilize the onboard sound clips that were provided with the leJOS platform. Students were given information about how the LEGO Mindstorms were built and configured with the appropriate sensors and motors.

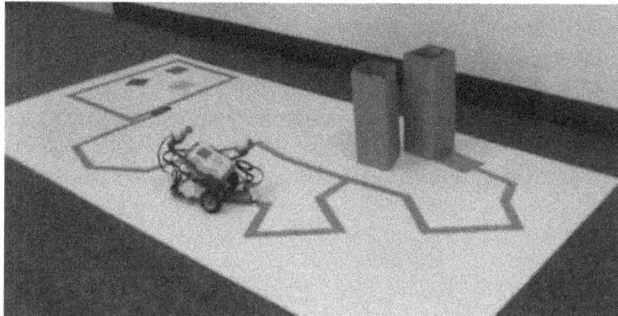

Figure 3. Amazing Bots Snapshot.

Students were provided with the following specifications for this project:

(1) The Sound Sensor or Bluetooth communications will be utilized to start the execution of the program for movement through the maze.

(2) The robot will need to detect and follow the PATH_COLOR tape. The color of the path is the one that is first detected by the robot.

(3) When the robot detects a WALL + NO_COLOR_CHANGE, the robot should continue travelling straight until it reaches the end of the tape (a T in the path) and then the robot should TURN RIGHT (90 degrees). The robot continues to follow PATH_COLOR tape.

(4) When the robot detects NEW_COLOR + WALL, it must turn around (180 degrees) and follow its PATH_COLOR path in reverse (continuing to follow a straight line when possible).

(5) It is expected that the robot will follow the specified tape line until the robot detects NEW_COLOR2 + NO_WALL, it will turn left (90 degrees) and enter a sandbox, which is outlined in a color that was previously detected (prior to reaching the sandbox). The robot must remain in the sandbox during the search.

(6) Within the sandbox, the robot will use a search pattern to find three NEW_COLOR items. These items will be in colors that have not been detected previously in the maze. When a new color is found, the robot will play a sound to identify the color was found. The developer will identify the sounds to be played prior to starting the maze.

(7) The application should stop execution after the third color in the sandbox has been found and the sound file has completed playing.

Keeping in mind that for their next project, students would need a mechanism that would allow the software applications in two robots to begin simultaneously to maintain synchronization with the dance movements of the Choreography project, students were asked to use the Sound Sensor or Bluetooth to start this project. A time limit to complete the maze was not specified and assessment for this project was based on the successful completion of the specified requirements.

3.2 Choreography

Students in a General Education Music Theory course and students in a Distributed Computing course were tasked with creating the digital musical scores in Sibelius and writing Java applications for the robot movements, respectively. The audio file would be played from a PC as background music with code that was uploaded to the brick being utilized for the robot movements of the dance. The design and implementation of the choreography would be the bridge between discipline areas. The final product was a robot dance where the movements of robot couples (two robots) were synchronized to the rhythm of the music [10].

The Music Theory students were introduced to fundamental concepts of music notation and terminology including: melody, rhythm, major and minor scales, intervals, chords, instrumentation, and proper setup of a musical score. These students were given preselected sheet music for the robot dance in which they needed to enter the musical notation with precision into Sibelius. The original score was further enhanced by the addition of instruments such as: flute, trumpet, saxophone, guitar, bass guitar, and utilized drum plug-ins. Using the Sibelius's integrated *Playback feature,* students had full control of their musical score by being able to control its tempo, dynamics, and other music nuances.

In preparation for this interdisciplinary robot dance project and while the Music students were creating the Sibelius and WAVE files, the IST students were completing the Amazing Robot project, described previously, to become familiar with the LeJOS Application Programming Interface (API), Java Threads, interaction with various sensors, but most importantly, how to pilot the robot to include right and left turns, forward and backward movements, arcs, and spins. This opportunity prepared the IST students with the knowledge they needed to communicate with the Music students when discussing the capabilities of creating the choreography for the robot dance. Although the Music students had an initial draft of the choreography completed, teams of students worked together to enhance and tweak the dance routines.

The IST students were required to utilize the leJOS NXJ environment to complete the Java code for the specified choreography that required robots to dance as a couple on a 6' X 12' dance floor. The *Playback* feature in Sibelius provided assistance with the timing that was needed to synchronize the robot dance movements with the music file. Together the IST and Music students observed the robot movements, listened to the music, and precisely documented the start/stop times for each movement as they followed the design of the choreography.

Assessment for this project was based on the correctness and completeness of the technical requirements of the project for each discipline along with the complexity of the choreography and how well the movements were synchronized to the song. Similar to the comparison presented by Do et al. [4], the music student is not expected to be a programmer, and the programmer is not expected to be a music student. Each member of the interdisciplinary team utilized their strengths for the success of the project.

3.3 Row Bots

For this undergraduate research project, four LEGO MINDSTORMS NXT robots march in a musical "round" as they play the "Row, Row, Row Your Boat." song. This project required that the original music file be created using Sibelius and then saved as a WAVE file. This WAVE file would then need to be converted, uploaded and played directly from the NXT brick along with the movements that would needed to be developed in Java utilizing the leJOS NXJ framework.

Each robot was required to move a specified distance based on the length of the uploaded sound clip and its position in line, wait for others to complete their task, turn in sequence, return to the starting location, turn in sequence again, and play an applause sound clip to finish the routine. The challenges of this project were the storage limitations on the brick, converting the audio file to a format that could be played on the brick, and synchronizing the movements of the robots during the marching routine.

The original audio file for the "Row, Row, Row Your Boat." song was approximately 6 seconds and had file size of 1.937 MB. The storage limitation on the NXT brick as defined by LeJOS is 256 KB, minus any arbitrary section assigned to the firmware [8]. The actual user-available storage on the NXT devices, with LeJOS installed, was observed to be roughly 190 KB for both the user-defined NXJ compiled source code and the uploaded audio file. We were faced with the challenge of how to load a user-defined music file onto the brick for playback. The amount of available memory was greatly insufficient to store the sound files and limits the music file for an NXT to approximately 5-6 seconds of audio. Since the LEGO Mindstorms NXT is capable of playing WAVE files that are formatted in 8-bit PCM samples, use a single channel, have a frequency between 5500 Hz and 16000 Hz, and are always played at 8000 Hz, despite the actual format of the audio data, the original music file needed to be converted.

The process of converting the audio file from Sibelius to the 8-bit PCM mono for playback on the LEGO Mindstorms NXT Brick can be accomplished by using Audacity (http://audacity.sourceforge.net/) or a trial version of GoldWave (http://goldwave.com/). First, the file should be converted from a Sibelius (.sib) file to a WAVE (.wav) file. Using Audacity Digital Audio Editor (version 1.2.6), we set the *Default Sample Rate* to 8000 Hz and *Default Sample Format* to 16-bit and the file format to "WAV"(Microsoft 8-bit PCM). The project rate was set to 8000 Hz. and the WAV audio file was opened. We then split the stereo track, deleted one of the tracks, and set the remaining track to Mono, with Sample Format of 16-bit and Sample Rate to 8000. This will extend the time of the audio file because you are slowing down the rate. To increase the speed of the Sound File, we highlighted the audio wave and changed the speed effect back to its original speed. After compressing the sound wave, by setting compressor ratio to 10:1 and Attack Time to .1 sec, the sound file was ready to be saved and uploaded to the NXT brick. Because of the amount of down sampling (from 44.1 kHz or 48 kHz to 8 kHz) the audio file, along with quality degradation, was observed to be significantly quieter than the original requiring an increase of volume. The size of the converted audio file was 98.4 KB, which allowed for uploading to the NXT brick.

Since the movements of the robots and the playing of the sound files would need to be coordinated, all four robots needed to start at precisely the same time. This required a process to synchronously start the application, delaying each successive robot incrementally, and threading requirements for simultaneous audio playback and robot movement. Each of the robots were given a unique identifier and once started would begin moving and playing with a progressive offset producing a musical round effect (i.e. NXT1 starts immediately, NXT2 starts at the end of the first musical measure, NXT3 one musical measure offset from NXT2, and NXT4 one musical measure offset from NXT3). Each of the robots would require a defined number of repetitions of both movement and audio playback. When the robot moving the farthest from the start had completed its routine, all four robots would turn 180 degrees and then return to the initial starting point while repeating the robot movements and audio playback actions. When all four robots had returned to the starting line, all of the robots would synchronously turn 180 degrees, play a converted and uploaded applause.wav file and then end execution of the program. A snapshot of the robots during this demonstration is shown in Figure 4.

Figure 4. Snapshot of Row Bots Demonstration.

Initially, the solution to starting the execution of the code synchronously relied on the use of the NXT sound sensor to detect a sound event that exceeded a predetermined threshold value, but was later replaced by communicating a start event through Bluetooth. We utilized the *NXTConnector* with a unique identifier and *DataOutputStream/DataInputStream* for synchronized communication between the PC and each of the NXTs. Since the leJOS *Sound* class implementation spawns a separate thread for audio playback, we utilized a separate thread for the NXT movement to prevent the main method from terminating prior to the completion of the full routine.

3.4 Streaming Performers

Once we could successfully create, convert, upload and play a music file on the NXT and we knew how to complete an NXJ project for executing the robot movements, we set a goal to stream both the music and robot movements from the PC to the NXT brick. This undergraduate research project utilized Sibelius to create the background music file, LeJOS NXJ to develop the Java applications for the choreography, and Bluetooth wireless technology to stream both music file and dance movements to the NXT. For this project the specified robot movements for the dance, similar to those utilized in the Choreography project, and one music file that would need to be split into segments that could be stored on the NXT brick were streamed to two robots.

Although memory storage is quite limited, the LEGO Mindstorms NXT is sufficiently equipped to store audio input via streaming.

Instead of saving audio files directly on the NXT, the audio can be streamed in segments via Bluetooth, played, and then the memory can be released to hold more audio. This was a challenging project as the leJOS *playSample* method did not work as we had expected. It appeared that the existing method resulted in the audio file being overwritten with newly streamed audio data prior to the playing or completion of the playing of the stored audio file. Since the Bluetooth device in the NXT was accepting information from a data input stream much faster than it was playing the stream, a new *playSample* method that accepted byte arrays and allowed input of the data format for the audio would need to be created.

To stream audio data from the PC to the NXT, we first paired the PCs with specific NXTs using the factory object for leJOS Bluetooth communication, *NXTCommFactory*, in tandem with the *NXTConnector* class. Since the NXT is waiting for a connection, the computer must act as the initiator and utilizes the leJOS *Bluetooth* class method *waitForConnection*, to allow the NXT to complete the pairing with the PC. The next step was to prepare the original audio file for streaming in a Java application on the PC by obtaining the file's WAVE format and extracting pertinent information to be used to replicate the original audio file's format on the NXT. The audio was transferred from the original file into a multi-dimensional byte array. This divided the audio file into byte arrays that represented a portion of digital audio data, presumably two second intervals of audio. The WAVE file header information, number of audio data arrays, and byte information was then streamed from the PC to the NXT. Once the first segment was fully streamed, a new memory location was created by the main thread for the second stream of information to ensure mutual exclusion between threads for the reading (playing) and writing (streaming) of audio data. As data streams were received, communication between the main thread and streaming thread ensured the streaming and playing of audio remain continuous and synchronized.

After the processing for streaming of music was complete, we needed to then stream the dance movements. It was much simpler to directly call methods for moving the NXT through the leJOS native *Motor* thread in the main thread on the PC, than use the leJOS *DifferentialPilot* on the NXT. This avoids the requirement of creating another thread for movement as the *Motor* thread directly accesses an already active, built-in thread and conserves valuable user memory by minimizing the program's file size, which in turn maximizes the length of music (essentially digital audio data) in byte array form that can be streamed and held in the NXT's user memory.

The song chosen to test the ability of the robot couple to synchronously dance and receive audio via streaming through Bluetooth was the "Hungarian Dance No. 5" by Johannes Brahms. Choreography to this song included dance steps such as sway forward, sway backward, spin, arc, shudder, and turn. To properly synchronize the dance steps to the music, the duration of each dance step was timed by inserting a date stamp at the beginning and end of each individual "dance step" method call, with the difference between these two times, in milliseconds, being the duration of each dance step. This duration would then be utilized to determine the number of bytes of audio data to stream for each dance step. If necessary, the audio data for each step was segmented into equal lengths of adequate bytes to ensure that the data would fit into the NXT user memory. The dance algorithm was utilized in conjunction with the completed

algorithm for the streaming and playing of music to ensure cohesiveness between the playing of music and dance routine.

3.5 Symphony in "R"
We were able to segment and stream one audio file, but wondered whether we could stream multiple audio files at the same time to the NXT. The goal of this undergraduate research project would be to stream four distinct sound files to four robots. Together these four Mindstorms NXT robots would act as an orchestra and play a four part harmony (woodwinds, upper brass, lower brass, and percussion) of "Fight On, State.". Sibelius was utilized to create the musical selections for each part, and leJOS NXJ for the development, formatting, streaming and playing of the audio files.

This project would require multiple simultaneous connections, buffering of audio on the NXT, and maintaining a synchronous playback (between robots) of the audio files. Similar to the Row Bots project, the audio files would need to be converted for playback on the NXT. We utilized leJOS *NXTComm* class. The convenience method *NXTCommFactory.createNXTComm(NXTCommFactory.BLUETOOTH)* created the Bluetooth connection through which NXT devices could be found using the *search(null, NXTCommFactory.BLUETOOTH)* method which produced a list of available devices and the information necessary to connect to them. After the pre-converted audio files were processed into byte arrays of appropriate size for streaming, four separate user-defined *AudioFileProcessor* threads for the processing of each audio file were constructed and initialized with total size in bytes, sample rate, and total packets to be streamed. A user-defined *AudioFileStreamer* thread was constructed and initialized with an ArrayList of *NXTConnectors*. The *AudioFileStreamer* represented a producer/consumer threading model to ensure that audio information received from each the *AudioFileProcessor* threads were properly queued and streamed to each of the NXTs. The largest and most efficient size of the byte array for continuous uninterrupted playing of music was determined to be 24,000 bytes (which allowed for the streaming of 24,000 bytes while playing a different 24,000 byte segment, for a total of 48,000 bytes of memory on the NXT). Due to the transfer rates of Bluetooth, a maximum of four NXTs could be streamed to simultaneously.

We experienced problems when trying to connect to multiple NXTs simultaneously using Bluetooth as some of the connections to the NXT would fail during execution. It was determined that the noted behavior can be overcome by ensuring that unique COM ports for sending and receiving (2 COM ports per device) are allocated and utilized during the Bluetooth Driver software installation and when the PC is pairing with the NXT.

4. SUMMARY AND FUTURE WORKS
Along the pathway to creating a LEGO Orchestra, we discovered there are many other music and animation projects that provide learning opportunities for students. The Amazing Bots and Choreography can be utilized together in a Java Programming course or integrated with a General Arts Music Theory course to provide fun and exciting projects for students. Within a more advanced curriculum, students who have interests in learning more about software development, threads, multimedia, or Bluetooth communications, projects such as Row Bots, Performing Robots or Symphony in "R" provide opportunities to coalesce technology with other disciplines. The timeline and complexity of future projects can be modified based on the course requirements and knowledge of the student participants. Student experiences within the technical and general education courses

were very positive and all suggested that we continue to offer these opportunities in future semesters.

Though the user memory on the LEGO Mindstorms NXT is quite small, there is a lot that can be done with it when used efficiently. Using the leJOS programming to develop programs for the NXT can challenge one's software development, robotics, and programming logic skills, all of which provide positive experiences for any developer. Additionally, the use of Bluetooth technology for communication between NXTs, or an NXT and a PC, opens a wide range of possibilities for application that utilize the LEGO Mindstorms NXT.

Although there is a newly released LEGO Mindstorms EV3 brick that has embedded 16MB flash memory, Bluetooth 2.1, an SD expansion slot, a USB 2.0 interface, and a Matric display with a loudspeaker [7], we still value the LEGO Mindstorms NXT for its limited resources. These storage constraints provide realistic problem-solving opportunities for our students as all problems cannot be solved by the purchasing of new equipment or upgrading to newer releases of software because budget limitations or vendor requirements may take precedence. This is a good learning experience for the students and will prepare them for the corporate world where timelines and budgets are critical to each project. As we move forward with new areas of application for interdisciplinary projects, we will continue to evaluate this new LEGO technology.

The success of these innovative and interdisciplinary projects has resulted in the awarding of internal research grants to support our efforts. Students are requesting opportunities to further these efforts via undergraduate research. We have been invited to present our efforts to campus advisory board members and the university board of trustees. In addition, our admissions office has requested that we demonstrate these projects at guidance counselor workshops and open house events to showcase undergraduate research and course projects to the local community for recruiting of new students into both the Music and IST programs.

We hope that the projects we presented in this paper inspire others to be creative and provide more opportunities for interdisciplinary projects that expand breadth of knowledge and areas of application for students pursuing technical majors. We look forward to the opportunity to show demonstrations of these projects at the conference.

5. REFERENCES

[1] Amoussou, G., Boylan, M., and Peckham, J. 2010. Interdisciplinary computing education for the challenges of the future. In *Proceedings of the 41st ACM technical symposium on Computer science education* (SIGCSE '10). ACM, New York, NY, USA, 556-557. DOI= http://doi.acm.org/10.1145/1734263.1734449

[2] L. Barker. 2009. Student and Faculty Perceptions of Undergraduate Research Experiences in Computing. *Trans.*

[3] Barr, V., Liew, C.W., & Salter, R. 2010. Building bridges to other departments: three strategies. In *Proceedings of the 41st ACM technical symposium on Computer science education* (SIGCSE '10). ACM, New York, NY, USA, 64-65. DOI= http://doi.acm.org/10.1145/1734263.1734285

[4] Do, E.Y., and Gross, M.D. 2007. Environments for creativity: a lab for making things. In *Proceedings of the 6th ACM SIGCHI conference on Creativity & cognition* (C&C '07). ACM, New York, NY, USA, 27-36. DOI= http://doi.acm.org/10.1145/1254960.1254965

[5] LeBlanc, M.D., Armstrong, T., and Gousie. M.B. 2010. Connecting across campus. In *Proceedings of the 41st ACM technical symposium on Computer science education* (SIGCSE '10), ACM, New York, NY, USA, 52-56. DOI= http://doi.acm.org/10.1145/1734263.1734280

[6] The LEGO Group. 2012. http://mindstorms.lego.com/en-us/whatisnxt/default.aspx

[7] LEGO Mindstorms EV3. 2013. http://mindstorms.lego.com/en-us/News/ReadMore/Default.aspx?id=476243

[8] leJOS Team. 2007 http://lejos.sourceforge.net/

[9] Lew, M.W., Horton, T.B., and Sherriff, M.S. 2010. Using LEGO MINDSTORMS NXT and LEJOS in an Advanced Software Engineering Course. *Proceedings of 23rd IEEE Conference on Software Engineering Education and Training,* 121-128.

[10] Smarkusky, D.L., and Toman, S.A. 2013. An Interdisciplinary Learning Experience: The Creation of a Robot Dance, *Information Systems Education Journal* 11, 5 (February 2013), 55-62.

[11] Smarkusky, D.L., and Toman, S.A. 2009. An interdisciplinary approach in applying fundamental concepts. In *Proceedings of the 10th ACM conference on SIG-information technology education* (SIGITE '09). ACM, New York, NY, USA, 224-228. DOI= http://doi.acm.org/10.1145/1631728.1631800

[12] Sobiesk, E.J, Blair, J.R.S., Cook, J.D., Giordano, J.C., Goda, B.S., Reynolds, C.W. 2006. Designing an interdisciplinary information technology program. In *Proceedings of the 7th conference on Information technology education* (SIGITE '06). ACM, New York, NY, USA, 71-76. DOI= http://doi.acm.org/10.1145/1168812.1168831

[13] Weiss, R., & Overcast, I. 2008. Finding your bot-mate: criteria for evaluating robot kits for use in undergraduate computer science education. *J. Comput. Small Coll.* 24, 2 (December 2008), 43-49.

Comput. Educ. 9, 1, Article 5 (March 2009), 28 pages. DOI= http://doi.acm.org/10.1145/1513593.1513598

Group Note Taking in MediaWiki, a Collaborative Approach

Dr. Michael Jonas
University of New Hampshire at
Manchester
400 Commercial Street
Manchester, NH 03101
603-641-4352
michael.jonas@unh.edu

ABSTRACT

We present a group note taking project designed to improve student learning. Getting students to actively participate in class can dramatically increase learning outcomes. Traditional lecture methods, where students passively take notes, are not the most effective ways for understanding new material in class. We organized students into groups to record weekly lectures and motivated them through various class based incentives resulting in a living document that captured a semester's worth of class material which helped improve student understanding of the material. We developed the infrastructure to capture these notes using the MediaWiki platform, an easy to use wiki environment. At the University of New Hampshire at Manchester (UNH-M), a commuter college in an urban setting, students tend to be older with their time split between classes and work. For these students, optimally utilizing class time is an important element for success and incorporating active learning methods applied in this work will help develop those skills.

Categories and Subject Descriptors

K.3.2 [**Computers and Education**]: Computer and Information Science Education – *computer science education, curriculum, and literacy.*

General Terms

Documentation.

Keywords

Active learning, note taking, group project, teamwork.

1. INTRODUCTION

We explore an active learning approach by engaging students in a semester long group note taking project to broaden the scope of knowledge they garner from an upper level computing course. In lieu of a course textbook, students will be tasked with capturing and constructing the lecture material into an online, wiki based, live document that will grow as we progress through the semester. We use MediaWiki, a tool that lends itself to an easy collaborative environment enabling students to seamlessly edit content.

SIGITE'13, Oct 10-12 2013, Orlando, FL, USA
ACM 978-1-4503-2239-3/13/10.
http://dx.doi.org/10.1145/2512276.2512312

We chose a course that combines programming language concepts with compiler construction application: CIS698 Advanced Perspectives on Programming, an elective course for UNH-M's Computer Information Systems majors. Motivation for this work arose from the lack of a good textbook that sufficiently covered the material for this course. Although a combination of textbooks would have been effective, both the added expense and the excess material skipped in both texts made the determination of creating a course specific web based document the ideal solution.

2. ACADEMIC SETTING

The University of New Hampshire at Manchester is an urban commuter campus in Manchester, the largest city in the state of New Hampshire. UNH-M has around 1200 non-residential commuter students with a more diverse population when compared to those from traditional residential colleges. Two-thirds of the students receive financial aid and on average are three or more years older than traditional college age students.

The large majority of UNH-M students attend school full-time while working more than 20 hours per week. Full time students on average carry a course load of 16 credit hours, i.e. four courses, but can take a maximum of 20 credit hours in a semester. It is important to keep these time constraints in mind when designing new course material that requires additional class attention.

3. MOTIVATION

Work on improving student engagement in several core computing courses at UNH-M is an ongoing effort. Innovating a Capstone course by introducing students to a group research project in a challenging field had as a primary goal to get students to work efficiently through collaboration [1][2]. More recently, incorporating micro-labs into the classroom to improve student professional development also helped classroom participation [3].

What motivated this collaborative note taking approach were both a lack of existing texts that covered the material in a way the instructor wanted and the level of difficulty of the material that, for a non-traditional computing program, could become too challenging if left in the conventional lecture/lab format. The idea was to engage students by having them join in the creation of a living document that not only captured material covered in class but also expanded on it, with the aim to enhance student knowledge beyond what they were initially capable of.

The ideal was to craft an online resource specifically for the Advanced Perspectives on Programming class that was developed by students for their peers and could be used in subsequent classes. Material that speaks to students from their point of view, highlighting areas in need of clarity that is sometimes difficult to see from the perspective of the instructor teaching the material. If this model is successful, other classes in the curriculum could follow with the same approach, having students become engaged not only in the learning process but in the teaching one as well. Because as writing is learning, so is teaching and mentoring.

3.1 Challenges

Getting students to take part in collaborative note taking required a proper approach. We introduced two ideas to help motivate students into actively participating in the project. First, a grade rubric was applied for student participation. Students were graded on both their group's contribution as well as overall quality of the final document. Many opportunities were available throughout the semester where students could contribute. Points were given if outlined requirements were met, but if students failed to receive full credit they could revise their work to fill in deficiencies. The main goal was not to have the project cause students to lose points but rather to have them continually refine their work until they received their full allotment of points, an important distinction.

A second mechanism was a perceived necessity based on the course semester plan. Students had only one exam, a final, at the end of the 16 week course, so many were concerned that without a textbook and a set of quizzes or a midterm to help gauge progress, they would be ill prepared to do well on the tested material. Although there were 4 homework assignments and a final project, the applied nature of those assignments left students lacking sufficient practice with broader concepts discussed during class lectures. In effect, students were left to rely on their own set of notes and therefore felt unsure how well this would translate into a successful study guide for the final exam. This made it somewhat easy to convince the class that a group generated study guide by students would be helpful in preparing for the exam.

4. APPROACH

At the start of the semester we developed a schedule where a total of 14 lectures would be captured. Class was divided into 7 groups, with 2 or 3 students paired up. Each group was assigned 2 different weeks, one in the first half of the semester and the other in the second half. Each group was tasked with capturing the lecture they were assigned. Students could organize their own group as they saw fit, delegating tasks such as topic research, writing, proof reading, and revising.

Students were urged to take ownership of their group's material, ask questions during lecture and engage in discussions on relevant topics during class. The more information students gathered in class, the clearer a task outlined for them during offline content writing. Students had the option to contact the instructor outside of class through office hours or email for clarification, but in-class time with both instructor and fellow students was encouraged to be the ideal environment to collect needed information.

It is important to note that this activity was a side project and students still faced homework assignments and a final project along with guided lab work, all of which accounted for 60% of their grade. Students did not have the luxury to solely focus on the note taking task during the week of their turn, so it was important that they find a way to optimize the information they gathered in class to help minimize outside class time on researching and filling gaps. Additional research on topics was expected, as a mere word for word transcription of the lecture was deemed insufficient to achieve the goal of fully capturing the essence of each topic.

4.1 MediaWiki

The use of a wiki based collaborative approach has been investigated as a platform for engaging students in active learning [4][5]. We use MediaWiki, an open source wiki platform, and find that its use creates a seamless environment where students can share their ideas with ease and do so without fear of either losing work or corrupting information as all changes are captured and tracked within its framework. The tracking feature also lends itself as a means to gauge student participation which becomes an invaluable tool both for motivational purposes as well as for evaluating each group's contribution to the final product.

With tracking, not only can the instructor keep informed of progress by individual students and groups, but also analyze how this is achieved. This open, collaborative environment provides an opportunity to continually monitor and improve student writing processes. A project standard was developed to openly share comments on work so the entire class could make improvements. Simply highlighting comments in italicized red colored text using HTML tagging provided a clear way to such communication.

5. CONCLUSIONS

We integrated a group note taking project into an upper level computing course. The goal was to improve student learning through active participation by creating a framework using MediaWiki to facilitate both seamless student collaboration and the ability to monitor their progress. We devised a set of incentives to ensure both optimal student involvement and the capture of a set of concise notes accurately reflecting the class lectures. We focused on teamwork in small groups to create possible peer mentoring relationships among students and help reduce overall time requirements needed for project completion.

6. ACKNOWLEDGMENTS

The author is grateful to his students who struggled to grasp the difficult concepts in a hectic and challenging environment.

7. REFERENCES

[1] Jonas, M., Capstone Experience – Lessons from an Undergraduate Research Group in Speech at UNH Manchester. in *Proceedings of the 2011 conference on Information Technology Education*, (West Point, NY, 2011) ACM, Pages 275-280.

[2] Jonas, M., Capstone Experience: Engaging Students in Speech Processing to excite them about STEM. in *Journal of Computing Sciences in Colleges*, (Springfield, MA, 2011) faculty poster, Volume 26 Issue 6, June 2011, Pages 180-181

[3] Jonas, M., Adding Micro Labs to Aid Professional Development in Information Technology Class Curriculum. in *Journal of Computing Sciences in Colleges*, (Hamden, CT, 2012), Volume 27 Issue 6, June 2012, Pages 166-172.

[4] Peters, V. and Slotta, J. Analyzing Student Collaborations in a Wiki-Based Science Curriculum. in *Proceedings of the 9th International Conference of the Learning Sciences*, (Chicago, IL, 2010), Volume 2, Pages 119-120.

[5] Forte, A. and Brukman, A., Constructing Text: Wiki as a Toolkit for (Collaborative?) Learning. in *Proceedings of the 2007 international symposium on Wikis*, (Montreal, Canada, 2007), ACM, Pages

Partially Flipped: Experiences Using POGIL

S. Jeff Cold
Utah Valley University
800 W. University Pkwy.
Orem, UT 84058-0001
+1(801)863-8851
coldje@uvu.edu

ABSTRACT

Flipped learning is a general term used to describe several kinds of teaching techniques designed to engage students and inspire deep learning. Flipped learning often means that the lecture is provided in a format available outside of the classroom while the homework or other activities are done in the classroom where students get help from the Instructor or fellow students. [1] When educators decide to start to flip a class, they discover that recording all of the lectures so that they can be streamed online is a daunting task. Many begin by flipping only one or two lectures, creating a partially flipped class to test how well it works. A teaching technique promoted by the National Science Foundation is Process Oriented Guided Inquiry Learning (POGIL). POGIL organizes students into teams of four or five team members. Each team member has a well-defined role to play while the team works through a POGIL activity. IT3510 is an Advanced Linux Administration class where POGIL activities were used as a partially flipped teaching technique. Several lessons were learned about implementing POGIL activities in an upper-division Information Technology (IT) course.

Categories and Subject Descriptors

K.3.2 [**Computers and Information Science Education**]: Information systems education.

General Terms

Management, Performance, Design

Keywords

Flipped classroom, POGIL, Education.

SIGITE'13, October 10–12, 2013, Orlando, Florida, USA.
ACM 978-1-4503-2239-3/13/10.
http://dx.doi.org/10.1145/2512276.2512314

1. INTRODUCTION

At the foundation of the POGIL project are seven process skills: teamwork, management, information processing, critical thinking, oral and written communication, problem solving, and assessment. Other process skills are important and can also be used to write process skills goals that provide direction for your POGIL activities. A POGIL activity is a document given to each team of four to five students. [2] At the top of the document is a clear title that communicates what students will be learning. The first paragraph of the POGIL activity briefly discusses why the activity is important. The purpose of the *why* is to motivate students to do the activity by demonstrating the relevance of the activity to concepts learned in lecture. The next section in the document will include any prerequisites needed to complete the activity. If a student did not see the lecture or read the required material, then they know up front that they are missing foundation concepts they need to know. Prerequisites are followed by learning outcomes. Learning outcomes clearly describe what the student is expected to be able to do at the end of the activity. [3] The rest of the activity document offers a series of questions that guide students through the activity. One of the team members has a job as Reader who reads the activity instructions and questions out loud to the team. Other team roles are Technician, Manager, Cheerleader, and Spokesperson.

POGIL was new classroom experience for students. One struggle experienced was that individuals within a team would stop to ask me questions whenever I came around near where the team was working. In POGIL, only the Spokesperson has the right to ask questions or speak for the team. This technique requires students work within the team structure. A benefit of this structure is that even if a student is not actively asking questions themselves, peripheral learning is loosely happening within this newly created community of practice. [4] Some of the advanced students not accustomed to working within a team environment found this constraint confining, preferring to move ahead in the activity by themselves.

IT3510 is a designated Service-Learning course [5] at our university. Students are required to complete a 20 hour project that applies advanced Linux skills used to address a computing problem for a community partner. A community partner is often a non-profit service-centric organization within the community. Because of the Service-Learning project requirement, up to a third of the students will drop the course. Once POGIL teams are organized at the beginning of the semester, POGIL team roles should and did rotate weekly. However, not only did the lack of attendance play havoc with missing POGIL team member responsibilities, but the POGIL teams themselves had to be re-organized about every three weeks during the semester. In one case, towards the end of a recent semester, there was only one POGIL team member left in his team.

POGIL activities use directed, convergent, and divergent questions. Writing carefully crafted POGIL activities that correctly guide student teams towards learning outcomes is challenging. POGIL activities are popular in Chemistry disciplines and Chemistry educators actively share POGIL activities. Whole POGIL workbooks are available for Chemistry classes. Similarly, a web site is available for computing educators to share POGIL activities at http://cspogil.org. At first there were few IT POGIL activities being shared on the site, but now there are more. As more IT educators create POGIL activity documents they are willing to share, the easier it will be to more completely use POGIL to flip a class.

2. REFERENCES

[1] McCue, R. *Flipped Classrooms Benefits - An Overview*. City, 2013. http://prezi.com/zuhnbl1smxsg/flipped-classrooms-benefits-an-overview/

[2] *Elements of a Typical POGIL Classroom Activity*. The POGIL Project, Lancaster, PA, 2012.

[3] Straumanis, A. *Benefits of Using POGIL, TEDx San Miguelallende, Mexico*. City, 2010. http://www.youtube.com/watch?v=XFYVmJYGJe8

[4] Lave, J. and Wenger, E. *Situated learning: Legitimate peripheral participation*. Cambridge University Press, New York, NY, 1991.

[5] Nejmeh, B. A. *Service-Learning in the Computer and Information Sciences: Practical Applications in Engineering Education*. John Wiley & Sons, Inc. , Hoboken, NJ, 2012.

An Early Introduction to Android App Development for CS1 using Sofia

Evelyn Brannock
1000 University Center Lane
Lawrenceville, GA 30043
678-939-9007
ebrannoc@ggc.edu

Nannette Napier
1000 University Center Lane
Lawrenceville, GA 30043
678-524-1511
nnapier@ggc.edu

ABSTRACT

An engaging context has been shown to improve student motivation and performance in introductory programming courses (CS1). Therefore, we incorporated a self-contained, one-week learning module on mobile app development into a CS1 course using Eclipse and Sofia (the Simplified Open Framework for Innovative Android Applications). The module was conducted in 2 CS1 sections for a total of 44 students. Overall, students responded positively, with all successfully modifying the provided app and running it on an emulator. In future semesters, the authors plan to repeat the study, conducting surveys to gather student perspectives on Eclipse and the Sofia module. The poster will describe the module, initial results, and future plans.

Categories and Subject Descriptors

K.3.2 [**Computers and Information Science Education**]: Computer science education – *curriculum*

Keywords

Android

1. SIGNIFICANCE AND RELEVANCE OF TOPIC

Our introductory programming class (CS1) course is the first in a two-part programming sequence required of all information technology majors at Georgia Gwinnett College (GGC). Unfortunately, the pass rates for our CS1 course have been as low as 58%. Literature shows that the introductory programming course is often a difficult course for students [1, 2]; in fact, some estimates show that 33% of students either drop or fail their first programming course [3, 4]. Since an engaging context can positively impact student performance and motivation [5], we wanted to incorporate mobile application development into our CS1 course.

In considering how to change the curriculum, we faced two key constraints. First, we valued authentic learning characterized by high relevance, ill-defined problems, and real-world tools [6].

SIGITE'13, October 10–12, 2013, Orlando, Florida, USA.
ACM 978-1-4503-2239-3/13/10.
http://dx.doi.org/10.1145/2512276.2512315

For this reason, we decided against using drag-and-drop approaches like App Inventor [7] and GameSalad [8]. Although these programs allow students to quickly build an app and can be used to teach programming concepts, they do not provide experience with Java or industrial strength development tools such as Eclipse. Because the majority of students taking our CS1 course would take the CS2 course using Java, it was important to provide a strong foundation in the language. Second, we did not want to completely reengineer our CS1 course to use a mobile applications theme. From a practical perspective, we had little time to devote to course redesign, limited expertise with mobile app development, and no ability to change textbooks for the current semester. In addition, we were concerned about adding more content and complexity to an already difficult course.

Given these constraints, we sought an approach that allowed us to use authentic tools, supported our existing course learning outcomes, and required minimal course rework. We added a one week module at the end of our CS1 course that would introduce students to mobile app development as an in-class activity. This module would also serve as a review of several concepts discussed during the semester.

2. COURSE CHANGES TO SUPPORT MOBILE APPLICATION DEVELOPMENT

The instructors' first challenge for the one week module was to find and evaluate a Java-based toolset to support the Android platform. Sofia, the Simplified Open Framework for Innovative Android Applications, developed by a team at Virginia Tech, was chosen because it gave the students the ability to fully transition their previous knowledge of the CS1 Java concepts without introducing the advanced concepts normally required to develop Android applications. The students could focus on using Java programming skills to build classes that are independent of implementation environment chosen and solve problems in the application domain, instead of worrying about advanced concepts such as event handling, binding GUI elements to Java code, and user interaction coding required to construct an Android application [9].

At GGC, CS1 is traditionally taught using a novice integrated development environment (IDE). Yet, from day one in CS2, they are expected to jump directly to Eclipse. Because the Sofia framework is integrated in Eclipse's Android Developer Tools (ADT) IDE, we required students to transition to the Eclipse environment shortly after midterms and Spring Break. To gently facilitate the change, the instructors demonstrated a pared down subset of the functionalities the students would find essential, provided instructions for home installation of Eclipse, and assigned a Lynda.com "Java Essential Training" video tutorial as homework [10].

In the second week of the CS1 course, the students had a console based, coding homework assignment that output a calculated restaurant bill total given the bill amount entered by the user. Although difficult when first assigned, by the end of the semester students viewed the program as simple. One of the sample projects offered in the Sofia framework coincidentally was a tip calculator. Because of this synergy and two class period time limit for the module, we determined we would utilize this pre-existing code, and have the students improve upon it, rather than build new code from scratch.

3. OVERVIEW OF ONE WEEK MODULE
The Sofia module consisted of three distinct, but closely intertwined, portions:
1. The installation of the Eclipse/ADT/Sofia environment on the student machines.
2. Completion of a worksheet that included multiple choice, fill in the blank and long answer questions. The open Google worksheet was designed to force each of the students to individually understand some simple concepts that were introduced with the use of ADT, an emulator, GUI/Widgets and Sofia.
3. Delivery of the Android Tip Calculator app. The first requirement to produce a more functional Tip Calculator app was for the students to familiarize themselves with the new capabilities offered in ADT, such as the Android Virtual Device Manager, the Sofia directory/project structure and the WYSIWYG GUI editor. They had to view and understand the two current Java classes in the src folder, the TipModel and TipCalculatorScreen files. They felt very comfortable with the TipModel class, as it was independent of physical implementation. It stored the private variables, the getters and setters, and necessary calculation methods. To understand the current app, they built and ran it, utilizing the emulator.

Next, the students began to modify. First they were challenged to find and add an image to the app, using the drag and drop capability of the palette. To make the app even more visual, they then changed the color of the text for the "Total". They did this by easily changing the Text Color property in a form; were excited to see the new generated XML, and how this was reflected in the screen editor. The students had to add a radio button for a 22% tip to the pre-existing tip hierarchical group. Then they had to add the code in the method to support the 22% tip. They were also assigned to improve the readability and maintainability of the code by removing the tip amount magic numbers that were hard-coded in methods, refactored as constants. The students were required to iterate through the development life cycle after each of the five improvements, emphasizing testing abilities. Upon completion, each team had to explain to the instructor the changes they made to achieve the requirements and demonstrate the running app to the instructor.

4. RESULTS AND FUTURE WORK
The module was used during the last week of two CS1 sections. There were 44 students participating across both sections.

Students worked in teams of 2-3 to complete the code and individually to complete the worksheet. All students completed the assignments in the time allowed. During the individualized demonstration time for each team, the instructors anecdotally noted an overall positive response with several students in the class asking for links to additional Sofia tutorials for self-study. An informal poll indicated that students would be interested in spending more time with Sofia in future classes. A CS2 class immediately followed one of the CS1 sections involved in the module. Showing an even broader impact, after seeing the CS1 students' work, one of the CS2 students came to the instructor, asked how to install the environment, and converted multiple previous CS2 console based assignments to apps on his own time.

The authors intend to repeat this module with CS1 students in the fall with a few changes. First, to allow more systematic study and reporting, we will collect end-of-semester surveys from students regarding the use of Eclipse and the Sofia module. Second, we will arrange with our Educational Technology department to install the appropriate tools on classroom computers to save time. Finally, we will adjust the pacing of the course to finish content in the CS1 course earlier so that students will have sufficient time for the Sofia module. As well, it is under consideration by the instructors to utilize Sofia/Android development in CS2. This engaging up-to-date approach can be used to teach important concepts such as inheritance and event handling instead of Swing.

5. REFERENCES
1. Douglas, J., R. McClelland, and J. Davies, The development of a conceptual model of student satisfaction with their experience in higher education. Quality Assurance in Education, 2008. 16(1): p. 19-35.
2. Furnham, A., A. Eracleous, and T. Chamorro-Premuzic, Personality, motivation and job satisfaction: Hertzberg meets the Big Five. Journal of Managerial Psychology, 2009. 24(8): p. 765-779.
3. Bennedsen, J. and M.E. Caspersen, Failure rates in introductory programming. SIGCSE Bulletin, 2007. 39(2): p. 32-36.
4. Bergin, S. and R. Reilly. The influence of motivation and comfort-level on learning to program. in Proceedings of the 17th Annual Workshop of the Psychology of Programming Interest Group (WPPI). 2005.
5. Guzdial, M. and A.E. Tew. Imagineering Inauthentic Legitimate Peripheral Participation: An Instructional Design Approach for Motivating Computing Education. in International Workshop on Computing Education Research 2006. Canterbury, United Kingdom: ACM.
6. Reeves, T.C., J. Herrington, and R. Oliver. Authentic activities and online learning. in Higher Education Research and Development Society of Australasia. 2002. Perth, Australia.
7. Appinventor.mit.edu. (n.d.). Retrieved May 29, 2013.
8. GameSalad.com. (n.d.). Retrieved May 29, 2013.
9. Stephen H. Edwards. 2013. Re-imagining CS1/CS2 with Android using the Sofia framework. In Proceeding of the 44th ACM technical symposium on Computer science education (SIGCSE '13). ACM, New York, NY, USA, 759-759.
10. Lynda.com. (n.d.). Retrieved May 29, 2013

Hands-on Privacy Labs

Svetlana Peltsverger
Southern Polytechnic State University
Marietta, GA
speltsve@spsu.edu

Guangzhi Zheng
Southern Polytechnic State University
Marietta, GA
jackzheng@spsu.edu

ABSTRACT

Laboratory exercises are important in all technical disciplines including information security. Development of reliable laboratory exercises covering rapidly changing topics takes a lot of time and resources. Instructors often prefer to cover an ever-changing topic using textbook materials and additional readings rather than developing a new lab exercise. Privacy is one of those topics. This paper presents a virtual environment developed for hands-on exercises that will complement theoretical coverage of privacy topics. In these exercises, students will investigate technical aspects of privacy such as user tracking, data aggregation, and various tools such as Firefox add-on Collusion.

Categories and Subject Descriptors

K.3.2 [**Curriculum**]

Keywords

Privacy, courseware, virtual learning environment

1. INTRODUCTION

Protecting consumer privacy has become a broadly recognized priority for both government and private industry (Consumer Data Privacy Bill of Rights, 2012). The explosion of online content and the growth of online services, including online banking and electronic health records expanded the surface of attacks on personal privacy. People expose their personal information when they use computers, smart phones and other devices in everyday business and personal life. Every time digital content is retrieved, a digital footprint is generated and can be used to trace the action to a particular individual or device.

Colleges and universities have realized the importance of privacy education. Many Computing and Information Systems courses began to cover privacy topics. However, many of them do not address privacy issues systematically and comprehensively [1]. Those courses do not offer students a complete picture of privacy from both data providers' and data collectors' perspectives. Moreover, most of the courses address privacy as a legal and policy issue and do not cover technical details, as technical implementation of privacy is difficult to learn and practice. A proposed coherent and consistent curriculum framework [1] was used to guide the development of key learning modules and labs to address major technical competencies defined in the

framework. The purpose of these technical learning modules is to demonstrate what happens "behind the scene," when Internet resources are used and how technology can be used to protect privacy. These labs are focused on the technical competencies that are least addressed in curricula. Students will learn not only how to protect customers' privacy and write privacy policies, but also how to develop technical/automatic procedures for their enforcement.

The purpose of the project is to create courseware to help students to learn potential privacy risks arising from user tracking. This paper describes the design of the learning environment and materials.

2. DEFICIENCY IN CURRENT WAYS OF TEACHING PRIVACY

Many universities use the Association for Computing Machinery's (ACM) curriculum model as a basis to plan their IT curriculum. ACM Information Technology Curricula (IT 2008) [2] calls for one core hour in Social and Professional Issues (23 core hours) for *SP. Privacy and Civil Liberties IT426*, which exclusively discuss privacy from a social, ethical, and legal perspective. "Reasonable expectation of privacy" is covered under "Information Assurance and Security", as a learning outcome in Forensics. Privacy is also mentioned under "Web Technologies Social Software" when talking about the use of cookies. The coverage of privacy is clearly scattered. It uses words like "describe" and "clarify" in learning objectives covering privacy. Authors believe that IT students not only must be able to describe, but also to design and implement privacy protection for information systems.

We also examined a number of courses, programs, and popular textbooks. Privacy is often covered from different and narrow perspectives, either as a compliance or ethical issue. Many programs have a dedicated course that covers Professional Practices and Ethics. One of the popular textbooks is the *Gift of Fire* by Sara Baase [3]. In one chapter dedicated to privacy the author covers Fourth Amendment, Privacy Regulations in US and Europe, Technology to Protect Privacy, Expectation of Privacy, Surveillance Technologies, Wiretapping and E-mail Protection, Designing Communications Systems for Interception, and ten more topics.

Many instructors would like to cover the topic from a more technical aspect, but a lack of teaching resources and environment limits them to do so. The development of appropriate courseware not only will benefit existing courses to add hands-on learning experience in technical aspects of privacy and data protection, but also opens up new opportunities in a more specialized and strengthened track.

SIGITE'13, October 10–12, 2013, Orlando, Florida, USA.
ACM 978-1-4503-2239-3/13/10.
http://dx.doi.org/10.1145/2512276.2512316

3. THE VIRTUAL ENVIRONMENT

Technical implementation of privacy is difficult to learn and practice. The main goal of this project is to develop an extensible delivery environment for privacy modules that help students to learn privacy through hands-on projects. This environment is a software package that makes it easy to add new lessons. Courseware is delivered via this virtual environment with a set of learning modules.

4. LEARNING MODULES

All educational materials are organized as learning modules. Each learning module consists of readings, demonstrations, hands-on assignments, discussions and assessments. As a prerequisite, students should have a fundamental knowledge of networking concepts (ports, protocols, HTTP, DNS), and basic web technologies, be able to use client-side technologies (forms, JavaScript) to implement web pages.

A study guide is provided to guide the completion of each module. The study guide consists of overview, learning outcome, lecture notes, a list of readings and tasks (with estimate of time) to complete.

A general learning modules plan has been developed and first two learning modules have been developed and implemented in the virtual environment: tracking keyboard and mouse action on the web and cookies and privacy concerns [4].

5. FUTURE WORK

A number of new modules are planned and under development. Currently we are working on a learning module on Data Aggregation Threats [5]. The objective of this module is to teach how users' profile data combined with usage data can be aggregated and become a threat to users' privacy. This module will demonstrate how a third party company can collect user tracking data from several sites and then target ads for one website owner or advertising networks (e.g. DoubleClick). A user behavior profile will be created and used for predicting user's future actions or detecting impersonation (when a user disguises herself/himself as another user).

The majority of big tracking sites are connected through third-party sites, e.g., tmz.com, wordpress.com, etc. connect Facebook and DoubleClick [6]. Students will use Firefox add-on Collusion (http://www.mozilla.org/en-US/collusion) to see real time interaction between Internet sites. In the module students will first study POSTs and GETs issued during their interaction with websites, then they will compare data they collected to the results collected by Collusion. Then students will analyze results and find potential privacy violations.

Our aim is to provide 8 to 10 learning modules for a complete courseware that are enough for an offering of a complete course in a regular semester. The framework and courseware is flexible and loosely coupled and can be independently used in web development courses, hacking courses, or a network/internet security course. There may be dependencies among learning modules; if so, they will be specified in a learning module road map (knowledge map). The learning environment is extendable and can support additional module development.

6. CONCLUSION

Learning privacy from a technical perspective is much needed and the knowledge is expected by students' future employers and society. IA curricular anticipates attention to technical aspects to complement the coverage, but instructors do not find enough resources. We have identified such need and have been developing a comprehensive framework and courseware for educators to use. The resulting framework and courseware can serve as a model for teaching students about potential privacy risks arising from user tracking. Developed laboratory exercises are crucial in understanding technical aspects of privacy. In addition to the release of the virtual environment and ready to go modules to instructors who need to enhance their courses with hands-on training, will make both the development efforts and the experience gained in this project available as well. The new environment allows adding new lessons as new privacy issues emerge. We will continue to develop the learning environment and soon release the completed version to the public.

7. REFERENCES

[1] Peltsverger, S., Zheng, G., "Defining a Framework for Teaching Privacy in Information Assurance Curriculum", Proceedings of the 16th Colloquium for Information Systems Security Education, Orlando, FL June 11-13, 2012,

[2] ACM Information Technology Curricula IT 2008, url: http://www.acm.org//education/curricula/IT2008%20Curriculum.pdf

[3] Baase, S. *"A Gift of Fire: Social, Legal, and Ethical Issues in Computing",* Prentice Hall, New Jersey, 2007.

[4] Toubiana, V., Verdot, V., & Christophe, B. (2012). Cookie-based privacy issues on google services (p. 141). ACM Press. doi:10.1145/2133601.2133619

[5] Ren, S. Q., Aung, K. M. M., & Park, J. S. (2010). A Privacy Enhanced Data Aggregation Model (pp. 985–990). IEEE. doi:10.1109/CIT.2010.181

[6] Tracking the trackers: who are the companies monitoring us online?, Interactive Technology http://www.guardian.co.uk/technology/interactive/2012/apr/23/tracking-trackers-companies-following-online

Developing HFOSS Projects Using Integrated Teams across Levels and Institutions

Heidi J. C. Ellis, Stoney Jackson
Western New England University
1215 Wilbraham Rd.
Springfield, MA USA
011-413-782-1748
ellis@wne.edu, stoney.jackson@wne.edu

Gregory W. Hislop
Drexel University
3141 Chestnut St.
Philadelphia, PA USA
011-215-895-2179
hislop@drexel.edu

Darci Burdge
Nassau Community College
Garden City, NY 11530
011-516-572-7383 Ext. 26826
darci.burdge@ncc.edu

Joanmarie Diggs
Igalia, S.L.
Spain
jdiggs@igalia.com

ABSTRACT

Studies have shown that the "near peer" experience where students of various levels are jointly involved in co-learning activities can motivate students and support wide learning. Humanitarian Free and Open Source Software (HFOSS) projects have shown promise for educating students using real-world projects within a global, professional community. Leveraging the near peer experience within an HFOSS project allows beginning students to get earlier exposure to large, complex systems while providing the more advanced students the opportunity to practice communication, coordination, and leadership skills. This poster describes initial steps towards the development of an HFOSS project by a mixed team of students of various levels and from three different institutions.

Categories and Subject Descriptors

K.3.2 [**Computers and Education**]: Computer and Information Science Education – *Computer Science Education*

Keywords

Open Source Software Projects, Vertical Teams, Student Projects

1. INTRODUCTION

Vertically integrated student teams comprised of more and less advanced students have the potential to improve student learning and excitement about computing [1]. "Near peers" are students that are one to several years senior to another student. The less advanced students are typically following in the steps of the more advanced students. As a result, the more advanced students have a unique understanding of the knowledge and viewpoints likely

held by the less experienced students. This benefits the less advanced students by allowing the advanced students to more easily identify and focus on the areas that are less well understood by the less advanced students. In addition, peer example and mentoring by advanced students provides motivation to inspire interest in computing and hopefully enhance learning. The more advanced students typically improve their communication and management skills via interactions with less experienced students.

Humanitarian Free and Open Source Software (HFOSS) projects have shown promise for educating students using real-world projects within a global, professional community [2]. IT students can learn much about developing, installing and configuring applications for a variety of platforms. Involving vertically integrated teams in HFOSS projects allows beginning students to get earlier exposure to large, complex systems while more advanced students have the opportunity to practice communication, coordination, and leadership skills.

2. THE MOUSETRAP PROJECT

In 2012, Joanmarie Diggs proposed a GNOME Outreach Program for Professors [3]. The goal of the program is to introduce professors to GNOME and free software by providing professors with ownership of a GNOME assistive technology project. The program provides support and mentoring for professors as they become familiar with the project. This poster reports on a pilot of the program that is being run across three institutions.

MouseTrap is an application that allows users with movement impairment to move the cursor. A webcam tracks user head motion and the cursor is moved accordingly. Originally created in 2008, development was halted in 2010 due to lack of developers. MouseTrap is written in Python and uses OpenCV.

The professors at the three institutions, Drexel University, Western New England University (WNE) and Nassau Community College (NCC), have involved students in the project resulting in an integrated team of students at various education levels across the three institutions. This team consists of a second year student from NCC, two third year students from WNE, and a fourth year student from Drexel. This team is operating in a vertically-integrated manner where the Drexel student is the most advanced and is taking the lead in development. She provides information and guidance to her teammates who look to her for direction.

Students were recruited to work on the project in late 2012 and began working on MouseTrap in earnest in mid-January 2013. The code is being updated to conform to the latest version of OpenCV. Students are holding weekly IRC meetings and progress is being logged on a wiki. Students are also building a knowledge base containing guidelines and tutorials related to the project that will aid other students in getting started in MouseTrap.

In this case, the near-peer approach is benefiting the less advanced students as they get to experience development principles in practice, perhaps before they are formally introduced to them. These students may also take their work more seriously as it is associated with the work of upper classmen (in addition to the cool factor). The more advanced students are able to apply development principles and the questions asked by less experienced students, guide them to create better, more detailed products. In addition, the more advanced students hone their management and training skills.

The poster reports on this pilot of the GNOME Outreach Program for Professors that uses the MouseTrap project. MouseTrap is currently being ported to Python 3 and is going to be used in a Software Engineering class at Western New England University.

3. ACKNOWLEDGMENTS

This material is based on work supported by the National Science Foundation under Grant Nos. DUE-1225708, DUE-1225738, DUE-1225688, and CNS-0939059. Any opinions, findings and conclusions or recommendations expressed in this material are those of the author(s) and do not necessarily reflect the views of the National Science Foundation (NSF).

4. REFERENCES

[1] Towhidnejad, M., Hislop, G.W., and Urban, J.E., "Using Vertically Integrated Project Teams: Inspiring Student Interest in Computing Careers." Proceedings, 2011 ASEE Annual Conference. June, 2011.

[2] Ellis, H.J.C., Hislop, G.W., Rodriguez, J.S., and Morelli, R.A., "Student Software Engineering Learning via Participation in Humanitarian FOSS Projects," Proceedings, 2012 ASEE Annual Conference. , June, 2012.

[3] Diggs, J., "Facilitating Student Participation in Free Software within Academic Courses," 2012 fossa Conference, Bois Blanc, France, Dec. 4-6, 2012. Ellis, H.J.C., Purcell, M., and Hislop, G., "An Approach for Evaluating FOSS Projects for Student Participation," *SIGCSE 2012, Technical Symposium on Computer Science Education*, Raleigh, NC, Mar. 2012.

The 2+2 Bachelor of Applied Science in Health Information Technology (BAS-HIT) – Continuation of the 2+2 BASIT Program

Rebecca H. Rutherfoord, Han Reichgelt, Chi Zhang, Ming Yang
Southern Polytechnic State University
Marietta, GA 30060
+1 (678) 915-7400
{brutherf, hreichge, chizhang, myang2}@spsu.edu

ABSTRACT

The need for programs in Health Information Technology has led Southern Polytechnic State University Information Technology Department to start a Bachelor of Applied Science in Health Information Technology (BAS-HIT). The program will allow students who have earned an Associate of Applied Science degree in Health Information Technology from an accredited technical college to enroll at Southern Polytechnic State University and obtain a bachelor's qualification with two years of additional study and no loss of credit. Students who graduate from this program should contribute in assisting the Atlanta Metro Area as the hub of Health Information Technology. This paper introduces the program development of a Bachelor of Applied Science in Health Information Technology. This follows the successful established 2+2 Bachelor of Applied Science in Information Technology (BASIT) program format, creates the credit to transfer evaluation credit and creates a tailored curriculum for the BAS-HIT students.

Categories and Subject Descriptors

K.3.2. [Computers and Education]: Computer and Information Science Education

Keywords

Health Information Technology (HIT), IT curriculum, 2+2 programs, transfer of courses

1. INTRODUCTION

For many states, 2+2 programs are designed to accept students who have completed their first two years and earned an Associate Degree (AS), to transfer to four year institutions to complete their Bachelors Degree (BS) [2, 3, 7]. In the state of Georgia, there are two separate college/university systems – University System of Georgia (USG) and the Technical College System of Georgia (TCSG). The TCSG comprises schools offering certificates, diplomas and Associate of Applied Technology (AAT) and Associate of Applied Science (AAS) degrees.

SIGITE'13, October 10–12, 2013, Orlando, Florida, USA.
Copyright © 2013 ACM 978-1-4503-2239-3/13/10...$15.00.
http://dx.doi.org/10.1145/2512276.2512318

Southern Polytechnic State University (SPSU) entered into an articulation agreement with the TCSG in 2008 to create a series of Bachelor of Applied Science degrees in several areas [7, 8]. The Information Technology department created a BAS in Information Technology (BASIT) that fully accepts the two year AAS and AAT degree credits earned in a computing field from any regional accredited TCSG schools. The students then complete the last two years at SPSU to receive their BASIT degree [4, 5].

As Health Information technology (HIT) professionals are in increasing demand. the Information Technology department at SPSU started an effort in health information technology in 2010 to design and implement a series of educational programs, including professional development courses, certificate programs, and degree courses [9]. As part of the effort in HIT, the IT department began exploring other ways to serve students who wanted to receive a bachelor's degree in HIT. By using the established articulation agreement between SPSU and TCSG, the department completed a new program – the BAS-HIT (Bachelor of Applied Science in Health Information Technology) for the students who wish to transfer from the two-year TCSG college to SPSU to complete their bachelor's degree.

2. TRANSFER OF CREDIT ISSUES AND ARTICULATION AGREEMENT

The American Association of Collegiate Registrars and Admissions Officers (AACRAO), the American Council on Education (ACE), and the Council for Higher Education Accreditation (CHEA) have published a joint statement on the transfer and award of credit [1]. The joint statement is intended to serve as a guide for institutions developing ore reviewing policies dealing with transfer, acceptance and award of credit.

One of the ways to help ensure quality in the transfer of courses is to examine the curriculum from the transfer institution, along with faculty and other pertinent accreditation criteria, whereas another is to accept courses only from accredited institutions. The state of Georgia has made a joint effort on smooth credit transfer between public institutions [6]. At Southern Polytechnic State University (SPSU) in Marietta, GA, we have chosen to look at accepting transfer students from accredited institutions from the TCSG and established an articulation agreement with most of the institutions within the TCSG. We accept the complete AAS or AAT degree in a computing field.

By following the success of the BASIT program [5], the BAS in Health Information Technology (BAS-HIT) has been created. The pathways from selected TCSG AAS/AAT degrees in HIT into related Bachelor's degrees will fully utilize the AAS courses that the students have taken at the TCSG by fully transferring them into the BAS programs.

3. COURSE OF STUDY

When creating our BASIT program a process was created whereby the general education course for transfer are evaluated by the Registrar's office and the major course would be sent to the BASIT coordinator for evaluation.

As in our established BASIT program, students transferring into the BAS-HIT program are required to complete their last two years – 60 semester hours, at SPSU. Students in the BAS-HIT program are required to obtain both breath and depth of IT education as the students in the BASIT and our regular four year degree program BSIT. This is driven both by the demands of employers of our graduates, the ABET CAC accreditation standards in IT, and the IT model curriculum.

The specialized courses for the major of HIT are very different from the other computing majors that can transfer to the BASIT program. In order to process the transfer of courses into the new BAS-HIT program, we follow the established process for transfer evaluation. More importantly, we examined the HIT curriculum at TCSG institutions. The transfer of credit is not done on a course-by-course transfer, but, instead, a group of major HIT courses taken as part of the AAS degree are transferred as a "technical block". This allows for the maximum number of transfer courses from the AAS-HIT degree. The students also transfer in several general education courses they completed as part of their AAS degree. Most students will transfer in 52-58 semester hours from their AAS degree – with a maximum of 37 semester hours of major HIT courses in the technical block.

The HIT students transferring from TCSG schools obtain depth before they obtain breadth; therefore we needed to restructure the courses that make up the BAS-HIT program. For example, students from TCSG have taken a series of specialized occupational courses, such as medical terminology, pharmacotherapy, medical coding and classification, among others. These courses are more healthcare-related, rather than technology-related. In order for the students to obtain breadth in IT and HIT specifically, the students take 2 programming courses, 3 lower-level IT courses, 2 upper-level computing courses, 6 upper-level IT courses including HIT practicum, 2 specialized HIT courses, and the additional required general education courses.

The ability for students to begin at a two-year technical college and then transfer to a four-year university to complete a bachelor's degree has already proven very successful in our regular BASIT program. We currently have approximately 175 BASIT students. We believe that we will see tremendous growth in this new BAS-HIT program as well.

4. CONCLUSION

The BAS-HIT program was introduced relatively recently. It is the start of the collaboration with other HIT program at TCSG schools. Many institutions from TCSG and USG offer healthcare-related programs, such as Nursing, Health Science, Public Health, Health Service Administration, Health Information Management, and Health Informatics, to name a few. From our interaction with the students from some of these programs, students showed their interest in knowing more about health informatics and health information technology to be better prepared for the increasing demand in the HIT field. Students who graduate from the newly created BAS-HIT program should support the efforts to establish the Atlanta Metro Area as the hub of Health Information Technology.

5. REFERENCES

[1] American Council on Education. 2001. Joint Statement on the Transfer and Award of Credit. Accessed on May 31, 2013 from http://www.acenet.edu/news-room/Documents/2001-Joint-Statement-on-Credit.pdf

[2] Florida Department of Education. 2006. 2+2 Pathways to Success. Accessed on May 31, 2013 from http://www.fldoe.org/articulation/pdf/Pathways_to_Success.pdf

[3] New England Association of Schools & Colleges, Commission on Institutions of Higher Education. 1980. Transfer and Award of Academic Credit. Accessed on May 31, 2013 from http://cihe.neasc.org/downloads/POLICIES/Pp75_Transfer_and_Award_of_Academic_Credit.pdf

[4] Rutherfoord, R. H. and Reichgelt, H. 2009. Creating a 2+2 Information Technology Degree Program – the Bachelor of Applied Science in Information Technology. Proceeding of SIGITE'09. Fairfax, VA. October 2009. 221-223.

[5] Rutherfoord, R. H., Reichgelt, H., and Wang, J. A. 2011. The 2+2 Bachelor of Applied Science in Information Technology Follow-up 2 Years Later – Dealing with Challenges. Proceeding of SIGITE'11. West Point, NY. October 2011. 149-153.

[6] Southern Association of Colleges and Schools, Commission on Colleges. 2003. Transfer of Academic Credit, A Position Statement. Accessed on May 31, 2013 from http://www.sacscoc.org/pdf/081705/transfer%20credit.pdf

[7] Southern Polytechnic State University. 2013. Articulation Program with Technical College System of Georgia. Accessed on May 31, 2013 from https://www.spsu.edu/tcsg/

[8] University System of Georgia and Technical College System of Georgia. 2012. Complete College Georgia. Georgia Higher Education Completion Plan 2012. Accessed on May 31, 2013 from http://www.usg.edu/educational_access/documents/GaHigherEducationCompletionPlan2012.pdf

[9] Zhang, C., Reichgelt, H. Rutherfoord, R.H., Brown, B. and Wang, J.A. 2012. Developing and Improving Interdisciplinary Health Information Technology Certificate Programs. Proceeding of SIGITE'12. Calgary, Canada. October 2012. 43-48.

A Transition Community for Deaf and Hard of Hearing Students in Information Technology Programs

Raja S. Kushalnagar　　　　　David E. Lawrence　　　　　Elissa M. Olsen

Information and Computing Studies Department, National Technical Institute for the Deaf
Rochester Institute of Technology, Rochester, NY 14623-5604
{rskics, delnet, emondp}@rit.edu

ABSTRACT

In the Information Technology (IT) field, deaf and hard of hearing (DHH) students are underrepresented and less academically successful compared to their hearing counterparts. DHH students face difficulty in handling the demands and expectations of college level classes, especially introductory programming courses. As a result, without appropriate support, most do not succeed in introductory programming courses. For this group, a combination of a transitional community and transitional programming course has been shown to improve their academic success. This paper describes 1) how the establishment of a community of peers with an appropriate academic support structure improves graduation persistence, 2) how a transition programming course with an appropriate support structure improves completion rates of the introductory programming sequence and 3) resources for instructors with DHH students in the classroom.

Categories and Subject Descriptors

K.3.2 [Computing Mileux]: Computers and Education. Computer Science Education

Keywords

Deaf and Hard of Hearing Students, IT Programming Sequence.

1. INTRODUCTION

There were about 138,000 deaf and hard of hearing (DHH) students in college nationwide in 2010 [1]. State and federal laws such as the Americans with Disabilities Act of 1990 enabled DHH students to attend the schools of their choice with support. As a result, over 38 years from 1972 and 2010, the percentage of DHH individuals attending college increased by over 400%. Though these improvements are a huge improvement, the percentage of deaf students pursuing bachelor's degrees continue to be much less than their peers. For example, in 2009, 60% of DHH high school graduates attended postsecondary education. Of these students, 57% attended two-year schools as compared to 48% for hearing students. By contrast, 33% of deaf students pursued baccalaureate degrees as compared to 47% of hearing students [1].

There are several reasons for this disparity. Many DHH students are steered to vocational or applied fields due to the belief they cannot succeed in more abstract fields such as IT or other STEM (Science, Technology, Engineering and Mathematics) programs.

This belief is shaped not only by their delayed English and mathematics competency but also because many have simply never had the opportunity to take courses that expose them to the high level of problem solving skills needed for courses like programming in IT. As a result if they do take programming courses, they are more likely to do poorly and discontinue their pursuit of an IT or STEM career. DHH students who get DHH specific peer and academic support have greater success in terms of better grades, higher persistence and graduation rates. The key characteristic for peer and academic support is to give them an accurate measure of their readiness for the rigors of computing disciplines along with appropriate peer support.

2. PEER AND ACADEMIC SUPPORT

Various studies with college students have shown that academic and social integration significantly affects academic persistence and graduation rates [2]. Due to communication barriers, especially in group settings, DHH students prefer to relate to other deaf students [3]. As deafness is low incidence, most universities have few deaf students. To mitigate the sense of isolation and alienation, and to boost student engagement, educators have tried learning communities among deaf and hearing students to encourage early academic and social integration. A learning community involves linking courses, instructors and students together to increase contact among students and faculty, and to create linkages between academic disciplines [4]. Studies at the National Technical Institute for the Deaf (NTID) have shown that students who participate in learning communities with similar communication and educational backgrounds have higher rates of class attendance, and keep up with homework and other course work. That is, the academic clustering fostered social connections with peers and to promote greater identification with the academic values of the institution [5]. At Rochester Institute of Technology (RIT), the Information and Computing Studies (ICS) department accepts DHH students who have ACT scores that show reasonable chance of success in college and places them in math and English courses based on in-house testing. For AS (Associate of Science) students interested in pursuing a baccalaureate degree, but not yet at the necessary math or English level, ICS provides a learning community of peer DHH students along with academic support in the form of simultaneous voice and/or direct signed instruction. During their first year, math, English and some technical courses are offered using direct classroom instruction to more easily understand the materials, catch up and excel in their studies. After they master the curriculum to be on par with hearing peers, the instruction shifts to voice only instruction with support of interpreters or captionists along with note takers in the classroom. A team of support faculty with a variety of communication modes assist these students throughout their AS and BS careers. In combination with peer support through formal and informal DHH student group meetings, this has been shown to lead to a higher percentage of graduates from those programs. This suggests that peer learning communities and language supportive academic support play key roles in successful completion of a baccalaureate program.

3. TRANSITION COURSE

Per ACM (Association for Computing Machinery) curriculum guidelines, students are required to completing a programming sequence focusing on algorithmic problem. The academic learning issues faced in computing courses is similar to the learning issues faced in mathematics and reading courses. Depending on the objectives and content area, a question or task may require integrating content knowledge, problems solving ability, laboratory experience and ability to apply information [6]. If these concepts and vocabulary are not fully captured, students are likely to do poorly. Most programming course knowledge is tacit, so only a fraction can be verbalized or signed during a lecture. Often students pick this up by integrating lecture material within their mental schema by discussion and practice with their peers. DHH students have fewer opportunities to integrate academic knowledge. A transitional programming course with language supportive instruction, enables DHH students learn the basic principles of programming. By the end of the transition course students are expected to construct simple programs and be prepared to complete the programming sequence.

4. METHODOLOGY

The goal was to determine if a transition community and transition course would impact the success rate in the IT programming sequence. We compared communication preferences and ACT scores and analyzed for pass/fail history for DHH students taking a programming sequence in IT or a related program in GCCIS.

4.1 Transition Community Course Analysis

Students were asked about their communication preferences at time of entry into RIT. The choices were to either to sign only, to sign and speak, or to speak only. About 50% of the students preferred to sign only, 25% preferred to sign and speak, and the rest preferred to speak only. Interestingly, there was no difference in graduation rate or passage rate among these groups. Although it might have been expected that students with a greater degree of communication inhibition with hearing peers would not succeed as well as those with less communication barriers, this was not observed. There was an observed trend of increased graduation and passage rate when they were more involved in the peer learning support group.

4.2 Transition Course Analysis

There was clear correlation between the average ACT score and degree level. The range of ACT scores for deaf students ranged from 15.19 for AOS (Associate of Occupational Studies; the shortest and least language intensive 2-year degree) to 20.15 for the AS (which focuses only on giving students a solid grounding in preparation for further studies in four year programs). For the baccalaureate degree, the average ACT score for deaf students in GCCIS was 25.95. In contrast, the average score of hearing students in GCCIS was around 28.

Our records for the introductory programming course offered by the Information Technology department go back to 1998. Before 1999, the ICS department did not offer a programming transition course for DHH students. As a result, the percentage of deaf students who obtained a passing grade in the first Information Technology programming sequence course was 28%. From 1999 onwards, the ICS department offered a mandated transition course for all DHH students transferring to the IT program take this course. As a result, the percentage of deaf students who obtained a passing grade on the first course of the programming sequence doubled from 30% to over 60% in 2000 and then rose slowly thereafter as transition course was fine-tuned to better fit the students' academic

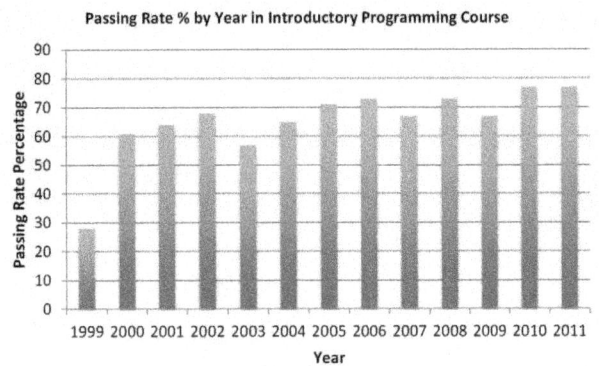

Passing Rate % by Year in Introductory Programming Course

and social needs. The transition course instructors, who both sign and voice developed and adopted strategies that focused on the two goals, e.g., content and social knowledge. The goal of content knowledge focused on enabling DHH students to pick up the content knowledge necessary to make the transition from applied computing to computational thinking. The goal of social knowledge focused on aiding students' self-awareness and social skills to make the transition to a mainstream environment with interpreters and or captionists.

5. RESOURCES

The following resources contain helpful suggestions from students and strategies that worked for other faculty.

http://www.rit.edu/ntid/teach2connect: This contains valuable resources to assist faculty in finding answers to questions they might have when working with DHH students in and outside of the classroom.

http://deaftec.org: DeafTEC provides resources for high schools and community colleges that educate DHH students in STEM-related programs.

REFERENCES

[1] G. Walter, "Deaf and Hard-of-Hearing Students in Transition: Demographics with an Emphasis on STEM Education." Rochester, NY, pp. 1–50, 2010.

[2] F. J. Dowaliby, W. M. Garrison, and D. Dagel, "The Student Integration Survey: Development of an early alert assessment and reporting system," *Research in Higher Education*, vol. 34, no. 4, pp. 513–531.

[3] J. A. Albertini, R. R. Kelly, and M. K. Matchett, "Personal factors that influence deaf college students' academic success.," *Journal of deaf studies and deaf education*, vol. 17, no. 1, pp. 85–101, Jan. 2012.

[4] V. Tinto, *Leaving college : rethinking the causes and cures of student attrition*. Chicago; London: University of Chicago Press, 1993.

[5] M. Stinson and S. Antia, "Considerations in educating deaf and hard-of-hearing students in inclusive settings.," *Journal of deaf studies and deaf education*, vol. 4, no. 3, pp. 163–75, Jan. 1999.

[6] R. J. Patz, "FOCUS ARTICLE: Building NCLB Science Assessments: Psychometric and Practical Considerations," *Measurement: Interdisciplinary Research and Perspectives*, vol. 4, no. 4, pp. 199–239, Oct. 2006.

Coordinating Artifacts in an Online Course Delivery System

David Burlinson
Winthrop University
Rock Hill, South Carolina
USA

burlinsond2@winthrop.edu

Marguerite Doman
Winthrop University
Rock Hill, South Carolina
USA
001-803-323-2692
domanm@winthrop.edu

Nicholas Grossoehme
Winthrop University
Rock Hill, South Carolina
USA
001-803-323-2113
grossoehmen@winthrop.edu

ABSTRACT
Development of online instruction has become a major goal of many universities. There are multiple aspects to delivering an effective online course [Carr-Chellman and Duchastel, 2000]. One of these is to provide guided web based sessions for tutoring, review or introduction of skill development. Materials provided can include question/answers (data), lecture (video), problems (textual input), and others. The instructional delivery of an online course can overlap many of these artifact types. These artifacts, designed to heighten student involvement, can clutter the screen, adding distraction. There is a challenge in concurrently presenting similar concepts of different artifacts in a meaningful way.

Our research investigates making the delivery of content through these technologies more effective. By linking review questions to the display of the content delivery, we propose that student attention will be more focused and content retention will increase.

Categories and Subject Descriptors
J.m[**Computer Applications**]: Applied Computing; Education; Computer-assisted instruction; Computer-managed instruction.

Keywords
Online education

SIGITE'13, October 10–12, 2013, Orlando, Florida, USA.
ACM 978-1-4503-2239-3/13/10.
http://dx.doi.org/10.1145/2512276.2512320

Can You Hear Me Now? – An Empirical Study on Using Social Media to Improve Student-Instructor Communication

Lei Li
Southern Polytechnic State University
1100 South Marietta Pkwy
Marietta, GA 30060
01-678-915-3915
lli3@spsu.edu

Rong Guo
University of West Georgia
1601 Maple St
Carrollton, GA 30118
01-678-839-5301
rguo@westga.edu

ABSTRACT

There are extensive research on the usage and effectiveness of social media in the classrooms. Many of those studies use questionnaires as main research methods. This paper conducts an empirical study on using social media, specifically Facebook and text messaging, to improve student-instructor communication in a distance learning environment. This study records the actual usage of social media tool for a treatment group and compares the students' performance of the treatment group with a control group. This study is a research-in-progress. The research design and implication of the study are discussed in details.

Categories and Subject Descriptors

K.3.2

Keywords

Social media, Higher Education, Distance Learning, Facebook, Text Messaging

1. INTRODUCTION

Social media refers to any media that help integrate technology into the lives of people for the purpose of communication [4]. More and more universities are using social media tools such as social networking, wikis, blogs, or video, to interact with or engage in students. [2] investigates the social media usage in higher education. For the 182 students and 64 faculty members in their survey, about 42% use Facebook, 32% use LinkedIn and 12% use Twitter for academic purposes. As for personal purposes, about 83% use Facebook, 36% use LinkedIn, and 30% use Twitter.

There is compelling evidence that social media is perceived as a valuable tool for students to be more engaged in the classroom, thereby improving their academic performance. [6] suggests that social media can provide a potential opportunity to enhance university life and community development. It can benefit the students to achieve success within the classroom. [5] states that social media can enhance student participation and learning

SIGITE'13, October 10–12, 2013, Orlando, Florida, USA.
ACM 978-1-4503-2239-3/13/10.
http://dx.doi.org/10.1145/2512276.2512321

outcome, as the context of the learning extends beyond the classroom into any learning environment that students participate in. [4] states that technology creates a more engaging and innovative classroom experience, which makes students more interested in the learning process. [3] found social media such as video and blogs can facilitate reflection and communication among students.

2. RESEARCH QUESTION FORMATION

Another exciting field that enjoys explosive growth is distance learning in higher education [1]. And effective communication is a key factor for online learning [7]. Even for well-constructed online courses, students may not be able to interact with the instructor well due to lack of real "face-to-face" meeting. For example, students may fail to submit an assignment on time even though instructor gives plenty of reminders on course delivery site. As the result, the students in online classes may perform less successfully than the ones who enroll in traditional classes.

Table 1 shows the grade distribution of a course at one author's institution over the last two academic semesters. The course is a skill-based introductory IT course that regularly offers multiple sections every semester. Even though the sections are taught by the same instructor using the same material, the students' passing rates in on campus sections are much higher than the rates of online sections. Passing grade is defined as letter grade of C or better while grade of D or worse is considered as failing grade. This course has a series of hands-on assignments which are usually due in a one-week window. As illustrated in table 2, it's not surprising that the completion rates of the assignments between traditional and online sections are follows the similar trend. When looking into the data deeper, many online students simply didn't complete the assignments. If they did complete the assignment, the passing rates are fairly good.

As matter of the fact, some students fail not because they don't know how to the assignments, but they simply forget about completing the assignment. It seems that one key factor for online student success is to keep them well informed. The instructor tried many ways to keep students up to date: a weekly overview that clearly lists all due items in that week; the assignment due dates that are marked on calendar a week ahead, an email and bulletin board reminder that is sent and posted two or three days before due date. However, it seems that those efforts aren't very effective. One possible reason is that all those are happening within the course delivery site, but many students don't login and check the site very often. In order to

Table 1. Overall Grade Distribution

	Traditional Sections		Online Sections	
Term	Spring 2012	Fall 2012	Spring 2012	Fall 2012
Enrollment	29	39	47	47
Passing rate	89.65%	79.49%	65.96%	61.70%
Failing rate	10.35%	20.51%	34.04%	38.30%

Table 2. Assignment Grade Distribution

	Traditional Sections		Online Sections	
Term	Spring 2012	Fall 2012	Spring 2012	Fall 2012
Completion rate	84.24%	85.78%	72.34%	70.41%
Passing rate upon completion	94.37%	90.43%	76.43%	80.01%

communicate with students more effectively, we need to speak their language. Naturally, social media seems to be a perfect solution.

Based on previous research, we expect social media such as Facebook and text messaging can promote better communication with student, thus improve their passing rate. The research question of this paper can be described as follows.

For an online IT introductory class, can social media such as Facebook and text messaging help the instructor communicate more effectively with students?

For an online IT introductory class, will the students who are offered social media such as Facebook and text messaging as additional communication tool perform better than the students who aren't offered such tools?

3. RESEARCH DESIGN

In order to test our research question, an empirical study is carefully designed.

Selection of Research Subject. The research subjects are drawn from several sections of a skill-based IT introductory course. Most students enrolled in this class are freshman or sophomore. They usually have limited experience with online classes and are most likely going to have problems. As matter of fact, those students have higher failing rate than the students in higher level online classes. Thus, those students are good research subjects.

All participating sections are taught by the same instructor using the same material. This eliminates potential mediating factors from different instructors and teaching materials. Each online section of the course generally enroll forty plus students which gives the study a relatively large sample size.

Selection of Social Media Tool. Based on previous research and informal in class survey, Facebook and text messaging are used in this study. They are also the most familiar tools to the students.

Research Design. The participating traditional sections are used for comparisons. The participating online sections are divided into two groups: a control group and a treatment group. The online course is well designed and satisfies rigorous Quality Matter ^{TM} standard. Within the course delivery website, the course has well established communication mechanisms: student emails are guaranteed to be replied within 12 hours; a bulletin board is set up for course updates; the due items are clearly listed in both weekly overview and calendar. In another words,

there are sufficient efforts inside the course management site for effective student-instructor interaction.

The course settings for the control group and the treatment group are the same except the treatment group is offered Facebook and text messaging as additional communication tools. For the treatment group, a class Facebook page is created. Students are encouraged but not required to use the course Facebook or text messaging. The instructor post course update such as assignment reminder on the course Facebook page using the same frequency as in the course management site. Student can also post questions on the course Facebook page. Student can also ask questions by texting the instructor.

The Facebook posting and text messages are recorded for later analysis. By the end of the semester, a questionnaire is administrated to the control group collecting feedbacks about the use of social media tools. The academic performance of the control group and treatment group will also be compared.

Questionnaire Design. The participation of survey is totally voluntary and anonymous. The questionnaire (see appendix) has three sections. Section one collects demographic information. Section two gathers students' preferred way of communicating with their instructor. Questions in section three investigate the usage and perceived effectiveness of social media tools. The display logic has been carefully added to the questionnaire. For example, if a student doesn't have a Facebook account, all questions related to the usage of Facebook won't be available to him/her.

Research Timeline. The data collection has been completed. We are working on cleaning the data and analyzing the survey result. A full version this study is expected to completed in the next FIGURES/CAPTIONS

4. DISCUSSION

This paper conducts an empirical study on the effectiveness of social media, in particular Facebook and text messaging, on improving student-instructor communication in an online learning environment. We expect that the findings would show empirical evidence that social media tools can help instructors get connected with the students better, thereby improving students' academic performance.

5. REFERENCES

[1]. Moore, M. G., and Kearsley, G. 2011. Distance education: A systems view of online learning. *Wadsworth Publishing Company*.

[2]. Records, H., Pritchard, J., and Behling, R. 2011, Exploring social media as an electronic tool in the university classroom, *Issue in Information Systems*, Vol. 12, Issue 2, 171-180.

[3]. Olofsson, A,. Lindberg, J., Stodberg, U. 2011, Shared video media and blogging: Educational technologies for enhancing formative e-assessment?, *Campus Wide Information Systems*, 28(1), 41-55.

[4]. Tadros, M., 2011, A social media approach to higher education, *Educating Educators with Social Media*, vol. 1, 83-105.

[5]. Wankel, C. 2011, Book Review: Educating Educators with Social Media, On the Horizon, 19(4), 350-354.

[6]. Wankel, L. & Wankel, C., 2011, Connecting on campus with new media, *Higher education administration with social media: including applications in student affairs, enrollment management, alumni relations and career centers*, 2, xi-xviii.

[7]. Woods Jr, R. H. 2002. How Much Communication Is Enough in Online Courses? Exploring the Relationship between Frequency of Instructor-Initiated Personal Email and Learner's Perceptions of and Participation in Online Learning. *International Journal of Instructional Media*, 29(4), 377-94.

Teaching in Amazon EC2

Carlos Gonzalez
Rochester Institute of Technology
Rochester NY, USA
cxg8647@rit.edu

Charles Border
Rochester Institute of Technology
Rochester NY, USA
cbbics@rit.edu

Tae Oh
Rochester Institute of Technology
Rochester NY, USA
thoics@rit.edu

ABSTRACT

As the trend of IT service consolidation continues to rise, organizations are now looking at hosting their services in the cloud to cut back on the costs of hosting their information systems locally. This presents an opportunity and challenge for higher learning institutions to prepare their students for the technology skills that are going to be in demand upon their graduation. In many aspects universities are already using virtual environments to teach many laboratory courses for distance students. However there is the need to introduce students to industry standard services that will better acquaint them with what is currently being used in the real world. This poster takes a look at the course 'Principles of System Administration' from the Networking Security and System Administration Department at Rochester institute of Technology and creates a foundation for moving the course over to the cloud using Amazon Web Services. It analyzes various cost scenarios, shortfalls of Amazon EC2 as a teaching platform, and proposes building a custom management system to better handle permissions.

Categories and Subject Descriptors

C.2.4 [**Cloud Computing**]

Keywords

Amazon EC2; elastic cloud computing; cloud computing; higher education; new technologies; teaching technology; virtual teaching; virtual environments; virtual labs

1. INTRODUCTION

Cloud computing is a technology that is on the rise[1][2] and will be used for years to come. For higher learning institutions this poses the challenge of preparing their students to be able to understand and utilize the technology as they move out into their careers. The largest challenge when teaching any new technology, however, is identifying where to start and what areas to focus on. It is important to begin teaching important concepts as soon as possible in order to allow students to further explore the different areas of the technology on their own. This project took a current pre-requisite course in the Networking, Security, and System Administration graduate program at the Rochester Institute of Technology (RIT) and introduced elements of cloud computing in a hands-on approach to give students a fundamental understanding of cloud computing using Amazon EC2 Web Services.

2. RELATED WORK

Using virtual labs is not a new concept in academia. The work of Stackpole et al. and Border [3–5] shows that virtual labs have been around since the mid 2000s to meet the needs of distance students who cannot attend classes physically. The work of Border[5] specifically outlines an online virtual lab environment that was developed for distance students but quickly became popular among local students as well, due to its ease of access and availability. That paper used VMware VCenter Lab Manager to provision configurations – sets of virtual machines with preconfigured settings and content – as templates for students in specific courses.

The work of Diaz [6] described student's satisfaction with a virtual lab environment for networking developed for PUCMM (Pontifica Universidad Catolica Madre y Maestra) students. His work focused on the level of satisfaction of students on their use of the virtual lab environment in comparison to a traditional hands-on environment. The students were asked to perform a lab (typically assigned in a networking class) but with one half using Amazon EC2 and the other using the traditional lab environment. At the end of the completed labs each student were asked to take a survey about their experience during the lab.

Similar to the above, Nunez [7] developed a Remote Virtual Lab on Amazon EC2 and used VMLogix as the management software on top of Amazon's infrastructure. The work focused on the experience of students when using this type of virtual environment. The thesis notes the shortcomings of the Amazon Web Services Console when it comes to ease of use and the steep learning curve when it is first introduced to students.

The thesis titled 'Creating local networks in the cloud' [8] took a similar approach to Nuñez[6] and Nuñez[7] in creating an instance of VMLogix on top of Amazon's Web Services to create a virtual networking lab environment. This work focused on the networking aspect of labs and more specifically using the TCP/IP network protocols in the cloud. Our project did not use the VMLogix software and relied instead on the Virtual Private Cloud (VPC) offered by Amazon Web Services.

All of these previous works demonstrate that the need for a virtual lab environment is a need that must be met. But more importantly they demonstrate that while there have been different types of approaches to teaching in the cloud there are not many that focus on teaching the cloud at the same time.

3. METHODOLOGY

The general methodology for the project involved 4 steps: creation of the lab materials, recruiting student volunteers, and setting up the Amazon EC2 environment for use by the student volunteers, and a survey to capture student's experience with the cloud environment. Using the feedback from students several scenarios for estimated costs were generated as well as a larger analysis of the effectiveness of Amazon EC2 as a teaching environment.

4. ANALYSIS

Amazon's EC2 service has a direct cost associated with the amount of use of instances and other resources. The lab developed in this project required students to use 2 small Ubuntu servers and 1 small Windows 2008 server. Based on data gathered during the project the average amount of time to complete this lab was 3 hours. The estimated cost for running the lab, based on the completion time by students, was $3.68.

The cost stated above, however, assumes that all instances are stopped immediately after the labs are completed and that the labs are completed all at once. For billing purposes Amazon charges partial hours as a full hour, which can also add to the total cost of the running the labs in the cloud. To provide a more realistic estimate we'll assume, taking into consideration partial hours, that a student will take 4 billable hours to complete the exercise. Using the same calculations of the original estimate the new total for the completion of the lab for one student is $0.98. Using a class sample size of 25 students this totals an estimated $24.50 for Lab 2.

This cost only includes the cost to run the instances and there are still other costs to consider. Elastic IP addresses are available to use in EC2 and are required for the second part of Lab 2 are charged at a rate of $0.01/hr. An account is only charged this amount for addresses that are not mapped to running instances. This is where it can become expensive for a class of 25 students who are not using the instances 24/7. For example we'll consider a scenario where Lab 2 is assigned to a class of 25 as an individual lab. Taking 332 hours (a two week period to complete a lab assignment) and multiplying them by 2 (one for the EC2 elastic IP and the other for the VPC elastic IP) and then multiplying it by 25 (amount of students) and the $0.01 charge we get an estimated $166.00 in charges for the unused elastic IPs. This is almost 7 times the amount that it costs to run the instances.

4.1 Amazon Cloud as a Teaching Platform

One of the most important aspects of this project was to determine the limitations and opportunities related to leveraging Amazon EC2 as a teaching platform. Ideally a system that is used for instructional purpose would allow an instructor to set fine-grained controls on what resources a student can access and what actions they can perform within the system. This is where EC2 falls short of other systems. Although you can setup groups in EC2 with permissions directly granted to each group, you cannot set access to only one set of amazon resources.

5. FUTURE WORK

Many of the issues with using Amazon EC2 for teaching a course is the amount of work that needs to go in from the instructor to setup the environment properly. The tasks would have to be repeated for each lab and then again for each term the class is taught. Additionally because students would be missing certain permissions, such as being able to terminate an instance, the instructor would also have to perform certain actions on demand.

A possible solution would be to create a dedicated instance and system that would automate some of the tasks that the instructor would have to perform routinely. The system could take in the names of students in the class and have them grouped if needed. Each student would have login credentials into the system to identify them. Once in the system they would have the option to instruct the system to delete an instance. The system would know which instances were created using a specific key pair and would check to see if that same key pair is the one assigned to the student. If the keypairs are the same the system would be able to terminate the instance for the student. If they are not, the system would prompt the student and take no further action.

The system could also help with the setup of each lab by using scripts that allocate the necessary addresses, VPCs, instances, and anything else. You can use Amazon's APIs to interact with the system with the same actions that are available using the web console. This allows for great flexibility in building a different structure of EC2 for teaching while still maintaining the direct access to cloud tools for students.

6. REFERENCES

[1] "Cloud Computing." [Online]. Available: http://www.comptia.org/research/cloud.aspx. [Accessed: 29-Mar-2012].

[2] "Gartner Survey Shows Cloud-Computing Services Represents 10 Percent of Spending on External IT Services in 2010." [Online]. Available: http://www.gartner.com/it/page.jsp?id=1438813. [Accessed: 30-Mar-2012].

[3] B. Stackpole, J. Koppe, T. Haskell, L. Guay, and Y. Pan, "Decentralized virtualization in systems administration education," in Proceedings of the 9th ACM SIGITE conference on Information technology education, Cincinnati, OH, USA, 2008, pp. 249–254.

[4] B. Stackpole, "The evolution of a virtualized laboratory environment," in Proceedings of the 9th ACM SIGITE conference on Information technology education, Cincinnati, OH, USA, 2008, pp. 243–248.

[5] C. Border, "The development and deployment of a multi-user, remote access virtualization system for networking, security, and system administration classes," in Proceedings of the 38th SIGCSE technical symposium on Computer science education, Covington, Kentucky, USA, 2007, pp. 576–580.

[6] K. Diaz Jorge, "Students' satisfaction when using a remote virtual lab based on Amazon EC2 for networking courses at PUCMM," Rochester Institute of Technology, United States -- New York, 2010.

[7] E. Nunez, "The development and deployment of a remote virtual lab based on Amazon Cloud for networking courses," Rochester Institute of Technology, United States -- New York, 2010.

[8] J. R. Sanchez E., "Creating local networks in the cloud," Rochester Institute of Technology, United States -- New York, 2010

Supporting Adult Learning: Enablers, Barriers, and Services

Chi Zhang and Guangzhi Zheng
Southern Polytechnic State University
Marietta, GA 30060
+1 (678) 915-3428
{chizhang, jackzheng}@spsu.edu

ABSTRACT

Adult learners are a large group for higher education including the computing and information technology programs. This paper provides a structured analysis of enablers and barriers to adult learning based on their characteristics and learning preferences. The paper proposes a general operational framework to support adult learners at different levels in educational institutions. The framework can be used as a guide for organizing adult learning support programs. Implications to IT education for adult learners are also discussed.

Categories and Subject Descriptors

K.3.0 [**Computer and Education**]: General

Keywords

Adult Learner, Adult Learning Theory, Andragogy, Higher Education.

1. INTRODUCTION

Adult learners are a large group for higher education. Adult learning is different from children's learning in that adult learners are more self-directed, having prior experience, and are internally-motivated to learn subjects that are more relevant to life and can be applied immediately. Understanding adult learners' characteristics can help institutions and instructors support adult students' learning and success.

As more working adults (especially many IT professionals) consider going back to college and taking distance or e-learning courses, it is essential for educators and administrators to recognize adult learner characteristics and learning profiles to meet their needs, and support adult students to reach their goals [3, 8]. The purpose of this paper is to summarize adult learner characteristics as enablers and barriers, and propose a structured support framework for educational institutions.

2. ADULT LEARNING THEORIES

Adult learning theories emphasize the importance of experience and self-directedness and imply that adult learners benefit most

SIGITE'13, October 10–12, 2013, Orlando, Florida, USA.
ACM 978-1-4503-2239-3/13/10.
http://dx.doi.org/10.1145/2512276.2512323

from experientially based constructivist-learning environments. The two important pillars of adult learning are andragogy and self-directed learning [8]. Knowles defined andragogy as "the art and science of helping adults learn" as opposed to the concept of pedagogy, the art and science of helping children learn [6, p. 43] whereas one of the best known self-directed learning models is Gerald Grow's Staged Self-Directed Learning (SSDL) model [5]. Self-directed learning provides a framework to match the teaching style and teaching methods to the learner's stage of self-direction. In essence, instructors play a role of facilitator or service manager in the educational process [2]. The role of facilitator is to challenge learners to examine their ways of thinking and doing regardless of their stage of self-direction.

3. ENABLERS AND BARRIERS TO ADULT LEARNING

Understanding the characteristics and needs of adult learners is a first step to provide better learning experience and support for them. Some of these characteristics can be barriers to their learning, and some others may provide benefits if they are appropriately addressed in teaching and course designs. We assess major enablers and barriers to adult learners at three levels (Table 1):

4. Proposed Framework for Adult Learner Support

We should create a cooperative climate of mutual trust and acknowledge the wealth of knowledge and experiences the adult learners bring to the class. Some teaching strategies and practices include *Active learning* [1], *Collaborative learning* [12], *Peer learning* [10], *Authentic learning* – relating learning to real world issues and problems [7], and *Personalized learning*, which provides flexibility and choices to accomplish course objectives [4, 9].

Two types of technologies are commonly used in the online learning environment which can help adult learners learn efficiently: learning management systems (LMS), a more formal and structured learning environment, and Web 2.0 applications including blog, wiki, social networking, online group, social bookmarking, online forum, content sharing, collaborative editing, online collaboration, etc. More importantly, it was found that organizational support and relevance of the course are two major factors influencing adult learners' decision to drop out or persist in online learning [11]. To enhance adult learners' learning and experience, a wide range of support and resources are needed as shown in Table 2.

Table 1. Enablers and Barriers to Adult Learners at Three Levels

	Enabler	Barrier
Personal	Rich life and work experience. Past experience motivates to learn. Goal-oriented. Strong motivation to improve knowledge and skills. Relevant to life	Poor academic preparedness. Lack of previous success. Are anxious about returning to school because of a long gap in education. Past experience may be biased or incomplete. Late adopter of technologies. Resistance to change. Ability to absorb new information due to aging.
situational	Less involved in campus activities; more concentrated. More open to discuss and communicate with peers.	Have multiple roles in life: work, family, financial responsibilities. Rigid schedules and limited time. Tight budgets (debt) and lack of support.
institutional	A variety of learning program options (e.g., online program, part-time program, accelerated training programs). Academic advising and other ancillary supports (e.g., counseling, career service, child care). Flexible course schedules.	Lack of information and support. Rigid course schedule and degree requirements. Teaching methods and course delivery that do not match adult learners' needs (e.g., more memorizing content, irrelevant to life, information cannot be applied immediately).

Table 2. Services to Support Adult Learners' Learning and Success

Level of support	Services to support Adult Learners' learning and success
Instructor	A variety of teaching methods and educational technology, accommodating class policy, relevance of the course
Academic program / Department	Flexible class schedules Distance learning options Career-related certificate program options Accelerated class options Part-time degree programs Academic advising Course credit for life experience (Prior Learning Assessment)
Institution	Financial aid packages Child care services Transportation options Course credit for life experience (Prior Learning Assessment) Academic, educational and career services Technology support

5. CONCLUSION

The principles and practices discussed in this paper apply to adult learners in the IT discipline as more IT professionals now come back to school for improving their skills, acquiring new skills or getting a certificate for promotion or changing fields. The teaching strategies and practices such as pair programming, capstone project, and online community, along with newer technologies, especially the advancement of web applications and resources have shown us an unprecedented potential to create learner-centered learning environments for IT students.

6. REFERENCES

[1] BONWELL, C.C. and EISON, J.A., 1991. *Active Learning: Creating Excitement in the Classroom*. The George Washington University.

[2] BROOKFIELD, S.D., 1986. *Understanding and Facilitating Adult Learning: A comprehensive analysis of principles and effective practice*. Open University Press, Milton Keynes.

[3] CERCONE, K., 2008. Characteristics of Adult Learners with Implications for Online Learning Design. *Association for the Advancement of Computing in Education Journal 16*, 2, 137-159.

[4] CHEN, C.M., 2008. Intelligent web-based learning system with personalized learning path guidance. *Computers & Education 51*, 2, 787-814.

[5] GROW, G.O., 1991. Teaching learners to be self-directed. *Adult Education Quarterly 41*, 125-149.

[6] KNOWLES, M.S., 1980. *The modern practice of adult education: From pedagogy to andragogy*. Englewood Cliffs: Prentice Hall/Cambridge.

[7] LOMBARD, F., 2007. Empowering next generation learners: Wiki supported inquiry based learning. In *Earli European practice based and practitioner conference on learning and instruction Maastricht, NL*.

[8] MERRIAM, S.B. and CAFFARELLA, R.S., 1999. Learning in Adulthood Jossey-Bass, San Francisco.

[9] NATIONAL EDUCATIONAL TECHNOLOGY PLAN TECHNICAL WORKING GROUP, 2010. Transforming American education: Learning powered by technology Washington, DC: Office of Educational Technology, US Department of Education.

[10] O'DONNELL, A.M. and KING, A., 1999. *Cognitive Perspectives on Peer Learning. Rutgers Invitational Symposium on Education*. ERIC.

[11] PARK, J.H. and CHOI, H.J., 2009. Factors Influencing Adult Learners' Decision to Drop Out or Persist in Online Learning. *Educational Technology & Society 12*, 4.

[12] SMITH, B. and MACGREGOR, J., 1992. What is Collaborative Learning? In *Collaborative Learning: A Sourcebook for Higher Education*, A.S. GOODSELL, M. MAHLER, V. TINTO, B.L. SMITH and J. MACGREGOR Eds. University Park, PA: National Center on Postsecondary Teaching, Learning and Assessment, 9-22.

Designing and Building Mobile Pharmacy Apps in a Healthcare IT Course

Bonnie MacKellar
Division of Computer Science, Mathematics and Science
St John's University
Queens, NY
718-990-4452
mackellb@stjohns.edu

Maria Leibfried
College of Pharmacy and Health Sciences
Dept. of Clinical Pharmacy Practice
St John's University
718-990-1965
leibfrim@stjohns.edu

ABSTRACT
An important skill for students in information technology (IT) programs is that of collaborating with domain specialists while designing IT solutions. This is particularly true in healthcare IT, where usability errors can impact patients' health. Here, we describe a course project in which healthcare IT students collaborated with pharmacy students in a task analysis session aimed at specifying the steps in two common pharmacy scenarios. The healthcare IT students then went on to design and implement mobile apps, using AppInventor that were based on the two scenarios. The process benefited both groups of students; the pharmacy students learned about the IT design process, and the healthcare IT students learned about pharmacy workflow as well as communicating with healthcare specialists.

Categories and Subject Descriptors
K.3.2 [Computers and Education]: Computers and Information Systems Education – *information systems education*

Keywords
Healthcare Informatics Education; Pharmacy Informatics Education; Mobile Application Development

1. INTRODUCTION
Learning how to work with domain specialists is a key skill for anyone who works in information technology. This is particularly the case in the specialized world of healthcare IT (HIT). The healthcare world is highly regulated, and has very specialized jargon and ways of doing things, which often differ significantly from procedures in other types of businesses. Add to that the fact that usability mistakes in IT systems can disrupt workflows in ways that impact patients' health, and it becomes clear there is a need for IT specialists and healthcare practitioners to be able to effectively communicate during the design of healthcare IT systems. Unfortunately, this is a skill that is difficult to teach, and is often not even present in standard healthcare informatics curricula. Learning how to communicate with IT specialists is even less likely to appear in the training programs for healthcare specialists, even though several related skills, such as participating in the design of electronic work queue systems and collaborating with informatics groups to design components of computer-based

Permission to make digital or hard copies of all or part of this work for personal or classroom use is granted without fee provided that copies are not made or distributed for profit or commercial advantage and that copies bear this notice and the full citation on the first page. Copyrights for components of this work owned by others than ACM must be honored. Abstracting with credit is permitted. To copy otherwise, or republish, to post on servers or to redistribute to lists, requires prior specific permission and/or a fee. Request permissions from permissions@acm.org.
SIGITE'13, October 10–12, 2013, Orlando, Florida, USA.
Copyright © 2013 ACM 978-1-4503-2239-3/13/10...$15.00.
DOI string from ACM form confirmation

order entry systems are described as emerging directions for pharmacy informatics education in [2].

At St John's University, we have an undergraduate major in HIT. In one of the required courses, we have been using mobile app development as a springboard to teach user interface and system design considerations for healthcare [3]. The students work on a major project using App Inventor, a programming environment that allows novice programmers to build applications for Android mobile devices [5]. It uses a block paradigm for specifying the logical steps in an app, similar to the Scratch programming language for children. In the past, students chose their own projects and the projects were designed and built without input from healthcare specialists. This year, we decided to concentrate on pharmacy as an application area and to use 5th year pharmacy students as our domain experts. This is beneficial not just for the HIT students, but also for the pharmacy students since they were able to learn firsthand the difficulties of explaining their needs to an IT specialist during the design process.

The College of Pharmacy and Health Sciences at St John's University is a large and thriving program. Students in the pharmacy program learn to work with and use HIT systems such as electronic medical record systems and computerized order entry systems. Since pharmacy applications are a large component of HIT systems, collaborating with faculty and students from this program is useful for our own program. Thus, we decided to collaborate with a group of 5th year pharmacy students, as well as a faculty member in the pharmacy program, in a task analysis session with the goal of breaking down the steps in two typical pharmacy scenarios into enough detail so that the health care informatics students could design and implement mobile apps supporting these scenarios.

2. METHODOLOGY
The professor for the HIT course and the collaborating pharmacy professor met a number of times before the course ran, in order to determine a structure for the design meeting and a set of scenarios. The two scenarios chosen involved the turnaround time for a new prescription in a community pharmacy, and the turnaround time for an intravenous medication order in a hospital pharmacy. There is a large body of literature on user-centered design and task analysis methods [1]; ultimately we chose the Collaborative Analysis of Requirements and Design (CARD) method [4]. We chose this method because it is simple enough to explain to students in a few minutes; we did not want to waste meeting time with lengthy explanations. In this method, participants work with cards which can represent a work activity, a workplace object, a person, an interpersonal activity, or a mental state. In a participatory analysis session, one of three types in the methodology, the domain specialists describe steps in their work and other group members ask questions. The session starts with

the participants brainstorming on a set of initial steps. Then, the participants work through the steps, one at a time. For each step, the corresponding card was laid out and discussed. We first asked if the step was a duplicate, in which case the card was removed, or if it was decomposable. If the step is decomposable, we added new cards for the substeps immediately. Then, we asked if the step could be blocked by anything, if it took variable lengths of time, and if it was a particularly difficult step. Exploring each of these questions, notes were added to the cards. As the students worked, the cards were taped to a board in order.

We ran the session with 8 pharmacy students and 6 HIT students. The students worked in two groups. One group worked with the scenario for a community pharmacy, detailing all of the steps involved in filling a prescription in that setting. The other group worked with the scenario for filling an order for an IV in a hospital setting. At the end of the two hour session, cards were taped everywhere on the boards. They were photographed and saved for future reference. A survey was administered at the end of the session to determine if the students had gained insights on communicating with members of the other discipline and whether they had learned about the processes of the other discipline. The majority of the students who returned surveys indicated that they gained insight into the way healthcare providers and HIT specialists can work together.

3. PROJECTS

The HIT students went on to design mobile apps that were linked to the scenarios discussed in the session. One mobile app is intended for a community pharmacy. The idea is that a pharmacist could enter key information into the app, and it would provide a time estimate for the prescription to be filled for the customer's use. As the process continues, if there are problems, such as a question that must be resolved with the physician, the pharmacist can easily update the app, causing a text message with a new time estimate to be sent to the customer. The other app is intended for a hospital pharmacy, to alert nurses on the floor with estimates of when an IV is expected to arrive.

The students worked on the apps in pairs. Two groups designed and implemented competing versions of the community pharmacy app. Two more pairs collaborated to produce the hospital pharmacy app. One pair developed the app that would be used in the pharmacy itself. As key events in the workflow for filling the IV order are met, a cloud database is updated with the new status of the IV and an estimate of remaining time. The other pair developed the corresponding app that nurses on the floor would use, which queries the database on a timed basis and displays status and time estimates for the IV.

The students had to pay particular attention to the user interfaces for these apps, since pharmacists and nurses will not use them if they are too complex. The key information must be easy to input without needing to type. The students had to produce and present an initial design to the class and also described it in detail on their design portfolios. The students, as well as the pharmacy professor, then critiqued the design. The students went on to implement their apps. In their final presentation on their portfolios, they were asked to explain how their design evolved in response to the critiques. Here are some examples of the apps.

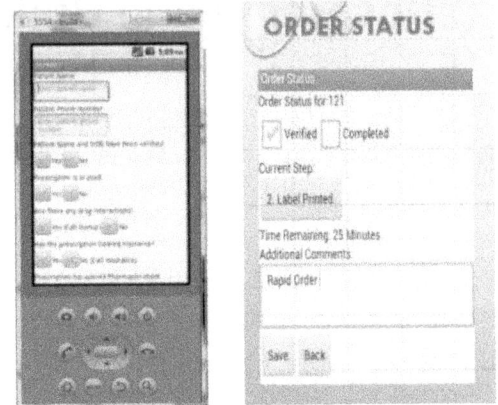

Figure1: Completed mobile apps

The 8 HIT students who finished the project were surveyed after completion. The survey included questions on prior programming experience, whether they felt the collaboration with the pharmacy students was valuable, their experiences working with AppInventor, and whether they felt that learning to develop mobile apps was beneficial to HIT specialists. All of the responding students answered yes to the question on whether they found learning mobile development to be a useful skill. The results from this survey will be presented in more detail on the poster.

4. CONCLUSION

In order to introduce healthcare IT students to the process of collaborating with healthcare specialists while designing IT systems, a pharmacy-oriented mobile app project was incorporated into a HIT course. Pharmacy students were recruited to act as domain specialists in a task analysis session. They worked with the HIT students to produce a detailed breakdown of the steps involved in two common pharmacy scenarios. The HIT students then went on to build mobile apps, using AppInventor, based on the scenarios. Surveys administered to the students indicated that the pharmacy students had benefited by learning more about the process of designing IT systems, and the HIT students benefited by learning about pharmacy workflows, and about communicating with healthcare specialists.

5. REFERENCES

[1] D. Diaper and N. Stanton, Eds., *The Handbook of Task Analysis for Human-Computer Interaction*. CRC Press, 2003.

[2] B. I. Fox, A. J. Flynn, C. R. Fortier, and K. A. Clauson, "Knowledge, skills, and resources for pharmacy informatics education.," *American Journal of Pharmaceutical Education*, vol. 75, no. 5, p. 93, Jun. 2011.

[3] B. MacKellar. "App Inventor for Android in a Healthcare IT Course", *Proceedings of the ACM Conference on Information Technology Education (SIGITE2012)*, ACM, Oct. 13, 2012, Calgary, Canada, 245-250.

[4] M. J. Muller, "Layered Participatory Analysis: New Developments in the CARD Technique," in *Proceedings of the SIGCHI Conference on Human Factors in Computing Systems - CHI '01*, 2001, 90–97.

[5] D. Wolber, "App Inventor and Real-World Motivation," *Proceedings of the 42nd ACM Technical Symposium on Computer Science Education(SIGCSE)*,601–606, 2011.

Project Selection for Student Participation in Humanitarian FOSS

Heidi J. C. Ellis
Western New England University
1215 Wilbraham Rd.
Springfield, MA USA
011-413-782-1748
ellis@wne.edu

Gregory W. Hislop
Drexel University
3141 Chestnut St.
Philadelphia, PA USA
011-215-895-2179
hislop@drexel.edu

Michelle Purcell
Drexel University
3141 Chestnut St.
Philadelphia, PA USA
011-215-895-2179
mjw23@drexel.edu

ABSTRACT
Student involvement in Free and Open Source Software projects provides rich potential for learning. However, the selection of such projects for use within a class can present difficulties due to the large number of available projects, and the wide range of size, complexity, domains, and communities in those projects. This workshop will provide guidance and hands-on experience in selecting a project based on a known methodology for project selection.

Categories and Subject Descriptors
K.3.2 [**Computers and Education**]: Computer and Information Science Education – *Computer Science Education*

Keywords
Open Source Software Projects, Faculty Development, Student Projects

1. INTRODUCTION
Many faculty members are excited by the learning potential inherent in student participation in a Free and Open Source Software (FOSS) project. Student learning can range from software development to technical writing to team skills to professionalism and more. The altruistic nature of humanitarian FOSS provides additional appeal to students by providing the ability to do some social good. However, selection of an appropriate project can be difficult due to the large number of humanitarian FOSS projects available, and the wide range of size, complexity, domains, and communities in those projects. We have developed an approach to FOSS project selection [1] based on several years of experience involving students in humanitarian FOSS projects. This workshop will provide participants with a hands-on experience in selecting such a project. Participants will understand the key aspects of FOSS projects that are important when evaluating a project for use in the classroom. Participants will also be guided through the process of identifying and evaluating candidate projects for their classes.

2. AGENDA
This workshop builds on prior workshops related to student participation in FOSS. These include several NSF-funded workshops on involving students in the development of Humanitarian FOSS. To the extent possible given the venue, the workshop will involve hands on work. The workshop will include discussion among participants. Topics will include:

1. **Overview of Student Participation in FOSS Projects**
   - Learning potential of student participation in FOSS communities
   - Ways that students can contribute

2. **Locating Projects**
   - How to get started looking for projects
   - Identification of information sources, Ohloh, SourceForge, etc.
   - Participants spend time identifying potential projects

3. **Model for evaluating FOSS projects**
   - Key evaluation aspects for humanitarian FOSS projects
   - Definition of evaluation criteria
   - Measures of the criteria and their application

4. **Examples of Model Application**
   - We show how the model is applied to two sample projects, one that is a good fit for student participation and another which is not a good fit

5. **Application of Model**
   - Participants will apply the model to the potential projects identified in step 2.

6. **Wrap Up**
   - Observations about results
   - Discussion about collaborating on projects

3. PRESENTER BIOGRAPHIES
3.1 Heidi Ellis
Dr. Ellis is Associate Professor and Chair of the Computer Science and Information Technology department at Western New England University. Dr. Ellis is one of the founding members of the Humanitarian FOSS (HFOSS) project which focuses on involving students in FOSS projects that improve the human condition. Heidi is PI/Co-PI on three NSF projects that support student involvement in HFOSS projects.

3.2 Gregory Hislop

Dr. Hislop holds faculty appointments in Information Science and Technology and Computer Science at Drexel University. He is PI on several NSF-funded projects that support student learning via participation in humanitarian FOSS projects (see xcitegroup.org). Dr. Hislop has 15 years experience leading development of curricula in SE, IS, and IT, and spent almost 20 years as an IT professional.

4. ACKNOWLEDGMENTS

This material is based on work supported by the National Science Foundation under Grant Nos. - DUE-1225708, DUE-1225738, and DUE-1225688. Any opinions, findings and conclusions or recommendations expressed in this material are those of the author(s) and do not necessarily reflect the views of the National Science Foundation (NSF).

5. REFERENCES

[1] Ellis, H.J.C., Purcell, M., and Hislop, G., "An Approach for Evaluating FOSS Projects for Student Participation," *SIGCSE 2012, Technical Symposium on Computer Science Education*, Raleigh, NC, Mar. 2012.

Workshop: Enhancing Information Technology Education (ITE) with the Use of 3D Printer Technology

Robert Lutz
1000 University Center Lane
Lawrenceville, GA 30043
678-744-5889
rlutz@ggc.edu

ABSTRACT
This workshop provides an introduction to three-dimensional (3D) printing. This tutorial will: cover the general background of 3D printing, summarize popular software tools, describe associated challenges and offer suggestions for application within information technology (IT) coursework. Attendees will get hands-on experience with 3D printing tools and will be able to print a limited number of items during the workshop. The workshop will also describe the author's experience integrating this authentic learning into several IT courses. (Participant Laptop Recommended)

Categories and Subject Descriptors
K.3.2 [**Computers and Information Science Education**]: Computer science education – *curriculum*

General Terms
Algorithms, Experimentation, Languages, Legal Aspects, Verification.

Keywords
3D Printing, Curriculum Innovation

1. INTRODUCTION
3D Printing is a very hot topic in the technical and consumer press. Students are drawn to and very excited to learn about this technology. Given the choice, this author's students have elected to work on harder projects when they involve a 3D printer. Authentic learning experiences also provide students an opportunity for authentic learning characterized by high relevance, ill-defined problems, and complex tasks [1-3].

With a background in mechanical engineering and numerically controlled (NC) machining, this author suspected that this technology might be effectively introduced in several courses he taught. Based on the author's experience integrating this into his curricula, this workshop will provide the following to attendees: general background, challenges, popular tools and resources used in 3D printing, 3D printing in IT education and hands-on activities.

2. WORKSHOP OUTLINE
2.1 General Background of 3D Printing
This segment will cover the following areas:
- Definition of additive manufacturing
- Brief history of 3D printing
- What's different and new here (printing assemblies, complex geometry, color printing)
- Different types of machines
- Different types of materials and the tradeoffs
- The internet community and 3d printing -- Thingiverse, Shapeways, i.materialize, Autodesk 123D Make, etc.
- The 3D printing workflow (scanning, CAD, slicing, plating, visualizing, etc.)
- Introduction to the G-Code language
- Terminology: what are infills, rafts, supports, bridges and plates?

2.2 Challenges with 3D Printing
This segment will cover the following areas:
- 3D printing times
- Parts that will not adhere to the machine's print surface
- Parts that will not fit together.
- Parts that fail
- Where's the UL approval? Is it really 400 degrees?
- A million things can go wrong
- Is this a consumer device or a hacker's endeavor?
- Printing small parts
- Bricking your printer!
- Commanding your printer to destroy itself
- Calibration, calibration, calibration
- Space for machine(s) and setup

2.3 Tools
This segment will cover the following areas:
- Processing environments: Sailfin, Reprap, etc.
- Slicing software: Slic3r, Skeinforge
- Modeling: Blender, Autodesk Inventor, Google SketchUp, TinkerCAD
- Autodesk's 123d Catch, 123d Creature, 123d Make
- Open source tools: Octoprint, Printrun/Pronterface, Repetier
- Raspberry Pi as a 3D print server

2.4 3D Printing in IT Education
- Students really love this topic!
- Things that can be prepared ahead of time
- Application in IT Survey Course
  - Discuss 3D printed guns
  - Discuss crowdsourcing

- o Incorporating the Raspberry Pi as a 3D print server
- o Pass around fabricated parts
- Application in Programming Courses
  - o Writing code that writes code
  - o Short-circuiting the traditional workflow with purpose-built software – A student project interfacing directly from Scalable Vector Graphics (SVG) to 3D printer [4].
  - o Programming the straight skeleton algorithms
  - o Infill generation algorithms
- In Digital Media Courses
  - o Create video documentaries of 3D printing projects
    - ▪ Build and use a DIY scanner
    - ▪ Create models with photogrammetric processing
    - ▪ Create time lapse videos of 3D build
  - o Discuss 3d guns
  - o Discuss crowdsourcing
  - o Pass around fabricated parts
  - o Time lapse video of a build sequence
- How to get started with a modest system
- Suggestions for initial projects and demonstrations

2.5 In the Workshop
- Pass around interesting 3D printed parts
- Build simple CAD models
- Download models from online services

- Download and run open source slicer and visualizer onto your own laptop
- A 3D printer will be available during the session to make a small number of parts and to demonstrate the 3D printing process. For attendees not able to print their parts during the session, interested attendees can complete the process inexpensively with an online printing service. (This mirrors what can be accomplished with students in IT classes).

3. REFERENCES

1. Schwartz, D., et al., *Towards the development of flexibly adaptive instructional design*, in *Instructional-design theories and models: a new paradigm of instructional theory*, C. Reigeluth, Editor 1999, Erlbaum: Mahwah, NJ. p. 183-213.

2. Preston, J.A., *Utilizing authentic, real-world projects in information technology education.* SIGITE Newsl., 2005. **2**(1): p. 1-10.

3. Reeves, T.C., J. Herrington, and R. Oliver. *Authentic activities and online learning.* in *Higher Education Research and Development Society of Australasia.* 2002. Perth, Australia.

4. Allen, S., et al., 2013. *Profxtruder: 3D Printing Directly from Scalable Vector Graphics (SVG)*, http://sdrv.ms/ZbhAy3.

Investigating the Effectiveness of Early Programming-Centric Models for IT Education

Edward Holden
Department of Information Sciences and
Technologies
Rochester Institute of Technology
Rochester, NY 14623
+1 585-475-5361
edward.holden@rit.edu

T.J. Borrelli
Department of Information Sciences and
Technologies
Rochester Institute of Technology
Rochester, NY 14623
+1 585-475-4784
tjbcis@rit.edu

ABSTRACT

Computer Science and Information Technology education offers significant challenges for both educators and students. Oftentimes students may not have much experience with logic, math and reasoning which may inhibit the transfer of knowledge in early stages. If, on the other hand, students have some prior experience, it may facilitate the understanding of early and mid-term concepts and will hopefully produce a more gradual learning curve for students to follow. This paper discusses a boot camp that was offered to incoming IT students and provides the results.

Categories and Subject Descriptors

K.3.2 [Computers and Education]: Computer and Information Science Education – computer science education, curriculum, information systems education

Keywords

Information Technology Education, Java, programming, teaching, programming experience, boot camp

1. INTRODUCTION

Rochester Institute of Technology (RIT) offers programs in several of its global campuses outside of the US. One of these programs is the Bachelor of Science in Information Technology (BS-IT) program, which is offered at the American College of Management and Technology (RIT-Croatia). There are two campuses, Dubrovnik and Zagreb. Although the program in the US is accredited by Middle States, through our university accreditation, and ABET, the RIT-Croatia program is not accredited by ABET. Middle States and the Croatian Ministry of Science, Education and Sports accredit the BS-IT program at RIT Croatia. The two programs are similar, but there are some notable

differences. The program at RIT-Croatia is taught by a combination of local faculty and US faculty from the main campus in the US.

One issue that has been noticed since the program's introduction in Croatia is that there has been a high attrition rate for students. This often manifests itself as a grade of D, F or W (DFW) in the introduction to programming course (IT1). Upon further investigation it was determined that high school students in Croatia were prepared differently than their US counterparts. One main difference is that Croatian students have seldom, if ever, had any hands-on computing and if they have had computing education it has been theoretical. In contrast, most of the US incoming first-year students have had some programming in their preparation.

An earlier study has shown that experience has a significant impact on performance in the first programming course [6]. Traditionally, eight out of ten US students will have some computing before they reach college. In one section of the boot camp that we conducted in Croatia only one student had any experience. Another difference is that some of the logic, mathematical and reasoning skills developed in secondary education in Croatia are not always on par with what would be expected by college-level students.

As we began to discuss the issues, we decided that a boot camp might help to overcome some of the retention problems, by providing some hands-on experience for the incoming students. We developed outcomes for students at the end of the boot camp. These outcomes were based on the shortcomings we had seen in the students' background in the past:

- Students will be able to solve basic problems.
- Students will be able to apply basic object oriented constructs.
- Students will be able to apply the procedural programming constructs of sequence, iteration and decision.
- Students will be able to apply Boolean logic to programming problems.
- Students will be able to use number systems for computing problems.
- Students will be able to use the lab computers for hands-on exercises.

We also wanted to encourage the students' excitement in the IT field and for the students to have some fun. With these desired outcomes, we proceeded to design the boot camp.

2. METHODOLOGY

A key component of the boot camp was hands-on experience, so we decided to investigate tools that would illustrate the concepts in the desired outcomes and would become an introduction to IT1.

Coordinating this internationally was an issue. We wanted to use faculty members who were familiar with our program who were also going to be in Croatia for the quarter. We needed to schedule the boot camp in such a way as to have the US faculty members be in Croatia for less than ninety days so that a visa was not required. To do this, we were able schedule three days in the week before the quarter started and still be out of the country before the visa requirement kicked in.

2.1 Scratch Programming

We began looking for programming environments that would introduce the concepts we wanted to cover. One programming environment that we found interesting was Scratch[1]. Scratch was designed to appeal to people who had not envisioned themselves as programmers. The main users of Scratch are between 8 and 16 years old although there are many adult users also [1].

The authors' goal of introducing "programming to those with no previous programming experience" [2] appealed to us and we believed that it would be a good introduction for our students. This goal had influenced "many aspects of the Scratch design. Some of the design decisions are obvious, such as the choice of a visual blocks language, the single-window user interface layout, and the minimal command set. Others are less obvious, such as how the target audience influenced the type system and the approach to error handling." [2]

The environment makes it easy for students to expand on their work and develop their own reasonably complex projects. The environment is totally visual and allows students to drag and drop code into their program (Figure 1). There are no error messages

Figure 2: The Scratch window

and students can easily step through the program one step at a time. The results are totally visual so that they can immediately see the impact of their activities.

Programming is done by snapping together command blocks representing statements, expressions and control structures, that control graphical objects called sprites. Sprites are moved on a background called a stage. The shapes of the command blocks suggest how they fit together, and the drag-and-drop system does not allow blocks to connect if the resulting operation would not make sense (Figure 2). Once Scratch projects are created they can be stored locally or shared on the web.

move 10 steps	A *command* block has a notch on the top and a matching bump on the bottom. Command blocks can be joined to create a sequence of commands called a *stack*.
mouse x	A *function* block returns a value. Function blocks do not have notches.
when space key pressed	A *trigger block* has a rounded top. It runs the tack below it when the triggering event occurs.
if	*Control structure* command blocks have openings to hold nested command sequences.

Figure 1: Scratch command blocks

Although Scratch is not object-oriented, since it does not support inheritance, it is said to be object-based. Sprites (objects) have state and behavior. This allowed us to introduce objects early in the boot camp.

One limitation of Scratch, for our purposes, is that we also wanted students to begin to experience the programming environment they would be using in the IT1 course. This introductory course uses Java as the programming language. In addition we wanted the students to gain some experience with a class-based environment. Scratch did not serve this purpose because of its focus on younger students, but it did look promising at introducing object concepts, procedural structures and fun.

2.2 Robots Programming

This led us to Robots[2]. Karel the Robot has been around since the early 1980's [3] and has had several iterations. Byron Becker used this for CS1 and described it in his paper [4] in 2001. His subsequent textbook provided a methodology for teaching Java OOP using Robots [5] (Figure 3).

Armed with Scratch and Robots we believed that we had the tools we needed to introduce the students to OOP and basic procedural programming constructs, two of our desired outcomes. Since Java is fully object oriented we can build on what is learned using Scratch. We then needed to fill in the other topics to accomplish the remaining desired outcomes.

To deal with the issue of problem solving, we decided to introduce a number of puzzles that would force the students to understand the data being presented and apply it logically to solve the puzzle. We had several of these puzzles that were introduced sporadically into the boot camp. These puzzles break up the sections of the course and tax the students' problem solving skills.

---

1   Scratch.mit.edu

2   http://www.learningwithrobots.com/

We also developed additional material that helped students to understand Boolean logic and number systems (binary, decimal, octal and hexadecimal). This was intended to be mostly a refresher for the students and included if-then-else, AND, OR, NOT, precedence, nested if statements and DeMorgan's law. We also covered basic flowcharting. These last topics were designed

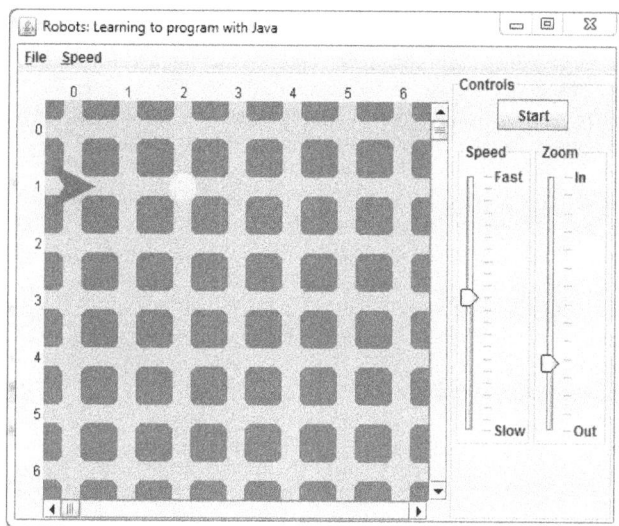

Figure 3: Robots

to fulfill the remaining desired outcomes.

3. THE BOOT CAMP

It was decided that the boot camp would run Tuesday through Thursday of the week before classes started. This time was adjacent to orientation activities that were planned on Friday. On the Monday before the boot camp, one faculty member in Zagreb and another in Dubrovnik set up the lab machines to support the boot camp. Since these computers were already set up for programming classes, the basics were already installed, specifically JGrasp[3] and Java[4].

The lab machines were Macs and all the software we needed is available for both Macs and PC's. The additional software changes included:

- Installing Scratch
- Adding the jar file for the Robots section
- Adding a folder for Javadocs for the Java Robots classes
- Adding the jar file to the CLASSPATH environment variable
- Adding a folder to the desktop for the programs we had written as examples for the student (Scratch and Robots)
- Adding a folder to the desktop for the students to save their own work

3.1 Day 1

The three-day boot camp was to run from 9:00 until 3:00 with a break for lunch. On the first day we began with a short lecture on classes and objects. We covered the topic broadly and included classes, objects, state (attributes), and behavior (methods). We

3   http://www.jgrasp.org

4   http://www.java.com/en/

used basic UML to model the classes and objects. We also talked about generalizing classes and inheritance. This section was intended to be interactive and we allowed students to design classes for common objects that they were used to seeing.

After lunch, as a warm up exercise, we began with a puzzle that would test their abstract reasoning skills and allow them to solve a more complicated problem. After this we introduced the Scratch environment. This was done through some lecture but more through examples. We designed and programmed a simple program that walked a sprite in the form of a cat across the stage. This was a simple exercise but it allowed the students to see how the programming concept of sequence played a part in a program. They also saw how the scripts define behavior and only act on the sprite (object) that contains them.

We continued developing this and added iteration. So instead of using several single move blocks they could iterate. They saw the power of iteration. The final step was to introduce decision. This allowed the sprite to detect that it was at the edge of the stage and turn around and head back. Putting these concepts together allowed the students to design some complicated scenarios.

We concluded the day with a project that allowed the students to develop their own programs with multiple sprites. All the students had programs that utilized the concepts taught this day in the course. One student developed a project that had a boy (sprite 1) throw a basketball (sprite 2) through a hoop with the ball returning to him to be thrown again.

So by the end of the first day, they were able to write Scratch programs exhibiting object usage and the programming constructs of sequence, iteration and decision.

The students were excited. Several wanted stay and others wanted to take Scratch home so they could play in the evening. For most it was their first experience programming and they felt a sense of accomplishment. They also enjoyed working with the computers in the lab.

3.2 Day 2

Using Scratch had given the students the ability to "write" programs in a visual way. On day two, we introduced Java and Robots. This meant that we needed to also have them work with an editor (JGrasp), a compiler, Javadocs for the class specifications, main methods and the cryptic error messages that Java generates; all of which we had avoided with Scratch. The students, however, were able to overcome these obstacles. We were careful to relate all the programming concepts back to what they had covered in Scratch. To our surprise the transition from drag-and-drop to actual coding was not as hard as expected.

We followed a similar path with Java and Robots as we had done with Scratch. We had a series of pre-developed programs that we designed and implemented as a class, stopping when a student experienced problems. We built up an example through several steps beginning by creating an object from a class in a main method, the one part missing from Scratch. We gave them the starter code with the main method.

The program was built up until they had used sequence, iteration (*for* loops) and decision. For decisions we used if-else statements with simple Boolean expressions. We added variables and println statements so they could have them as tools in developing their programs.

We introduced another puzzle after lunch similar to the puzzle from the first day. We concluded the day by having them develop a program from our specifications.

3.3 Day 3

We began day 3 by having them design and implement their own Java Robots program. They were required to apply the concepts they had learned the previous day.

The rest of the day was spent covering Boolean logic and number systems with exercises. There was also another puzzle. This part of the boot camp was less interactive and could probably be improved by introducing more hands-on programming exercises. We also could have used more time at the end. If we conduct the boot camp again, we will make changes here.

4. RESULTS

For comparison purposes, students who were repeating IT1 were excluded from the data because they already had some experience. Only new, first-year students were included in the data. This allowed us to keep the samples consistent from a student perspective.

The results of the boot camp were mixed. At the end of the course students were excited about starting the IT1 course the next week. In addition, many students seemed to easily relate the concepts learned through Scratch and Robots to the work we were having them do in IT1. Also, the enthusiasm for the subject seemed to continue throughout the programming course.

Later in the year in an interview with selected students who had taken the boot camp, we asked if the boot camp was helpful with the introductory course. The students without experience thought that the boot camp did help them get off to a good start with the Java course.

Students with experience, however, did not think it was very helpful. One student who had previous experience with PHP said that converting to Java was easy, since it had the same concepts. "The big problem was that we used JGrasp, then at the beginning of the course we used BlueJ. We should eliminate BlueJ[5] and just use JGrasp in the courses." These students believe that BlueJ just shelters them from using main methods so learning with JGrasp was better. They thought that the transition from BlueJ to JGrasp was not easy. They believed that since the boot camp used JGrasp, we should just continue with JGrasp. "Continue the momentum," was the comment.

We had introduced BlueJ into our IT1 course when we switched to an objects-first approach. Perhaps we should rethink that decision when students have been through the boot camp.

Both experienced and inexperienced students believed that one thing that the boot camp did accomplish was to give a good introduction to the IT1 course, so it was beneficial from that perspective. "It made me more comfortable," was one quote.

In analyzing our results, we had difficulty in that we have little control over the faculty teaching the IT1 course. At the Dubrovnik campus, the instructors teaching the courses before the boot camp (2011) and after the boot camp (2012) were from our main campus in the US and had a consistent teaching and evaluation style. This was not true at the Zagreb Campus where the IT1 course in Java was taught by a local adjunct faculty member in 2011, who was replaced by a full-time, tenure-track faculty member in 2012. Another difference was that in Zagreb a different instructor taught the boot camp and the IT1 course. So comparing the results, particularly in Zagreb, is suspect. With that in mind, however, we had the comparison shown in Table 1.

Table 1 compares the results from 2011 and 2012 for Dubrovnik (DBV), Zagreb (ZGB) and combined total. None of the comparison results allow us to rule out the null hypothesis, that there was no difference between 2011 and 2012, except in Zagreb where the results were negative. As mentioned earlier, Zagreb may have used inconsistent teaching and evaluation methods between 2011 and 2012. For this reason the comparisons for both Zagreb and the combined total may be invalid.

Table 1: Results in IT1 after the boot camp

	Dbv 2011	Dbv 2012	Zgb 2011	Zgb 2012	Tot 2011	Tot 2012
Number Students	10	9	13	15	23	24
ABC	4	5	10	7	14	12
DFW	6	4	3	8	9	12
Percent ABC	40%	56%	77%	47%	61%	50%
Average	1	2.1	2.4	1.1	1.8	1.5
Median	0	3	2	0	2	0.5
p-value	0.158		0.013		0.483	

If we compare just Dubrovnik, the p-value still does not rule out the null hypothesis but the actual results are interesting. The percentage of A, B and C (ABC) grades for the small sample went from 40% to 56%, the average grade went from D to C, and the median grade went from 0 (F or W) to a 3 (B).

Although not shown in Table 1, if we compare Dubrovnik, 2011 (10 students) with the combined total for 2012 (24 students), where we know we had consistent teaching and evaluation, then we see the that the number of A, B and C grades improved from 40% to 50%, average from 1 to 1.5 and the median from 0 to 0.5. Again, the data does not allow us to reject the null hypothesis (p-value = 0.167).

Although these results were disappointing, we do believe that they, together with student and instructor feedback, indicate that there was an improvement in student performance. Also, as previously mentioned, some comparisons with Zagreb are difficult due to the conflating variables of having different faculty members teach from year-to-year and from boot camp to the IT1 course itself. Also, with such a small sample size, it is difficult to obtain meaningful statistics.

One interesting note is that one student who sat in on the first day of the boot camp decided to change majors since he did not like what we were doing. He was able to do this before the first day of classes. Without the boot camp he would have gone part way through the quarter before he realized he had selected the wrong major.

5. DISCUSSION

The authors believe that there is a positive difference in students after the boot camp. This is based on the student response in the boot camp, in the initial Java course and after the course was completed. The data alone, however, does not prove this. Part of the difficulty here is the small sample size that was available. It may be beneficial to look at several years of data to be able to draw meaningful conclusions.

Some changes and modifications to the boot camp that are being considered for the future include: not using BlueJ for students after boot camp, but instead using JGrasp to continue with the momentum from boot camp and present the students with a consistent development environment. Another possible change is to improve the last day to allow for the inclusion of more hands-on activities thus making the last day a more natural continuation of the previous two days. Another thought was to extend the contact-hours of boot camp and meet for five days instead of three. This will allow for both more logic and reasoning background as well as additional hands-on activities.

6. FUTURE WORK

Moving forward, RIT will be switching to semesters from year 2013-2014 onward. This change will affect the IT1 class since now 15 weeks of material will be presented instead of 10. However, it is the opinion of the authors that students can still benefit from the inclusion of a boot camp under the semester model. Since the need for having previous experience for the students remains the same, the goals of the boot camp remain the same also.

7. REFERENCES

[1] Mitchel Resnick, John Maloney, Andrés Monroy-Hernández, Natalie Rusk, Evelyn Eastmond, Karen Brennan, Amon Millner, Eric Rosenbaum, Jay Silver, Brian Silverman, and Yasmin Kafai. 2009. Scratch: programming for all. *Commun. ACM* 52, 11 (November 2009), 60-67. DOI=10.1145/1592761.1592779 http://doi.acm.org/10.1145/1592761.1592779

[2] John Maloney, Mitchel Resnick, Natalie Rusk, Brian Silverman, and Evelyn Eastmond. 2010. The Scratch Programming Language and Environment. *Trans. Comput. Educ.* 10, 4, Article 16 (November 2010), 15 pages. DOI=10.1145/1868358.1868363 http://doi.acm.org/10.1145/1868358.1868363

[3] Richard E. Pattis. 1981. *Karel the Robot: A Gentle Introduction to the Art of Programming* (1st ed.). John Wiley & Sons, Inc., New York, NY, USA.

[4] Byron Weber Becker. 2001. Teaching CS1 with karel the robot in Java. In *Proceedings of the thirty-second SIGCSE technical symposium on Computer Science Education* (SIGCSE '01). ACM, New York, NY, USA, 50-54. DOI=10.1145/364447.364536 http://doi.acm.org/10.1145/364447.364536

[5] Byron Weber Becker. 2006. *Java: Learning to Program with Robots*. Course Technology Press, Boston, MA, United States.

[6] Edward Holden and Elissa Weeden. 2004. The experience factor in early programming education. In *Proceedings of the 5th conference on Information technology education* (CITC5 '04). ACM, New York, NY, USA, 211-218. DOI=10.1145/1029533.1029585 http://doi.acm.org/10.1145/1029533.1029585

Does Language Choice Influence the Effectiveness of Online Introductory Programming Courses?

Waleed Farag, Ph.D.
Indiana University of Pennsylvania
Computer Science Department
Indiana, PA 15705
+1 (724)357-7995

farag@iup.edu

Sanwar Ali, Ph.D.
Indiana University of Pennsylvania
Computer Science Department
Indiana, PA 15705
+1 (724)357-7994

sanwar@iup.edu

Debzani Deb, Ph.D.
Winston-Salem State University
Computer Science Department
Winston-Salem, NC 27110
+1 (336)750-2496

debd@wssu.edu

ABSTRACT

The growing introduction of online courses and degrees places high emphasis on the need for thorough assessment of these offerings. This paper focusses on researching a reliable answer to whether changing the programming language used in online introductory programming courses from C++ to Java will have an impact on their effectiveness or not. The paper uses four distinct data sets to measure course effectiveness and implements an experimental, in-depth analysis procedure to come up with an answer to the posed research question. The data collected from classes, using C++, constitute the control group while data collected when Java was used constitute the experimental group. The first set uses data collected from students that express their perception of the effectiveness of various online course parameters. The second set directly measures students' achievement of course outcomes and compares the measured levels across the studied groups. The third set compares a number of students' success and interactivity indicators while the last set measures the student satisfaction with the course and the instructor. The obtained results for all studied performance measures asserted that there were no statistically significant differences between the control and experimental groups. Such findings can be deemed significant for IT-programs given the popularity of the studied languages and the fact that the study focused mainly on online offerings which are on the rise.

Categories and Subject Descriptors

K.3.2 [**Computers and Educations**]: Computer and Information Science Education - *computer science education, self-assessment.*

Keywords

Programming language choice, Online programming courses, Evaluating student's perception and satisfaction, Measuring course learning outcomes.

SIGITE'13, October 10-12 2013, Orlando, FL, USA
Copyright 2013 ACM 978-1-4503-2239-3/13/10...$15.00.
http://dx.doi.org/10.1145/2512276.2512293

1. INTRODUCTION

Online course delivery (usually referred to as E-learning) is a contemporary trend in education that has flourished over the past decade and has opened a wide variety of learning opportunities. The flexibility of such offerings is very appealing to both students and educators alike. Moreover, online delivery usually has a very positive impact on students' enrolment due to the attraction of non-traditional ones. Therefore, many higher education institutions have started to offer several courses in various majors online. At the same time, the exponential proliferation of such offerings poses many challenges to be overcome. Furthermore, the direct and indirect ramifications of the increasing use of such new delivery mechanism need to be carefully studied.

Given such wide-spread proliferation of online delivery, one should keep in mind that it is a novel mechanism for knowledge transfer that has its own characteristics and peculiarities. Such characteristics can be completely different than those of traditional delivery mechanisms. Therefore, many of the assumptions and findings that generally apply to traditional mechanisms might not apply to online environments. As will be discussed next, there have been many attempts by various researchers to study the effect of programming language choice on traditional programming courses. To the best of our knowledge, there are little if any attempts to conduct comprehensive studies that address such effects when delivering these courses online. Therefore, this research is an initial trial to fill this existing gap and to reliably answer a fundamental research question that has broad impact on the IT and scientific fields.

This paper describes the design, implementation, and results of a new research study with the aim of comprehensively evaluating the impact of language choice on online introductory programming offerings. Our initial research hypothesis can be stated as: Changing the programming language used in an introductory programming course from C++ to Java will have an impact on the effectiveness of the course. Such hypothesis was based on common observation that the early introduction of Object Oriented Programming (OOP) concepts (which is unavoidable in case of using Java) usually introduces learning difficulties for some students. Such hypothesis was also based on our assumption that the nature of the online environment and the lack of physical interaction between students and the instructor might stress these difficulties.

To test the proposed hypothesis, a wide spectrum of performance metrics was devised. Broadly speaking, both direct assessment and indirect assessment metrics were adopted. The indirect assessment metrics were measured by collecting data from students taking these courses that reflect, from students' perspectives, their perception of (first set) and satisfaction with (second set) the course and its contents. On the other hand, the direct assessment metrics use data derived from the students' actually performances when taking these courses. Two sets of data were analyzed for the purpose of direct assessment. The first one was used to measure and compare the levels of achieving the course Intended Learning Outcomes (ILOs) in the control group (using C++) and the experimental group (using Java). The second set compares a number of students' success and interactivity indicators across the two studied groups. These four sets of data were then used in performing in-depth, comprehensive statistical analyses in order to test the above-mentioned research hypothesis. The paper primarily discusses the details of the statistical analyses and the conclusions drawn from the obtained results. A brief literature review of the emergence of online delivery, its recent trends, and representative research studies focusing on the selection of programming languages are presented below.

The past few years have seen many attempts to deliver programming courses online by a number of academicians. Some representative examples of these trials are given in [1, 4, 15]. One of the noticeable recent trends in online delivery is the introduction of Massively Open Online Course (MOOC) systems in which a recent example is edX [14]. These courses enrolling thousands of students are a positive indicator of the increasing popularity of online course delivery.

The choice of the programming language for introductory computer programming courses has long been researched in traditional settings. One of these early publications can be found in [11] where contributors stressed the profound impact of the adopted programming language upon students' success in the discipline. Another recent study [13] collected and analyzed data regarding the use of various languages and reasons for such use among other studied variables. That research highlighted the fact that language choice is an important factor that can be influenced by varying conditions such as pedagogical benefits and marketability. Bhattacharya and Neamtiu [2] presented a study that comprehensively assessed the impact of using C and C++ on the development and maintenance of a set of open source software. The study concluded that the use of C++ led to less complex and easier to maintain software. In [12], the importance of choosing a proper programming language for CS1 was discussed along with various factors that need to be considered when making that decision. Farooq et. al [8] proposed a frame work for assessing the first programming language and stressed the significance of such choice.

From this brief, non-comprehensive survey, one can notice that online delivery is definitely on the rise. In addition, the studies conducted on the choice of language in tradition classroom settings realized the importance of such choice and analyzed its impact. Given that, this paper presents an inclusive study of language choice in a fully online environment.

2. STUDY DESCRIPTION

This study focuses on our introductory programming course which is a traditional introduction to algorithm development and programming. It covers basic programming concepts such as data types, allocation, expressions, I/O then advances to discuss decision making, looping, structured data types, functions, recursion, OOP, and simple GUI concepts.

To ensure the homogeneity of the study and to exclude extraneous factors, the study focuses on a number of relatively recent offerings of this course taught by the same instructor covering similar concepts. The control group data were collected from five different sections of this course taught in 2010 and 2011. These five sections were taught fully online using the C++ programming language [3]. The online course features a comprehensive syllabus that highlights the self-paced nature of the course while clearly expounds all policies and expectations. Course asynchronous activities include programming projects, laboratory environment, online programming exercises, and several discussion forums. Synchronous activities including chat sessions, phone calls and Live Classroom (LC) were also lightly used. Details of this course can be found in [7].

The experimental group data were collected from recent two sections of the same course taught fully online in 2012 and 2013 but used Java [10] as the chosen programming language. The language switch was the result of a decision taken by our Department to change our curriculum. These two sections featured almost identical contents to the control group sections described above with the exception of augmenting the Java online course with additional Multimedia-based contents. The two Java sections representing the experimental group were also taught by the same instructor using the same teaching style and Learning Management System (LMS).

As stated before, the research hypothesis posed by this study is that the language switch will result in some differences when measuring various course assessment factors. In order to verify such hypothesis, the following sections present detailed, in-depth statistical analyses and comparisons between the two studied groups using the following four devised effectiveness indicators: students' perception of various online course delivery metrics, levels of achieving the intended learning outcomes (ILOs), a set of student success metrics, and the degree of students' satisfaction with the course. These sections will also discuss in details the interesting findings of these analyses.

3. EVALUATING STUDENTS' PERCEPTION OF COURSE EFFICACY

In order to come up with a reliable, quantitative assessment of how students perceive the effectiveness of the course, a set of two surveys was designed. The first one studies the students' approval of each of the eleven fundamental course components and tools in effectively facilitating learning throughout the course. These questionnaires use a 4-level Likert-scale with value 1 codes the "Strongly Disagree" response while value 4 codes the "Strongly Agree". Examples of these course components include the syllabus, programming projects and exams. The second survey proposed in [16] adopts a constructive learning model known as COLLES. The later survey assesses the quality of the students' online experience in six central categories: relevance, reflection, interactivity, tutor-support, peer-support, and interpretation (making sense). Questions in this second survey use a 5-level Likert-scale with value 1 codes the "Almost Never" response while value 5 codes the "Almost Always", the highest score. Under each of these six categories student are asked to rate four subcategories for a total of 24 variables. In addition, the first survey assesses the ratings of 11 additional variables yielding an overall of 35 variables to be analyzed. In order to be able to draw proper conclusions, the subcategories variables under each of the main categories are combined to come up with a single figure that represents the category in the analysis. For instance, all four variables under the relevance metric were combined into one value (relevance_combined) representing relevance in all subsequent analyses. All test statistics [9] in this research were conducted using IBM SPSS Statistics Version 20.

To ensure that the data in both groups conform to parametric assumptions, the following tests were conducted: normality (Shapiro-Wilk) test and Homogeneity of variance (Levene's) test. Table 1 shows the results of these tests along with the mean value (μ) and the sample size (N) in each group for all seven studied factors. Note, p is test significance value, and df is the degree of freedom. Normality test results in Table 1 show that the data for all factors are normally distributed with the exception of three factors: reflection (see Figure 1 which shows a distribution with obvious negative skewness and positive kurtosis), tutor support and making sense where Shapiro-Wilk produced significant results with $p < 0.05$. Additionally, the Levene's test across both groups for all factors produced non-significant results ($p > .05$); and thus, variances are homogenous.

Table 1. Results for various statistical tests for both groups

	μ	N	Shapiro-Wilk			Levene's test			
			test	df	p	test	df1	df2	p
course–C++	2.96	27	.98	27	.75	.06	1	34	.81
course–Java	2.63	9	.98	9	.98				
relevance-C++	3.61	33	.94	33	.07	1.65	1	40	.21
relevance-Java	3.44	9	.93	9	.50				
reflect-C++	3.90	33	.93	33	.03	.00	1	40	.98
reflect-Java	3.56	9	.93	9	.46				
interact-C++	3.17	33	.97	33	.58	.76	1	40	.39
interact-Java	3.53	9	.97	9	.93				
tutor-C++	3.05	33	.85	33	.00	.01	1	40	.93
tutor-Java	2.67	9	.78	9	.01				
peer-C++	3.12	33	.95	33	.10	.81	1	40	.38
peer-Java	3.19	9	.98	9	.96				
sense-C++	3.59	33	.91	33	.01	.36	1	40	.56
sense-Java	3.42	9	.77	9	.01				

An important remark from Table 1 comes from comparing the means of both groups for all factors. For instance, the means for the peer support factor are 3.12 and 3.19 for the C++ and Java courses respectively. These mean values are very close which are also the cases for almost all other factors. In order to verify the statistical significance of such observation, the independent-samples t-test was used in the four normally distributed factors. The t-test for all of these four factors found no significant differences between the two studied groups. For instance, the

findings of the t-test for the course-components combined factor (first entry in Table 1) are reported as such: On average, students taking the C++ online class have higher perception ratings of the course-component combined factor ($\mu = 2.96$, SE = 0.13) than students taking the Java online class ($\mu = 2.63$, SE = 0.25). This difference was NOT significant $t(34) = 1.29$, $p > 0.05$. Moreover, the effect size (r) is 0.22 which represents a small effect.

For the remaining three factors (reflection, tutor support and making sense) the non-parametric Mann-Whitney test was used. It produced insignificant differences between the control and experimental groups for all three factors. The result for making sense combined factor can be stated as follows: The students' perception of the degree of students and tutors make good sense of each other's online communications in the C++ classes (Median = 3.75) did not differ significantly from the same degree reported by students taking the Java classes (Median = 4.00), U = 132.00, $z = -.51$, ns ($p = .63$). The effect size (r) is .07 which represents a small effect.

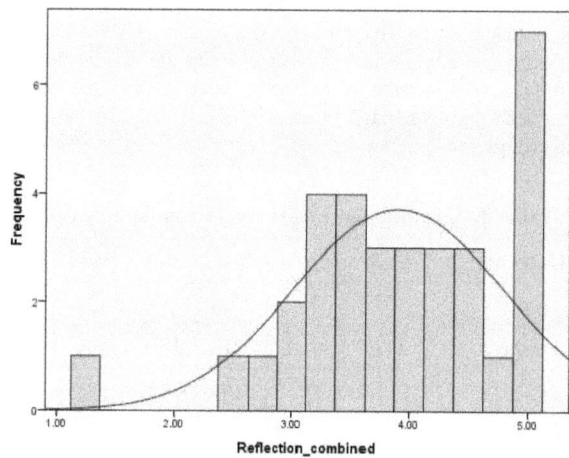

Figure 1. Non normal distribution of C++ reflection factor

4. COMPARING ACHIEVMENT OF COURSE LEARNING OUTCOMES

In this section, the achievement of the four main Intended Learning Outcomes (ILOs) that students need to acquire/exhibit upon completion of this course will be measured and analyzed for both groups. These outcomes are listed below:

1. Put into practice effective use of an Integrated Development Environment to edit, compile, and run programs (O1).
2. Demonstrate the ability to develop algorithms from problem specification and apply various structured programming techniques to proficiently transform them into programming code (O2).
3. Illustrate the ability to use debugging and testing techniques to locate and fix errors to ensure program correctness (O3).
4. Recognize the proper use of the language's constructs and apply this knowledge in creating effective programs (O4).

Equivalent ILOs in both groups signify that both student populations have acquired comparable knowledge and skills upon completion of the course. To measure each outcome, a set of graded activities are selected as a measure for this particular outcome. Each student's achievement in this set is measured to come up with a percent value indicating how well a student attains such an outcome. Then, a number of thresholds were used to differentiate Exemplary (E), Adequate (A), Minimal (M), and Unsatisfactory (U) performance. This procedure is applied to the four outcomes and on every student in the course to develop an EAMU vector for each ILOs. The EAMU model was proposed in [5] and has been used in a previous research study [6] that compared the achievements of ILOs in face-to-face and online classes. For example, in a C++ online offering of the course in spring 2011 the computed EAMU vector for the first outcome (O1) is [7, 1, 1, 0] meaning that out of the 9 students who passed the course, 7 exhibited exemplary attainment of outcome 1, 1 at the adequate level, one minimal and zero unsatisfactory.

To compare the achievement of the course ILOs across the studied groups and try to spot any impact of the used programming language, simple descriptive statistics are first derived then studied. For each group, the EAMU vectors for all offering are accumulated to produce a single EAMU vector for each outcome. In the five sections offered using C++, 44 received a passing grade while that number is 17 in the two sections that used Java. The accumulated EAMU vectors for each outcome along with the percentage of each level are listed in Table 2 for both groups.

Table 2. Accumulated EAMU vectors and percentages

Outcome	EAMU vectors	%E	%A	%M	%U
O1-C++	[33 5 3 3]	75%	11%	7%	7%
O1-Java	[12 3 1 1]	71%	18%	6%	6%
O2-C++	[22 10 8 4]	50%	23%	18%	9%
O2-Java	[10 6 0 1]	59%	35%	0%	6%
O3-C++	[24 9 3 8]	55%	20%	7%	18%
O3-Java	[12 4 0 1]	71%	24%	0%	6%
O4-C++	[16 17 8 3]	36%	39%	18%	7%
O4-Java	[5 10 1 1]	29%	59%	6%	6%

A quick look at the percentage values in Table 2 shows that the two groups exhibit close achievement levels. For example, in outcome 1, the percentages of students who achieved Exemplary (E) performance are 75% and 71% in the C++ and Java classes respectively. We can also spot some differences such as the M (Minimal) percentages for outcome 2 (18% and 0%). In order to verify the significance of these observations, further statistical analyses need to be applied. First, each EAMU vector for each offering is transformed to a scalar value using a devised formula that encourages good performance (E and A) while reprimands minimal and unsatisfactory performance. For details of that formula, please refer to [6]. For each course offering, a scalar value was computed that represents achievement of a specific ILO. These scalars are then analyzed (using Shapiro-Wilk and Levene's tests as done in the previous section) to check whether the transformed data conform to the parametric test assumptions

or not. That analysis revealed that the data for all four outcomes are normally distributed within each group. In addition, the variance is homogenous for the first three outcomes but not for the fourth one. Therefore, the Independent Samples t-Test was used to compare the achievement levels for the first three outcomes while the Mann-Whitney non-parametric test was used to compare outcome 4. The results of these tests are presented in Table 3 where SE is the standard error and r is the effect size which provides a measure of the importance of the effect [9].

Table 3. Results of t-test and Mann-Whitney for all four ILOs

Outcome overall	Descriptive values		Test (t for t-test and U for Mann-Whitney)			
	μ	SE	t	df	p	r
O1-C++	.46	.02	.48	5	.65	.21
O1-Java	.44	.05				
O2-C++	.37	.03	-.96	5	.38	.40
O2-Java	.41	.01				
O3-C++	.38	.03	1.51	5	.19	.56
O3-Java	.45	.02				
	Median		U	z	p	r
O4-C++	.328		5.00	.00	1.0	0
O4-Java	.316					

In Table 3, all tests' significances (p values) are greater than .05 which indicates that both groups exhibit similar distributions. For instance, the results of the t-test for outcome 2 can be reported as follow: On average, students taking the online C++ class scored slightly lower in achieving the ILO2 (μ = 0.37, SE = 0.03) than students taking the online Java class (μ = 0.41, SE = 0.01). This difference was NOT significant t(5) = -.96, p > 0.05. Also, the effect size (r) is .40 which represents a medium effect. Similarly, the insignificant Mann-Whitney results can be stated as follow: the achievement levels of ILO4 for students taking the C++ online class (Median = .328) did not differ from the same levels for students taking the Java online class (Median = .316), U = 5.0, z = .0, p > .05. Again, the results in this section lead us to reject our research hypothesis and confirm that both groups have similar distributions of the achievement levels of all studied ILOs.

5. COMPARING STUDENTS' SUCCESS AND INTERACTIVITY

In this section, we further analyze a number of performance metrics that generally indicates the degree of students' success and interactivity. In such analyses, we try to spot any statistically significant differences. The chances of student receiving highest grade (A), failure grade (F), or withdrawing from the course (W) are first compared across both groups. The data for these three factors are analyzed as categorical data. For example, those students who received A in the course are represented by one category while those who received B are another category and so on. To analyze these data, Chi-Square (X^2) test was used and the results are given in Table 4. For example, Table 4 shows that the percentages of students who withdraw from the course were 37% and 44% when using the C++ and Java respectively. X^2 tests for all three factors produced insignificant result (p > .05). The results for the failure factor can be stated as follow: there was NO significant association between the programming language used and whether or not students receive a final grade of F in the class X^2 (4) = .256, p = .992. The computed odds ratio of 1.18 indicates that the odds of students receiving F in the online Java class were 1.18 times if they were taking the C++ class which supports the insignificant Chi-square test results (see Table 4).

Table 4. Chi-square test results for three success factors

Success Factor	%	Chi-Square test results			
		X^2	df	p	odds ratio
A-C++	48%	.14	3	.99	0.98
A-Java	47%				
F-C++	33%	.26	4	.99	1.18
F-Java	37%				
W-C++	37%	.72	1	.40	1.34
W-Java	44%				

Another factor focusing on comparing the overall grade percentage in both groups is then analyzed. Data for the C++ class were not normal in addition to the significance of the Levene's test indicating that the groups do not have homogenous variance. Thus, Mann-Whitney non-paramedic test was used and produced non-significant results. The test statistic outcome can formally be reported as follows: students final grades in the C++ class (Median = 89.35) did not differ significantly from those enrolled in the online Java class (Median = 87.22), U = 354.00, z = -.322, ns: p > 0.05, r = -0.04. This was also apparent in the close values of the average final grades in the C++ and Java online classes, 85.14 and 86.13, respectively. Lastly, we use the frequency of utilization of course online resources as a rough indicator to the interactivity of students then compare that across both groups. The interactivity data were parametric and thus the t–test was used and led to the following conclusion: on average, the interactivity level for students taking the C++ class (μ = 1342.95, SE = 94.75) did not differ significantly from the corresponding level for students taking the Java class (μ = 1201.33, SE = 169.02), t(87) = .78, p > .05 (ns). The effect size (r) is: 0.08 which represents a small effect.

6. COMPARING STUDENTS' SATISFACTION IN BOTH GROUPS

This section focuses on comparing the levels of students' satisfactions when taking the online C++ course with their satisfactions when taking the Java-based one. The student evaluation instrument employed at our institution was used to perform the following analyses. The employed student evaluation instrument assesses more than 23 performance metrics and for the purpose of this study, only eight important metrics of those 23 are examined. The selected eight metrics are: course organization, effective communication, willingness to give help, increasing knowledge and skills, giving appropriate feedback, learning of valuable skills, willingness to take another course with the same

instructor, and the overall instructor rating. The first seven metrics use a 4-level Likert-scale similar to the one described in section 3 and are collectively called measure #1. On the other hand, the eighth metric, instructor rating, uses a 5-level Likert-scale in which value 5 codes the "Superior" rating while value 1 codes the "Poor" rating, the lowest one. The eighth metric will be analyzed by itself and is referred to as measure #2.

The computed mean values of measure #1 were 2.82 and 2.79 for the C++ and Java cases, respectively. Similarly, these values were 2.85 and 2.78 for measure #2. To test the significance of these close mean values, the data will be further analyzed. The collected data are first tested using Shapiro-Wilk normality and Levene's homogeneity of variance tests as done in previous sections. The results of these test confirmed the parametric nature for both measure #1 and measure #2 factors. Therefore, to compare the obtained means values, the independent samples t-test was used as before and its results are reported in Table 5.

The obtained results for measure #1 can be stated as: on average, students taking the C++ online class have slightly higher evaluation of measure #1 (μ = 2.82, SE = 0.24) compared to students taking the Java online class (μ = 2.79, SE = 0.27). This difference was NOT significant t(20) = .07, p > 0.05. Moreover, the effect size (r) is 0.02 which represents a negligible effect. Likewise, the results for measure #2 can be stated as: on average, students taking the C++ online class have slightly higher ratings for the course instructor (measure #2) (μ = 2.85, SE = 0.37) compared to students taking the Java online class (μ = 2.78, SE = 0.52). This difference was NOT significant t(20) = .11, p > 0.05. Moreover, the effect size (r) is 0.03 which represents a negligible effect.

Table 5. Results of t-test for satisfaction measures #1 and #2

Studied Factor	Descriptive values		t-test results			
	μ	SE	t	df	p	r
measure #1-C++	.2.82	.24	.07	20	.95	.02
measure #1-Java	2.79	.27				
measure #2-C++	2.85	.37	.11	20	.91	.03
measure #2-Java	2.78	.52				

In other words, there was no significant difference between the students' overall satisfaction when taking the C++ online class compared to the same class when Java is used as the adopted programming language. This interesting result is further supported by the computed effect size (r) for both measures #1 and #2.

7. CONCLUSIONS

This paper presented interesting findings of a comprehensive research study aiming at evaluating (using multitude of performance measures) the impact of language choice on the effectiveness of introductory online programming courses. In this experimental study, our initial hypothesis was that there will be differences between the two studied groups: the control group in which C++ was used in the course and the experimental group in which the adopted language was Java. In order to verify that hypothesis, the paper employed both direct and indirect assessment techniques followed by extensive, in-depth statistical analyses of the collected data comprised of four distinct data sets. Two data sets were used in the indirect assessment; the first one was used to assess the perception of students via a number of online specific performance metrics. None of the analyzed seven measures showed any significant differences across the two studied groups. The second indirect data set was used to compare students' satisfaction levels when taking the C++ class with the same levels when taking the Java class. The obtained test statistics results indicated that there were no significant differences between the two groups for the two used performance measures.

On the other hand, the direct assessment has also used two data sets. The first one measured the degree of achieving the course Intended Learning Outcomes (ILOs) and compared these levels in both groups. In conformance with the above results, the obtained statistical results asserted that there were no significant differences between the groups for the four examined ILOs. The last direct data set was used to measure a number of parameters that are indicative of students' success and interactivity in both groups. Again the employed statistical analyses affirmed that both distributions are the same. In summary, the obtained results for all studied performance measures led us to the rejection of our initial research hypothesis. In other words, there were no significant differences between the control and experimental groups. This conclusion is deemed the main contribution of this paper.

Lastly, we need to highlight a couple of limitations in this study. The first one is the employed sample size which was relatively small in some experiments. This was dictated by the facts that the Java course was only offered twice and the participation in these surveys is totally voluntarily (a requirement of our institution IRB). We plan to collect more data as the course continues to be offered. Second, the obtained results and the drawn conclusions were mainly for the studied cases (using C++ and Java). Caution should be exercised when trying to generalize our conclusions on other programming languages without further investigation.

8. REFERENCES

[1] Armitage, W., Boyer, N., Langevin. S., and Gaspar, A. 2009. Rapid conversion of an IT degree program to online delivery: impact, problems, solutions and challenges. In *Proceedings of the SIGITE Conference on information technology education* (Fairfax, Virginia, October 22 - 24, 2009). ITE '09. ACM, New York, NY, 100-107. DOI= http://doi.acm.org/10.1145/1631728.1631758.

[2] Bhattacharya, P. and Neamtiu, L. 2011. Assessing programming language impact on development and maintenance: A study on C and C++. In *Proceedings of the 33rd ICSE'11 International Conference on Software Engineering* (Honolulu, Hawaii, May 21–28, 2011). ICSE'11 ACM, New York, NY, 171-180. DOI= http://doi.acm.org/10.1145/1985793.1985817.

[3] Dale, N. and Weems, C. 2010. *Programming and Problem Solving with C++*. Jones & Bartlett Publishers.

[4] El-Sheikh, E. 2009. Techniques for engaging students in an online computer programming course, *J. of Systemics, Cybernetics and Informatics*, 7, 1, 1-12.

[5] Estell, J. 2007. Streamlining the assessment process with the faculty course assessment report, *Workshop in the 37th ASEE/IEEE Frontiers in Education Conference* (Milwaukee, WI, October 10 - 3, 2007), IEEE, W1A-1. DOI= http://doi.ieeecomputersociety.org/10.1109/FIE.2007.4418236

[6] Farag, W. 2012. Comparing achievement of intended learning outcomes in online programming classes with blended offerings In *Proceedings of the SIGITE Conference on information technology education* (Calgary, Canada, October 11 - 13, 2012). SIGITE '12 and RIIT'12. ACM, New York, NY, 25-30. DOI= http://doi.acm.org/10.1145/2380552.2380561.

[7] Farag, W. and Ali, S. 2010. Online delivery of the first programming course in an undergraduate computer science degree: Is it Possible? In *Proceedings of the Pennsylvania Association of Computer and Information Science Educators Conference (*West Chester, PA, April 9-10, 2010). 24-31.

[8] Farooq, M., Khan, S. and Abid, A. 2012. A Framework for the Assessment of First Programming Language, *J. Basic and Applied Scientific Research*, 2, 8 (2012), 8144-8149.

[9] Field, A. 2009. *Discover Statistics Using SPSS*. SAGE Publications Ltd, London, UK.

[10] Horstmann, C. 2011. *Java for Everyone*. John Wiley & Sons.

[11] Jones, R., Cooper, D., Friedman, D., Holt, R., and Robinson, P. 1993. Issues in the choice of programming language for CS 1. In *Proceedings of the SIGCSE twenty-fourth technical symposium on Computer science education* (Volume 25 Issue 1, March 1993). SIGCSE '25. ACM, New York, NY, 301. DOI= http://doi.acm.org/10.1145/169073.169531

[12] Kaplan, R. Issues in the choice of programming language for CS 1 In *Proceedings of the SIGITE Conference on information technology education* (Midland, Michigan, October 7 - 9, 2010). SIGITE '10. ACM, New York, NY, 163-164. DOI=http://doi.acm.org/10.1145/1867651.1867697

[13] Mason, R., Cooper, G., and Raadt, M. 2012. Trends in introductory programming courses in Australian universities – languages, environments and pedagogy In *Proceedings of the Fourteenth Australasian Computing Education Conference* (Volume 123, Melbourne, Australia, January, 2012), 33-42.

[14] MIT-edX 2012. Retrieved May 31, 2013 from http://web.mit.edu/press/2012/mit-harvard-edx-announcement.html.

[15] Pears, A., Seidman, S., Malmi, L., Mannila, L., Adams, E. Bennedsen, J., Delvin, M., and Paterson, J. 2007. A survey of literature on teaching of introductory programming, In *Proceedings of the Annual Joint Conference on Integrating Technology into Computer Science Education* (Dundee, Scotland, June 25 - 27, 2007) ACM, New York, NY, 204-223. DOI= http://dx.doi.org/10.1145/1345443.1345441.

[16] Taylor, P. and Maor, D. 2000. Assessing the efficacy of online teaching with the Constructivist On-Line Learning Environment Survey, In Proceedings of the 9th Annual Teaching Learning Forum (Perth, Australia, February 2 - 4, 2000).

Diversity in the Game Industry: Is Outreach the Solution?

Amber Settle
DePaul University
Chicago, IL
(312) 362-5324
asettle@cdm.depaul.edu

Monica M. McGill
Bradley University
Peoria, IL
(309) 677-4148
mmcgill@bradley.edu

Adrienne Decker
Rochester Institute of Technology
Rochester, NY
(585) 475-4653
amdigm@rit.edu

ABSTRACT

Over the last decade, the International Game Developers Association (IGDA) has considered the lack of diversity in the game industry workforce a quality of life issue. Using the results of our recent study on demographics of undergraduate students in game degree programs, we compare our data against data reported in the 2005 IGDA Quality of Life survey. The most significant result of this study is that gender diversity in the current group of undergraduate students studying games is statistically the same as that reported within the industry seven years ago, with an approximate 8 to 1 ratio of males to females. The number of black and Asian students was higher than in the industry survey, and the number of Hispanic and other ethnic and racial groups was only slightly lower. Our data shows that there is a greater diversity in sexual orientation and of reported disabilities than in the industry survey results. We describe effective initiatives for recruiting and retaining women in related fields and suggest that similar efforts might address the imbalance in the game industry.

Categories and Subject Descriptors

K.3.2 (Computer and Information System Education)

Keywords

Games, demographics, undergraduate students, diversity, curriculum, gender

1. INTRODUCTION

Over the last decade, there has been general agreement that a lack of diversity exists in the game industry workforce, with game designer Anna Anthropy recently describing the typical game-making cycle as "Straight white developers make games that straight white reviewers market to straight white players, who may eventually be recruited to become the new straight white developers and reviewers" [2]. Recent topics on industry sites indicate that workforce diversity is one of the top five topics in the game industry in 2012 [10].

Diversity has been considered a quality of life issue by the International Game Developers Association (IGDA), which has conducted two full-scale industry surveys on the topic [12, 13]. It is the wise and resourceful business leader who knows that diversity is not just an issue of fairness, but is an issue of competitiveness that can create broader market share and increase revenues [9]. The foundation of this lies in multiple theories

widely recognized and promoted in the fields of sociology and human psychology as well as in business models. In fact, encouraging diversity is crucial for innovation, as so clearly stated by William A. Wulf: "Research tells us that creativity does not spring from nothing; it is grounded in our life experiences, and hence limited by those experiences. Lacking diversity on an engineering team, we limit the set of solutions that will be considered and we may not find the best, the *elegant* solution" [25, p. 595].

The root cause for this lack of diversity within the game industry has been considered and it has been linked to the lack of diversity of and in games that are being produced. Game journalist N'Gai Croal of Newsweek recently drew the conclusion that "...clearly no one black worked on this game" when discussing how race was depicted in Resident Evil 5 [18]. Researchers Williams, Martins, Consalvo, and Ivory have also made the connection between in game representations and developers when they stated that "[w]ith the exception of African Americans, the representation in games bears a strong resemblance to the game developer workforce itself." [23, p. 830]

Using the results of a recent study on demographics of undergraduate students studying games, we compare and analyse the data against diversity in the game industry workforce. The overarching question that guided our analysis was "How does the composition of undergraduate students studying games compare/contrast from the composition of the game industry workforce?" The results of this analysis are presented in this paper first. We follow this with a discussion of initiatives for retaining and recruiting underrepresented groups in related fields of study.

2. METHODOLOGY

We developed the Game Industry Employee Pipeline Survey for this study. Many of the questions were taken directly from the 2005 IGDA survey "Game Developer Demographics: An Exploration of Workforce Diversity" and the 2011 IGDA Industry Survey with permission [12, 13]. The survey consisted of nine demographic questions: one question about favorite high school subjects, four questions about religious preferences, sexual preferences, and political views, and two questions about disabilities. The survey elicited information about student perceptions of diversity in the game industry.

The initial population for this cross-sectional study included undergraduate students in game degree programs in the US, UK, and Canada. The institutions initially contacted included public, not-for-profit private, and for-profit private institutions that offered undergraduate degrees in games and included institutions of various sizes and locations with the specific intention of having data from students at a variety of institutions. Faculty at four institutions in the US, one institution in the UK, and one institution in Canada completed this process of IRB approval required by the study. Upon institutional review board approval, the surveys were distributed to students within participating institutions between March 1, 2012 and September 20, 2012. To gather data, the survey instrument was created using an online survey tool. Only participants who agreed to the letter of consent that appeared on the survey's first page were able to complete the survey.

Using SPSS, we analysed the data using descriptive statistics. We then used GraphPad to run chi-square tests and independent samples t-tests to compare our results against the 2005 IGDA Survey results, since the 2011 survey data has not been published.

3. RESULTS

There were a total of 313 valid responses to the surveys from U.S. and UK institutions from the 1240 emailed, a 25.2% response rate. We compare our results to the 2005 IGDA Survey results. The response rate from Canada was too low, and that data is not discussed here.

3.1 Demographics

3.1.1 Gender

Gender is an area of diversity that has received particularly high attention recently. Comparing results of gender among undergraduate students (males=87.2% and females=12.8%) to the results of the 2005 IGDA Diversity survey (males=88.5% and females=11.5%), we find χ^2 (1, N=313) = 0.50, p=0.48, indicating no statistical difference between the two groups.

3.1.2 Ethnicity

Comparing results of ethnicity among undergraduate students to the results of the 2005 IGDA survey, we find an extremely statistically significant difference, χ^2 (4, N=296) = 34.23, p=0.00. The results (Table I) show that undergraduate students have a wider range of ethnicity than the 2005 industry workforce.

TABLE I.   ETHNICITY

	IGDA Survey	Pipeline Survey
White	83.3%	76.7%
Black	2.0%	6.4%
Hispanic/Latino	2.5%	2.4%
Asian	7.5%	10.5%
Other	4.7%	4.1%

3.1.3 Sexual Orientation

With respect to sexual orientation, a very statistically significant result was found (χ^2 (1, N=304) = 35.99, p=0.00). Results indicate that undergraduate students were more likely to have more diversity in sexual orientation than reported in the industry survey.

TABLE II.   SEXUAL ORIENTATION

	IGDA Survey	Pipeline Survey
Heterosexual	92.0%	85.9%
Lesbian/Gay	2.7%	1.3%
Bisexual	2.7%	6.9%
Decline to specify	2.6%	5.9%

No significant difference was found in the number of transgendered individuals, with slightly less than 1% identifying that they were.

3.1.4 Disabilities

Undergraduate students were more likely to report that they had some form of disability than respondents from the industry survey, with a statistically significant difference found between the two groups (χ^2 (1, N=288) = 45.65, p=0.00). However, for the types of disabilities reported, no significant difference was found (χ^2 (6, N=71) = 4.77, p=0.57).

TABLE III.   DISABILITIES

	IGDA Survey	Pipeline Survey
Non-disabled	87.0%	73.6%
Disabled	13.0%	26.4%

TABLE IV.   TYPES OF DISABILITIES

	IGDA Survey	Pipeline Survey
Cognitive	30.0%	37.0%
Sight	9.0%	13.0%
Hearing	6.0%	4.0%
Mental	31.0%	38.0%
Mobility	4.0%	1.0%
Other	11.0%	7.0%

3.1.5 Minority Women

Among female respondents to both surveys, women in the game industry were typically white at 77.4%. Asians were the second largest group among women, at 9.7%. Blacks comprised a mere 3.3% and Hispanic/Latinos 2.3%, with other minorities at 7.3%. When compared against the student data, white women were the majority still, but at a lower percentage at 66%. There were more black women, Asian women, and other minority women (percentage wise) studying games than responded in the 2005 industry survey. However, Hispanic/Latino women, who comprised 2.3% of the women in the industry, are absent from the undergraduate student study.

TABLE V.   ETHNICITY OF WOMEN

	IGDA Survey		Pipeline Survey	
	Count	Percent	Count	Percent
White	541	77.4%	25	66%
Black	23	3.3%	4	11%
Hispanic/Latino	16	2.3%	0	0%
Asian	68	9.7%	6	16%
Other	51	7.3%	3	8%

3.2 Diversity Perspectives

We explored the results of diversity perspectives by gender against that of the IGDA survey to determine if any statistical differences could be found. Several questions were posed on the

IGDA survey about perceptions/opinions on diversity in the game industry (see Tables VI, VII and VIII). We asked three identical questions (1, 5, and 7) and asked similar questions reframed for undergraduate students (2, 3, 4, and 6). To compare, the original data from the 2005 survey was downloaded and loaded into SPSS. The five-point Likert scale responses were scaled down to four responses in order to conduct a straight comparison against the student data, which only used a four-point Likert scale. To do this, we transformed the data to match (Strongly Agree–4, Agree-3, Disagree-2, and Strongly Disagree-1). The Neutral category for this question was treated as missing data and was not used in the calculations.

TABLE VI.   DIVERSITY QUESTIONS

#	IGDA Survey	Pipeline Survey
1	The game industry workforce is diverse.	The game industry workforce is diverse.
2	The company I work for is diverse.	My program at my university is diverse.
3	My current project/team is diverse.	Project teams in my game degree program are diverse.
4	It appears that diversity is important to my employer.	In one or more of my courses, we have discussed diversity.
5	A diverse workforce has a direct impact (broad appeal, quality, etc.) on the games produced.	A diverse workforce has a direct impact (broad appeal, quality, etc.) on the games produced.
6	My future project/team needs to have more diversity.	My program would benefit from more diverse students.
7	Workforce diversity is important to the future success of the game industry.	Workforce diversity is important to the future success of the game industry.

3.2.1 Gender

In 2005, males in industry agreed slightly that the workforce is diverse (M=2.57, SD=0.82, N=4252) and females were less in agreement (M=2.25, SD=0.87, N=529). However, both male and female students views of the diversity in the industry were much higher, with males reporting at M=3.12, SD=0.75, N=266 and females at M=2.65, SD=0.66, N=40). This is a highly significant difference for men (p=0.00, t(4516)=10.66) and for women (p=0.00, t(617)=2.85).

Males in industry agreed that a diverse workforce has a direct impact on the games produced (M=3.03, SD=0.79, N=4101). Among undergraduates, no significant difference in this agreement could be found (M=3.05, SD=0.81, N=265). However, in 2005 females reported a much stronger agreement to this question (M=3.38, SD=0.64, N=559). Undergraduate females were less likely to agree with this than males in 2005, females in 2005, and undergraduate males (M=2.9, SD=0.88, N=39).

Males in industry agreed that workforce diversity is important to the future success of the game industry (M=3.10, SD=0.81, N=4231) and this was also true of male undergraduate students (M=3.06, SD=0.78, N=266). However, similar to the last question, females in the industry in 2005 reported that they more strongly agreed (M=3.46, SD=0.64, N=577) with the statement than female undergraduate students (M=3.25, SD=0.67, N=40).

Since the other questions were similar, but not identical, we leave it to the reader to interpret the results.

3.2.2 Ethnicity

In 2005, whites in the industry agreed slightly that the workforce is diverse (M=2.51, SD=.81, N=3807) and non-whites were even more in agreement (M=2.63, SD=0.88, N=1024). White and non-white students agree that the game industry workforce is diverse (whites M=3.08, SD=0.73, N=224 and nonwhites at M=3.00, SD=0.82, N=69). This is an extremely significant difference for both whites (p=0.00, t(4029)=10.29) and for non-whites (p=0.00, t(1091)=3.39).

No significant differences could be found for questions five and seven between the 2005 industry survey data and current students (Table VIII). Whites in 2005 and current students agreed that a diverse workforce has a direct impact on the games produced, while non-whites had stronger agreement. Whites agreed that workforce diversity is important to the future success of the game industry and non-whites had stronger agreement.

4. ANALYSIS

Here we provide an integrated summary of the results and offer a set of limitations that should be considered when interpreting the data and planning future work.

4.1 Summary

One significant result of this study is that gender diversity in the current group of undergraduate students studying games is statistically the same as that reported within the industry in 2005. The results are more promising with respect to ethnic and racial diversity. The number of black and Asian students in our survey was higher than in the 2005 industry survey, and the number of Hispanic/Latino/Latina respondents and other ethnic/racial groups was only slightly lower. This may indicate that there is a growing ethnic diversity in the pipeline.

The ethnic composition of women is surprising, with white women making up only 66% of all women studying games and black and Asian women making up 11% and 16%, respectively. Hispanic women appear to be non-existent in the student groups.

Our data shows that there is a greater diversity in sexual orientation among students than in the previous study of the game industry. Similarly, our study shows a greater degree of reported disabilities by students than in the industry study. It could simply be that diagnosis of disabilities, particularly some cognitive disorders such as autism spectrum disorders, has been improved over time [14]. The stigma associated with disabilities has shifted over time and students may be more willing to disclose their status [11, 21]. The academic environment may also encourage a greater rate of disclosure of disabilities. Many higher education institutions provide services to students with disabilities [6].

Our study confirms many of the 2005 results regarding diversity perspectives. Male workers and students agree that diversity has an impact on the games produced and that workforce diversity is important. On both questions, female workers were more likely to agree with the statement than undergraduate students. Female students are less likely to agree to these issues than any of the other groups. Another similar result to the IGDA survey is equal agreement for all ethnic and racial groups about the impact of a diverse workforce on the type of games produced and on the future success of the game industry.

Some diversity perspectives differed from the IGDA survey. Male and female students were more likely to agree that the game

TABLE VII. DIVERSITY PERSPECTIVES BY GENDER

Question	Gender	2005 IGDA Survey Results			Student Survey Results			Comparison	
		N	Mean	SD	N	Mean	SD	p	t
1	Male	4252	2.57	0.82	266	3.12	0.75	0.00	t(4516)=10.66
	Female	579	2.25	0.87	40	2.65	0.66	0.00	t(617)=2.85
2	Male	3881	2.76	0.81	266	3.03	0.69	0.00	t(4145)=5.31
	Female	475	2.77	0.83	40	2.55	0.85	0.11	t(513)=1.61
3	Male	3826	2.65	0.82	265	2.88	0.68	0.00	t(4089)=4.46
	Female	477	2.70	0.84	40	2.53	0.64	0.21	t(515)=1.25
4	Male	3195	2.79	0.83	265	2.57	0.89	0.00	t(3458)=4.12
	Female	425	2.89	0.80	40	2.38	0.81	0.00	t(463)=3.85
5	Male	4101	3.03	0.79	266	3.05	0.81	0.69	t(4365)=0.4
	Female	559	3.38	0.64	39	2.9	0.88	0.00	t(596)=4.41
6	Male	3217	2.80	0.82	265	2.88	0.79	0.13	t(3480)=1.53
	Female	431	3.07	0.74	40	3.1	0.59	0.80	t(469)=0.25
7	Male	4231	3.10	0.81	266	3.06	0.78	0.43	t(4495)=0.78
	Female	577	3.46	0.64	40	3.25	0.67	0.04	t(615)=2.02

TABLE VIII. DIVERSITY PERSPECTIVES BY WHITE VERSUS NON-WHITE

Question	Gender	2005 IGDA Survey Results			Student Survey Results			Comparison	
		N	Mean	SD	N	Mean	SD	p	t
1	White	3807	2.51	0.81	224	3.08	0.73	0.00	t(4516)=10.29
	Non-white	1024	2.63	0.88	69	3.00	0.82	0.00	t(617)=3.39
2	White	3425	2.74	0.81	224	2.97	0.71	0.00	t(4145)=3.48
	Non-white	931	2.82	0.82	69	2.90	0.83	0.11	t(513)=0.78
3	White	3382	2.62	0.81	224	2.85	0.67	0.00	t(4089)=4.16
	Non-white	921	2.78	0.82	69	2.74	0.78	0.21	t(515)=0.39
4	White	2827	2.79	0.81	224	2.53	0.89	0.00	t(3458)=4.58
	Non-white	793	2.87	0.86	69	2.59	0.91	0.00	t(463)=2.58
5	White	3577	3.02	0.78	223	3.00	0.80	0.69	t(4365)=0.37
	Non-white	1083	3.24	0.75	69	3.16	0.89	0.00	t(596)=0.85
6	White	2792	2.76	0.80	223	2.83	0.77	0.13	t(3480)=1.26
	Non-white	856	3.05	0.81	69	3.12	0.74	0.80	t(469)=0.69
7	White	3705	3.09	0.80	224	3.03	0.76	0.43	t(4495)=1.09
	Non-white	1103	3.34	0.77	69	3.25	0.81	0.04	t(615)=0.94

industry workforce is diverse. This may be explained by the fact that workers have direct experience in the industry and the students may not, or it may be that a more diverse pipeline has convinced the students that the industry will be similarly diverse. Similarly, white and non-white workers agree slightly that the industry is diverse, but white and non-white students were much more likely to agree that the industry is diverse.

4.2 Limitations

Some limitations of this study are worth considering when interpreting the results. There is the assumption that these students will seek employment in the game industry, and that these students, regardless of their status, will apply for and be considered equally for such employment.

We used data from the 2005 IGDA survey, since results of the 2011 survey remain unpublished. This data seems to still be valid given the amount of discussion on diversity in the game industry in recent months. The IGDA survey was open to all occupations in the game industry, including human resources and other areas that have typically had more female participation, while the student demographic survey included only those who were intending to be directly involved in the design and development of games. By including programmers, a field in which women are typically underrepresented, this group would be expected to contain fewer women. It could be, therefore, that the pipeline shows greater promise than the results might initially indicate.

The institutions that were part of this study and the participants from those institutions may not be representative of the entire population of students studying games. Institutions included in the survey may have low populations of Hispanic/Latino/Latina students in the student body, which could skew the data. Further, the entire data set is based on self-reported data. Some of the questions in the instrument ask participants to provide sensitive information and may have influenced students to not answer truthfully or choose options for "declining to answer". Finally, the instrument has not been validated, so the results of the questions asking for perspectives on diversity must be interpreted carefully.

5. DISCUSSION

Though widespread discussions of diversity in the game industry are relatively new, it is has long been recognized as an issue within many industries. This includes other areas of entertainment such as film direction and production, as well as related disciplines in science, technology, engineering, and mathematics (STEM). The importance of diversity has become more high profile as the need for STEM workers has increased and the pool of potential students has decreased [20, 24].

Recruiting underrepresented groups is seen as one approach to increase the overall STEM student population. Recruitment of students is of particular interest since it has been shown that there is a strong relationship between degree specialization and employment field for workers in science and engineering areas [20, pp. 16-17]. In the US, attention to this issue has expanded beyond STEM educators, resulting most recently in a high-profile "Educate to Innovate" campaign by the President [7].

The call for an improvement in gender diversity in the game industry became particularly strong in 2012. The highly negative reaction to a Kickstarter project exploring negative stereotypes of women in games posted by Anita Sarkeesian resulted in wide discussion of sexual harassment in the games culture and industry. The Twitter hashtag #1reasonwhy became associated with many stories of gender discrimination in the industry, and the resulting calls for diversity and inclusion was named by Gamasutra as one of the 5 trends that defined the game industry in 2012 [10].

In the following sections we discuss the current state of diversity in STEM fields, an umbrella under which game development is often included in post-secondary institutions, to provide information for comparison. We then discuss outreach efforts undertaken by educators and others in technology-focused disciplines, highlighting the difficulty in improving diversity and look at what this might mean for academic institutions.

5.1 Diversity in STEM fields

The demand for STEM occupations remains strong, with growth in the US in science and engineering jobs predicted to increase 20.6% through 2018 [20]. At the same time, the diversity among science and engineering employees remains nearly stagnant. Gender diversity in science and engineering has seen minor improvements, with female workers now constituting 27% of the population, as compared to 23% in 1993 [20, p. 40]. Information about workers' sexual orientation and disability status was not included in the science and engineering workforce report, but other sources indicate that disabled computing students are a

small group with approximately 12% of computing undergraduates identifying as disabled [3].

Scrutiny of diversity in technology-focused fields took on a renewed urgency when university enrollments dropped after 2000 [24]. This was true especially for gender diversity, as female participation in computer science peaked in the mid-80s at around 37% and has fallen and remained low since, currently hovering around 15% [24, 26]. This represents a move in the opposite direction from overall female university enrollments, which have grown to 57% [3]. Likewise, while the minority population in the US is growing, their presence in computing remains low. In 2009, racial/ethnic minorities represented only 19.4% of undergraduate computing degrees [3]. The situation is dire for minority women, who receive only 5.6% of computing degrees [3].

Concern about inclusion is not limited to computer science. Women remain underrepresented in information technology (IT) occupations and the gap has grown. In 1991, 36% of IT jobs were filled by women but in 2008 only 25% of IT jobs were [22]. There is a pay gap, with the highest gender pay gap for web developers and programmers standing at 14.05% [22]. Also troubling is the churn of female IT job holders, with only 33% of female degree holders remaining in a STEM job two years after graduation [22].

5.2 Outreach efforts in technology disciplines

With the decline in university enrollment in technology programs came a strong focus on improving outreach to underrepresented populations. One of the strongest efforts has been on behalf of gender diversity, and some institutions have seen dramatic improvement in female student representation. Harvey Mudd College, for example, now has a female student population of approximately 40% [1]. A similar program at Carnegie Mellon University saw increases in female computer science representation rise from 8% in 1995 to 42% in 2000 [8]. Programs and courses that demonstrate how computing is relevant and useful in applications have shown particular promise with female students [1]. One of the most prominent examples of this is Georgia Tech's Media Computation program [19].

Making the high school curriculum more attractive to women and minorities has been a goal of a new advanced placement computer science course [5]. The course aims to expose students to a wider set of computer science topics and demonstrate the relevance of those topics in modern society [15]. Teacher education and professional development is a large part of these efforts, and the National Science Foundation has created a program to fund projects focused on preparing computer science teachers, with a goal of having 10,000 teachers ready by 2015 [4].

6. CONCLUSION

When putting this information into context, two questions must be answered. The first is whether or not a diverse workforce is important, while the second is, if it is deemed important, what steps can and should be taken to address it.

To address whether or not a diverse workforce is important, we reference Forbes and the World Economic Forum. The World Economic Forum's Global Agenda Council on Competitiveness focused on two issues this year, with one of them being the "[s]tructural and institutional reforms to overcome barriers to competitiveness." [16]. The Forbes report explains that a diverse workforce (gender, ethnicity, and disabled) has great bearing on competitiveness in industry [7, 9]. If the game industry holds the same economic and business tenets, then a diverse workforce is important to competitiveness within it as well.

What steps, then, can and should be taken to effectively address diversity in the game industry? STEM initiatives that have been implemented over the last decade present a comprehensive effort to recruit and retain underrepresented groups in the field both at the secondary and post-secondary levels, and some even sooner [8, 17]. The majority of these initiatives have been designed and implemented by educators who are equipped to develop outreach programs. Governments and industry have supported these initiatives, adding legitimacy as well as resources. We encourage leaders in the game industry and academics to join in an effort to develop a framework for addressing this issue.

7. ACKNOWLEDGEMENTS

We acknowledge and thank the following academics for their time and resources in shepherding the IRB process at their respective institutions and recruiting participants: Briana Morrison, Southern Polytechnic State University; Jacques Carette, McMaster University; Mark Eyles, University of Portsmouth, United Kingdom; and Siobhan Thomas, London South Bank University.

8. REFERENCES

[1] Alvarado, C., Dodds, Z., and Libeskind-Hadas, R. 2012. Increasing Women's Participation in Computing at Harvey Mudd College, *ACM Inroads*, 3:4, December 2012.

[2] Anthropy, A. "Token video game characters distract from real stories," Gamasutra, http://www.gamasutra.com/view/news/178977/Token_video_game_characters_distract_from_real_stories__Anna_Anthropy.php#.UH7Wyn_LiUF, accessed December 2012.

[3] Camp, T. 2012. Computing, We Have a Problem ..., *ACM Inroads*, 3:4, December 2012.

[4] CS 10K Initiative, http://www.computingportal.org/cs10k, accessed December 2012.

[5] CS Principles, http://www.csprinciples.org/, accessed December 2012.

[6] Collins, M.E. and Mowbray, C.T. 2005. Higher Education and Psychiatric Disabilties: National Survey of Campus Disability Services. American Journal of Orthopsychiatry, 75:2, pp. 304-315.

[7] Educate to Innovate. 2012. The White House, http://www.whitehouse.gov/issues/education/k-12/educate-innovate, accessed December 2012.

[8] Fisher A. and Margolis, J. Women in Computer Sciences: Closing the Gender Gap in Higher Education, http://www.cs.cmu.edu/afs/cs/project/gendergap/www/index.html, accessed December 2012.

[9] Forbes. 2012. Diversity & inclusion: unlocking global potential. Retrieved December 2012 from http://www.dpiap.org/resources/pdf/global_diversity_rankings_2012_12_03_20.pdf

[10] Graft, K. 2012. The 5 trends that defined the game industry in 2012, Gamasutra, http://www.gamasutra.com/view/news/182954/The_5_trends_that_defined_the_game_industry_in_2012.php#.UMn3em_Ad8E, accessed December 2012.

[11] Green, S. et al. 2005. Living Stigma: The Impact of Labeling, Stereoptypes, Separation, Status, Loss, and Discrimination in the Lives of Individuals with Disabilities and Their Families. Sociological Inquiry, 75:2, pp. 197-215.

[12] IGDA International Game Developers Association. 2005. Game Developer Demographics: An Exploration of Workforce Diversity. Retrieved October 15, 2011 from http:// www.igda.org/game-developer-demographics-report

[13] IGDA International Game Developers Association. 2011. Game Industry Survey 2011. Retrieved December 2011 from http://www.research.net/s/IGDA_Industry_Survey_M2Research

[14] Mandell, D.S., Novak, M.M., and Zubritsky, C.D. 2005. Factors Associated with Age of Diagnosis Among Children with Autism Spectrum Disorders. Pediatrics, 116:6, pp. 1480-1486.

[15] Margolis, J., Ryoo, J.J., Sandoval, C.D.M., Lee, C., Goode, J., and Chapman, G. 2012. Beyond Access: Broadening Participation in High School Computer Science, *ACM Inroads*, 3:4, December 2012.

[16] Murphy. 2012. Keeping focused on the global competitiveness agenda. World Economic Council. Retrieved December 2012 from http://forumblog.org/2012/11/keeping-focused-on-the-global-competitiveness-agenda/

[17] New Image for Computing: Report on Market Research. 2009. WGBH Educational Foundation and the Association for Computing Machinery, http://www.acm.org/press-room/membership/NIC.pdf, accessed December 2012.

[18] Packwood, D. 2011. News America Media. Hispanics and Blacks Missing in Gaming Industry. Retrieved December 7, 2012 from http://newamericamedia.org/2011/09/gamer-to-game-makers-wheres-the-diversity.php

[19] Rich, L., Perry, H., and Guzdial, M. 2004. A CS1 course designed to address interests of women, *SIGCSE Bulletin*, 36:1, pp. 190-194.

[20] Science and Engineering Indicators. 2012. Chapter 3: Demographics of the S&E Workforce, National Science Foundation. Retrieve December 2012 from http://www.nsf.gov/statistics/seind12/c3/c3s4.htm

[21] Susman, J. 1994. Disability, stigma and deviance. Social Science & Medicine, 38:1.

[22] Trauth, E. M. 2012. Are There Enough Seats for Women at the IT Table? *ACM Inroads*, 3:4, December 2012.

[23] Williams, D., Martins, N., Consalvo, M., and Ivory, J. 2009. The virtual census: representations of gender, race and age in video games. New Media & Society, 11:815. Retrieved December 7, 2012 from http://nms.sagepub.com/content/11/5/815.full.pdf+html

[24] Vegso, J. 2005. Interest in CS as a Major Drops Among Incoming Freshman, *Computing Research News*, 17:3, May 2005.

[25] Wulf, W.A. 2000. How shall we satisfy the long-term educational needs of engineers? *Proceedings of the IEEE*, 88:4, pp. 593-596.

[26] Zweben. S. 2011. Undergraduate CS Degree Production Rises; Doctoral Production Steady: 2009 – 2010 Taulbee Survey, *Computing Research News*, 23:3, May 2011

MOOC as Semester-long Entrance Exam

Arto Vihavainen, Matti Luukkainen, Jaakko Kurhila
University of Helsinki
Department of Computer Science
P.O. Box 68 (Gustaf Hällströmin katu 2b)
Fi-00014 University of Helsinki
{ avihavai, mluukkai, kurhila }@cs.helsinki.fi

ABSTRACT

MOOCs (massive open online courses) became a hugely popular topic in both academic and non-academic discussions in 2012. Many of the offered MOOCs are somewhat "watered-down versions" of the actual courses given by the MOOC professors at their home universities. At the University of Helsinki, Department of Computer Science, our MOOC on introductory programming is exactly the same course as our first programming course on campus. Our MOOC uses the Extreme Apprenticeship (XA) model for programming education, thus ensuring that students are proceeding step-by-step in the desired direction. As an additional twist, we have used our MOOC as an entrance exam to studies in University of Helsinki. In this paper, we compare the student achievement after one year of studies between two cohorts: the MOOC intake (n=38) and the intake that started their studies during the fall (n=68). The results indicate that student achievement is at least as good on the MOOC intake when compared to the normal intake. An additional benefit is that the students admitted via MOOC are less likely to drop out from their studies during their first year.

Categories and Subject Descriptors

K.3.2 [**Computers and Education**]: Computer and Information Science Education *Computer Science Education*

General Terms

Experimentation

Keywords

entrance exam, admission, first-year experience, student achievement

1. INTRODUCTION

MOOCs or massive open online courses have been a source for an intense debate recently in academia, both in administration and among teachers (see e.g. [5]). MOOCs come in

a variety of forms; however, most of the current high-profile MOOCs tend to be based on short lectures (8-12 min videos, animations and screencasts) interspersed with quizzes that are used to keep up the students' attention to the learning material[1]. A key issue in MOOCs is to facilitate and allow massive attendance.

MOOCs have been aptly described as "textbooks on steroids" [6]. In other words, the students that are successful in MOOCs tend to be autodidacts, to the extent that e.g. more than 70% of the starting MOOC students already have an undergraduate or postgraduate degree [13].

Our MOOC at the University of Helsinki Department of Computer Science differs from typical MOOCs in two key aspects [16]:

- Students start by installing a real-world programming environment and start to program immediately. All learning materials are built to support hands-on programming. The emphasis is heavily on a learning process that allows and requires the learners to produce working solutions. There are hundreds of programming assignments that the students are expected to construct during the course.

- By successfully completing the MOOC and participating in an interview, a student is granted admission to the university to major in Computer Science.

In Finland, the students choose their major before entering a university, making the decision often based on a relatively vague idea of the area and whether the studies suit the student. Using a traditional entrance exam as a way to select students provides insufficient results[2] as some of our first-year students fail to succeed in e.g. the very first required programming courses, effectively forcing them to seek another study.

The most important part of MOOC as semester-long entrance exam is the *process of learning to program*, during which the student sees if CS/IT is the desired area of study for her. Successfully completing the MOOC provides us and the student herself the evidence that shows that she has the aptitude for CS/IT.

---

[1] A notable exception are so-called connectivist MOOCs that rely more on facilitated discussions among networked learners [14, 7, 12].

[2] Attempts to pinpoint identifiable markers for aptitude to succeed in CS/IT studies have yielded non-conclusive results (see e.g. [10, 1, 15, 8]), making it impossible to derive a set of markers for revising the traditional entrance exam.

In practice, our MOOC is exactly the same course as the entry-level programming course in our university. This in itself acts as a validation measure to see whether a student is able to handle the first and often the most challenging courses.

In the first 18 months of operation, our MOOC has had 2109 participants, from which some 200 students have applied for a study position. The MOOC in programming was first used as an entrance exam in spring 2012. In addition to the new admission path via MOOC, the traditional admission procedure was kept intact and also offered to high-school students.

In this paper, we compare the success of students admitted via a MOOC to the traditional entrance exam-based intake. As our work on using MOOCs as an entrance exam to university studies has been active only for a short while and we are still adjusting the level that we require from the MOOC participants for them being admitted, we have deliberately chosen not to include statistical analysis to avoid drawing premature conclusions at this stage.

2. EDUCATIONAL SYSTEM IN FINLAND

Before starting undergraduate higher education in Finland, students typically have 12 years of schooling. During those 12 years, there is only one standardized test: the matriculation exam after the 12th grade. Major subject is chosen before starting the University studies.

Universities can use the results of the matriculation exam to grant study rights. However, most study disciplines in the universities use the matriculation exam results only as a small addition to university- and subject-specific entrance exams, especially in highly desirable subjects. In STEM subjects, the admission is typically more generous due to the lack of applicants. Admission can be granted based on either 1) solely the entrance exam, 2) solely the matriculation exam, or 3) a combination score from entrance exam and matriculation exam. At the Univ. Helsinki Dept of Computer Science most of the admitted students have taken the entrance exam (402 applicants in 2013) and received some extra points based on their matriculation exam. Entrance exams for CS/IT – and other subjects as well – are classic pen-and-paper tests conducted in a lecture hall under strict surveillance so that candidates are using only their brains to answer the exam questions.

As computer science (computing, or any IT-related topic) is not among the mandatory study subjects in high school in Finland, it is not part of the matriculation exam [3]. Therefore, the entrance exam to CS/IT does not contain programming per se; instead it contains logical problems and essay writing. Many of the students who are admitted to computer science do not have an accurate image of the subject, and many drop out soon after their studies have started.

Another issue worth noting is that there are no tuition fees for anyone in Finland (from elementary schools to universities). Instead, the government supports students by a monthly allowance for living expenses, including rent support. As CS/IT is not among the most highly sought-out study subject, some students apply for CS/IT as a fallback

position, and accept the study right in order to get the student benefits. Instead of studying CS/IT, they use the extra year for e.g. preparing for an entrance exams to a more preferable study subject.

In order to alleviate the problem of having an incorrect mental image of CS/IT studies, we wanted to allow high-school students (esp. grades 10 to 12) in Finland to experience CS/IT studies. Therefore, we opened up our introductory programming course (CS1) to the whole country[4], targeting especially high-school students who have no programming education in their schools, or who seek more advanced courses than their local high school offers[5].

The most significant benefit is that the MOOC participants get a more realistic view of the studies they would be encountering if they took CS/IT as a major subject, and can themselves evaluate if they are up to it. By completing the MOOC in programming, the students show us at the department that they are both competent and persevering enough to study CS/IT. Therefore, it is only natural to grant those students full study rights for a degree.

3. MOOC AS AN ENTRANCE EXAM

Starting the MOOC is straightforward, as there is no need to provide any other information than a valid email address when registering. If the student seeks admission, she is required to enter full personal information. The option for applying for the study right is available for the first two months.

3.1 Course Content and Pedagogy

The MOOC in programming is content-wise exactly the same as our CS1, which is taught in Java using an objects-early approach. The course contains 12 weekly exercise sets, and covers topics typical to any introductory programming course; assignment, expressions, terminal input and output, basic control structures, classes, objects, methods, arrays and strings, advanced object oriented features such as inheritance, interfaces and polymorphism, and familiarizes students with the most essential features of Java API, exceptions and file I/O[6].

During the MOOC, the participants work on over 150 programming exercises, which are further split into over 350 tasks. The students that are applying for the study rights must correctly solve 80% or more of the weekly tasks in order to be invited to the interview. The material is handed out online in a book-like format, with a few screencasts, and its sole purpose is to help the students work on the exercises; the main working method for the students is programming.

The learning-by-doing orientation comes from using the Extreme Apprenticeship (XA) [17] method in the course implementation. XA is based on cognitive apprenticeship [3, 2] and approaches programming as a craft that needs to be

---

[3]Many schools offer computing as an elective course. However, as there is no national curriculum for courses in computing, courses often concentrate on the use of computer applications and computer literacy. The situation in Finland as such resembles many other countries, e.g. USA [20].

[4]As is typical for MOOCs, there are no restrictions for participation. Our MOOC is in Finnish language, so the natural audience is mostly in Finland.

[5]In case a participant does not want to apply for a study right but would like to have a certificate of accomplishment, we have facilitated the schools in Finland to provide examinations. High schools use the certificate for granting school credits.

[6]The course material and exercises are available at http://mooc.fi and licensed under the Creative Commons BY-NC-SA -license.

honed continuously. Two core values in XA are "practice as long as necessary" and "continuous feedback". In our earlier XA-based courses [11], the feedback has been provided by human advisors (teachers). In the MOOC, the participants program in an industry-standard programming environment that contains a plugin, which provides help for the students (for additional details, see [18]).

3.2 Interview and Programming Task

Once the students have worked through the required number of programming tasks, they are invited to an interview. The interview is a two-part process: first, the students work on a programming task in a live setting, and after that are interviewed by two members of the faculty. The programming task is done in a lab, where a supervisor can help participants with e.g. operating system or programming environment-related issues, and correct potential misunderstandings regarding the task. The students are free to use any available material which can be found on the internet, e.g. the course material. However, asking for help in solving the programming task is not allowed.

The participants had a total of 2 hours for the task, which was as follows for the interview held during spring 2012.

Programming task: a text analyzer

Create an application that can be used to analyze text file contents. The application should contain at least the following features:

- calculating the number of words in a file

- finding and printing the most common word(s) in a file

- finding and printing the longest word in a file

If you wish, you can also create additional features.

The program should be able to analyze several files during a single execution, and it should also be able to handle large files. You can test your application for example with Kalevala, which is available at

http://www.gutenberg.org/cache/epub/7000/pg7000.txt

You can decide what sort of a user interface the application provides, however, we suggest that you build a text-based user interface. Below is an example of how the application could work:

```
Enter filename, empty input exits the program
> kalevala.txt
commands: longest, words, most-common, help
command > words
67443
command > longest
longest word is: kautokengän-kannoillansa
command > most-common
most common word is: on
>
finished processing kalevala.txt

Enter filename, empty input exits the program
> test.txt
commands: longest, words, most-common, help
```

```
command > help
commands: longest, words, most-common, help
command > words
7
command >
finished processing test.txt

Enter filename, empty input exits the program
>
Thank you!
```

After the programming task, the students are interviewed for up to 30 minutes by two faculty members. The faculty members discuss the students' program design choices and possible issues with e.g. performance with the student. During the interview, the faculty also attempts to form an understanding of the student's background, and reasons for applying to the department of computer science. Things that are of interest are e.g. existing programming background, the student's vision regarding her life after five years from now, and existing educational background.

3.3 Selection of Students

During spring 2012, most of the students that did over 80% of the exercises in the MOOC in programming and applied for study rights also fared well in the actual interview. Most of the participants were able to complete the programming task fully, and only a handful of the participants had issues with e.g. program design or did not have a working program at all. Out of the 52 students that applied for a study position during spring 2012, 49 study rights were granted. Out of the 49, 38 students started their studies during fall 2012, and the remaining 11 had varying reasons not to start their studies: they are still in high school, they postponed the start due to the mandatory military service, or they took another, preferred study position.

The number of applicants via the traditional path has been in hundreds for years. Therefore, we are not expecting an uncontrollable need to scale up the interview process. Currently, the interviews involved with the MOOC entrance have been conducted by two faculty members without extra resources.

4. DATA

Our data contains study records from students that have started their studies at the Department of Computer Science at the University of Helsinki in August 2012. As some of the students postpone their start due to the military service, focus on other studies than Computer Science, or have transferred courses from earlier studies (e.g. open university), we include only students that have either attempted or completed the introductory programming course during the academic year 2012-2013.

The study records cover the period from August 1, 2012 to May 24, 2013. We examine two separate groups. The first group (MOOC, n=38) contains students that have been admitted via the programming MOOC that was organized during spring 2012. The second group (NORM, n=68) contains students that were admitted via the traditional path, namely the entrance exam, matriculation exam, or a combination of both. The MOOC group has the introductory programming

CS/IT Courses		
	MOOC (n=38)	NORM (n=68)
Credits		
overall	1257	1629
mean	33.08	23.96
std	11.32	15.3
median	32.5	24
Courses passed		
overall	346	452
mean	9.11	6.65
std	2.95	4.02
median	9	7
Courses failed		
overall	66	157
mean	1.74	2.31
std	1.83	2.37
median	1	2
Grade stats		
mean	4.04	3.79
std	1.15	1.2
median	4	4

Table 1: Student performance in CS/IT-related courses.

Math Courses		
	MOOC (n=38)	NORM (n=68)
Credits		
overall	273	350
mean	7.18	5.15
std	7.49	7.63
median	5	0
Courses passed		
overall	46	62
mean	1.12	0.91
std	1.19	1.25
median	1	0
Courses failed		
overall	30	50
mean	0.79	0.74
std	0.74	0.66
median	1	1
Grade stats		
mean	3.39	3.37
std	1.2	1.45
median	4	4

Table 2: Student performance in mathematics courses.

and advanced programming courses (a total of 9 ECTS[7]) included in the data, as the courses have been added to students' records when they were granted study rights, i.e. 1st of August 2012. We offered the MOOC for all students that were admitted as well. The second group (NORM) does not include students, who took the MOOC during the summer (n=15), as their effective study time would be 3 months longer than the other students in NORM group, causing additional deviation in the data.

For each study subject (CS/IT, Math, all), we report the number of credits, number of courses passed, number of courses failed, and grades for each category. The grades range from 1 (pass) to 5 (excellent), and the grade averages exclude failed courses. Our university does not force courses to be graded on a bell curve. On the contrary, student grades are based on the true performance of the student using an explicit criteria.

When looking at the data, one should keep in mind that the study path for first-year students is designed for students taking the programming courses during the first semester. This means that the students that have been admitted via MOOC have received no benefits from a tailored study path.

4.1 CS/IT Courses

Table 1 contains the students' performance in CS/IT courses. When considering the number of credits that students have gathered during the study period, the average is almost identical when we include the knowledge that MOOC students have taken the introductory programming courses earlier. The standard deviation in the number of credits, which is higher for the NORM group, indicates that there is more variance within the NORM group. In essence, it indicates that there are students that end up failing their first

[7]European Credit Transfer and Accumulation System. An academic year corresponds to 60 ECTS, and one ECTS credit point equals 25-30 hours of student work.

programming courses and do not proceed at all, as well as students, who fare well in their studies.

On average, the students admitted via a MOOC pass more CS/IT courses than the NORM group, and end up failing less courses. On average, MOOC students have one fail per five passed courses, while the NORM group has one fail per three passed courses. The standard deviation in both passed and failed courses is also smaller for the MOOC group; on average, the MOOC students fare better than the NORM students. This is also seen in the grade statistics; although there is not much difference, and the median grade is 4 on a scale from 1 (pass) to 5 (best) for both groups, the average grade is slightly higher for the MOOC group.

4.2 Mathematics Courses

In Table 2, we see the students' performance in mathematics courses. Although mathematics is not a mandatory minor subject, completing at least 10 ECTS of mathematics is mandatory. Typically, students enroll in a course called Introduction to University Mathematics, which covers the essential mathematics required for the course on Data Structures (CS2), where e.g. algorithm run-time analysis is one of the focus areas.

On average, both student groups have completed at least 5 ECTS of mathematics during their first year of studies. The MOOC students have taken over 7 ECTS worth of mathematics, while NORM students have 5.15 ECTS. Note, however, that the standard deviation is high for both groups, which means that it is very likely that there are students in both groups that have either not passed any mathematics courses, or have passed more than one mathematics course.

When looking at the number of passed courses, the median for the MOOC students is 1, and the median for NORM students is 0. This means that one half or more of the NORM students have not succeeded in passing any mathematics courses. This is problematic, as although mathematics is

	All Courses	
	MOOC (n=38)	NORM (n=68)
Credits		
overall	1675	2296
mean	44.08	33.76
std	17.58	21.96
median	43	32.5
Courses passed		
overall	434	599
mean	11.42	8.81
std	4.24	5.27
median	11	9
Courses failed		
overall	101	214
mean	2.66	3.15
std	2.16	2.73
median	2	3
Grade stats		
mean	3.94	3.73
std	1.13	1.18
median	4	4

Table 3: Student performance in all courses.

not a formal requirement for CS2, it is highly beneficial for students to understand the contents of the Introduction to Mathematics course as they take on Data Structures.

The grade averages for both groups are almost alike; the only difference being the slightly higher standard deviation for the NORM group.

4.3 All Courses

Table 3 contains information on all the courses that the students have taken during their first year of studies. It contains both the CS/IT courses and the mathematics courses, and in addition other courses that the students may have taken. Students are able to choose almost any course from any discipline, so minor studies vary a lot among the students. Among the students that have started their studies in 2012, we have students taking courses related to e.g. politics, economics, literature, psychology, languages and law.

Overall, the students in the MOOC group fare slightly better on average than the NORM group, but the NORM group has more variation. On average, the MOOC students have gathered 44.08 ECTS during their first year (35.08 if programming courses are not included), while the NORM students have gathered 33.76 ECTS. There is a small, but noticeable difference, and the median is 43 for MOOC (34 if programming courses are not included), and 32.5 for NORM[8].

When looking at the number of courses passed, and the number of courses failed, the MOOC students fare better on average, while the NORM students have a larger variation. The MOOC students have one fail per four passed courses, while the NORM students have one fail for slightly less than

---

[8]It should be noted that the student should complete 60 ECTS per academic year in order to graduate according to the model curriculum. In practise, a slow start and advancement of CS/IT studies (as well as large dropout rate) is a common problem in Finland. Even the most competent students tend to start working in the IT industry while studying, thus delaying their graduation.

three courses. Again, some students perform well, while others perform poorly. The grade statistics are almost alike, on average the grade of MOOC students is 3.91, while the grade average for NORM students is 3.71.

In addition, when considering the amount of students that have received less than 10 ECTS during their first two semesters, i.e. have done only the programming course or less, only one out of the 38 MOOC students did not complete anything outside the programming courses. When considering the students in the NORM group, a total of 12 students (17.6%) have gathered less than 10 ECTS. We must note that we consider only the students that started their studies and participated in the introductory programming course; in reality, the number is higher.

5. DISCUSSION AND FUTURE WORK

Our initial analysis of students that have been admitted via the MOOC indicates that they are failing less courses and gaining slightly more credits than the students admitted via the traditional path. However, lots of variance in the student groups exist, and both of the groups have so-called high performers and low performers. As we compared the MOOC students to students that have attempted or succeeded in the introductory programming courses during the academic year 2012-2013, our initial analysis excluded the admitted students that did not study at all (e.g. entered military service or started to study another subject at the university) or chose to start their studies early by participating in a voluntary MOOC during summer 2012.

At the University of Helsinki, Department of Computer Science, we receive some 500-600 study applications per year. A majority of the applicants seek a study right via the entrance exam, while some apply directly using their matriculation exam score. Typically less than 200 students are admitted, and of these, on average, less than 130 students accept the study right. Thus, CS/IT is not the number one choice for the study for many of the applicants. Moreover, some 20-30 students do not start any CS/IT courses, even if they accept the study right. When we compare these traditional figures to our first MOOC intake, in which over 93% of the applicants were accepted and started their studies accordingly, the MOOC intake is far superior in matching the students to an appropriate and desired area of study.

Having the students successfully perform introductory programming courses already before they start their studies gives the students a head start over their fellow students. It also acts as a preliminary verification on the students' motivation to study CS/IT. In addition, the students are not getting stuck to the "filter" of learning to program that is a cause for challenges for many in their early studies.

As the awareness of our MOOC as an entrance exam is increasing, we are currently in the process of increasing the number of students admitted via the MOOC. In spring 2013, a total of 66 students were admitted. In addition to improving the intake, we are also working on the students' first year experiences so that the MOOC students have more relevant courses to work on. Even though our MOOC has proven to be beneficial for us, we are not aiming to stack up on online education: we want all of our students to participate in the academic community and therefore emphasize the social support during the degree studies, helping them in the transition from a high school to the university [19].

We see a strong indication that one of the important success factors in first-year CS/IT studies is foundational programming skills. These skills can be practised already before the formal start of the degree studies. Universities with a similar admission system to ours that are facing challenges with student intake and performance (e.g. students dropping out during first semester, students not opting for CS/IT-studies) may benefit from a long-term programming exam, which is administered already during the high-school studies (cf. e.g. [4, 9]).

Acknowledgements

This research is partially funded by the Technological Industries of Finland Centennial Foundation. We gratefully acknowledge the anonymous reviewers for their valuable feedback.

6. REFERENCES

[1] M. E. Caspersen, K. D. Larsen, and J. Bennedsen. Mental models and programming aptitude. In *ACM SIGCSE Bulletin*, volume 39, pages 206–210. ACM, 2007.

[2] A. Collins, J. Brown, and A. Holum. Cognitive apprenticeship: Making thinking visible. *American Educator*, 15(3):6–46, 1991.

[3] A. Collins, J. Brown, and S. Newman. Cognitive apprenticeship: Teaching the crafts of reading, writing, and mathematics. In *Knowing learning and instruction Essays in honor of Robert Glaser*, volume Knowing, 1 of *Psychology of Education and Instruction Series*, pages 453–494. Lawrence Erlbaum Associates, 1989.

[4] T. Crick and S. Sentance. Computing at school: stimulating computing education in the UK. In *Proceedings of the 11th Koli Calling International Conference on Computing Education Research*, Koli Calling '11, pages 122–123, New York, NY, USA, 2011. ACM.

[5] J. Daniel. Making sense of MOOCs: Musings in a maze of myth, paradox and possibility. 2012. http://www.academicpartnerships.com/docs/default-document-library/moocs.pdf.

[6] K. Devlin. The future of textbook publishing is us, 2012. http://devlinsangle.blogspot.fi/2012/08/the-future-of-textbook-publishing-is-us.html.

[7] S. Downes. What is a connectivist MOOC. 2012. http://www.connectivistmoocs.org/what-is-a-connectivist-mooc/.

[8] G. E. Evans and M. G. Simkin. What best predicts computer proficiency? *Commun. ACM*, 32(11):1322–1327, Nov. 1989.

[9] B. Franke, J. Century, M. Lach, C. Wilson, M. Guzdial, G. Chapman, and O. Astrachan. Expanding access to k-12 computer science education: research on the landscape of computer science professional development. In *Proceeding of the 44th ACM technical symposium on Computer science education*, SIGCSE '13, pages 541–542, New York, NY, USA, 2013. ACM.

[10] P. Kinnunen, R. McCartney, L. Murphy, and L. Thomas. Through the eyes of instructors: a phenomenographic investigation of student success. In *Proceedings of the third international workshop on Computing education research*, ICER '07, pages 61–72, New York, NY, USA, 2007. ACM.

[11] J. Kurhila and A. Vihavainen. Management, structures and tools to scale up personal advising in large programming courses. In *Proceedings of the 2011 conference on Information technology education*, SIGITE '11, pages 3–8. ACM, 2011.

[12] A. McAuley, B. Stewart, G. Siemens, and D. Cormier. The MOOC model for digital practice. 2010. http://davecormier.com/edblog/wp-content/uploads/MOOC_Final.pdf.

[13] MOOCs@Edinburgh Group. MOOCs @ Edinburgh 2013: Report nr. 1, 2013. http://hdl.handle.net/1842/6683.

[14] G. Siemens. What is the theory that underpins our MOOCs? 2012. http://www.elearnspace.org/blog/2012/06/03/what-is-the-theory-that-underpins-our-moocs/.

[15] Simon, S. Fincher, A. Robins, B. Baker, I. Box, Q. Cutts, M. de Raadt, P. Haden, J. Hamer, M. Hamilton, R. Lister, M. Petre, K. Sutton, D. Tolhurst, and J. Tutty. Predictors of success in a first programming course. In *Proceedings of the 8th Australasian Conference on Computing Education - Volume 52*, ACE '06, pages 189–196, Darlinghurst, Australia, Australia, 2006. Australian Computer Society, Inc.

[16] A. Vihavainen, M. Luukkainen, and J. Kurhila. Multi-faceted support for MOOC in programming. In *Proceedings of the 13th annual conference on Information technology education*, SIGITE '12, pages 171–176. ACM, 2012.

[17] A. Vihavainen, M. Paksula, and M. Luukkainen. Extreme apprenticeship method in teaching programming for beginners. In *Proceedings of the 42nd ACM technical symposium on Computer science education*, SIGCSE '11, pages 93–98. ACM, 2011.

[18] A. Vihavainen, T. Vikberg, M. Luukkainen, and M. Pärtel. Scaffolding students' learning using Test My Code. In *Proceedings of the 18th ACM conference on Innovation and technology in computer science education*, ITiCSE '13, pages 117–122, New York, NY, USA, 2013. ACM.

[19] P. Wilcox, S. Winn, and M. Fyvie-Gauld. 'It was nothing to do with the university, it was just the people': the role of social support in the first-year experience of higher education. *Studies in higher education*, 30(6):707–722, 2005.

[20] C. Wilson, L. A. Sudol, C. Stephenson, and M. Stehlik. Running on empty: The failure to teach k-12 computer science in the digital age. Association for Computing Machinery. 2010.

Incorporating an Entrepreneurship Concentration into the Undergraduate IT Curriculum

Jeff Crawford, Ken Mayer, Fortune Mhlanga
Lipscomb University
School of Computing and Informatics
One University Park Drive
Nashville, TN 37204
{jeff.crawford, kenneth.mayer, fortune.mhlanga} @lipscomb.edu

ABSTRACT

This paper presents our approach to implementing structures that encourage innovation and entrepreneurship behaviors within the Lipscomb University student population. An early step in this process is presented in this paper: extending our undergraduate Information Technology (IT) curriculum with a concentration on entrepreneurship. Specifically, the paper clarifies where our IT courses address specific dimensions of innovation (a precursor to entrepreneurship), how the curriculum can be extended to effectively incorporate entrepreneurship, and where facilitating conditions can be implemented to reinforce entrepreneurial behavior in our student population. The curriculum changes and ideas presented here have a number of long- and short-term benefits for Lipscomb University as a whole and our IT program in particular. The paper ends by soliciting input on several issues that can maximize the effectiveness of this innovative program.

Categories and Subject Descriptors

K.3.2 [Computers and Education]: Computer and Information Science Education-*computer science education*.

Keywords

Entrepreneurship, innovation, IT curriculum

1. INTRODUCTION

Lipscomb University (hereafter referred to as Lipscomb) has recently undergone a radical redesign of its undergraduate Information Technology (IT) program[i] within the School of Computing and Informatics. The IT program was revamped from a *"one size fits all"* vertical or silo model to a horizontal model program that facilitates individualized customization. Working within Lipscomb's requirement that all students complete a minor of study, customization has been achieved by offering five concentrations for IT majors that, in part, enable them to get a general business minor. The new program has been designed to attract and retain students with extremely diverse interests. One

core change has been to implement structures that encourage innovation and entrepreneurial behaviors within our student population. An early step in this process has involved creating an Entrepreneurship concentration for students majoring in IT.

The idea of incorporating IT Entrepreneurship as a concentration has been partly motivated by environmental factors that support IT innovation and entrepreneurship education. Market conditions have encouraged Lipscomb's School of Computing and Informatics to re-evaluate the structure and focus of our IT program. The United States experienced a recession in 2008, the effects of which are still felt today in two specific ways. First, sources of state revenue have been negatively and dramatically impacted. For example, local governments within Tennessee (TN) have been hit especially hard, with the majority of TN counties experiencing a significant decline in annual sales tax revenue for 2009 and 2010 [14]. Second, the U.S. job market has endured a significant constriction. Again using TN as an example, recent U.S. Department of Labor statistics show a post-recession reduction of more than 17% of manufacturing jobs [4]. These challenging economic factors have driven government leadership to pursue initiatives that encourage growth and innovation [15]. One common focus has been to encourage innovation and entrepreneurship activities, often through the novel application of IT [8].

The rest of the paper is organized as follows. Section 2 presents our IT entrepreneurship concentration. It also describes the nature of our IT curriculum within the context of how it impacts specific dimensions of innovation. Section 3 presents some potential benefits to those IT students who opt for the Entrepreneurship concentration. It also outlines short- and long-term benefits of encouraging an entrepreneurial spirit among undergraduate students. Section 4 concludes the paper with call for input on five specific questions related to the future direction of our IT Entrepreneurship concentration.

2. INTRODUCING AN IT ENTREPRENEURSHIP CONCENTRATION

Responding to market demands, Lipscomb recently placed an emphasis on the entrepreneurship discipline by instituting a Center for Entrepreneurship in 2011. The Center offers both undergraduate majors and minors in Entrepreneurship, with a special focus on two core aspects of the discipline: business and social entrepreneurship[ii]. University investments in faculty and structures surrounding Entrepreneurship allow the IT program to leverage high levels of expertise outside our college to effectively prepare IT students for a career in IT-driven entrepreneurship.

2.1. Curriculum Changes in Support of Entrepreneurship

All undergraduate IT students are required to select one of six available three-course (9-hour) concentrations starting in their junior year. Concentrations offered include Business Informatics, Health Care Informatics, IT entrepreneurship, Leadership and Organizational Behavior, Sustainability Performance Informatics and Web Development. The IT Entrepreneurship concentration presented in this paper comprises the following three courses taught through our Center for Entrepreneurship faculty:

- **The Entrepreneurial Enterprise:** *This cornerstone course introduces students to entrepreneurship, the pursuit of value-creating opportunities without regard to the current control of assets. The course examines the entrepreneur's approach to life and the knowledge and skills necessary for that approach to create value. Students will be able to recognize and evaluate entrepreneurial opportunities. At the end of the course, students will develop a business model for one of those opportunities.*
- **Promotional Strategy:** *Analysis of the uses of various promotions in formulating an overall consumer communication strategy. Topics include advertising, publicity and sales promotion, creative strategies, evaluation of results and the advantages and disadvantages of differing types of media and vehicles in reaching the target audience.*
- **Managing the Entrepreneurial Enterprise:** *This course focuses on the business processes that an entrepreneurial enterprise needs to implement at start up and on the approach to maturing these processes as the enterprise grows. The course emphasizes human resources processes and surveys legal, operations, technology, and services processes that a successful firm must practice. Students will explore which human resources should be employees of the firm and which the firm should outsource, will understand various approaches to compensation and employee organization, and will be able to determine the appropriate legal structure for an entrepreneurial venture. At the end of the course, they will develop an organizational plan for a growing firm through its firm's three years of existence.*

The entrepreneurship courses supplement an IT curriculum focused on understanding and effectively utilizing IT in a myriad of contexts.

2.2. Our IT Curriculum in Perspective

IT presents both an opportunity and constraint for enabling economically valuable innovation. The opportunity for IT-related higher education departments is clear –encourage entrepreneurial activities by educating students on how to innovate with IT. While higher education has done an admirable job designing and implementing an IT curriculum that produces technically proficient students, there has been an inconsistent (and at times, negligent) attention paid to the ways in which IT competencies can enable innovation. Simple strategic changes to the existing IT curriculum can encourage innovation behaviors. We conceptualized addressing this by examining how IT impacts specific dimensions of innovation.

According to MIT researcher Eric Brynjolfsson, contemporary IT has shifted the nature of innovation along four interrelated dimensions: measurement, experimentation, sharing and replication [6]. Innovation opportunities exist where entities are able to utilize IT to rapidly collect and make sense of highly complex data (*measurement*). Further, IT is an innovation game changer in that it provides an inexpensive mechanism for the rapid testing and re-testing of innovative ideas and initiatives (*experimentation*). Contemporary IT also has the potential for encouraging innovation through its information sharing capabilities, allowing individuals to connect and combine information in unique and exciting ways (*sharing*). Finally, IT allows individuals to quickly and inexpensively scale innovations once they have been identified (*replication*). IT programs clearly have an opportunity to train students to exploit market opportunities through these four innovation dimensions.

2.2.1. Innovation characteristics in relation to the IT curriculum

Table 1 lists the coursework for our IT undergraduate program, indicating its potential for addressing each innovation dimension outlined by Brynjolfsson. It illustrates where IT-driven innovation can be addressed in our IT curriculum. The courses listed in Table 1 exclude general education requirements and concentration courses.

While at times taught directly (e.g., innovation through experimentation in Marketing), innovation has often been addressed in tangential ways within the IT curriculum. For example, the idea of innovation through measurement is often addressed in project management during discussions on utilizing lessons learned.

Table 1. IT Curriculum in relation to Brynjolfsson's innovation dimensions

IT Curriculum Subject Area with Example Courses	Measure-ment	Experiment-ation	Sharing	Replication
IT Fundamentals				
• Future of computing	X			
• Intro. to computer programming				
• Fundamentals of information security				
IT Management				
• Project management	X	X	X	
• Systems analysis & design				
• Principles of technology management				
IT Competency				
• Object-oriented system design & programming		X		X
• Web application development I				
• Network principles				
• Wireless networks & mobile systems				
Data Competency				
• Data structures & algorithms	X			X
• Database management systems				
Analytical Competency				
• Survey of calculus		X	X	
• Calculus I				
• Discrete mathematics				
• Elementary statistics				
Business Competency				
• Foundations of business				
• Financial accounting				
• Managerial accounting	X	X	X	
• Principles of management				
• Principles of marketing				
• Consumer behavior				
• Economics				

Regardless of minor (or concentration, thereof) selected, all IT majors graduate with the skills and knowledge necessary to innovate with IT (measurement, experimentation, sharing and replication). For example, all IT majors are required to complete a senior project where they design and implement a software product. While Table 1 illustrates where innovation can be addressed through existing IT courses, innovation capabilities alone are not sufficient to enable successful entrepreneurship activities within the student population. This is where the three Entrepreneurship courses discussed earlier are expected to make a critical contribution.

Entrepreneurship, most commonly defined as "the identification, evaluation and exploitation of opportunities" [12, p. 12], is more than simple innovation. It requires a strategic long-term approach that supports growth from the idea surfaced during episodes of innovation to a marketable product. Most IT undergraduate programs address basic business understanding through introductory business courses in Accounting, Finance, Economics, Marketing and Management. However, topic coverage in these courses only provides a taste of the tools and skills required for an effective entrepreneur. For Lipscomb to comprehensively train students in the skills and mental models essential for successful IT entrepreneurship, an extension to the current curriculum is necessary.

The introduction of a concentration in IT Entrepreneurship now means that those students choosing the concentration are infused with an entrepreneurial mindset that understands how to effectively move idea to product. However, curriculum changes alone are only part of Lipscomb's overall effort to train students towards entrepreneurship. Literature on Entrepreneurship education clearly suggests that coursework alone is an insufficient means of producing *effective* entrepreneurs [2]. Facilitating conditions must exist if we are to maximize the likelihood of a student's transition to an effective entrepreneur.

2.2.2. IT Curriculum Facilitating Conditions that Encourage Entrepreneurship

Entrepreneurship is an inherently risky process, illustrated by the observation that "only 48.8 percent of the new establishments started between 1977 and 2000 were alive at age five" [11]. Many argue that Entrepreneurship is more nature than nurture, art instead of science, which directly impacts how it should be taught [5; 7; 9]. To this end, structures are being leveraged to help students learn the "art" of IT entrepreneurship.

2.2.2.1. Applied coursework
Two specific courses that encourage entrepreneurial learning have been implemented within the IT program. First, graduation requirements specify that all IT majors must complete an internship. Students choosing an IT Entrepreneurship concentration have the opportunity to select an internship that fits their specific interests, with the idea that they would learn from individuals who have an expertise in entrepreneurship [3]. Further, faculty interactions before, during and following the internship experience provide a means of ensuring that students can achieve entrepreneurial learning goals. Second, IT majors participate in a senior project course where they must work with a predefined client to create and implement a live solution to a real world problem. The course requires that students demonstrate

innovation skills, but also demands that they fulfill a "market need" by meeting client requirements.

2.2.2.2. Cross-discipline exposure
Because of its small size, Lipscomb's culture encourages and supports cross-discipline interaction among faculty. With this rich environment as a backdrop, The IT School implemented an undergraduate research initiative in 2012 that partners select IT undergraduate students directly with research faculty. One important goal of this program is to create an environment where students can explore business opportunities from an IT perspective, exercising their entrepreneurship skills to identify, test and (potentially) produce a marketable product. The undergraduate research program is not a requirement for the IT Entrepreneurship concentration, but rather an opportunity for those students who demonstrate an interest and motivation to extend their entrepreneurial skillset. Importantly, the design-based learning opportunity enabled through this research initiative provides an important means of reinforcing and growing an entrepreneurial mindset [9].

2.2.2.3. Social entrepreneurship opportunities
The current generation of undergraduate students, often referred to as The Millennials, are characterized by a strong motivation to work towards a social good [10]. Additionally, a core part of Lipscomb's mission relates to how students use the education they have received: "knowledge acquired and skills gained are to be used to bless the lives of others". These two factors create a reality where students choosing to study at Lipscomb often arrive on campus with a strong motivation to serve. Lipscomb facilitates student service-orientation through a service-learning program that provides undergraduate students with "academically appropriate" service-learning opportunities. In order to graduate, all undergraduate students at Lipscomb must complete two service-learning experiences. As such, IT students with a social entrepreneurship mindset are provided a context where they can utilize their entrepreneurial skillset towards a self-selected social good.

2.2.2.4. Academic competitions
Students are also provided opportunities to become involved with University-sponsored student organizations that demand the use of entrepreneurial skills. For example, Lipscomb sponsors a local chapter for Students in Free Enterprise (SIFE), where students come together in teams and "apply business concepts to develop outreach projects that improve the quality of life and standard of living for people in need" [13]. Additionally, the IT program encourages select students to participate in competitions sponsored by organizations such as the Association for Information Technology Professionals [1]. Competitions like these provide an entertaining, but intensive environment where entrepreneurial skills can be tested and shaped. While students are not required to participate, they are offered ample opportunities to practice those entrepreneurial skills discussed in the classroom.

3. BENEFITS OF AN IT ENTREPRENEURSHIP CONCENTRATION
The IT Entrepreneurship concentration is expected to enhance our IT program. By offering this new concentration, students who have an entrepreneurial disposition will now have access to formal training that helps them become an effective entrepreneur.

Rather than simply training students on how to innovate with IT, the concentration will reinforce skills necessary to take their innovation from infancy to maturity. Clearly, we expect a subset of students to benefit from this extension to our curriculum. This change also has a number of benefits for Lipscomb as a whole, and our IT program in particular. While many of the gains will be quickly realized, a number are more long-term in nature.

3.1. Short-term Benefits of Encouraging Entrepreneurial Spirit of Undergraduate Students

The new focus on IT entrepreneurship has direct implications for the culture within IT faculty and students. First, growing an entrepreneurial mindset within some IT students is expected to encourage a more robust problem-solving mentality among the more general IT student population. Sharing the IT Entrepreneurship student experience with others will help students move from focusing on a general view of IT innovation (e.g., what can I do with IT?) to an active problem-identification / solution development perspective (e.g., how can I solve a specific problem with IT?). Second, student entrepreneurial success should serve as a catalyst for other IT students interested, but not trained, in entrepreneurship. By seeing what is possible, students less inclined towards entrepreneurship will be able to extend and shape their perspective in order to be more effective IT professionals. Finally, the concentration will, by nature, mean that IT students are likely to involve students from other departments to solve non-IT problems, i.e., healthcare, graphic design, or political science.

IT faculty are also impacted by this change in the short term. The process of creating an IT minor has demanded that faculty deeply consider how entrepreneurship fits within the IT major. One unexpected outcome of this process has been a realization that IT-enabled innovation (through measurement, experimentation, sharing and replication) is a core aspect of our IT curriculum. Further, we have also become cognizant that entrepreneurial skills extend beyond simple innovation. This has required our faculty to break down several departmental walls and find ways to more effectively collaborate with faculty from other departments and colleges.

Finally, training and equipping students with an IT entrepreneurship mentality means that graduates will be more likely to make a distinctive and decisive impact when they leave Lipscomb. Rather than facilitating a consumption mindset, an IT entrepreneurship focus should produce students who are more likely to be value creators in the communities where they take residence.

3.2. Long-term Benefits of Encouraging Entrepreneurial Spirit of Undergraduate Students

There are also a number of long-term benefits related to this curriculum change. For example, entrepreneurial activities pursued while in the School of Computing and Informatics have the potential for financial and/or social gains. We envision the partnership with Lipscomb's Center for Entrepreneurship as a vehicle through which technology and applications developed entirely at Lipscomb, or in collaboration with its faculty/staff, can be commercialized to develop income streams to support

programs within the School of Computing and Informatics. IT-driven entrepreneurship can also provide an unparalleled example to visitors and prospective donors of the school's commitment to technology, its direct involvement in the IT business complex, and its willingness to engage in community and economic development.

IT-driven entrepreneurship is also expected to deliver a significant recruiting advantage for prospective students and their parents because of its uniqueness among institutions of Lipscomb's size and focus. Specifically, the program will demonstrate to prospective students that they will have a safe environment from which to experiment with entrepreneurial endeavors very early in their careers.

In the very long-term, we anticipate that the new focus on IT entrepreneurship will allow students to become effective and successful entrepreneurs. Their success will translate into economic and/or social gains in their direct sphere of influence.

4. FUTURE DIRECTIONS

The changes described in this document have been implemented as of Fall 2012. While we anticipate positive outcomes from this important addition to our IT program, we have a number of open questions about how to most effectively mature the program. In particular, we would appreciate insights from those in the academic community with regards to the following questions:

1. Beyond simple metrics such as enrollment numbers, how should we measure success of the IT entrepreneurship concentration?
2. What role should industry play in the IT entrepreneurship concentration? How can we leverage our industry contacts to enhance entrepreneurship opportunities for our student population?
3. What institutional structures / policies should be implemented to support and protect University-student-industry R&D initiatives?
4. How should business and social entrepreneurship be addressed within the curriculum? Specifically, should these be treated as separate concentrations or dealt with through a generic "IT entrepreneurship" concentration?
5. With regards to our IT entrepreneurship concentration, what are the most effective ways to involve other disciplines within the university?

5. BIBLIOGRAPHY

[1] Association for Information Technology Professionals. Contest Information for AITP National Collegiate Conference. *Accessed on September 5, 2012.* http://aitpncc-contests.org/?page_id=11.

[2] Balan, P. and Metcalfe, M., 2012. Identifying teaching methods that engage entrepreneurship students. *Education & Training 54*, 5, 368-384.

[3] Cooper, S., Bottomley, C., and Gordon, J., 2004. Stepping Out of the Classroom and Up the Ladder of Learning: An Experiential Learning Approach to Entrepreneurship Education. *Industry and Higher Education 18*, 1 (February), 11-22.

[4] Donahoe, J. Tennessee lost 68,000 manufacturing jobs during the recession. *Accessed on September 5, 2012.*

http://www.bizjournals.com/memphis/news/2012/07/11/tennessee-lost-68000-manufacturing-jobs.html.

[5] Henry, C., Hill, F., and Leitch, C., 2005. Entrepreneurship education and training: Can entrepreneurship be taught? Part I. *Education & Training 47*, 2/3, 98-111.

[6] Hopkins, M.S., 2010. The Four Ways IT Is Revolutionizing Innovation. *MIT Sloan Management Review 51*, 3 (Spring2010), 51-56.

[7] Katz, J.A., 2008. Fully Mature but Not Fully Legitimate: A Different Perspective on the State of Entrepreneurship Education. *Journal of Small Business Management 46*, 4, 550-566.

[8] Nashville Technology Council. About Us. *Accessed on September 5, 2012.* http://www.technologycouncil.com/about/.

[9] Neck, H.M. and Greene, P.G., 2011. Entrepreneurship Education: Known Worlds and New Frontiers. *Journal of Small Business Management 49*, 1, 55-70.

[10] PwC Consulting. Millennials Survey: Key Findings. *Accessed on September 1, 2012.*
http://www.pwc.com/gx/en/managing-tomorrows-people/future-of-work/key-findings.jhtml.

[11] Shane, S., 2009. Failure is a Constant in Entrepreneurship. In *The New York Times.* http://boss.blogs.nytimes.com/2009/07/15/failure-is-a-constant-in-entrepreneurship/.

[12] Shane, S., 2012. Reflections on the 2010 AMR Decade Award: Delivering on the Promise of Entrepreneurship as a Field of Research. *Academy of Management Review 37*, 1, 10-20.

[13] Students in Free Enterprise. About SIFE. *Accessed on September 5, 2012.* http://www.sifeusa.org/about_sife_usa.

[14] Tennessee Advisory Commission on Intergovernmental Relations. The Residual Impact of the Recession on Local Government Taxes. *Accessed on September 4, 2012.* http://www.tn.gov/tacir/Special html Reports/slowdown.html.

[15] Tennessee Department of Economic and Community Development. Jobs4TN Announcement. *Accessed on September 4, 2012.* http://www.tn.gov/ecd/Jobs4TN.html.

---

[i] Unlike Computer Science, IT programs frequently supplant higher-level mathematics and engineering course work with business-related subjects such as Accounting and Marketing. IT differs from Management Information Systems in that it exists outside the College of Business.

[ii] Business entrepreneurship typically focuses on positive financial ROI (return on investment) while social entrepreneurship most often focuses on positive social outcomes.

Migrating a Voice Communications Laboratory to a Virtualized Environment

Ronny Bull [*]
State University of New York
Institute of Technology
100 Seymour Rd.
Utica, NY 13502
bullr@sunyit.edu

ABSTRACT

Due to a recent surge of student interest in the field of Voice over IP (VoIP) communications, new and innovative methods were required to be employed in order to keep pace with the increasing enrollment in the Voice Communications course offered at the State University of New York Institute of Technology. The traditional Voice Communications laboratory setup was obsolete and created a bottleneck hindering the students' capability to learn due to increasing class sizes. Under the previous setting, students were required to work in large groups on two shared servers in order to gain hands-on experience. This inevitably caused students to receive unequal portions of hands-on time with the allocated resources. To remedy the aforementioned issues, a centralized virtualization approach was proposed and implemented.

Categories and Subject Descriptors

K.3.2 [**Computer and Information Science Education**]: Computer Science Education, Information Systems Education, Curriculum, Lab Environments

Keywords

Laboratory Environments, Voice Communications, VoIP, Virtualization, Networking, IT Education, Telecommunications

1. INTRODUCTION

The evolution of virtualization technology has made a huge impact on the world of computing. In the business world, many companies are migrating towards server consolidation techniques that harness the power of virtualization to save space and energy, cut costs, reduce downtime, and

---

[*]The entire set of Voice Communications laboratory exercises that utilize the VLE are available at: `http://web.cs.sunyit.edu/~bullr/classes/NCS416/labs`

lower administrative overhead[2, 9]. With today's advances in computer technology, entire rooms of servers can be consolidated down to a single rack of modern high performance servers that are configured in a virtualization cluster therefore providing an increased level of service than what was previously available. This technology has also proven useful in education where entire laboratories have been virtualized, freeing up physical space and funding for other uses[1, 5, 6, 7, 12, 13].

The Virtualized Laboratory Environment (VLE) developed for the Computer Science Department at the State University of New York Institute of Technology (SUNYIT) is a centralized virtualization[6] approach which was designed with these goals in mind. However, the primary goal was to empower students by providing them convenient access to the resources they need to succeed. One of the initial implementations was the migration of the Voice Communications course offered to Telecommunications and Network Computer Security majors into the VLE. Previously, students were placed into groups of four to six. These groups were required to perform laboratory exercises on two Pentium 4 class Asterisk machines. All of the groups were required to share the available resources, however only one group at a time would be able to use the resources to complete the assignment. Under the new VLE, Voice Communications students are each provisioned their own set of Asterisk virtual machines to utilize during the semester. Every student receives an equal amount of access to resources required by the laboratory exercises, and can use them on their own schedule. Students also have greater opportunity to experiment on their own without affecting other's work since each student's set of virtual machines are located within an isolated environment.

2. VIRTUALIZED LABORATORY ENVIRONMENT OVERVIEW

Work on the VLE began in the summer of 2011 as part of the author's Computer Science Master's Thesis work at SUNYIT. The system was initially constructed with three custom built servers using the open source Xen Cloud Platform (XCP)[14] product from Xen.org. One of the servers was allocated to the SUNYIT CS Department to utilize for department server consolidation. The other two servers were pooled together and used to host laboratory machines for Network Computer Security (NCS) students. Each student was provisioned four virtual machines that they were able to use simultaneously on an isolated VLAN to perform laboratory exercises throughout the semester. After noting the success of the VLE's implementation of the NCS course laboratories, two more servers were added to the system for general student use. One was dedicated for CS students who require project or research machines whereas the other was dedicated to the Voice Communications course.

The VLE builds upon of the existing VLAN infrastructure implemented on the CS network. The VLAN architecture supports virtual machines directly placed on subnets associated with their purpose and isolation requirements (figure 1). For instance, if a machine's purpose is a production server, it could be placed on one of the production networks. If a faculty member requires a virtual machine for research, the virtual machine could be assigned to the faculty subnet. This provides the instructor with easy access along with a level of isolation. Student virtual machines are completely isolated from the production network and are usually assigned to a VLAN that is located behind a protected gateway that provides very restrictive network access. Some courses may require students to have a set of virtual machines that run operating systems with known vulnerabilities so that they may be exploited and should not be accessible externally. In these situations the virtual machines are restricted to an isolated VLAN with no external access to ensure that the integrity of the CS department's network can be maintained.

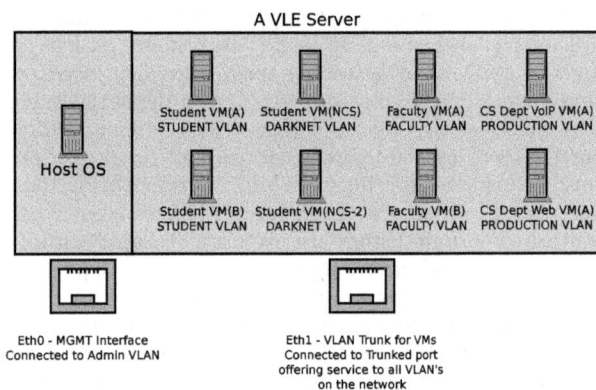

Figure 1: Abstraction of typical VLAN usage on a VLE server.

VLAN integration within the VLE supports the transition of virtual machines between subnets as needed. For example a planned production server could be developed on an isolated VLAN, moved to another VLAN for testing, then finally moved to the production VLAN when it is ready for deployment. Virtual machines may also be assigned more than one virtual network interface, allowing them to access multiple VLANS.

Scalability and centralized virtual machine management are integrated into the VLE as well. Server pools can be created that allow multiple servers to be joined together in a cluster sharing resources to host virtual machines. New servers can be added to the pools as long as they have the same CPU features and chipset as the other servers in the pool. The use of Linux Logical Volume Manager (LVM) partitioning allows administrators to scale storage space by adding more hard drives to the servers as needed to meet the needs of increasing storage demands.

The entire VLE is centrally managed by the use of the Citrix XenCenter[3] product as well as an open source product known as OpenXenManager[11]. These applications allow administrators to manage servers, pools, and virtual machines from one central location. The use of virtual machine templates facilitates quick deployment of single virtual machines for students in a matter of minutes. Once a course master template is created, an entire class worth of virtual machines, approximately forty to fifty machines, can be deployed in under an hour. Administrators can export virtual machines and templates so that they can be backed up over a network or imported into other Xen servers to be used to create new virtual machines. Students may also request an export file of their virtual machines at the end of the semester so that they may import it into one of the popular desktop virtualization products such as VMWare Workstation or Oracle VirtualBox to continue experimenting on their own.

A particularly useful feature of the VLE system is that it allows the students access to their virtual machines anywhere in the world via a Java enabled web browser and Internet access. Students can access their virtual machines and control them from a web portal using the open source XVPAppliance product[15]. This web portal not only provides the students with VNC console access to their virtual machines, but it also gives them the authority to perform tasks such as powering on or off their machines as well as rebooting them. Their virtual machines can be totally isolated from the Internet yet be accessible by the students through this portal using their standard CS login credentials. This allows them to work at their convenience, on their time, and without requiring physical access to their machines. Typically physical machines are located on campus in a locked laboratory that is only accessible at certain times.

3. TRADITIONAL VOICE COMMUNICATIONS LABORATORY SETUP

Traditionally the Voice Communications course was taught with both lecture and laboratory based portions. In the laboratory environment, students took turns in groups working on two legacy Pentium 4 computers running Asterisk, each containing a single port FXO card connected to an analog phone line for PSTN access (figure 2).

Each group worked through the semester editing the proper configuration files located in /etc/asterisk. During a laboratory session, once the first group was finished with a laboratory exercise they would clear the configuration files and were responsible to reset the machines back to their original state. Then the next group would utilize the machines and perform the same laboratory exercise. The hands-on exercises would cover topics such as setting up the dual machines to send and receive phone calls over the SIP protocol and create a communication link between the two servers using the IAX protocol to simulate a main branch to remote branch setup. Other laboratories taught the students to configure features such as voice mail, call waiting, and utilizing the FXO cards to provide access to the PSTN.

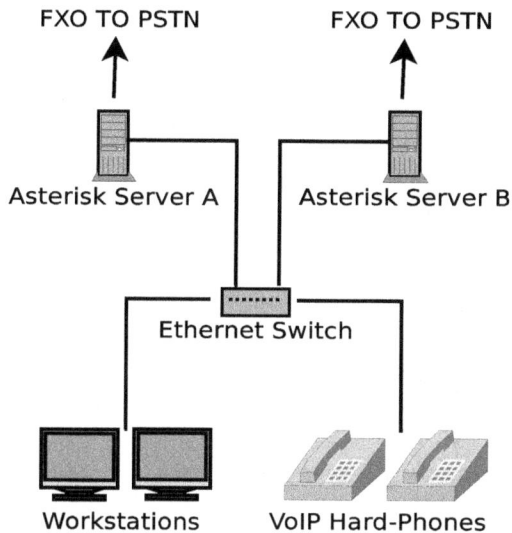

Figure 2: Traditional Voice Communications laboratory setup.

This setup worked well for a number of years with small classes of eight to ten students when VoIP technology was emerging on the scene. However in today's society, an explosive growth in the global usage of VoIP technology[8] has sparked a greater interest in Telecommunications and Network Computer Security students' desire to learn and understand it. This rise in interest is evident in SUNYIT's Voice Communications course enrollment which has doubled to around twenty-five students per semester. Consequently, the current two server setup was quickly becoming a bottleneck in the students' capability to experiment with and learn the technology.

Automating the configuration file cleanup was one proposed solution to deal with current shortcomings. The idea was to write login scripts that swap in a set of configuration files each time a group logged into the machines which belonged to them. This would eliminate some of the issues that were caused by a previous group's activities. The responsibility would be removed from the students and instead be offloaded to the script. Both of the machines would be initially loaded with Asterisk and a default set of configuration files. When a group logged in, a backup of the configuration files would be saved to a safe location and the group's configuration files would then be loaded into /etc/asterisk. Upon logging out, the group's configuration files would be stored to their home directory in the .asterisk-configs directory and the default configuration files would be copied back to /etc/asterisk for the next group. Though this solution would eliminate confusion caused by switching groups, it still did not solve the physical constraints caused by twenty-five students attempting to work on a single set of computers. It also did not eliminate the issue of one group possibly altering the operating system causing issues that are not addressed by the automated script.

The second solution proposed was to use the Virtualized Laboratory Environment to create virtual machines for the students to use. This solution eliminates all of the issues

that were created by using the two physical machines as well as removes the physical bottleneck issue as discussed previously.

4. VIRTUALIZED VOICE COMMUNICA-TIONS LABORATORY SETUP

The migration of the Voice Communications laboratory to a centralized virtualization solution provided each student the ability to gain hands-on experience with the Asterisk open source PBX software under an easily managed and scalable system. Each student is provisioned two virtual machines loaded with the AsteriskNow Linux distribution created by Digium[4], the creators of Asterisk. The distribution consists of a minimal CentOS installation preloaded with Asterisk and provides the option to install the FreePBX web management interface. Students are allocated one of each type of installation. Primarily the laboratories are all performed with the command line only version, however students are provisioned a FreePBX enabled version to experiment with. All of the virtual machines are located on an isolated VLAN that is dedicated for student laboratory use only. All external access into the laboratory subnet from the outside is blocked by the use of a gateway/firewall server *(figure 3)*. The laboratory virtual machines do have Internet access via the gateway, however due to the restrictions on external access no ports may be forwarded to the virtual machines on the subnet.

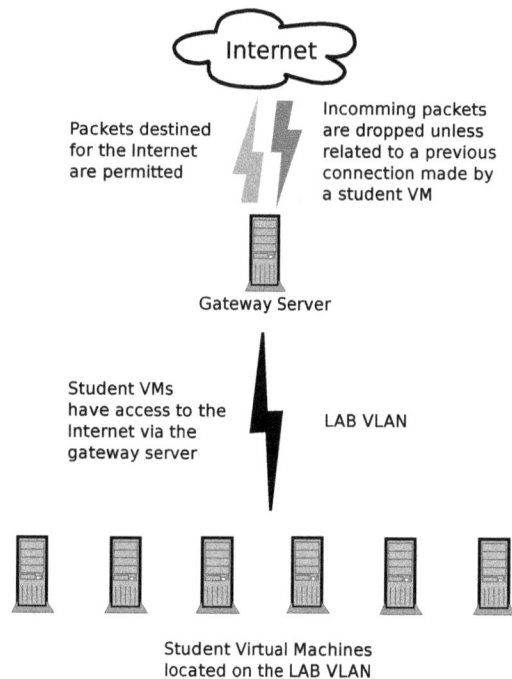

Figure 3: Basic overview of the virtual laboratory gateway setup.

Students can access the console on their machines either remotely by using the web portal offered by the VLE or by using SSH on one of the physical laboratory computers that are connected to the same subnet as the virtual machines. The FreePBX web interface on each of the student's virtual machines is only accessible from within the laboratory subnet. Students may gain access by connecting personal laptops at approved locations or use the physical laboratory computers that are connected to the subnet. Savvy users may use an advanced form of SSH tunneling through a series of department servers and the laboratory gateway to access their FreePBX web interface and SSH console from outside of the restricted laboratory subnet. However, this is a technically advanced procedure and instructions are provided as an optional laboratory exercise for those who are interested.

It is important to note that students may use various means to configure their virtual servers remotely, but cannot connect remote SIP devices to their servers due to the restrictions on external access to the laboratory subnet *(figure 4)*. Therefore students must connect all SIP devices (ie. soft-phones and hard-phones) directly to the laboratory subnet in order for them to work with their Asterisk virtual machines. No SIP proxy is provided. This restriction helps to prevent abuse, exploitation, and overloading of the network resources.

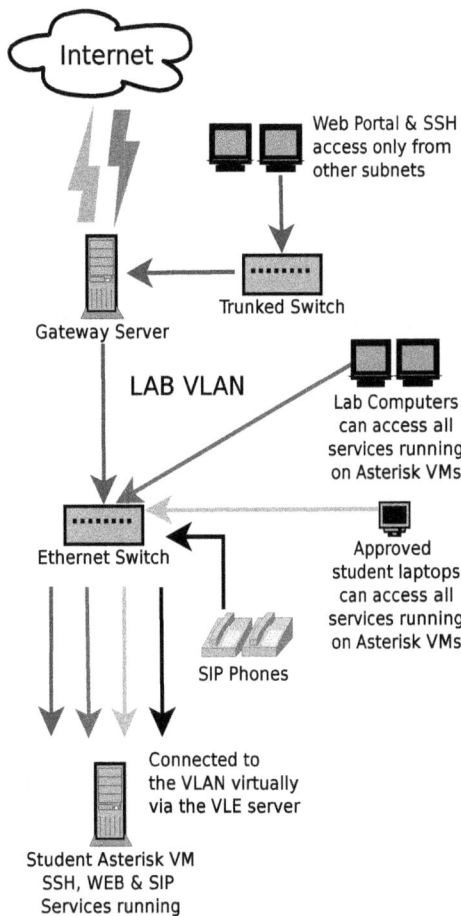

Figure 4: Laboratory VLAN access restrictions

Since all of the Asterisk machines are now virtual, students still need an avenue to gain experience with using the IAX protocol to connect two Asterisk servers, as well as using a FXO trunk to gain external PSTN access. This issue was solved by adding a physical Asterisk server to the lab-

oratory subnet that contains multiple 4-port Digium FXO cards connected to analog PSTN phone lines. Students are able to connect their virtual Asterisk servers to the master Asterisk trunk server using the IAX protocol allowing them to gain access to one of the available FXO ports so that they may make and receive calls using the PSTN *(figure 5)*.

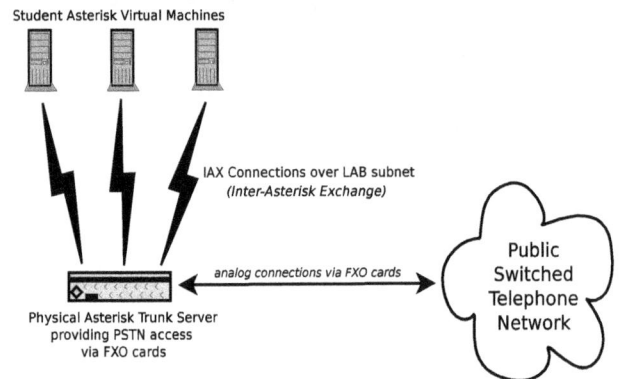

Figure 5: Student virtual machines connecting to a trunking server over the IAX protocol to gain PSTN access via FXO cards.

Adhering to objectives in the traditional Voice Communications laboratory setup, students are provided with a series of laboratory exercises that are intended to teach them how to access their machines, initially configure their server, as well as create and use SIP extensions with soft and hard phones. They learn how to deploy features such as call waiting, voice mail, auto-attendants, and hard-phone provisioning. The main difference between the traditional setup and the VLE is that each student now has his or her own Asterisk server to work with and the ability to work at their own pace without competition for physical resources.

5. PERFORMANCE REMARKS & SYSTEM MONITORING

Each VLE server was custom built in house using the following hardware:

- Motherboard: SUPERMICRO MBD-X9SCM-O Server Motherboard (Sandy Bridge) w/2 integrated 1000MB Intel Network Interface Cards

- Processor: Intel Xeon E3-1240 @ 3.30GHz Quad Core w/ HyperThreading

- RAM: 16 GB Crucial DDR3 SDRAM ECC Unbuffered Server Memory

- Hard Drives: 2x Seagate Momentus XT 500GB Hyrbid

- Rack Mount Case: Antec Take 4+ 4U w/ 650W Power Supply (Quiet Computing)

Total cost per server: $1331.46

A single VLE server built from the above listed hardware can support upwards of one hundred virtual machines running simultaneously, given that each virtual machine is allocated a minimal amount of memory *(128MB or less)* so that there is enough available memory to start and run them all.

With additional memory a VLE server could technically support additional concurrently running virtual machines, or allow more memory to be allocated to each of the running virtual machines. The VLE server that is utilized for the Voice Communications class has been proven to easily support a class of twenty-five students each running two virtual machines that are allocated 256MB of memory.

Server monitoring, metrics, and alerting for the VLE as well as all other servers and lab computers located on the Computer Science network are performed by a Gentoo Linux virtual machine running Nagios[10]. Nagios is an enterprise level IT infrastructure monitoring service that can be used to keep track of server resources such as CPU, memory, and disk utilization. It can also be configured to monitor services running on a host, as well as send out alerts when those services are no longer detected. An agent is setup on each host that requires monitoring, and corresponding rules are put into place that perform actions such as collecting data and sending out email alerts based on certain criteria. Graphs are also produced that provide historical views *(4 hrs, 25 hrs, weekly, monthly, and yearly)* of the collected data. *Table 1* depicts what is being monitored on each VLE server, as well as the corresponding alert thresholds that have been set.

Service	Warning	Critical	Alert
Disk Space /	3224 MB	3627 MB	Email
Disk Space XenStore	200 GB	75 GB	Email
Server Load Average 1	15	30	Email
Server Load Average 5	10	25	Email
Server Load Average 15	5	20	Email
NTP Time Offset	1 min	5 mins	Email
SSH Service on eth0	N/A	No Response	Email
SSH Service on eth1	N/A	No Response	Email
Round Trip Times	3000 ms	5000 ms	Email

Table 1: Nagios monitoring of VLE servers.

By constantly monitoring the VLE servers administrators are able to determine if the servers are capable of handling the current semester load. The use of Nagois also provides the administration team with immediate alerts of potential problems, failures, or other events that require attention. Warning and critical alerting thresholds allow administrators fine grained control over how and when they should be alerted. If a monitored service hits the warning threshold an alert is dispatched before a potential problem actually occurs. The warning threshold is typically set to a level that will still provide uninterrupted service, however that level tends to be close enough to the critical threshold that the early warning alert may provide an administrator enough time to resolve a potential issue before it becomes a real problem. If the critical threshold is hit then another alert is dispatched warning the administrative team that immediate attention is required.

Nagios provides a visual rendering of historical data in the form of graphs. *Figure 6* depicts a one week overview of the time it takes a single ICMP packet to reach the Voice Communications VLE server and return to the Nagios server. This measurement was taken in the middle of the semester during peak usage. It is referred to as Round Trip Time *(RTT)*, and is important because not only does it tell an

administrator that the server is online and responding, but it also provides insight as to how well the server's network interface and the network in general are handling the virtual machine traffic load.

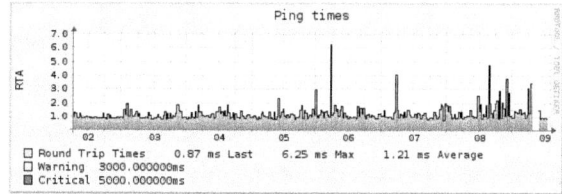

Figure 6: Round Trip Times over one week.

6. ISSUES & STUDENT FEEDBACK

Throughout the course of the semester the students experienced a very minimal amount of issues when performing their laboratory exercises using the VLE. Only two issues surfaced that were due to the VLE implementation. The first was a problem with the XVPAppliance web service. Students were reporting issues with gaining console access to their virtual machines via the web portal. This turned out to be that the reporting students were using an open source version of Java that was not compatible with XVPAppliance. The solution to this issue was to inform all students that they must be running the latest version of the Oracle Java web browser plug-in in order to access their virtual machines from the VLE web portal. The second issue that appeared was during a laboratory exercise that was intended to provide students with hands-on experience installing the AsteriskNow distribution into a virtual machine. This seemed to be a good exercise for the students at the time, however the installations took a very long time due to the excessive amount of disk I/O traffic generated from twenty-five virtual machines performing an operating system installation simultaneously on the same set of mirrored hard drives. This issue was not experienced in any of the other laboratory exercises that utilized the VLE due to the fact that they are not disk I/O intensive. A future enhancement to the VLE that would help to alleviate this issue could be the addition of high speed network attached storage that utilizes multiple drives in a high performance and redundant RAID array configuration such as RAID-10. This would spread the disk I/O activity across multiple hard drives reducing the bottleneck caused by the single mirror that is currently in use.

The majority of the feedback obtained from the students at the end of the semester was very positive, and included recommendations to use the VLE for future Voice Communications classes as well as to expand its use to other course offerings. Students enjoyed the fact that they had individual laboratory resources that were available to them around the clock both on campus and remotely, which gave them the ability to experiment beyond the laboratory sessions and gain hands-on experience on their own time.

7. CONCLUSION

The virtualized solution empowers the students and allows them a greater opportunity to learn and succeed. It also optimizes sparse resources students depend on for a high quality course experience. The optimization comes from the scalability of the virtualized environment making it suitable for generous class sizes. Cumbersome laboratory setups can be replaced with templates to create new virtual machines for students on the fly. When the semester is over, cleanup is easy by removing the unused virtual machines to free resources for next semester. If the operating system has been updated or changed, only the master template needs to be addressed. Every machine created from the updated template will be an exact copy making deployment a simple task. The use of this approach in a Voice Communications laboratory setting allows an instructor to reduce bottlenecks created by shared hardware as well as gain more space in the laboratory for devices such as switches and hard-phones that the students can use to interface with their virtual machines. Students only require a space to connect a computer to the restricted subnet to use a soft-phone or configure their virtual machines after removing the physical machines. Funding that would have gone into purchasing more physical computers for use as Asterisk servers for the students could be routed into purchasing hard-phones and other VoIP equipment for the students to experiment with. It is the author's experience that a school can purchase three to four mid-ranged enterprise class hard-phones for the price of a low end computer.

8. REFERENCES

[1] ANDERSON, B. R., JOINES, A. K., AND DANIELS, T. E. Xen worlds: leveraging virtualization in distance education. In *ITiCSE '09 Proceedings of the 14th annual ACM SIGCSE conference on Innovation and technology in computer science education* (2009), pp. 293–297.

[2] BARHAM, P., DRAGOVIC, B., FRASER, K., HAND, S., HARRIS, T., HO, A., NEUGEBAURER, R., PRATT, I., AND WARFIELD, A. Xen and the art of virtualization. *ACM SIGOPS Operating Systems Review - SOSP '03 37*, 5 (December 2003), 164–177.

[3] CITRIX SYSTEMS INC. Citrix Xen Center. Retrieved June 13, 2011 from `http://community.citrix.com/display/xs/XenCenter`.

[4] DIGIUM. AsteriskNow. Retrieved September 21, 2011 from `http://www.asterisk.org/asterisknow`.

[5] KETEL, M. A virtualized environment for teaching it/cs laboratories. In *ACM SE '10 Proceedings of the 48th Annual Southeast Regional Conference* (2010), pp. 92:1–92:2.

[6] LI, P. Centralized and decentralized lab approaches based on different virtualization models. *Journal of Computing Sciences in Colleges 26*, 2 (December 2010), 263–269.

[7] LI, P. Selecting and using virtualization solutions: Our experiences with vmware and virtualbox. *Journal of Computing Sciences in Colleges 25*, 3 (January 2010), 11–17.

[8] MADSEN, L., MEGGELEN, J. V., AND BRYANT, R. *Asterisk: The Definitive Guide.* O'Reilly Media Inc., California, 2011.

[9] MCDOUGALL, R., AND ANDERSON, J. Virtualization performance: Perspectives and challenges ahead. *ACM SIGOPS Operating Systems Review 44*, 4 (December 2010), 40–56.

[10] NAGIOS. Nagios - the industry standard in it infrastructure monitoring. Retrieved August 10, 2011 from `http://www.nagios.org`.

[11] OPENXENMANAGER SOURCEFORGE PROJECT. OpenXenManager. Retrieved June 13, 2011 from `http://sourceforge.net/projects/openxenmanager/`.

[12] STACKPOLE, B. The evolution of a virtualized laboratory environment. In *SIGITE '08 Proceedings of the 9th ACM SIGITE conference on Information technology education* (2008), pp. 243–248.

[13] WANG, X., HEMBROFF, G. C., AND YEDICA, R. Using vmware vcenter lab manager in undergraduate education for system administration and network security. In *SIGITE '10 Proceedings of the 2010 ACM conference on Information technology education* (2010), pp. 43–52.

[14] XEN.ORG. Xen Cloud Platform. Retrieved June 6, 2011 from `http://www.xen.org/products/cloudxen.html`.

[15] XVP SOURCE. XVPAppliance. Retrieved June 8, 2011 from `http://www.xvpsource.org`.

Integrating Authentic Learning into a Software Development Course: An Experience Report

Evelyn Brannock
1000 University Center Lane
Lawrenceville, GA 30043
678-939-9007
ebrannoc@ggc.edu

Robert Lutz
1000 University Center Lane
Lawrenceville, GA 30043
678-744-5889
rlutz@ggc.edu

Nannette Napier
1000 University Center Lane
Lawrenceville, GA 30043
678-524-1511
nnapier@ggc.edu

ABSTRACT

This paper describes our experience integrating an authentic learning project into a junior-level software development course. During the course, students applied full software development life cycle processes to meet a campus need – providing classroom clicker support without purchasing additional hardware. The paper provides the motivation for this approach, summarizes relevant developments in classroom response systems, details the design of the class project, and shares our results. Finally, we offer reflections describing both intended and unintended outcomes of this experiment.

Categories and Subject Descriptors

K.3.2 [**Computers and Information Science Education**]: Computer science education – *curriculum*

Keywords

Software development life cycle, software engineering course, curriculum innovation

1. INTRODUCTION

Students are frequently motivated by projects where their efforts can positively impact a client or broader user community [1-3]. These experiences also provide students an opportunity for authentic learning characterized by high relevance, ill-defined problems, and complex tasks [4]. As such, senior-level capstone projects have been used within computing curriculum to provide students some experience in developing software for a real-world client [5, 6].

The implementation of these courses can vary considerably between institutions. For instance, they can range in length from a semester project to a year. The client role could be fulfilled by internal departments, non-profit organizations, or open source communities [7, 8]. Some schools have strong institutional support for engaging community partners and supporting faculty

and students, while others rely purely on the instructor to sustain efforts [9]. Despite this variation, reported studies consistently attribute benefits to students such as the ability to apply

foundational skills, increased appreciation for importance of teamwork, and exposure to critical software tools – all leading to better preparation for software development jobs [10-12].

Considering these benefits, we sought to incorporate authentic learning experiences early in the software development curriculum at Georgia Gwinnett College (GGC), a public four-

year undergraduate institution in the southeastern United States. In particular, our software development students take three project-based classes: Software Development I (SD I), Software Development II (SD II), and the capstone Software Development Project (SDP). In each of these classes, students participate in projects where they work on teams to develop applications for internal clients or student groups. For example, SD I students created the GGC Connect application which provides functionality such as finding rooms on campus, looking up faculty directory information, and finding the current schedule for the gym [13]. The SD II class created the TsoiChem application to support chemistry students in accessing unique podcasts, flashcards, and videos [14].

This paper reports in detail on our experience managing and implementing an authentic learning project in the SD I course. We describe both the course objectives and the project design from initiation to final assessment. We provide an example of this approach by detailing the Clicker Project completed by students in Fall 2011. We conclude with lessons learned.

2. SOFTWARE DEVELOPMENT COURSE

2.1 Objectives

SD I is the first course in a sequence that teaches students to use the software development life cycle. Prior to taking this junior-level course, students are required to have passed two semesters of Java programming with a grade of C or higher. Therefore, they will know how to program individual, small-scale projects but would have had limited exposure to team-based projects. At the end of the course, students in SD I should be able to (1) gather and analyze user requirements; (2) plan and track project development; (3) understand professional practice of software development, industry trends and ethical issues; and (4) collaboratively develop a simple system using an object-oriented approach.

The long-term goal of SD I is to prepare students for software development careers and enable them to seek challenging industry work. The immediate goal involves consolidating knowledge from their lower-level courses while adding newly learned concepts about team-based software development processes. We also hope to increase interest in the discipline, increase critical thinking skills, and enhance the student's appreciation for the intricacies of the software development process.

2.2 Project Design

Unlike capstone courses, we were only able to devote roughly one-third of the course to the authentic learning project. The other two-thirds of the course consisted of theoretical topics such as systems analysis, requirements gathering, software processes, testing, and teamwork. For instance, students were informed of the industry failure rate for projects, as quoted to them from Standish in the CHAOS report [15]. For these topics, students were asked to read a software engineering textbook, complete hands-on assignments, and conduct independent research on software tools. A mid-term and final exam were given to assess students' understanding of these concepts.

Simultaneously with the production of a running system, the SD I course also requires that theoretical concepts and terms are covered in the course. A summary timeline for the theoretical work follows in Table 1:

- Week 1 – Introductions and course overview. This included the outline of the four major projects that would be due throughout the semester.

One	Evaluating, Utilizing and Presenting on an Open Source CASE Tool of their choice (accomplished in teams via a simple case study project implementation, presentation later in the semester and report on efficacy of the tool chosen).
Two	Contributing to Testing in Free and Open Source Software via assignment of a bug in a real-world open source project (JUnit was used), including verification of the bug, effective test cases for the bug, improved bug report, and solution plan).
Three	Research on a Current Software Engineering Topic, requiring a synopsis of an academic paper, accomplished in teams of two. Students could choose from an instructor provided list of possible papers.
Final	Developing a Web-enabled Software Clicker, discussed in this paper which included deliverables of running, tested application in a version control system. The final project required not only code artifacts, but the requirements, analysis, and design documentation, a user manual, and installation guide. Three teams of 5 to 6 students would be responsible for this final project.

Table 1

- Week 2 – The object oriented life cycle model and other life-cycle models, CASE tools, and high level UML overview Part 1.
- Week 3 – High level UML overview completion.

- Week 4 – Requirements and analysis workflows.
- Week 5 – Design and implementation workflows.
- Week 6 – Tools of the trade including aids such as SourceForge, and version control.
- Week 7 – Mid-term.
- Week 8 – Testing, including introduction to testing with JUnit, and overview of the JUnit open source product for open source project.
- Week 9 – CASE tool project presentations.
- Week 10 – Reusability and design patterns.
- Week 11 – Maintenance.
- Week 12 – Project Management, and team dynamics
- Week 13 – Phases of the Unified Process, planning for a project, CMM, Cost-Benefit Analysis, software metrics and integration.
- Week 14 – Corporate visit to a successful software vendor.
- Week 15 – Demonstration of Final Project by teams.

For the project, the instructor took responsibility for identifying the project and serving as the primary liaison with the client. The instructor then led students through the following steps:

1. Understand needs and constraints
2. Form teams
3. Propose technical project plan
4. Implement solution
5. Assess work

In the next section, we describe in detail an example of how these steps came together during Fall 2011 semester for SD I. This is followed by reflection on the lessons learned from this experience.

3. THE CLICKER PROJECT

Classroom response systems (CRS), as known as 'clickers', are technological devices used in classrooms for a variety of purposes. Clickers, in their simplest implementations, allow instructors to establish a poll electronically. Students participate in a poll by asserting their responses through an electronic device. In more elaborate scenarios, the clickers are used in other ways, including: psychological experiments, attendance taking, data collection, and response timing [16, 17]. Use of clickers has been observed to increase attendance, class participation, student attention and to promote student engagement in the classroom; furthermore, Taneja concludes that clickers increase both students' learning outcomes at a higher level and student satisfaction [17].

At our institution, hardware clickers are a popular but scarce resource which must be checked out from the library by a faculty member. Since all of the classrooms for the Introduction of Computing courses are equipped with computers, the use of a web-based application to replace the physical clickers seemed to mesh well with our needs.

3.1 Understand needs and constraints

At the beginning of the project, the instructor (the first author) provided background to students on the importance to clickers in the pedagogical process. Next, the instructor explained the goal of the project as providing a software-based alternative. At this point, students were told that they needed to gather more specific requirements by interviewing the client (the second author) during the next class period. This precipitated an active lecture on how to effectively interview users most effectively. Templates for interviewing were provided, and decision trees for interviewing were introduced.

When the client came to the class, he again explained the need for the software. Students used their prepared interview guide to further clarify needs and wants. Three primary technological goals were asserted. First, the application must be server based with a "zero footprint" on the student machines. Second, no additional software will need to be installed on the student machines in introductory class beyond the standard laboratory configuration. Finally, the application must be anonymous so that students can feel free to answer.

Additionally, the following secondary requirements were established: the service must be highly scalable, the interface must be easy to use, and the instructor needs to be provided with a histogram of responses with a show/hide capability. Overriding all of these three goals was the client's non-functional requirement that the application be intuitive and very simple to use.

Additionally, the student developers were specifically exempted from integrating the developed clickers to existing test banks, Learning Management Systems (LMS) or presentation applications such as PowerPoint. Storing or reporting on performance statistics was also considered outside of the scope of this first iteration of the project.

3.2 Form Teams

After receiving this overview of the project, the instructor assigned students to one of three teams. Each team would propose, implement, and present an independent solution. To assist in forming teams, the instructor asked students to rate themselves on a scale of 1 to 3 for the following roles: project manager, network specialist, developer, user interface design, systems analyst, and tester. A program, written by the instructor, placed them in a group according to their rankings. It was the hope of the instructor that every group would have someone that could substantially contribute for all of the necessary skill-sets required in the SD life cycle. Each group, inclusive of all skill-sets, had an equal rating according to a sum when all was done. However, one group did not have an apparent Project Manager, but a student volunteered to fill the role, as other students were relying on him.

To minimize the number of client interactions, the instructor served as primary liaison with the client. If there were questions the instructor could not answer, only the team project manager was allowed to communicate with the client. As the teams delved into the project, they identified many questions about functionality, such as "Can I allow an instructor to pose a multiple choice question, with the possible choices from A-Z?" They also had questions regarding the infrastructure such as "What are the restrictions of the institution's firewall?"

3.3 Propose Technical Project Plan

The first team deliverable was a high-level project plan. The instructor met with representatives from each of the teams to review their proposed architecture. Multiple technologies were used, including Java Web Start and Ruby on Rails. Once this approval had been obtained, each team needed to produce a rudimentary requirements document based upon a provided template. Minimum requirements and analysis artifacts included a description of non-functional requirements, use cases, either activity or sequence diagrams, and class diagrams. The instructor provided feedback on these documents before providing approval to start implementation. Students were expected to refine these

documents throughout the semester and turn in updated versions with their final project deliverables.

3.4 Implement solution

After all teams had submitted their requirements documents, the client again visited the class to interact with the teams. Each team presented a brief overview of their proposed architecture and user interface design (if available). The client provided some initial feedback and responded to additional questions that arose.

With feedback from the user, the students began to code. Groups, which were placed together without necessarily knowing each other before, began to produce a final application. They had to plan multiple meetings outside of the classroom. Not surprisingly, there were some complaints ("My team member is not producing", "I expected this on a certain date"). At the same time, there were also the words of comfort: "A team member stepped in and completed this, even though they weren't supposed to." Through this experience, students saw firsthand the importance of non-technical skills to the success of the project.

3.5 Assess work

The final deliverables for each student team included revised requirements documentation, a user manual, an installation manual, the working application, and a demonstration for the client. In fact, a contest was held which was judged by the client and external professors. Figure 1 shows the user interface from both the instructor and student perspectives.

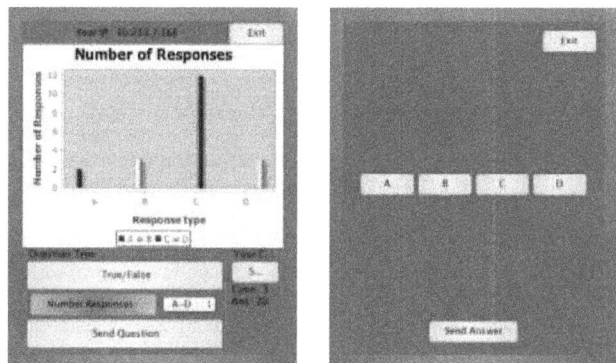

Figure 1: Instructor and Student Apps, respectively

The application was deployed by the Center of Teaching Excellence at our institution. Two professors utilized the application the next semester as part of the initial roll out.

4. DISCUSSION
4.1 Lessons Learned

This experience provided many neat, and sometimes unexpected, learning opportunities for both students and faculty.

1. Students considered the importance of branding software application.

It is important to give the application a "snappy" marketable name and make sure the user appreciates the skills they bring. The students were in charge of the application and they chose the name that they felt would have the most impact. The class had a lot of fun deciding what the project would be called. Georgia Gwinnett College General Grizzly Consensus (or GGC[2]) was decided on. Other names were offered, General Consensus,

Polarware, Survey Says and Claw Clicker were proffered, but GGC² was decided on by majority.

2. *Instructors should consider the early involvement of stakeholders.*

Office of Education Technology (OET) is responsible for the configuration and management of campus desktops. The application the students produced is highly reliant on the environment and network capabilities offered to the students in courses that may utilize the application. Therefore, input from OET would have improved the final product, and illustrated to the students the importance of the blessing of the implementer.

3. *Course delivery method makes a difference.*

The SD I class was offered once a week, at night, for a 3 ½ hour session. The amount of conceptual material, combined with the time the teams needed to work together on the application, and guidance required from the instructor, made this challenging. To address this, we could adopt a team teaching approach that divides the course between two instructors; one that focuses on the conceptual portion of the course, and another that focuses on the project and project artifact delivery of the course. This approach is well worth examining to improve the amount of feedback given and the learning experience of the students.

4. *The project motivated students both in and out of the course.*

The importance of the project and its applicability to the campus helped them to understand that they needed to make sure the application succeeded. They had to learn the value of supporting their application, past the time of their "commitment". Two members of the winning team continued to improve the application in their free time after the semester ended, before it was installed on a server available to other instructors, which astonished the course instructor. As well, a research course was created to increase the portability of the application and allow it to also target mobile devices. If a project provides an authentic learning experience, is meaningful, and solves a real-world problem for their own institution, students will perform. Additionally, the judged contest appeared to foster competition and improved the functionality, quality, and usability of the delivered solutions. The gift card prize offered was secondary to the prestige of winning.

5. *Never underestimate the creativeness, ingenuity and resolve of strong developers.*

In several instances, the teams pursued the project with novel, effective and unexpected approaches. In the first case, although the students were strongly encouraged to pursue an architecture built on Java WebStart, two teams employed alternate methodologies, namely *node.js* and *Ruby on Rails*. They still conformed to the project's functional and non-functional requirements. In another case, students employed both source code control and issue management using the Google Code environment, which provided significant benefit to students viewing the project in a successive term. A third example emerged when one team produced a non-functional user interface prototype and demoed it on an Apple iPad.

4.2 Impact and Future Work

The success of the students was reflected in later semesters of the course as well. The fact that professors were using a creation of the students helps attract potential Software Development recruits. As well, the influence extended outside of the SD realm. Introductory students that used the application were impressed and inspired that their peers created this. In Fall 2012, another

group of SD I students experimented with bug fixing and functional improvements on the contest-winning code base. In Spring 2013, this version of the code was used as a basis for a complete re-write of the system by a small team of undergraduates doing independent study. This group is conducting exploratory work on interfacing the clickers to brain computer interface (BCI) devices.

Other future plans include supporting other platforms, such as the iPhone, iPad and Android. The application can also be used as a case study for other courses, such as SD II, Human Computer Interaction and even Networking.

5. CONCLUSION

Software Development students were responsive and challenged by the tasks given to them. An enthusiasm was fostered, because this was a real world application that the students could envision being used by the institution as a useful contribution. The students not only performed for the course, and the grade for the course, but because of the students' enthusiasm, unanticipated results outside of the classroom were achieved. The students entered their application into a contest, they continued to fix bugs after the course ended, and they were able to include the application in their career portfolio.

6. REFERENCES

1. Pinkett, R.D., *Strategies for motivating minorities to engage computers*, in *Carenegie Mellon Symposium on Minorities and Computer Science*1999, MIT Media Laboratory.
2. Schwartz, D., et al., *Towards the development of flexibly adaptive instructional design*, in *Instructional-design theories and models: a new paradigm of instructional theory*, C. Reigeluth, Editor 1999, Erlbaum: Mahwah, NJ. p. 183-213.
3. Preston, J.A., *Utilizing authentic, real-world projects in information technology education.* SIGITE Newsl., 2005. **2**(1): p. 1-10.
4. Reeves, T.C., J. Herrington, and R. Oliver. *Authentic activities and online learning.* in *Higher Education Research and Development Society of Australasia.* 2002. Perth, Australia.
5. Burns, R., L. Pollock, and T. Harvey, *Integrating hard and soft skills: software engineers serving middle school teachers*, in *Proceedings of the 43rd ACM technical symposium on Computer Science Education*2012, ACM: Raleigh, North Carolina, USA. p. 209-214.
6. Cicirello, V.A., *Experiences with a real projects for real clients course on software engineering at a liberal arts institution.* J. Comput. Sci. Coll., 2013. **28**(6): p. 50-56.
7. Liu, C., *Enriching software engineering courses with service-learning projects and the open-source approach*, in *Proceedings of the 27th international conference on Software engineering*2005, ACM: St. Louis, MO, USA. p. 613-614.
8. Polack-Wahl, J.A., *Incorporating the client's role in a software engineering course.* SIGCSE Bull., 1999. **31**(1): p. 73-77.
9. Lambright, K.T. and A.F. Alden, *Voices from the Trenches: Faculty Perspectives on Support for Sustaining Service-Learning.* Journal of Higher Education Outreach and Engagement, 2012. **16**(2): p. 9-45.
10. Liu, J., J. Marsaglia, and D. Olson, *Teaching software engineering to make students ready for the real world.* J. Comput. Sci. Coll., 2002. **18**(2): p. 43-50.

11. Tan, J. and J. Phillips, *Incorporating service learning into computer science courses.* J. Comput. Small Coll., 2005. **20**(4): p. 57-62.

12. Ikonen, M. and J. Kurhila, *Discovering high-impact success factors in capstone software projects*, in *Proceedings of the 10th ACM conference on SIG-information technology education*2009, ACM: Fairfax, Virginia, USA. p. 235-244.

13. *GGC Connect application.* Available from: https://play.google.com/store/apps/details?id=edu.ggc.it&hl=en.

14. Tsoi, M.Y. and S. Dekhane. *TsoiChem: A Mobile Application To Facilitate Student Learning in Organic Chemistry.* in *International Conference on Advanced Learning Technologies.* 2011. Athens, GA: IEEE Computer Society.

15. The Standish Group, *Extreme Chaos*, 2001.

16. Murphy, T., *Success and failure of audience response systems in the classroom*, in *Proceedings of the 36th annual ACM SIGUCCS fall conference: moving mountains, blazing trails*2008, ACM: Portland, OR, USA. p. 33-38.

17. Taneja, A., *The influence of personal response systems on students' perceived learning outcomes and course satisfaction.* J. Comput. Small Coll., 2009. **25**(2): p. 5-11.

Winds of Change: Toward Systemic Improvement of a Computer Science Program

Steven Nordstrom
nordstrosg@lipscomb.edu

Arisoa Randrianasolo
asrandrianasolo@lipscomb.edu

Eddy Borera
ecborera@lipscomb.edu

Fortune Mhlanga
fsmhlanga@lipscomb.edu

School of Computing and Informatics
Lipscomb University
One University Park Drive
Nashville, TN, USA

ABSTRACT

Computer science programs at small, liberal arts universities often have difficulty with effectively managing change, and attracting and retaining top students and faculty. They also sometimes struggle to provide a relevant and appealing curriculum while maintaining an appropriate level of academic rigor. This paper presents a restructuring of our department and computer science degree program, identifies several key areas of our curriculum which needed attention, outlines our improvement areas, and proposes a self-assessment strategy for gauging the effectiveness of the program changes over time.

Categories and Subject Descriptors

K.3.2 [**Computer and Information Science Education**]: Curriculum

Keywords

Curriculum, Experiences, Assessment

1. INTRODUCTION

Small computer science programs have a unique set of constraints not typically found in larger programs. Notably, when CS is offered by a predominately liberal arts university, issues include but are not limited to: fewer faculty, fewer CS program courses due to increased liberal arts and general education course requirements, less than spectacular laboratory facilities, and a lack of funded, graduate-level research programs. Often, CS programs at universities such as these have to find creative ways to stay relevant with extremely limited resources.

Over the last two years, the programs at our small liberal arts university which have seen the most growth are the professional graduate degree programs. Master of Science program enrollments within the department of Computing and Information Technology have been on a meteoric rise (over 70 graduate students AY2012, up from zero enrollment just two years prior) and it was known that the associated enrollment increases would present challenges related to faculty and staff, new roles and responsibilities, and new opportunities for growth.

It was decided by the university in the summer of 2011 that the department would undergo a transformation to a more self-sufficient school to better support the growth within these programs. The new school, heretofore referred to as the School of Computing and Informatics (SCI, or simply, the School) would subsume the department, and would direct the former department's undergraduate and graduate degree programs.

These intended changes to the structure of the department provided an opportunity to survey the landscape of the undergraduate programs currently offered, and to make revisions where possible. It was decided by the School that from an administrative perspective, changes to program curriculum could be made much more easily in bulk while the winds of change were already blowing. A rapid self-study was undertaken to identify any major improvements to be made and to develop plans to realize those improvements. An added benefit of this self investigation was the opportunity to look closely at the programs that were not independently accredited and to investigate curriculum and faculty issues that would allow those programs to work toward accreditation.

At its inception, two important building blocks of the SCI were to recruit talented faculty and to expand and strengthen curriculum choices for its students. The number of substantive faculty in the School has since grown from three to 10. The School continues to strengthen existing curricula and has since expanded curriculum choices. On the undergraduate piece, it has grown from four degree programs (computer science, information security, information technology, Web application development) at inception, to seven degree programs in the fall of 2013, with the addition of informatics, information technology management and software engineering. The School is now beginning to build on the original department's traditional strengths in information technology and Web development to establish significant presence in the areas of scientific computing, theory of computation, artificial intelligence, and software engineering. At the graduate level, we have grown from two MS degree programs (healthcare informatics and information security) at inception, to three with the addition of information technology management. Student population was at 85 undergraduate students at the beginning of fall 2011. This number is now roving around 145, with 95 at the undergraduate level and 50 at the graduate level.

This paper summarizes the changes to the computer science program curriculum, faculty roles, student engagement efforts, and self-assessments during the restructuring and establishment of the School. It identifies several key areas of the curriculum which needed attention, outlines improvement areas, and proposes a self-assessment strategy for gauging the effectiveness of the program changes over time.

2. RELATED WORK

Downey and Stein [2] illustrate through their development of an Engineering with Computing curriculum how programs can maximize the capabilities of a small number of CS faculty while still providing breadth in relevant CS topics at an acceptable level of depth. This strategy is key for understanding how to make the best use of faculty and resources at hand to teach what we consider to be the most critical and relevant portions of CS given a limited course offering. Zhang *et. al.* [9] show that a senior seminar course used to enhance student readiness to join a profession or continue to graduate school can support a more streamlined assessment process and even be a driving force for reform throughout the CS curriculum.

Toward increasing student engagement, peer led team learning (PLTL) strategies that put undergraduate teaching assistants in leadership roles in the classroom have been shown by Santa Maria and Banerjee [8]to be an effective way to improve student satisfaction and learning, and Horwitz *et. al.* [4] show PLTL to be highly effective in engaging women, minority, and traditionally under-represented students in introductory computer science courses.

Finally, the establishment of regular research activities within the School is imperative for promoting faculty and student scholarship. Given that the SCI has limited access to funded graduate research programs, there is promise in a recent study by Matzen and Alrifai [7] showing a strong preference by CS faculty for undergraduate research programs tailored specifically for undergraduates rather than simply scaling down regular graduate research activities. This requires a desire by the faculty to be active participants in the development, care, and feeding of an undergraduate research program. One way to facilitate this is through the establishment of undergraduate faculty research groups within the School. Fitzgerald *et. al.* [3] show by example that the establishment of regular research groups can be enriching to the faculty experience in terms of camaraderie, productivity and of quality of research output.

3. CURRICULUM CHANGES

The School currently provides seven undergraduate degree programs: computer science (CS), software engineer-

ing (SE), information security (SEC), information technology (IT), information technology management (ITM), informatics (INF) and Web application development (Web App Dev). A number of possible improvements to our CS degree plan were identified that when put together, make it both stronger academically and better suited for our incoming students. The changes, in part, bring our computer science curriculum into better alignment with the educational recommendations of the Association of Computing Machinery (ACM) and the Institute of Electrical and Electronics Engineers (IEEE)-Computer Society [5], and with the Accreditation Board for Engineering and Technology (ABET) [1] requirements for computer science program accreditation. They are also very much in line with the Computer Science Curricula 2013 (CS2013) Strawman draft [6], which redefines the essentials necessary for a modern computer science curriculum. Our curriculum changes should at least meet the final CS2013 Core-Tier 1 requirements considered essential for all CS degree granting programs.

3.1 Course Title Alignment

The following computer science course numbers, titles (and designations) were changed to make the course numbers consistent and commensurate with the level at which the course should be integrated and the titles were changed to more closely reflect the nature of the courses.

As noted in Table 1, some of the CSCI designated courses were changed to IT or SEC courses as they are more aligned to those designations.

3.2 CSCI Courses removed from CS program

The following courses were removed from the old CSCI degree plan:

- *IT 1403 (The Future of Computing)* is now repurposed for use in the IT and Web App Dev degree plans. CS majors will instead take *CS 1122 (Introduction to Computer Science)*. Traditionally, the first few courses in the computer science curriculum have focused exclusively on computer programming, without introducing students to the areas of application they may subsequently expect as professionals. This new introductory course provides broad exposure to the fundamental concepts found throughout the field of computer science. It is designed to be fun and engaging while introducing core concepts of CS through illustrative games, demystification lectures, and problem solving activities.

- *IT 2043 (Information System Applications)* teaches an introduction to IS applications such as Microsoft Word, Powerpoint, Excel, and Access, and is now repurposed for use only in the Web App Dev degree plan. It is assumed that CS students will either be already prepared and conversant with the Microsoft suite of applications or they can pick those skills up very quickly on their own.

- *CSCI 4613 (Senior Project)* is now repurposed for use in the IT and Web App Dev degree plans. Computer science majors will instead take *CS 4163 (Senior Seminar in Computer Science)*. CS 4163 subsumes CSCI 4613 by providing students with the opportunity to gain a realistic perspective of career fields

Table 1: New Course Designations and Titles

Old Course Designation and Title	New Course Designation and Title
CSCI 1513 Structured Programming	CS 1213 Introduction to Computer Programming
CSCI 2113 Intermediate Programming	CS 1233 Object-Oriented System Design and Programming
CSCI 3113 Data Structures	CS 2233 Data Structures and Algorithms
CSCI 3213 Data Base Management Systems	CS 2243 Database Management Systems
CSCI 3353 Introduction to Software Engineering	CS 3223 Software Engineering
CSCI 3413 Numerical Algorithms	CS 3433 Numerical Methods
CSCI 3513 Computer Organization	CS 2313 Computer Organization
CSCI 3613 Network Principles	IT 3313 Network Principles
CSCI 3703 Introduction to GUI Programming	IT 2233 User Interface Design
CSCI 3713 Information Security	SEC 2313 Fundamentals of Information Security
CSCI 3803 Introduction to AI and Expert Systems	CS 4453 Artificial Intelligence
CSCI 4113 Comparative Programming Languages	CS 3413 Comparative Programming Languages
CSCI 4213 Operating Systems	CS 3523 Operating Systems
CSCI 4613 Senior Project	IT 4613 Senior Project

of personal interest in computing, from both industry and graduate school perspectives. At the same time, it also gives instructors the opportunity to assist students with computing career explorations and the possibly to gain assistance with a special project or research of mutual interest.

3.3 CS / SEC / IT Common Courses

The following courses remain in the common requirements of all CS majors, although some of the titles and designations have been realigned to reflect a new designation and/or revised title (cf. Table 1 for old titles and designations):

- CS 1213 Introduction to Computer Programming
- CS 1233 Object-Oriented System Design and Programming
- CS 2233 Data Structures and Algorithms
- CS 2243 Database Management Systems
- CS 2313 Computer Organization
- CS 3223 Software Engineering
- CS 3523 Operating Systems
- CS 4453 Artificial Intelligence
- CS 395V Internship in Computer Science
- SEC 2313 Fundamentals of Information Security
- IT 2223 Web Application Development I
- IT 3313 Network Principles

3.4 Additional Common CS Courses

The following seven courses were added to the common requirements of all CS majors:

- CS 1122 Introduction to Computer Science *(new course)*
- CS 2252 Competition Programming *(new course)*
- CS 3213 Design and Analysis of Algorithms *(new course)*
- CS 3413 Comparative Programming Languages*
- CS 4163 Senior Seminar in Computer Science *(new course)*
- CS 4213 Compiler Construction *(new course)*
- CS 4413 Fundamentals of Automata and Formal Language Theory (new course)

*Although CS 3413 existed in the previous program as CSCI 4113, due to its elective nature it had not been taught in over four years. It is now a compulsory course in the new CS program.

3.5 CS Concentration Areas

The old CSCI program was a more general, one-size fits all computer science degree program. This vertical or silo-based model has been diversified to form a new, more horizontal program which facilitates individualized customization. This new model is, to a great extent, designed to attract and retain students with extremely diverse interests. These concentration areas have been tailored to align with the areas of expertise and likely interests of existing and newly hired faculty, respectively.

CS students will select one of nine available three-course (9-hour) concentrations, as noted in Table 2:

The beauty of the above concentration areas is that five of the nine concentrations are built based on required courses from the other three degree plans within the School of Computing and Informatics, one of which includes existing courses offered by another department's Electrical and Computer Engineering (ECE) degree plan, and induce no additional overhead on SCI faculty. Three of the concentrations (Computer Theory, Game Development, and Mobile Computing) introduce and require completely new courses distinct from the ones listed above. One concentration area (Database Systems and Security) introduces two new courses if the Computer Theory concentration is satisfied. The potential also exists to include other concentrations in the future.

3.6 Math and Physics Requirements

MATH 2183 (Elementary Statistics) was removed from the CS requirements; students are instead required to take the more rigorous MATH 3123 (Mathematical Theory of Statistics) course. Accordingly, all CS students will now be required to take the following six math courses:

- MATH 1314 Calculus I
- MATH 2103 Discrete Mathematics
- MATH 2314 Calculus II
- MATH 2903 Logic, Proof and Mathematical Modeling
- MATH 3123 Mathematical Theory of Statistics (new required MATH course)

Table 2: Concentration Areas

Computer Networking	Computer Systems	Computer Theory
IT 3323 Wireless Networks & Mobile Sys	CS 3333 Mobile & Distr Computing Sys	CS 4423 Computability & Complexity Theory
IT 4323 Modern Telecommunications	EECE 3813 Digital Computer Design I	CS 4433 Algorithmic Graph Theory
SEC 3323 Cryptography	EECE 4254 Microprocessors	CS 4443 Database Theory and Applications
Database Security	Database Systems and Security	Game Development
SEC 3313 Intro to Policy & Procedures	CS 4443 Database Theory and Applics	CS 3253 Game Development I
SEC 3323 Cryptography	SEC 3323 Cryptography	CS 3263 Game Development II
SEC 4313 Database Security	SEC 4313 Database Security	CS 3273 Collaborative Serious Games Devt
Mobile Computing	Network Security	Software Engineering
CS 3243 Mobile Device Programming	SEC 3323 Cryptography	CS 3233 Intro to GUI Prog & Graphics
CS 3333 Mobile & Distr Computing Sys	SEC 4323 Network Security	IT 3223 Web Application Development II
CS 4013 Future Mobile & Social Comp Sys	IT 3323 Wireless Networks & Mobile Sys	IT 3233 Web Server Technologies

- MATH 3213 Linear Algebra (new required MATH course)

All CS students will also be required to take the following two calculus-based physics courses:

- PH 2414 General Physics I (with Lab)
- PH 2424 General Physics II (with Lab)

3.7 Electives

The remaining hours will be added to the number of advanced CS / SEC / IT elective courses required for the degree, for a total of five upper-level elective hours. To help meet the need for five upper-level elective hours, we have added a new two-hour elective course (3252 Programming Challenges). Students can also choose courses from other concentrations other than theirs as electives. In addition, CS 401V (Independent Study in Computer Science) is of variable credit (1-3 hours) and is also repeatable for up to six credit hours. This course can also be used to introduce 1- or 2-hour language lab courses.

4. FUTURE AND ONGOING WORK

Work is ongoing in the areas of increasing undergraduate student engagement and assessment activities. We are seeking ways to increase student engagement in scholarly work, which we hope will lead to more participation in funded graduate work and increased placements in top-tier companies. We are also continuing work on a plan for comprehensive program outcome measurement by including more robust alumni involvement in the CS program's assessment process.

4.1 Undergraduate Research

While the School already has three professional graduate programs, the ability to establish a viable research reputation is somewhat limited by the absence of full-time graduate assistants; and without a fully-funded graduate research program, it is not feasible to have graduate teaching/research assistants. On the other hand, it is possible to establish a reputable program of undergraduate research in which students make limited, but recognizable, contributions to a broader research program. In the computing sciences, this is particularly true if research is cast in terms of applications development.

The School of Computing and Informatics is in the process of establishing a formal program of applied undergraduate research directed by two faculty members (presumably this would be part of a research project within the School). The opportunity to participate in this program would be granted to students on a competitive basis. Because the opportunity to participate in research activities at the undergraduate level is known to be a significant draw for prospective top-tier students, the existence of the program would also be used as a recruiting tool. The presence of top-tier undergraduate students on campus would, in turn, be used to recruit top prospective faculty who would be expected to bring their research portfolios to the university.

4.2 Assessment

In keeping with our goal to seek ABET accreditation, a formal effort is underway to evaluate the School's mission, student learning outcomes, and program educational objectives as they relate to the newly reworked computer science degree program. In addition, this plan seeks to further our self-assessment efforts by implementing the following new or improved mechanisms (note: A (*) indicates a new metric not currently implemented by the existing self-assessment initiatives of the SCI):

- Student enrollments and graduation rates
- Second-year attrition rate study*
- Pass rates on ETS Major Field Test (MFT)*
- Enhanced career / job placement tracking
  - Day-of-graduation placement percentages
  - Six-month placement percentages
  - Three-year and Five-year alumni surveys*
- Faculty scholarship tracking
  - Publication tracking*
  - Education-related scholarship and professional development*
  - Professional society participation*
- Student engagement
  - Active ACM student branch members*
  - UPE membership statistics*
  - Student participation in the School's events*

Our belief is that while the measurement tools we use to assess the effectiveness of the program changes outlined in this paper will certainly undergo continuous refinement, the collection of data needs to begin straightaway, as we currently have a selection of students completing the old CSCI program while new flights of students start entering the new CS degree plan.

5. CONCLUSIONS

Several improvements to our CS program have been put in place recently to serve a number of goals, 1.) to better align with ACM recommendations and ABET accreditation requirements, 2.) to make better use of existing and new faculty utilization, and 3.) to increase student engagement in our programs. Anecdotal evidence from existing students is extremely positive, and we have seen that our students have been craving these changes for some time. Requiring more in-depth, academically challenging courses is appealing to many of our top students, while the prospect of increased exposure to modern topics of CS such as gaming and mobile devices has caused genuine excitement among our students who are, shall we say, less enthusiastic about theoretical rigor.

The opportunity to enact widespread change in undergraduate programs does not come around often; we have done our best to maximize the impact of this opportunity and it is our hope that by revamping the program in the ways described we will be able to demonstrate a measurable increase in the knowledge, success, and engagement of our students. We solicit the feedback of the computer science education community at large, and we welcome feedback and your comments. Finally, as we proceed with further improvements, we hope to participate in an ongoing, open exchange of ideas toward computer science curriculum reform in general.

6. REFERENCES

[1] ABET Computing Accreditation Commission. *Criteria for Accrediting Computing Programs.* http://www.abet.org/DisplayTemplates/ DocsHandbook.aspx?id=1805, Oct. 2011.

[2] A. Downey and L. Stein. *Designing a small-footprint curriculum in computer science.* In *Frontiers in Education Conference, 36th Annual*, pages 21 –26, oct. 2006.

[3] S. Fitzgerald, B. Hanks, and R. McCauley. Collaborative research in computer science education: a case study. In *Proceedings of the 41st ACM technical symposium on Computer science education*, SIGCSE '10, pages 305–309, New York, NY, USA, 2010. ACM.

[4] S. Horwitz, S. H. Rodger, M. Biggers, D. Binkley, C. K. Frantz, D. Gundermann, S. Hambrusch, S. Huss-Lederman, E. Munson, B. Ryder, and M. Sweat. Using peer-led team learning to increase participation and success of under-represented groups in introductory computer science. *SIGCSE Bull.*, 41(1):163–167, Mar. 2009.

[5] Interim Review Task Force (ACM and IEEE-Computer Society). *Computer Science Curriculum 2008: An Interim Revision of CS2001.* http://www.acm.org/education/curricula/ ComputerScience2008.pdf/view, Dec. 2008.

[6] Joint Task Force on Computing Curricula (ACM and IEEE-Computer Society). *Computer Science Curricula 2013* (strawman draft). http://ai.stanford.edu/users/sahami/CS2013, Feb. 2012.

[7] R. Matzen and R. Alrifai. Defining undergraduate research in computer science: a survey of computer science faculty. *J. Comput. Sci. Coll.*, 27(3):31–37, Jan. 2012.

[8] R. Santa Maria and S. Banerjee. Using undergraduate teaching assistants in introductory computer courses. *J. Comput. Sci. Coll.*, 27(6):61–62, June 2012.

[9] W. Zhang, T. Beaubouef, and K.-p. Yang. Revamping computer science seminar course for comprehensive assessment of student learning. *J. Comput. Sci. Coll.*, 27(5):17–23, May 2012.

Author Index

www.ingramcontent.com/pod-product-compliance
Lightning Source LLC
Chambersburg PA
CBHW061417210326
41598CB00035B/6240